DEREGULATING THE HEALTH CARE INDUSTRY

DEREGULATING THE HEALTH CARE INDUSTRY
Planning for Competition

Clark C. Havighurst

BALLINGER PUBLISHING COMPANY
Cambridge, Massachusetts
A Subsidiary of Harper & Row, Publishers, Inc.

This book was prepared with the support of the Federal Trade Commission. Any opinions, findings, conclusions, or recommendations are those of the author and do not necessarily reflect the views of the Federal Trade Commission. The Federal Trade Commission retains a royalty-free, non-exclusive and irrevocable right to reproduce, publish or otherwise use and to authorize others to use this work for government purposes.

International Standard Book Number: 0-88410-736-1

Library of Congress Catalog Card Number: 81-15011

Printed in the United States of America

Library of Congress Cataloging in Publication Data

Havighurst, Clark C.
  Deregulating the health care system.

  Includes index.
  1. Health planning—Law and legislation—United
States. 2. Medical laws and legislation—United
States. 3. Competition—United States. 4. Medical
policy—United States. 5. Medical economics—United
States. I. Title.
KF3825.5.H38   344.73′0321   81-15011
ISBN 0-88410-736-1   347.304321   AACR2

DEDICATION

To the memory of my father,
HAROLD C. HAVIGHURST
(1897–1981)

ACKNOWLEDGMENTS

Major support for my work on this book was provided by the Federal Trade Commission both under a contract for a study in 1977 and during a sabbatical leave in 1978–79, when I was a part-time resident consultant to the Bureau of Competition. The final phases of the work, particularly the extensive effort needed to take account of the 1979 amendments to the federal health-planning legislation, were supported by Grant No. HS01539 from the National Center for Health Services Research, U.S. Department of Health and Human Services. Of course, neither sponsor necessarily shares any of the views expressed herein.

Some material in this book has appeared, often in substantially different form, in other places. Appreciation for the right to reprint that material is hereby expressed to the American Enterprise Institute for Public Policy Research, the *American Journal of Law and Medicine,* the Hoover Institution, *Law and Contemporary Problems,* the *University of Toledo Law Review,* and the *Utah Law Review.**

---

*In two instances, the reprinted material is too widely scattered to be readily attributed in footnotes. Thus, the references are supplied here. "Prospects for Competition Under Planning-cum-Regulation," in *National Health Insurance: What Now, What Later, What Never?* 329 (M. Pauly ed. 1980) (published by the American Enterprise Institute), and

Other acknowledgments are of a less obligatory and more personal nature. Glenn M. Hackbarth, my colleague in the Program on Legal Issues in Health Care at Duke, has shared every thought, though not necessarily every opinion, and has provided many ideas that I have now so thoroughly internalized that I cannot reconstruct his precise contribution and must simply say that it was great. Other professional friends, colleagues, and coauthors to whom I am particularly indebted for having helped to shape my thinking on these many subjects are Randall Bovbjerg, James F. Blumstein, Alain C. Enthoven, and Walter McClure.

A particular professional and personal debt is owed to Lawrence S. Lewin and Jack Needleman of Lewin & Associates, Inc., for the opportunity to participate in their work leading to enactment of the State of Utah's Pro-competitive Certificate of Need Act of 1979. More than anything else, that legislation gave my ideas the credibility in the real world that was needed to get Congress to take them seriously in the 1979 health planning amendments.

Finally, although my family—Karen, Perry, and Marjorie—and my secretary, Jacksie Plambeck, are not as consumed as I am by interest in national health policy, it should be recorded that, if this book makes any difference, they have made a contribution to it.

Clark C. Havighurst

Durham, North Carolina
August 1981

"Health Planning for Competition: Implementing the 1979 Amendments," 44 *L. & Contemp. Prob.* 33 (1981).

TABLE OF CONTENTS

Part II   Drafting Health Planning and Certificate-
of-Need Legislation to Foster Competition

Chapter 5
Charging the Planner-Regulators to Weigh Competitive
Values

INTRODUCTION

This book began to take shape in 1977 as a study of health planning and certificate-of-need laws undertaken for the Federal Trade Commission. The subsequent history of that study has been one of catching up with important events that, even though it was never published, it helped to trigger. In particular, the 1979 amendments to the National Health Planning and Resources Development Act of 1974 adopted not only the study's basic notion of competition-sensitive regulation but even some of the proposed statutory language contained in the version that I supplied to congressional staff. These amendments significantly altered the thrust of federally mandated health planning-cum-regulation, bringing it substantially into line with the study's original thesis. Having achieved its chief purpose while still a mere draft, the study had to be substantially recast and reworked to warrant the present publication.

Thus, the study has become, in large part, an explication of the procompetition provisions of the 1979 health planning amendments and a guide for health planners and health system regulators to use in carrying out their new statutory responsibilities; inevitably, the book will also arm providers and their lawyers and other protagonists in the regulatory process with new arguments for and against allowing competition in particular circumstances.

1

Because the regulatory strategy outlined will succeed only if regulators are persuaded or induced to participate in bringing about their own displacement by market forces, I have felt the need to make the book in part a work of advocacy, emphasizing competition's real potential for imposing appropriate discipline on this complex industry. This advocacy of competition has necessarily led me to consider larger health policy issues and to propose policy changes that are needed before competition can be truly serviceable. The result is a book that addresses several additional audiences, including federal and state policymakers and all those who are interested, intellectually or practically, in these policy questions.

THE ESSENTIAL CONCEPT OF COMPETITION IN HEALTH SERVICES

Though falling short of being a technical treatise on the economics of health sector competition, this book proceeds on the basis of a paradigm of a market for insured health services. This concept, which is beginning to take hold in health policy discussions, envisions a multiplicity of competing health plans and financing arrangements that vie for consumer favor by differently organizing services and differently allocating decisionmaking among plans, providers, and patients. The common denominator in this paradigmatic market is not any particular organizational form, such as the health maintenance organization. Neither does the ultimate key lie primarily in the notion of consumer choice, although plan accountability to consumers in the marketplace is indeed a sine qua non of a competitive market. Instead, the crucial competitive arena, which has been neglected in most thinking about this industry, is the interface between competing health plans and providers. Until the full potentialities for aggressive competitive bargaining at that interface are realized, providers will remain effectively insulated from competitive accountability to consumers for the overall cost as well as the quality of care.

Competition among providers is currently weak precisely because conventional health care plans have eschewed competition in the procurement of providers' services. For complex reasons, such plans conceive their function as either "reimbursing" providers (note how the terminology implies that the transaction is noncommercial) or indemnifying consumers for incurred costs. Under either approach, the plans fail to transmit consumer cost concerns across the plan-provider interface, thus abdicating their role as the consumer's purchasing agent. These health plans must learn, under increasing competitive pressure, to give effect to cost concerns in one of two ways. Either they must act as cost-conscious negotiators and purchasers of providers' services or they must structure their benefits and premiums so that consumers face more of the cost implications of their discretionary choices. Although problems exist, competition's potential for inducing effective private action on the cost problem is very great.

THE USES OF THEORY AND EXPERIENCE IN HEALTH POLICY ANALYSIS

It is regrettable that we lack a fully developed appreciation of the economics and dynamics of health sector competition. The main problem is of course our lack of experience with uninhibited competition that economists could study and laymen could appreciate. One result of our inexperience has been a chronic weakness in our ability to recognize the presence of competition when it is operating and the significance and causes of its absence when it is not. Another difficulty is that the policy argument for relying on competition in this industry rests more on theory, anecdotes, impressions, and speculation than on social-scientific proof that competition in this field inevitably lowers prices, raises quality, and contributes to rational utilization of resources. Although there is little reason to doubt that empirical evidence, if it were available, would confirm the limited claims that I make in this book by analyzing incentives and institutional factors, empirical studies would be valuable in giving a sense of magnitudes, establishing the theory's validity, increasing its credibility, and isolating possible flaws in its application. But the absense of conclusive empirical evidence is hardly an objection to proceeding with a policy whose theoretical basis seems strong, especially when that policy is readily reversible or when its adverse effects, if any, are not likely to be catastrophic. This book's advocacy proceeds on this basis, asking only that competition be given a sympathetic hearing in specific cases.

The genius of the 1979 health planning amendments is precisely that they make no ultimate judgment on competition's efficaciousness but instead simply reopen the possibility that regulation will allow competition to do those things that it proves, or appears, able to do well. Previously, the health planning law and other emerging policies in the health care industry effectively foreclosed this possibility by seeming to embody a powerful presumption in favor of command-and-control regulation and against ever allowing market forces to operate freely. Whereas the market strategy has at least a good theoretical foundation, both the theoretical and the empirical basis for embracing regulation as an exclusive policy have always seemed to me shaky. Not only were the regulatory measures initially selected unproved in the health sector, but they were analogous to regulatory mechanisms that had proved unsatisfactory in other industries and could be seen as theoretically and politically unsound. Even as the regulatory noose was being tightened, anecdotal and statistical evidence of such regulation's ineffectiveness in health care applications began to accumulate, confirming theoretical analyses predicting that regulation would fail to achieve anything like optimal and efficient levels of health care spending.

In addition to being unpromising on its own terms, the seemingly definitive choice of regulation in the health legislation of the 1970s was apparently based on a misinterpretation of the historical record concerning the market's capabilities. Although the competitive market had undeniably failed to perform well, that empirical fact could not warrant a decision to regulate unless the causes of that failure were irremediable. In fact, little attention was paid to the several specific ways in which government itself, through such policies as incentive-distorting tax subsidies, nonenforcement of the antitrust laws, and poorly designed public financing programs, had contributed to the market's malfunctioning. Policymakers also ignored the contribution of the industry itself, which had used its political power and its de facto antitrust immunity assiduously to ensure the failure of government and the private sector to develop cost-effective financing mechanisms. With the historical record correctly interpreted, a comparison of market theory and experience with regulatory and monopolistic alternatives now seems strongly to support a policy of changing incentives, curbing industry prerogatives, and relaxing command-and-control regulation in order to give market forces a chance to show what they can achieve under proper conditions.

Critics of the market strategy have usually written it off in a few paragraphs by citing ways in which real-world markets depart from the theoretical ideal. There is no longer any excuse, however, for facile dismissal of the market strategy on such simplistic grounds as that consumers are ignorant, that third-party payment makes price competition unworkable, or that physicians control demand. The heart and soul of the market strategy is not the simple theory of first-year economics but the practical likelihood of competitively induced change—most particularly in those areas that the critics like to highlight: the availability to consumers of information and decisionmaking assistance, the cost-effectiveness of financing systems, and the constraints on provider decisionmaking. While important empirical questions can be raised about the likelihood and extent of such changes and the conditions necessary to bring them about, most critics of the market strategy have assumed that no significant change is possible—at least anytime soon. But it is hard to doubt that major changes would quickly occur if health policy and the multitude of health planners and regulators suddenly became dedicated to removing the causes, rather than suppressing the symptoms, of the cost problem.

Because no general decision for competition or command-and-control regulation was made in the 1979 amendments, planners and regulators, in carrying out their new duties, must employ both theory and experience in deciding when competition should be allowed to operate. Although this book offers more theoretical than empirical support for competition, experience accumulated by planners and regulators experimenting with competition in local markets could soon supply a secure basis for knowing when competition can be relied on without undue risk. Probably the most hopeful aspect of the health planning amendments' procompetitive thrust is that the amendments will allow experiments with competition under regulatory oversight and will thus provide the empirical evidence needed to flesh out the theory and reduce it to practice. To an optimistic market advocate, this looks like a path to ultimate deregulation, undertaken on a service-by-service, market-by-market basis by planners and regulators truly committed to bringing this market under the most satisfactory of our alternative mechanisms of social control.

ETHICAL ISSUES AND CONCERNS

In addition to my confidence in both the theory and the evidence underlying increasing reliance on competition to allocate health resources, I feel strongly supported by ethical principles whose validity transcends the empirical issue of whether competition would work major or only modest changes in the health care industry's performance. Thus, I think a majority of people would find it nearly as hard as I do to deny the attractiveness of letting people choose for themselves within wide, though definite, limits set by such residual regulation as physician licensure and consumer-protection regulation of individual insurance contracts. While such a choice-oriented policy lets people bear the bad consequences of their choices as well as enjoy the rewards (including the savings from economizing), catastrophic mistakes would surely be rare in a system with sound incentives. To my mind, this is the most attractive way, ethically, to deal with the ubiquitous and extraordinarily difficult tradeoffs that characterize this complex industry. Given the symbolism involved in health care, such tradeoffs severely undercut the legitimacy of any economizing effort that benefits someone other than the individual whose health might possibly be affected. Really effective cost containment seems ethically and politically tolerable only where one does it for one's self—and even then only within certain limits. Because people—that is, consumers—can pool information, can join together voluntarily for the purpose of making informed choices, can gain allies and hire agents to help them in deciding, and can rely on reputable middlemen, their widely perceived ignorance and helplessness seem a false issue, particularly when one considers the shortcomings of the political and monopolistic alternatives.

Even setting aside the poor record and prospects of regulatory and professionally contrived solutions to the cost problem and discounting the strength of the theory underlying the market strategy, I would go so far as to argue that consumer choice is an ethical imperative. Thus, I would ultimately deny the relevance of "empirical" questions designed to elicit a complete description of the system as it would evolve and function under competition. To the extent that such questions are asked in order to permit the questioner or some public body to judge whether a system based on choice would be desirable, they miss the ethical point. To my mind (and others need not share this view to accept the general analysis on pragmatic grounds), the competitive process, precisely because it is based on choice, validates the outcome whatever it may turn out to be. Thus, the only relevant empirical issues would be those relating to the process itself—whether people were freely choosing with correct incentives and had a meaningful range of choice available to them. While there is a great deal more that might be said, it may all come down to the simple proposition that such an intensely personal matter as what to do about disease should be kept within the realm of private choice.

The market-oriented proposals in this book have some undeniably disturbing implications for the health care system's ability to care for underinsured populations. The market strategy, however, does not in itself deny the claims of equity and social justice. Indeed, it contemplates that government would continue to discharge its responsibilities in this regard and requires only that it do so in ways that preserve both the principle of choice and the essential incentives to economize. Nevertheless, competition would impair the system's ability to generate from healthy premium payers and paying patients the excess revenues that are currently used to cover the cost of treating the less healthy and those who both cannot pay and lack adequate public support. Thus, government would be called on in a competitive system to provide new direct subsidies to replace the hidden ones previously depended upon. Although I do not think that this equity problem and the inevitable undercutting of social insurance concepts make competition undesirable, it would be unconscionable and unwise for government to ignore these and other side effects (on medical education and research, for example) to which competition and the pursuit of efficiency give rise.

THE POLICY MILIEU

This book should appear at an opportune time. Interest in encouraging health sector competition has increased dramatically in the recent past. The Ninety-sixth Congress, in particular, deserves credit for raising fundamental questions about whether the heavy hand of regulation could do as well in this industry as the invisible hand of competition. Indeed, it was only in 1979 that Congress's own deregulatory right hand finally came to realize what its regulatory left hand was doing in health care—namely, tightening its grip even as other industries were moving toward deregulation. Congress seems likely to continue in this deregulatory vein, and, at this writing, the Reagan administration has embraced market-oriented health policies in general terms.

The sudden shift in ideological orientation in the federal establishment brings with it a new set of problems that this book was not originally intended, but may help, to alleviate. Whereas excessive enthusiasm for regulation was the problem that this book was originally intended to address, there now appears to exist an opposite danger that Congress, in its deregulatory and antifederalist fervor, might overreact and eschew any active role for the federal government in reforming the health services industry. Moreover, a more conservative and economy-minded Congress could easily fail not only to provide needed new subsidies for health services to underserved populations but even to replace the hidden internal subsidies on which such populations have long depended but which strengthened competition could jeopardize. Whether it will be possible to prevent the pendulum from swinging back too far is not clear, but this book's policy prescriptions should be viewed as having that object in mind.

A new possibility suddenly appearing on the policy agenda following the 1980 elections is outright repeal of the federal health planning legislation. This book provides a rationale for maintaining the health planning and regulatory effort a while longer and using it as a bridge to orderly deregulation. To my mind, the Reagan administration's soundest policy would be to insist, under threats including the possibility of program termination, on wholehearted compliance by the planners and regulators with the procompetitive mandate of the 1979 amendments. Such a policy would surely induce the planner-regulators to adopt a perspective similar to that urged in this book. It would also nicely balance a national policy favoring competition and deregulation with another conservative value, namely local decisionmaking and experimentation. Though not embracing pure laissez-faire, the 1979 amendments can be viewed as a decisive reopening of the possibility that competition will one day—not immediately in every community, to be sure—effectively rule this important industry. This book should help people understand how that denouement is possible and why it would be the best possible outcome.

I hope that, in addition to improving the credibility and understanding of competition among health policymakers, planners, and regulators, the book's thesis will find some support among health care providers. Many providers may simply see the strengthening of market forces as a lesser evil than regulation, but many others will, I think, recognize that the accountability to consumers and their agents that is enforced by competition is simply right and just and that such accountability is consistent with the medical profession's and the larger industry's professed ideals. Most interest groups will oppose the market strategy's full implications, of course, and they can hardly be blamed for clinging to power and for resenting pressures (such as antitrust enforcement) to alter cherished institutions. Nevertheless, while the market solution is not likely to be the first choice of many people, the realism that induces them ultimately to accept it as a second-best solution should help the nation's health care system to maintain its position as first-best in the world.

REGULATION AND COMPETITION AS ALTERNATIVE MECHANISMS OF SOCIAL CONTROL

1 FACING THE CHOICE BETWEEN REGULATION AND MARKET FORCES

Although it is common to speak of a health care "system," the United States is still rather far from having anything as unitary as that term implies. Indeed, the public health movement has long regarded the fragmentation of the health services industry as a grave defect, offering the observation that the industry is a "*non*system" to clinch the argument for a public takeover or heavy regulation. But, despite the regulatory efforts of recent years, centralized control has yet to remedy this alleged deficiency, and current political trends suggest that efforts to rectify it through government-administered controls may finally have run their course. In the current environment, it is no longer feasible—if indeed it ever was in the American context—to mold the diffuse and intractable health care industry into anything that could fairly be called a "system."

It is the thesis of this book that health policymakers—including the system's planners and regulators, many of whom were brought up in the public health tradition—would do well to begin viewing competition as a vehicle for turning the health care industry's fragmentation into a virtue. If properly nurtured, competition could supply the impetus for restructuring the industry, not into a single centrally controlled system but into a variety of competing systems. Competing health care plans and financing

13

mechanisms could take many forms. Indeed, their only common characteristic would probably be that in each of them the elements of medical care would be somewhat more organized and integrated with financing than in the "cottage industry" deplored so frequently in the past. Such systems would be the product of private, not government, initiative and would be subject to the dictates of consumer demand, not government bureaucrats. As so conceived, the health care sector of the economy is more accurately characterized as an "industry" than as a "system."

Maintenance of active competition among several more or less discrete and integrated health care plans and financing arrangements holds great promise for improving the industry's overall performance. On the one hand, competition should help to improve many aspects of health care that come under the general heading of "quality." On the other hand, it should intensify innovation in cost containment by insurers and other health plan operators and should improve providers' efficiency in the delivery of services. With proper restructuring of tax and other public subsidies, a competitive system should assure that new economizing incentives are translated into lower unit prices, that cost-effective inputs are chosen and used efficiently, that available services are utilized appropriately, and in general that closer attention is paid to getting adequate value for each dollar spent. Aside from its promise of efficient economic performance, such a marketplace of competing health care plans would also serve as a forum in which consumers and providers of health care could accommodate the myriad tradeoffs and economic and philosophical conflicts that are inherent in the provision and consumption of personal health services. In a unitary system, such issues become political battlegrounds and are resolved—inappropriately, it would seem—on the basis of collective rather than individual preferences. For a variety of reasons, then, a competitive health care industry should have wide appeal in a free society increasingly concerned about efficiency in the use of scarce economic resources.

CHARTING A COURSE TO A COMPETITIVE REGIME

Approaching such a competitive world from where we are at present is, of course, a difficult problem. To reach the goal of a smoothly functioning competitive market for health services would require sweeping changes in federal and state legislation, in regulatory behavior at the federal, state, and local levels, and in the way services are bought and paid for in both public and private financing programs. Because of the necessity for orchestrating changes at all levels of government and throughout the far-flung private sector, immediate and total deregulation would be difficult to accomplish and, moreover, might be a questionable policy until conditions are established to permit market forces to operate smoothly throughout the industry. Instead of embracing a radical overturning of all controls on industry performance, this book advocates a system of competition-sensitive regulation that could reasonably be expected to achieve deregulation eventually. The main focus is on the ways in which the industry could be helped, while still under some regulatory restraints, to evolve, service by service and market by market, toward greater and more constructive competitiveness. Universal deregulation of the industry is embraced only as a future prospect whose realization depends on developments that cannot be entirely foreseen.

The central subject of the book is the major health planning and regulatory effort that was originally undertaken in the United States pursuant to the National Health Planning and Resources Development Act of 1974 (referred to hereafter as Public Law 93–641).[1] In particular, the focus is on the state certificate-of-need laws enacted in compliance with Public Law 93–641. These regulatory laws, which impose public controls on health care providers' capital investments and new service offerings, have a greater impact on competition than any of the other regulatory measures now being pursued in the health care industry. Not only do state and local certificate-of-need agencies control market entry by would-be competitors and expansion by existing ones, but they also set the tone for local markets through their planning activities and otherwise. Such agencies regularly face decisions on such questions as whether to encourage competition or tolerate monopoly, whether to allow initiatives by outsiders or prefer established providers of services, whether to constrain supply artificially or allow it to adjust to market demand, and whether to leave a matter to consumer choice and private incentives or impose a collective judgment. The approach taken by health planners and regulators to these and other questions will reveal certain premises concerning how change is expected to occur, and these premises will in turn be influential in determining the climate for competitive initiatives and independent action.

Despite the disappointing track record of health system planners and regulators in fostering competition in the past—even where it might have served consumers well—, this book contemplates that they might play a constructive part in deregulating the industry. The specific basis for viewing the health planning and regulatory system not as an obstacle to competition, which it undeniably has been, but as a possible vehicle for replacing regulation with a competitive regime is the new legislative mandate given by Congress to the planners and regulators in 1979. Enacted while this book was being written, the National Health Planning and Resources Development Amendments of 1979[2] went quite far toward bringing Congress's directives to the health care system's planners and regulators into line with the book's basic precepts. Thus, what began as a brief for legislative change has ended up as a guide for carrying out the new statutory mandate. The working hypothesis throughout most of the book is that, if the planner-regulators engage in the kind of competition-sensitive regulation that federal law now seems to contemplate, meaningful deregulation could reasonably be expected to occur in due course, though not before essential reforms in the private sector and in public and private financing mechanisms were either in place or in prospect.

Unfortunately, the view that the planners and regulators can be successfully enlisted in the cause of deregulation, either as voluntary recruits or under the law's compulsions, is open to challenge, since changing regulatory habits and ingrained ideology may take more than an act of Congress. Nevertheless, although doubts about whether dyed-in-the-wool regulators could be persuaded to undertake free-market-oriented regulation might have been justified in the political climate prevailing before the 1980 elections, the new political environment may be more conducive to changes in regulators' behavior. Indeed, if the Reagan administration and Congress should finally reveal themselves as committed to procompetitive regulation along the lines indicated in the 1979 amendments, planners and regulators would, for the first time, be under pressure from Washington to justify their continued existence by contributing in a positive way to the restoration of market forces.

Despite the probable difficulty of getting the health care system's planner-regulators to implement a procompetitive regulatory strategy, deregulation may be easier to accomplish in this way than by some more revolutionary stroke. As Chapter 15 explains, the idea of seeking a regulatory path to deregulation rests primarily on a belief that strong federal leadership is needed to effectuate deregulation on a responsible basis. Outright repeal of Public Law 93–641, such as some people have proposed, would eliminate the federal compulsion to regulate but would not achieve deregulation, because state regulation would be left largely in place. Even though some states might repeal their certificate-of-need laws, the attachment of institutional providers and other interests to these anticompetitive statutes would probably prevent their repeal in most states. Moreover, the current trend toward giving the states both greater responsibility for Medicaid costs and greater flexibility in controlling those costs may invite more command-and-control regulation at the state level rather than less. For these reasons, the federal government, in order to assure true deregulation, would have to prohibit state regulation, and it seems unlikely that the Reagan administration or Congress would want to take such a preemptive step. It is far from clear, then, that responsible deregulation can be achieved simply by terminating federal involvement. Although it would require strong leadership by the Department of Health and Human Services (DHHS) to alter the prevailing command-and-control philosophy, the thesis of this book is that existing federal legislation already provides a sound framework within which deregulation can be responsibly pursued.

PUTTING REGULATION IN PERSPECTIVE

The initial objective of this book is to obtain for competition some recognition as a planner's tool and to assure it a fair regulatory hearing on its merits. Unfortunately, competition is likely to be viewed as a legitimate contender for a prominent role in guiding the health care industry's economic performance only if regulation's generic imperfections are recognized. Regulation's shortcomings are therefore cataloged briefly here[3] in order to dispel both the commonly held view that political mechanisms enjoy superior legitimacy in this field and the illusion that regulatory programs automatically define, and inexorably effectuate, the public interest. Unless regulation can be viewed critically and not as its own excuse for being, the outcome of a competitive process will never be seen as preferable to a regulatory decision.

Increasing public recognition of the high costs of regulation finally triggered a bipartisan deregulation movement in the mid-1970s. Indeed, that movement appears to have marked a historic shift away from the view, prevailing since the Progressive era, that regulatory legislation represents ipso facto a vindication of the public interest over private greed. Regulation has finally been recognized as having, too often, a destructive effect on efficiency and thus an adverse effect on consumers as a group. In the traditionally regulated industries, such as the airlines, trucking, the railroads, telecommunications, and energy, economic regulation (of prices, entry, and so forth) has frequently been found to benefit the regulated industry and other special interests at consumers' expense and to cause other harms as well. The nature and causes of these regulatory failures must be outlined briefly here both to inculcate a proper skepticism about regulation in general and to establish the context for the critique of health sector cost-containment regulation in Chapter 2.

Long experience in the regulated industries has led finally to a recognition of the political obstacles to discovering and effectuating "the public interest" through the use of regulatory commissions. It is now widely accepted that consumers are at a vast disadvantage in aggregating and obtaining appropriate attention to their numerous small interests in legislative and regulatory matters. Industry trade associations, on the other hand, are keenly aware of where their interests lie and have often manipulated the political system to assure that regulation's net effect on them is not adverse, even when the public has succeeded in raising an issue concerning industry performance. Not only are industry interests influential in the framing of legislation, but regulated firms have a comparative advantage in making the regulators' lives more difficult once a regulatory scheme is enacted. This has usually led to systematic accommodation of their interests. Even when the consumer's interest is represented in some effective way, the political setting of the agencies encourages them to seek compromise, a propensity that results in recognition being given to interests more in proportion to their "clout" than to their merit. Perceiving their task primarily as one of mediating among interest groups, the agencies have shrunk from the harder tasks of defining what really constitutes the public interest and compelling the affected interests to abide by their definition. As political scientist Theodore Lowi has said, regulation with these dynamic features "replaces planning with bargaining."[4]

On those occasions when regulators pursue their view of the public interest with unusual vigor, they may still find that it is beyond their power to make much of a difference. Due to bargains struck in the process of enactment, their statutory powers may be insufficient to accomplish major changes, and the burdens of day-to-day administration and the limits of agency resources may prevent attention to long-range planning and implementation of aggressive policies. The practical impossibility of controlling all the inputs and outputs of the regulated firm and of acting quickly or in anticipation of events may also cause regulatory efforts to be unavailing or inconsequential. George Stigler and Claire Friedland, noting that regulators are obviously busy, remind us that "the innumerable regulatory actions are conclusive proof, not of effective regulation, but of the desire to regulate."[5]

Ineffectiveness is not the worst hazard by any means, since regulation can cause positive harm. Many of its harms will be so hidden from public view as to make their amelioration unlikely. Because of their political environment, regulators usually attach higher priority to addressing known harms than to preventing harms that are not visible to the public eye. Indeed, they may even be inclined to eliminate visible costs by substituting higher hidden ones. Simple technical inefficiency—less output per unit of input—is one such insidious threat under regulation; not only is inefficiency invited by the "cost-plus" character of most rate controls, but it is almost perfectly hidden from public or regulatory attention. Even when regulation's costs are palpable, their rectification may still be hard to bring about for political reasons. Once such costs have become stable items in household and governmental budgets, it is hard to generate the political pressure needed to overcome the resistance of the interests that would be hurt by their elimination.

Regulators' most destructive inclination is probably the one that leads them to protect regulated interests against outside competition, including desirable new technology and promising organizational innovations. Usually the regulators have seen themselves as defenders of an existing "system" whose capacity to serve must be maintained in the public interest against all seemingly subversive influences. This protective attitude reflects more than the industry's influence over the regulators, since regulators usually develop a natural sympathy for the industry and particularly for its problems when confronted with an external threat. Because the industry's capital is perceived as having been entrusted to the regulators' safekeeping, its protection is viewed as an obligation. In the final analysis, the power to prevent the competitive market from working to the regulated firms' disadvantage is an important item in the regulators' stock in trade, a primary source of their ability to obtain the cooperation of private interests that is needed to attain other regulatory goals.

Another fault to which regulators must plead guilty is the encouragement of excessive investment of society's resources in the regulated activity. Maintenance of very high quality standards, higher than an informed public would insist on if given the choice between slightly higher quality and a significantly lower price, is one way in which this can occur. Another regulatory practice contributing to excessive industry size is the imposition of requirements that certain services be rendered even though they cannot pay their own way. The internal cross-subsidies needed to finance such unprofitable activities have long been endemic in regulated industries, leading to severe allocative inefficiency. Maintenance of regulated firms' financial ability to cross-subsidize desirable services has necessitated regulation to discourage price cutting and competitive market entry. Regulatory protectionism has thus found an additional rationale in the need to foreclose competitors allegedly bent on "skimming the cream" off the regulated firms' market.

It is curious, to say the least, that mechanisms of economic regulation similar to those that have performed so poorly in other regulated industries—and that, in particular, have caused them to absorb excessive resources—were seized on to correct inflation and excessive growth in the health care industry. As Chapter 2 demonstrates, the choice was not a sound one. Certainly enough has already been said to establish that regulation does not inevitably define and serve the public interest. Only if economic regulation is perceived as a seriously flawed but occasionally necessary social instrument can a sound comparative evaluation of competition's potential in the health care industry proceed.

THE CURRENT CONTEXT OF POLICY CHOICES

It can be postulated, for analytical purposes, that there is some-where a socially appropriate—even an optimal—allocation of health care resources and level of health care spending that health policy should be designed to approach. That allocation of resources and level of spending cannot be objectively identified, however, and therefore analysis is more usefully directed at eval-uating the merits of various allocative processes than at assessing actual results, which we lack a benchmark for evaluating. The analysis in this book looks critically at both the political—that is, regulatory—processes and the market processes that are available for allocating resources to health care uses, and seeks to find the most promising mix of policies and procedures. Stressing the in-centives at work and the opportunities available for people to re-veal their preferences and the strength thereof, the analysis concludes that market forces have a substantial comparative ad-vantage in the long run.

The deregulation movement that began in the mid-1970s has made it increasingly possible for choices between regulation and competition to be weighed without a heavy presumption in favor of the regulatory approach. A landmark in the restoration of bal-ance in such policy debates was a book by Charles L. Schultze, chairman of President Carter's Council of Economic Advisers. In *The Public Use of Private Interest*,[6] Schultze discussed at length what he viewed as the political system's undue propensity to adopt the "black box" approach to social intervention. He object-ed to the political preference for "grafting a specific command-and-control module—a regulatory apparatus—onto the system of incentive-oriented private enterprise,"[7] instead of attempting to design techniques of intervention that preserve some of the vir-tues of the free market. Since Schultze's book was written, a sub-stantial political shift has occurred so that the presumption, if there is any, may now run against regulation rather than in its favor. As long as such a presumption is not accompanied by too heavy a burden of persuasion, that stance would appear to serve the public interest well.

Schultze's insightful explanation of how the political process previously yielded biased prescriptions points naturally toward adoption of a more balanced approach to policy choices in the health care sector. This book's primary objective is to strengthen the resolve of health system planners and regulators to explore the possibilities for mixed solutions that avoid, in Schultze's words, an "output-oriented, command-and-control approach to social intervention which is not only inefficient, but productive of far more intrusive government than is necessary."[8] In addition to promoting regulatory decisions that are more receptive to the idea of competition in local markets for health services, the book also contains a message for those interested in using nonregulatory initiatives to encourage competition's emergence as a useful force in local markets. Thus, health planners, consumer groups, and coalitions of major purchasers of health benefits will find here many clues, as well as some direct advice, concerning how to bring about private, competitive innovations that will more effectively deter inappropriate spending on health services.

Important legislative issues will also be more intelligently addressed if the choice between regulation and market forces is made with Schultze's precepts in view and this book in hand. For example, the states, which are required by Public Law 93–641 to adopt and administer certificate-of-need programs satisfying extensive federal conditions,[9] must amend their laws to reflect the 1979 amendments' recognition of competition's potential.[10] While federal law and policy dominate the field at the moment, it would be desirable if, rather than simply echoing the federal requirements concerning the weight to be given to competitive values, the states would add the weight of their own independent support for a procompetitive policy. The certificate-of-need law enacted in Utah in 1979 prior to the enactment of the federal amendments (see Appendix A) provides a potentially interesting model for a state-sponsored competition-sensitive regulatory program. The need for independent state action in support of finding a regulatory path to deregulation would increase in the future if

Congress should repeal or again alter the thrust of the federal legislation.

Whether state and local political support for the concept of competition will be forthcoming in many places could prove decisive in determining whether the strategy of introducing competition will be aggressively and creatively pursued. Reductions in federal budgetary support for local health planning already presage a shift of policymaking responsibility on these questions back to the states. Such a shift would raise significant new doubts about competition's prospects because, at the state and local levels, politics may easily guarantee sacrifice of competitive values. It could, for example, fall victim to established providers' preference for a more protected environment, to panicky attempts to contain Medicaid budgets through Draconian regulatory controls, or to some planner-regulators' desire to exercise as much direct authority as possible—even when more defensible results could be gained by deferring to consumer choices in a competitive environment. In general, it is hoped that Schultze's general approach, as adapted to the health care sector, will find a receptive audience in at least a substantial minority of the states so that experimentation with intensified, cost-conscious competition can proceed.

Finally, there are the larger issues of national health policy. These will also be viewed differently if approached from the analytical perspective adopted here. With the Reagan administration's accession to power came a major shift in the philosophy of the executive branch from a strong presumption in favor of health sector regulation to an equally strong presumption against it. Although the full implications of this ideological shift are not yet clear, the time may be ripe for a balanced reappraisal of health policy questions with a view to improving the ability of market forces to discipline the industry. This book is intended to inform the continuing debate on that subject and to influence decisions that will determine just how far back the policy pendulum will be allowed to swing from the previous commitment to regulation toward complete laissez-faire. In addition to examining the role of competition and health planning-cum-regulation in making the transition to an effective marketplace, the book includes pronouncements on the other major policy issues that must be addressed.

NOTES

1. 88 Stat. 2225 (1975) (codified at 42 U.S.C. §§300k-300t (1976)). References to Public Law 93–641 hereafter will be to sections of the Public Health Service Act. Unless otherwise indicated, such references include all amendments through August 1981, including the Omnibus Budget Reconciliation Act of 1981, Pub. L. No. 97–35, §§933-37, 95 Stat. 357, 570–72 (to be codified in scattered sections of 42 U.S.C.).

2. Pub. L. No. 96–79, 93 Stat. 606 (codified in scattered sections of 42 U.S.C.) This enactment will usually be referred to hereafter in the text as the 1979 amendments and in footnotes as Pub. L. No. 96–79.

3. What follows is a brief summary and adaptation of Havighurst, "Federal Regulation of the Health Care Delivery System: A Foreword in the Nature of a 'Package Insert'," 6 *U. Tol. L. Rev.* 577 (1975) (adapted with permission).

4. T. Lowi, *The End of Liberalism* 101 (1969).

5. Stigler & Friedland, "What Can Regulators Regulate? The Case of Electricity," 5 *J. L. & Econ.* 1 (1962).

6. C. Schultze, *The Public Use of Private Interest* (1977).

7. *Id.* at 13.

8. Schultze's book was summarized under the same title in *Harper's*, May 1977, at 43, from which this particular quotation is taken. *Id.* at 61.

9. Public Health Service Act §1523(a)(4)(B), *as amended. See* North Carolina *ex rel.* Morrow v. Califano, 445 F. Supp. 532 (E.D.N.C. 1977), *aff'd mem.,* 435 U.S. 962 (1978).

10. The deadline for state compliance in Public Health Service Act §1521(d), *as amended,* was most recently extended by Pub. L. No. 97–35, §936(b) (1981).

2 THE SPECIAL PROBLEMS OF HEALTH CARE COST-CONTAINMENT REGULATION[1]

Economic regulation of the health care sector was undertaken in the late 1960s and 1970s to deal with rising health care costs. Although neither the circumstances occasioning such regulation nor the mechanisms adopted were identical to the circumstances and mechanisms of regulation in other industries, many of the same problems surfaced, and some new ones appeared. This chapter seeks to show in a somewhat impressionistic way why regulation is unpromising as a way of solving the industry's cost problems.

COMPARING HEALTH SECTOR REGULATION WITH OTHER REGULATORY EXPERIENCE

Early doubts expressed by scholars and others about the probable efficacy of cost-containment regulation in the health care industry were somewhat unfocused because they were based on extrapolation from experience in other industries.[2] Those early doubts were not wide of the mark, however, and accumulating evidence about health sector regulation has shown their essential validity. Whereas the most thoughtful early critics anticipated some cost-containment impact from regulation and argued only that it would be woefully inadequate to the need, the most careful studies that have been done so far have shown practically no measurable effects on costs from certification of need[3] and professional standards review organizations (PSROs);[4] even hospital rate setting, which had only to prove that it was superior to retrospective cost reimbursement, has yet to be declared a major improvement.[5] These disappointing regulatory results, some of which are examined and explained in Chapter 3, seem attributable in part to the same general failings of regulation that were identified in Chapter 1.

As in other regulated industries, the design of regulation in the health care industry has reflected the influence of providers. In general, health system regulators have been given only weak powers to control costs and effectuate change as industry lobbying, both in Congress and in most states, has prevented the enactment of the heavy regulatory weapons, primarily rigorous rate controls on hospitals, that might have had some success. Thus, aside from a few state hospital rate-setting programs, planners and regulators have had to depend to a large extent on their powers of persuasion to curb cost escalation. Certificate-of-need laws, enacted largely at the hospitals' own behest, were intended to deal only with the expanding supply of facilities and services and rarely provide explicit mechanisms for reducing the excess capacity that is widely believed to exist. Utilization controls were adopted only for care provided under public programs and are administered by professional groups largely unconcerned about costs. Even where hospital rate regulation has been enacted, it has usually had some support from hospitals seeking to legitimize their costs and to facilitate recovery of those costs from third-party payers.

The Certificate-of-Need Process: Planning Versus Political Bargaining.

Under Public Law 93–641, certification of need for new facilities and services has been carried out by the states through a process that is spelled out in considerable detail in federal law and regulations. Under the federal requirements, a state must create a "state health planning and development agency" (hereafter, the state agency or SHPDA) to administer the regulatory program. Although the state was to be the ultimate decisionmaker on certificate-of-need applications, the state agency was required to receive advice on all such applications from local "health systems agencies" (HSAs). HSAs are federally designated and funded planning agencies serving one of over two hundred federally defined "health service areas." Usually they are private nonprofit corporations and not governmental instrumentalities. Legislative moves in 1981, which are discussed in Chapter 15, substantially reduced the prominence of HSAs and raised doubts about their future. Nevertheless, HSAs remain in place as perhaps the most notable feature of the regulatory process established under Public Law 93–641. Functioning as a kind of satellite of the state agency, a traditional regulatory body, the HSA was conceived as a solution to the problem of undue influence of regulated interests over the regulators. As such, it deserves some attention in this political assessment of regulation's prospects.

Even before Public Law 93–641, certification of need, the centerpiece of several states' regulatory effort, was implemented by conferring new powers and influence on provider-dominated health planning bodies and state health departments. Although additional consumer interests were often introduced into the planning process, the agencies continued to include providers as substantial participants in decisionmaking, thus confirming that bargaining with providers was the intended modus operandi. By formalizing the providers' role, the process reinforced what has seemed to be a substantial deficiency of regulation in other fields—namely, the regulators' inability to act in the public interest without accommodating in substantial ways the private interests of the regulated.

In Public Law 93–641, Congress carried the interest-group bargaining model of regulation to new extremes, providing in explicit and burdensome detail for the representation of various consumer and provider constituencies on the governing boards of local HSAs.[6] Having the character of minilegislatures, these boards would naturally see their function as one of balancing competing interests, thus belying the image of the agencies as bodies engaged in "hard" planning. Although the law seemed also to embody, schizophrenically, the technocratic planning ideal—calling for a high level of professionalism in agency staffs and highly specified health systems plans, for example—, the decisionmaking mechanisms adopted constituted such an invitation to politicization that the agencies could not reasonably be expected to define objective goals and enforce their realization.

Even though politicizing health planning and certification of need has struck many as progressive and democratic, the minilegislature model of the HSA governing body is particularly unpromising as a cost-containment mechanism. Some of the shortcomings of the policy of entrusting decisions to bargaining among well-organized constituencies are revealed in the weakness of the assumption that the relative strengths of individual groups' preferences can be accurately registered and given due effect in such bargaining. Manifestly, majority voting on a one-group, one-vote basis does not lend itself to achieving this ideal.

Another questionable assumption is that all relevant interests are adequately represented in an HSA. In fact, regulation of health facilities and services has been structured in such a way as to give cost containment poor representation. Whereas the benefits of each proposed project will be brought to the attention of the local HSA, that agency is likely to see only a fraction of any saving that might be achieved by turning it down. This occurs because, under the prevailing financing system, an economizing decision would benefit distant taxpayers and premium payers whose interests are not well represented in the local deliberations. Even the state agency, which takes final action on certificate-of-need applications and serves a wider constituency including taxpayers, will inadequately reflect the diffused interest in cost, much of which is borne nationally. (For example, the federal government has long borne the lion's share of Medicaid costs.) Thus, the externalization of the costs of local decisions strongly suggests that, unless an economizing ideology supplies an offsetting influence,[7] political forces at the local level will be biased in favor of spending in many cases where the benefits do not justify the outlay.

There is an even more fundamental prescription for failure in cost containment implicit in the HSAs' reliance on quasi-legislative decisionmaking based on majority voting. Because such voting permits coalitions of interest groups to gang up on others, one could expect HSA members to engage in "logrolling," or vote trading, to organize coalitions in support of particular spending proposals that would otherwise command only minority support.[8] Because HSAs act sequentially on certificate-of-need applications, the decisionmaking process seems positively to invite this practice. It is a sobering irony that logrolling in an HSA has powerful cost-escalating tendencies, precisely the opposite of the effect apparently desired by Congress. Congress's own experience with "pork-barrel" legislation demonstrates how legislative logrolling can distort the allocation of public funds.[9]

Perhaps one could reasonably hope that logrolling behavior consistent with the legislative analogy will not occur in HSAs despite powerful reasons to engage in it and that, due to ideological or other factors, the strong assumption of self-interested voting that underlies the theory of vote trading will not hold in the HSA context.[10] Unfortunately, such hopes do not seem well grounded. Questionnaire responses in 1977 indicated that vote trading had in fact occurred in HSAs; of sixty respondents, eighteen (30 percent) said they had identified vote trading, seven saying it was rare and eleven saying it occurred occasionally.[11] Of course, vote trading would not be necessary as long as proposals supported by any substantial community group were approved nearly automatically either by the HSA or at the state level. Thus, the evidence cited in Chapter 3 indicating the ineffectiveness of certificate-of-need laws suggests that participants have had no particular need to sharpen their political skills. On the other hand, if HSAs' influence in certificate-of-need regulation threatened to become greater, increasingly explicit vote trading could reasonably be expected to emerge to retard its impact. From all appearances, HSAs are increasingly viewed as political bodies, and it seems likely that participants' political sophistication in garnering support for projects—through ex parte contacts with decisionmakers, for example[12]—would increase in proportion to the necessity.

In general, certificate-of-need regulation seems too political to succeed. One possibility is that the political character of HSAs would give their recommendations a legitimacy that induces undue deference by state officials, resulting in the rubber stamping of actions that reflect the interplay of political forces rather than sound health planning. Alternatively, sound HSA advice might be effectively ignored at the state level, where political influence may also operate.[13] The net effect of the two-tiered decision process may be to give established interests two points at which to bring their influence to bear and to bargain for a satisfactory result. All in all, the mechanisms established by Congress in Public Law 93–641 seem to contain many of the elements that contribute to regulatory failure.

Regulation's Costs

Regulation's hidden costs in other industries have important parallels in the health care system. Simple inefficiency, bred in part by regulation that confirms and supports third-party payers' practice of reimbursing incurred costs, is widely believed to be a serious problem. Other costs, also largely hidden, are the internal subsidies that flow within hospitals. Some of these subsidies would probably be approved by the public, particularly those that support indigent care, education, and research, but they have never been quantified or scrutinized. Even though internal subsidies have long been a hallmark of economic regulation, the health care industry may be more interlaced with cross-subsidies at the moment than other regulated industries have been.

Health sector regulation has also reflected the protectionist tendencies of other regulatory endeavors. Hospital capital investments have often been seen as dedicated to a philanthropic purpose, which the regulators have felt called upon to further. Thus, the nonprofit and community-service nature of established hospitals has helped to legitimize regulators' defense of them against alleged cream skimming, often by proprietary providers. Moreover, competition has been perceived—correctly, in many circumstances—to yield adverse cost consequences and only questionable benefits. Finally, a strong belief that empty hospital beds attract additional patients who do not really require hospitalization has also supplied a warrant for curbing "duplication"—that is, competition. For these reasons, the protectionism that has characterized other regulated industries has infected certificate-of-need regulation, even to the extent of excluding or harassing such desirable innovations as health maintenance organizations (HMOs). Most of this book is concerned with encouraging the industry's planner-regulators to overcome their restrictive and protective impulses and to allow competition to operate when the public interest so requires.

There appears to be a real likelihood that health sector regulation, like regulation in other industries, has contributed to rather than prevented industry overexpansion. Quality-oriented regulation, such as PSROs have tended to pursue, may well have fostered the use of excessively expensive inputs and encouraged utilization levels that would not be justified by a comparison of marginal costs and benefits. There is also good reason to think that internal subsidies have lowered the price and thus encouraged the use of some services that are not worth their cost. Just as the logrolling possibilities in HSAs facilitate excessive spending, the quality imperative discussed later in this chapter suggests the same hazard. Finally, as Chapter 3 reveals, jurisdictional limits on the regulators' power may make them unable to prevent providers from spending, in some way, all of the resources that the dysfunctional financing system puts at their disposal.

Health sector regulation, it turns out, has been poorly designed to deal with the resource misallocation that occasioned it. Indeed, analogous economic regulation in other industries has proved more a cause of, than an obstacle to, the dedication of excessive resources to the activity being regulated. Unless health sector economic regulation can be fundamentally redesigned, it must be expected that it will continue to foster more and better services and ever higher quality. If the reader thinks this sounds good, he has missed the overriding point: that health care can absorb, and demonstrably has absorbed, too much of society's resources and will continue to do so as long as regulators of the health care sector behave as other regulators have behaved.

The "New" Regulation and Its Significance for Health Care

A wave of new regulatory initiatives enacted in the 1960s may be thought to solve many of the generic problems of regulation cited in Chapter 1. These laws, which dealt primarily with safety, health, and environmental problems, reflected little industry influence over the legislative process, and their implementation against industry interests has been so aggressive that it may no longer seem reasonable to worry that health sector regulation, a product of the same era, may benefit the regulated interests at the expense of the public or fail to give the public a full measure of relief.

A critical feature of the new regulation is its focus on problem areas that transcend industry lines. With industrial interests diffused and often in conflict with each other, lobbies of citizens concerned about the particular problem and professing to represent the public interest were able to dominate the legislative process and to keep pressure on the agencies through publicity, political activism, and litigation. The powerful political appeal of the safety, health, and environmental values being defended—all highly symbolic and resistant to tradeoff against mere dollars—practically guaranteed that regulation would not be watered down to suit the regulated interests. There is now good reason to think that much of this regulation has gone to economically irrational extremes, imposing costs on industry (and ultimately on consumers) that are greater than the associated benefits could possibly warrant. Indeed, the legislation itself, conforming to the extreme views of citizen lobbies and reflecting the imperatives of the health and safety rationales, frequently precluded the use of benefit/cost analysis, thus seeming to invite the excesses that appear to have occurred. Failures of the new regulation appear to be of a very different order than the problems under the old.[14]

The new era has also brought about some change in the nature of the old regulation. Deregulation has made considerable headway, and there is more vigilance today against the regulatory mistakes and abuses of the past. Predictions of regulatory performance are much less reliable than they once were because new political constituencies have formed and others have weakened. Nevertheless, the hazards remain very much as they have always been. In the new circumstances, careful analysis of particular regulatory schemes in light of the balance and character of operative political forces seems essential in making any assessment.

For the most part, the design of regulation in the health care sector resembles that of the old regulation. Regulation is essentially directed to the myriad problems of a single industry rather than to a specific health, safety, or environmental problem that cuts across industry boundaries. The regulatory approaches used to achieve cost control differ only slightly from those employed in traditional public utility regulation. Thus, analogies to the old regulation and its problems still seem more pertinent than analogies to the new.

Experience under the new regulation does, however, reveal the force that health and safety claims exert in a regulatory environment and the extraordinary difficulty of facing tradeoffs between these claims and dollar costs. What is particularly striking is that, in health care cost containment, the health and safety arguments weigh in favor not of the regulators, as in the new regulation, but of the regulated interests—the providers of care and the patient populations whose care the regulators seek to ration. Unlike traditional public utility regulators, the regulators of the health care system are not engaged simply in limiting industrial profits. With the symbolic values nearly all on the producers' side, the health care system's planner-regulators are left to fight for cost containment in a potentially unfriendly political environment. The rest of this chapter explores at some length the significance of the tradeoff problem for regulatory performance.

It thus appears that cost-containment regulation in the health sector features the worst aspects of both the old and the new regulation. Oriented to a single industry armed with ample political clout, it closely resembles the old regulation, and may easily share the latter's tendency to define issues in such a way as to promote the industry and its desirable services and to discourage meaningful competition. On the other hand, dealing with health and safety issues in an intensely political climate and without a developed capacity for coping with complex tradeoffs, it threatens to suffer from excesses similar to those of the new regulation and hence to tolerate a good deal of spending to achieve health benefits that are not worth their cost. The combination of these elements seems most unpromising.

The Relevance of Parallels to Other Regulatory Experience

Although the problems of health sector regulation parallel the failings of regulation in other industries, it must ultimately be evaluated on its own terms. It is possible to argue, for example, that regulation has never been allowed to take its final form and could be strengthened in readily apparent ways to achieve cost-containment objectives. Also, it can be argued that regulators need more time to solve difficult problems and to develop the skills needed to bring an intractable industry into line. Even though current political trends make it unlikely that regulators will be given more powers or much additional time, no final policy choice has been made. In any event, the purpose here is to compare regulatory and market-oriented strategies, a task requiring that the alternative approaches be evaluated without unfairly discounting one or the other strategy for possibly transitory political obstacles to its realization.

Although regulatory experience in the health sector is still somewhat inconclusive, it is now possible to move well beyond imperfect analogies to other regulatory programs and to assess governmental cost-containment regulation in the health care field on its own merits. Deferring discussion of empirical evidence until Chapter 3, the following analysis relies primarily on improved understanding of what regulation in this industry must seek to achieve and of the practical obstacles it must confront. While analogies to other regulation have been useful in framing the pertinent questions, it is now clear that health sector regulation is in many respects sui generis. Among other things, it employs some unusual regulatory mechanisms, particularly HSAs, that were designed in large measure specifically to avoid the problems of domination by vested interests which regulation had encountered in other settings and about which the early critics of regulation had warned. Although some institutional considerations may suggest that regulation in the health sector could outperform regulation in other industries, the cost-containment job that regulators have been asked to do with respect to health care is far from easy compared to other regulatory assignments.

RATIONING HEALTH CARE: A POLITICAL "HOT POTATO"

Although the regulators' task in the health care industry is variously stated, the job to be done involves nothing less than rationing health care—preventing patients from receiving and providers from providing care that they believe would be beneficial. Whereas the rationing of commodities such as sugar or gasoline involves simply giving equal portions to each consumer within broad functional categories defined by objective circumstances, rationing health care requires parcelling out medical services in accordance with relative need. Because this entails comparing incommensurables and making myriad social valuations in a context fraught with potential personal tragedy, the political problems of explicitly rationing health services are potentially substantial.

Rationing health care is not a regulatory function that is likely to be popular with or easily understood by a public which has been told that there is a right to health care and which has come to expect a high standard of care and easy access to it. In effect, the regulators have been charged with reducing, one way or another, what have come to be seen as the most tangible indicia of quality in medical care—namely, the quantity and intensity of services rendered both in individual cases and in the aggregate. They have been asked to say no to more and better health services under circumstances where everyone immediately concerned in a specific treatment decision is inclined to say yes because, with widespread third-party payment, they do not face the costs. Although some means of limiting the consumption of health services is clearly required, public regulation may be incapable of achieving this specific goal.

Semantic Clues to the Regulatory Problem

The rationing objective is usually obscured in the rhetoric describing the function of various regulatory programs in the health sector, raising doubts about how effective regulation can be. For example, PSROs are usually said to be primarily concerned with the quality of care, not cost containment. Under the banner of "quality assurance," some "unnecessary" care and costly "overutilization" can perhaps be eliminated, but the medical profession's de facto control of PSROs assures that cost considerations and the rationing objective will be kept distinctly secondary. It has been argued that PSROs could better ration services if they were not seen as regulatory agencies at all but instead were perceived as agencies to define and appropriately limit the coverage of federal health programs.[15] What is striking is that it has been politically impossible to maintain this latter conception of PSROs as rationers of federal financing concerned with bene-fit/cost ratios. As a result, lines have been drawn on the basis of whether medical decisions are defensible under professional norms, not whether the federal government has some obligation to underwrite their costs.

The stated goals of certificate-of-need regulation likewise indi-cate that regulation will fall short of achieving meaningful ration-ing. Certificate-of-need agencies are usually charged merely with preventing duplication and forestalling the construction of "un-needed" facilities. They are seldom, if ever, publicly instructed to create artificial shortages, yet meaningful cost containment re-quires that supply be curtailed not to meet, but to contain, de-mand.[16] Responses to a questionnaire circulated to HSA administrators by the author in 1977 confirmed the expectation that the rationing objective would not be achieved. Forty of for-ty-four respondents felt that "to eliminate duplication of services and save the costs of underutilized capital assets" was a better statement of the purpose of certificate-of-need laws than "to limit the availability of facilities as a means of forcing providers to make hard choices about their use."[17]

Similarly, the ostensible purpose of most hospital rate-setting agencies is to squeeze "inefficiency" out of the system, not to force hospitals to cut back services. Nevertheless, some cutbacks are certainly essential if costs are to be appropriately controlled. Reducing hospital revenues would be a way of enforcing neces-sary rationing, but, because regulators are reluctant to declare that goal, there is reason to doubt that they can achieve it.

The semantic obscurity under which regulation is practiced in the health care sector reveals the political and social touchiness of the subject being regulated. A powerful taboo surrounds public discussion of tradeoffs between citizens' lives and health, on the one hand, and the public's financial resources, on the other. This taboo causes regulators to be reluctant to fight many battles in the "quality/cost no-man's-land"—that area where, although ad-ditional medical inputs are undeniably beneficial, there is real doubt that the benefits are worth the cost.[18] Even though effec-tive cost-containment regulation seems to call for the sophisticat-ed techniques of benefit/cost analysis, regulators will naturally shy away from such tools because their use would require placing explicit values on individuals' lives and health.[19] Given their political vulnerability, the lack of public understanding, and their own moral trepidation in the face of providers' claims, regulators are unlikely to be able consistently and forthrightly to address the tradeoffs involved in rationing health care and to have due regard for other uses of resources.

Shifting the Rationing Burden to Providers

One consequence of regulators' difficulties in challenging directly what passes for "quality" in medical care is that, to be effective, regulators must somehow avoid addressing the medical merits of specific cases and concentrate on grosser forms of control. One reason why PSROs are unlikely to make more than a marginal contribution to cost containment is that they purport to assess the medical merits of individual utilization decisions, which can usually be questioned only if one is willing to compare the benefits and the costs of treating an individual patient. Much greater hope for cost control is currently reposed in limiting the availability of health facilities (through certificate-of-need programs) and the amount of hospital budgets (through rate setting), two approaches that impose resource constraints on providers and thereby shift to them the difficult task of rationing care among those who seek it. Indeed, regulation in the health sector has shied away from asking the public authorities to make the hard case-by-case decisions and has moved in subtle ways toward making providers do the rationing. Precisely because the regulators, like Ado Annie in *Oklahoma,* "cain't say 'no,'" they have sought to shift the burden of doing so to the providers. The PSRO program does this explicitly, but certification of need and hospital rate-setting programs do it as well.

The policy of forcing providers to do the rationing job is based on an unarticulated assumption that limiting the resources available to providers can induce them to allocate those resources to their best uses, providing those services that are most valuable to patients and omitting those services that are least valuable. But hardly any thought has been given to whether providers can realistically be expected to serve primarily public needs rather than their own interests and values in performing this allocative function. Despite this, regulation has been implemented in a way that perpetuates the very provider dominance which has produced excessive emphasis on high-technology acute care rendered in institutional settings while neglecting more routine needs of large populations and which has therefore been an important source of the health sector's problems in the first place. It is far from clear that the limited consumer participation provided for in health planning and resource development can overcome provider influence on any issue where the claims of quality are plausible.

Providers' economic interests and their traditional "cost-is-no-object" orientation make it doubtful that they can be counted on to cooperate fully in helping the regulators achieve their rationing objective. Indeed, far from sparing the regulators embarrassment in their efforts to limit the health sector's spending proclivities, providers can be expected to expose the regulators' veiled attempts to erode what providers will characterize as the quality of care. In exercising their substantial discretion in the allocation of regulation-limited resources, providers may find it convenient to threaten cutbacks in just those highly visible areas where the regulators are most vulnerable and under the most pressure to keep the resources flowing. Thus, the politics of such regulation could easily produce a "hot potato" game in which providers, who are better insulated against political temperatures, can force public decisionmakers to take the heat. Under these circumstances, socially appropriate stringency is not likely to be achieved.

CAN COST-CONTAINMENT REGULATION BE BOTH PALATABLE AND EFFECTIVE MEDICINE?

Saying no to other people's health care and to arguable qualitative improvements in the care available in a community is so difficult, both politically and ethically, that it is unreasonable to expect public officials to succeed in regulation that entails explicit rationing. Nevertheless, there is a possible cost-containment strategy that would shield such officials from having to engage in explicit nay-saying and thus reduce their exposure to charges of callous neglect of specific health needs. Despite this strategy's relatively greater potential for effectiveness compared to yes-or-no regulatory decisions, its political prospects are very much in doubt. Recent history reveals both serious efforts to administer this strong medicine and an equally strong political dislike for the remedy thus prescribed.

The Apparent Necessity for Arbitrariness in Regulation

The first generation of health care cost controls imposed in the 1970s was apparently not sufficiently effective to legitimize the costs incurred under them. Perceiving the inadequacy of these measures and seeking more effective control, government began to turn increasingly to its only available counterstrategy against providers' adamant rejection of a role in rationing services. That strategy was to move toward more arbitrary forms of regulation that would avoid the necessity for yes-or-no choices affecting specific services, patients, or populations. By confining itself to making only "macro" choices, government hoped to minimize opportunities for confrontations with providers over specific quality/cost tradeoffs and to force providers to accept the rationing burden without recourse. The leading examples of escalating arbitrariness in regulation were the Carter administration's 1977 proposals to put a 9 percent cap on annual hospital cost increases and another cap on aggregate capital investments by hospitals.[20] Another demonstration of government's felt need to reduce regulators' discretion—and thus their political exposure—was the National Guidelines for Health Planning of the Department of Health, Education and Welfare (DHEW), particularly the highly quantitative guidelines originally proposed.[21] What is noteworthy about these proposals is that they sought to place absolute limits on spending increases and facilities' availability, thus permitting virtually no appeals based on health needs or other considerations. Much of the argument against the proposals was based on their arbitrary character.

The Carter administration could justify arbitrariness of this sort only by claiming that an emergency existed. This in turn required charging providers with gross irresponsibility in spending the public's funds. Thus, Secretary Joseph Califano's strong assertions about the "fat" and inefficiency in hospitals, in addition to being a distortion, could be seen both as an attempt to justify extreme measures and as an expression of frustration about regulation's achievements to date. Indeed, taken together, the Carter proposals were a clear confession of the failure of the regulatory approaches originally conceived for the health sector. Although regulation was originally intended to embody a tough-minded, planning-oriented approach to medical care, this did not materialize and, for the reasons stated above, seems never to have been in the political cards. Judging from Secretary Califano's remarks, government regulators apparently found it politically preferable, rather than face the hard tradeoffs openly on their merits, to appear overtly antiprovider, even dictatorial. They apparently thought it better to have any adverse impacts on quality chalked up to their general obtuseness rather than to be accused of callous cost consciousness in resolving health care spending issues on a case-by-case basis.

The logical extension of the policy of arbitrariness in regulation, had that policy been adopted, would have been the adoption of the ultimate cost-containment device embodied, most notably, in Senator Edward Kennedy's health security proposal of the mid-1970s. That device is a congressionally determined fixed budget for the health care system as a whole. As the ultimate in arbitrary regulation (it is really more a management tool than a regulatory measure), the fixed budget approach does promise effectiveness of a sort in cost containment. However, the predictability it achieves is not quite the same thing as cost control since Congress might find it hard to deny the claims of the many interest groups affected. Indeed, the setting of annual budget allocations is more a political than a scientific undertaking, and there could be no assurance that Congress would have any more success in setting a proper health budget than it has had in dealing with national defense or other categorical programs. In the nature of things, political bargaining over such a budget would always begin at whatever spending level had already been attained, thus dimming the prospects for any but very gradual corrections of a resource misallocation.

Even if the fixed budget approach seemed a good way to control total costs, there would remain the problem of allocating that budget to a myriad of possible uses. Allocation would be entrusted to the system's internal political processes, with consequences that are again extremely difficult to assess. Many of the same intractable decisionmaking difficulties that currently exist would remain, and it seems likely that, despite all efforts to introduce

citizen participation, providers would continue to exercise dispro-
portionate influence over the uses to which resources are put, if
not over absolute levels of spending. Thus, despite employment of
a fixed budget and central planning, the British National Health
Service long remained more heavily committed to high-technology acute care than was appropriate given that system's limited
resources and unmet needs in such areas as elective surgery and
long-term care for the elderly, the chronically and mentally ill,
and the handicapped.[22]

Despite its shortcomings, regulatory arbitrariness has had a
strong appeal to those who were firmly committed to regulation
of the health services industry. As the first regulatory interventions failed to achieve the expected victory, the necessity for
bringing more firepower to bear seemed undeniable. But, although the logic of the regulation advocates' case for escalating
the war on providers was strong, Congress ultimately refused to
go along.

Congress Digs In Its Heels

If regulation were in fact necessary to deal with the problem of
health care costs, then arbitrariness in regulation would seem desirable as a strategic response to providers' ability to win most
skirmishes over specific health care spending issues. Precisely because providers command the political heights overlooking the
quality/cost no-man's-land, government could reasonably elect to
employ strategic rather than merely tactical weapons in the battle for cost containment. Nevertheless, even though arbitrariness
is probably the most responsible regulatory policy available, it
has obvious objectionable features. Recognition of these features
has not only prevented its adoption but has stimulated a fundamental reexamination of the premise that regulation is necessary
or desirable as a device to solve the cost problem.

The Carter administration's hospital cost-containment bill was
defeated in Congress in 1979. During the extended negotiations
over the bill, its provisions were watered down to the point where
it would have had little effect on costs in any event. Most of the
changes were designed to reduce the essential element of arbitrariness and make room for exceptions. Although the bill had many
flaws, Congress's refusal to accept the concept of fixed limits con-

firmed the judgment that regulation cannot be both effective in controlling costs and politically palatable. The National Guidelines for Health Planning were also ultimately revised to eliminate their more arbitrary features.[23] Again it appeared that, despite the virulence of health care cost escalation, the United States was not ready for controls that departed fundamentally from the original ideal of regulation based on planning, fine tuning, and sensitivity to local conditions.

In rejecting the new departure in health regulation represented by the Carter cap proposals, Congress was by no means expressing its satisfaction with the status quo. Indeed, the individual leaders in the congressional fight against the hospital cost-containment legislation became prominent in the health policy debate shortly thereafter as sponsors of innovative reform measures that, instead of strengthening government control, would have addressed the recognized problems by eliminating distortions in consumers' incentives and increasing opportunities for consumer choice.[24] Thus, it was confrontation with the necessity for accepting extreme arbitrariness in regulation as the price for effective cost containment that, more than anything else, triggered the new interest in health sector competition that emerged in the Ninety-sixth Congress and was reflected in the 1979 health planning amendments. Although belief in the necessity and desirability of regulation still persists in many places, the failure of the Carter proposals, embodying the last best hope for achieving effective regulation, appears to have marked a watershed in national policy. Congress is now unimpressed by regulatory proposals in this field and is leaning toward terminating or reducing the scope of existing regulation.

VALUE IMPLICATIONS OF THE CHOICES IN HEALTH POLICY

Not only are there powerful pragmatic and political reasons for not relying heavily on regulation to control health care costs, but there are also some ethical issues that, though debatable, also suggest the need for second thoughts about the wisdom of employing regulation as the dominant mechanism of social control. Ultimately, the choice of regulation to control the health care industry implies a judgment on the appropriateness of substituting collective decisionmaking for private choices regarding the intensely personal matter of how an individual's health is to be cared for. Although a full treatment of these issues would be out of place here, no discussion of this subject should leave them entirely implicit.

Regulation Versus Private Choice

One of the most important observations one can make about health care is that it varies greatly in value, some of it being of priceless benefit and other care not being, in any defensible sense, worth its cost. Although this insight was long neglected in the campaign to establish the existence of a right to health care, versions of it appeared increasingly in health policy discussions in the 1970s. Nevertheless, its full implications were slow to sink in. For example, many observers who gave lip service to the insight that only limited benefits are yielded by much health care remained fervently attached to the symbolic goals of comprehensive benefits and equality of access to high-quality services. Yet the emerging sophistication about health care's value should have suggested placing less emphasis on providing the poor with an ideal standard of health care and more emphasis on providing them with other things, many of which, such as better housing and nutrition, might be more conducive to improved health.

The new awareness about medicine's uncertain benefits was also slow to overcome the tendency of policymakers and other observers to disparage private choices between health care and other things. Yet increasing skepticism among commonly recognized authorities about the value of health care at the margin suggests (1) that the range and subjectivity of consumer preferences with respect to medical care do not necessarily signify consumer ignorance or irrationality and (2) that different people can come rationally to different conclusions about what quantity and quality of services to buy. Although individual consumers' decisions can always be questioned, most consumer choices are made with the benefit of professional advice or by employment (or other) groups whose sophistication is less subject to doubt. Moreover, private choices are made with information concerning personal preferences that obviously is not available to anyone except the individuals involved. In a free society, private decisions might be viewed as having comparative or even absolute legitimacy on this account alone.

As a substitute for private decisions, regulation leaves much to be desired. Not only does it suffer from irremediable ignorance about individual cases—both the precise medical circumstances and the subjective preferences of the parties affected—but it also lacks data on societal preferences concerning the value of health care in comparison with other possible uses of society's limited productive capacity. Although it is common to attribute irrationality only to consumers, it is clear that irrationality systematically afflicts health system regulators because politicized regulation allows symbolism to overwhelm forthright benefit/cost comparisons. Moreover, the interest-group bargaining implicit in the American concept of regulation perpetuates a high degree of provider influence, leaves out many other pertinent values and interests, and assigns weights on the basis of power and influence, not merit. It is doubtful that health sector regulators can earn higher marks for knowledge, rationality, general soundness, or democratic validity than consumers making decisions with professional and other available advice and under appropriate incentives to conserve resources.

The Values of the Planner-Regulators Themselves

A major obstacle to reintroducing market forces and consumer choice as useful guides for system development is the value system of the planner-regulators themselves. Though assessing values is difficult, the public health orientation of most planners has inclined them toward a command-and-control approach rather than a market-facilitating role. Indeed, health care system planners and regulators appear to be drawn in large numbers from what has been pejoratively labeled by some neoconservatives, particularly Irving Kristol, as "the new class."[25] The value system attributed to the new class would incline them away from embracing a market-oriented approach to the health care system's various problems. Moreover, although the new class purports to represent consumer interests, their values are so different from those of consumers that they cannot claim to be simply seeking to replicate by regulatory means the results of a smoothly functioning marketplace. On the other hand, the biases that the new class brings to the regulatory endeavor might offset some of the political pressures on which this chapter's assessment of regulation's prospects is largely based. For these reasons, the new class deserves brief discussion.

The new class, as the term is used in sociological assessments, refers not so much to an identifiable class of individuals as to the value system that seems to underlie certain new directions in policy development that began in the 1960s, particularly in the area of government regulation of business. Nevertheless, these values are attributable to many of the upper middle class who have rejected the commercial world in favor of careers in the public sector and in nonprofit organizations closely allied with government and who largely exercise the power and authority that increasingly reside in these institutions. The value system of the new class, while difficult and perhaps dangerous to generalize about, appears to attach less weight to actual consumer choices than to the preferences of self-appointed consumer advocates. By the same token, regulatory choices are likely to be viewed as presumptively sounder than the results yielded by even a smoothly functioning market. Paul H. Weaver has described the ethos of the new class as "so systematically statist, so indifferent to the liberal promise of individual autonomy and social abundance, so hostile to the achievements and aspirations of so many liberal institutions that it strikes me as being more heresy than not."[26] It seems clear that the values of the new class go beyond mere paternalism, approaching self-righteous authoritarianism.

Among the contributions of the new class to American society has been the new wave of regulatory legislation of the 1960s and early 1970s in the areas of the environment, health, and safety. Earlier discussion contrasted this new regulation with the old public-utility-type regulation, and the point was made that the health-and-safety rationale, which has been so effectively wielded by the new class to overwhelm industry-expressed concern about benefit/cost tradeoffs, appears in health sector regulation to weigh on the side of the regulated industry and against the regulators. This observation, coupled with other similarities between health sector regulation and the old regulation, particularly its orientation to a single and well-respected industry, enhances the concern expressed here that regulation cannot be counted on to solve the health care industry's cost problems. Perhaps the greatest imponderable in this assessment is the political ability of the new class to employ the regulatory process to give effect to its perceptions that medical care is both overrated and inappropriately distributed, that health care providers are an irresponsible elite, and that technology is suspect. The mission of the new class in health care, as in the new regulation, is clear—to enforce both its conception that less is better and its antipathy to, in Weaver's words, "acts of consumption by consenting adults."[27]

While it is easy to agree with the new class that, in health care at the moment, less would very often be better, there is reason to doubt two things: First, one may ask whether, given a free hand, the new class would know where to stop economizing or how to recognize the exceptional case where more is better. Second, one may wonder how the political forces would balance out and whether the new class, lacking a specific constituency but clever enough to shape the questions and manipulate the system, could gain and keep control of the regulatory process. A great deal obviously would depend on chance and fortuitously distributed political skills, a fact that should itself weaken our faith in the outcome. Moreover, although the new class might provide an overdue counterweight to the quality imperative, to provider interests, and to the historic dominance of the medical profession's values,[28] it can give no assurance that is has better answers or can allocate resources as well as a reformed competitive marketplace.[29]

The Reagan administration's appearance seems likely to doom the new class to reduced influence and indeed to a high level of unemployment. To a large extent, the Reagan budget-cutting effort and the campaign against overregulation are a reaction against the values of the new class. Insofar as the health care sector is concerned, there would seem to be good reason to let consumers speak for themselves and to reduce the role of the new class in the allocation of resources.

The Value Implications of Provider Dominance

Another danger in health sector regulation is that provider values will weigh heavily in decisionmaking. Providers' political influence has already guaranteed them an explicit role in health planning, and the integration of planning and regulation assures them substantial influence in regulatory decisions. The structure of regulation thus contemplates what regulatory politics would assure in any event—namely, that provider interests will be balanced off against consumer interests in a largely political context. Because provider preferences are necessarily incorporated in the regulatory calculus, it is impossible to maintain the pretext that health planning and regulation are intended simply to approximate the results that would obtain in an ideal competitive marketplace. Thus, instead of being a device for replicating the results of provider competition to meet consumers' effectively expressed demands, regulation is a process in which interest groups bargain for advantage. Because providers possess a greater ability than most consumer groups to organize and to defend their interests in such political bargaining, their influence can be expected to be very great.

Despite providers' rhetoric, the values that they bring to the bargaining process are not entirely congruent with those of patients and the general public. Providers and consumers would not see eye to eye, for example, on cost containment or on the desirability of price competition and might differ over such matters as the priority to be given to expensive high-technology medicine. Even though the interests of different provider groups are often in conflict, there is a strong preference for resolving these differences through collective negotiations rather than competition. Health planning-cum-regulation provides an opportunity for providers to bargain both among themselves and with others over differences that exist and to insist on one-dimensional symbolic values, such as quality, that neglect important but sensitive countervailing considerations, such as costs. Thus, although provider-dominated regulation may not produce an entirely monolithic system, the pluralism that is tolerated nevertheless denies consumers the opportunity to express many entirely reasonable preferences. The concessions that are sometimes made to permit consumer choice and nonprice competition, while important, should not obscure the options and values that are sacrificed.

Regulation has often seemed a positive step because it has tended to narrow the discretion of providers and has brought a new set of interests to the bargaining table. It is therefore argued that any influence that providers may retain under regulation is less than they would have in the absence of regulation and that regulation is to be valued precisely because it gives countervailing interests an opportunity to be heard and respected. The fallacy in this argument is not that regulation is never a useful counterbalance to provider dominance. Instead, the problem with regulation has been that better ways were, and are, available to weaken the power that providers have historically possessed. Thus, the case for a competition-promoting strategy rests on the use of other means to strengthen the consumer voice. Indeed, the policy of promoting competition should be understood not just as an alternative to regulatory controls but as an alternative to provider domination as well. Chapter 4 notes the factors that have allowed providers to dominate the system in the past and shows how public policy can systematically remove the causes of the industry's failure to serve consumer interests in the past. It is a vital insight that the choices in health policy are not just between regulation and the provider-dominated status quo but include competition as a quite distinct, and distinctly preferable, third option.

CONCLUSIONS: PROSPECTS AND ALTERNATIVES

Even the most pessimistic or skeptical observer cannot be sure that regulation will inevitably be totally ineffective in the health care industry or that no change in the direction or pace of cost escalation will occur as control mechanisms take hold and mature. It is likely, after all, that some regulators would prove adept in managing the political environment and in developing a constituency for cost-containment efforts and that some providers would adopt relatively responsible attitudes or would at least tolerate regulation designed to change the behavior of deviant providers. Thus, regulation may sometimes seem to have had a beneficial effect when compared with past experience in a particular area or with contemporaneous experience in places where regulation has been less intensive or less skillful or where providers have been more recalcitrant. But such apparent successes are likely to be marginal in magnitude and difficult to replicate universally. Proponents of regulation have nevertheless singled out the seemingly successful programs to prove the efficacy of their chosen methods and have viewed unimpressive average perform-ance only as evidence of the need to try harder and to invest more money in the regulatory effort. They have also yielded to the temptation, noted in Chapter 1, to equate vigorous regulatory activity, such as frequent denial of certificate-of-need applica-tions, with regulatory success, when in fact regulation may have had only minimal impact on its most important targets—that is, on cost and capital investment.

Regulation will frequently seem advantageous because it is measured only against the alternative of doing nothing, not against other promising policies that might have been, but were not, tried. Indeed, when adopted at the national level, regulation forecloses experimentation, not only making success or failure hard to recognize but also making the optimum strategy undis-coverable. While it is possible that some kind of equilibrium might eventually be reached where pressures to control costs and pressures to increase them were in rough balance, there would be no reason whatsoever to think that the political processes yield-ing that result had come anywhere near finding the socially opti-mal level of spending on health care. Instead, excessive spending on health care, buying too much of a good thing, is likely to con-tinue as a direct consequence of the strategic advantage that pro-viders enjoy as a result of their control of the high ground overlooking the quality/cost no-man's-land.

Regulation has failed to solve the resource allocation problem in the health sector precisely because it proceeds on wrong prem-ises concerning the capabilities of public decisionmakers. But, even if it should succeed in imposing effective controls, it would do so at the expense of important values. While holding out the promise of a right to health care, it would simultaneously define that right narrowly and arbitrarily and would almost certainly deny or indirectly curtail consumer rights to purchase care that they might wish to have but which the regulators chose not to make available. Regulation's chief tendency is thus toward nar-rowing consumers' range of choice, enforcing a false consensus, and obscuring the wide variations that exist in both consumer preferences and medical practice. Contrary to what both the po-litical debate and professional ideology imply, there is no "one right way" to deal with most health problems. Rather than relying on government alone to chart our course, it would seem more appropriate in a pluralistic society to widen opportunities for consumer choice under meaningful cost constraints.

NOTES

1. Portions of this chapter are adapted from Havighurst, "Health Care Cost-Containment Regulation: Prospects and an Alternative," 3 *Am. J.L. & Med.* 309 (1977). For a critique of that article and a strong rejoinder, *see* Weiner, "Governmental Regulation of Health Care: A Response to Some Criticisms Voiced by Proponents of a 'Free Market'," 4 *Am. J.L. & Med.* 15 (1978), and Havighurst, "More on Regulation: A Reply to Stephen Weiner," 4 *Am. J.L. & Med.* 243 (1978).
2. *See, e.g.,* Havighurst, "Regulation of Health Facilities and Services by 'Certificate of Need'," 59 *Va. L. Rev.* 1143 (1973); Noll, "The Consequences of Public Utility Regulation of Hospitals," in Institute of Medicine, *Controls on Health Care* 25 (1975).
3. Empirical research on regulation is discussed in Chaper 3.
4. *See, e.g.,* Congressional Budget Office, *The Effect of PSROs on Health Care Costs: Current Findings and Future Evaluations* (Background Paper, June 1979).
5. *See* Biles, Schramm, & Atkinson, "Hospital Cost Inflation under State Rate-Setting Programs," 303 *New Eng. J. Med.* 664 (1980); Sloan & Steinwald, "Effects of Regulation on Hospital Costs and Use," 23 *J.L. & Econ.* 81 (1980).
6. *See* Public Health Service Act §1512(b)(3)(C), *as amended.*
7. *See* D. Altman, R. Greene, & H. Sapolsky, *Health Planning and Regulation: The Decision-Making Process* 149–55 (1981) (indicating HSAs in New England have adopted economizing as a goal but have had little influence).
8. *See* Riker & Brams, "The Paradox of Vote Trading," 67 *Am. Pol. Sci. Rev.* 1235 (1973).
9. *See generally* J. Ferejohn, *Pork Barrel Politics: Rivers and Harbors Legislation, 1947–68* (1974); J. Jackson, *Constituencies and Leaders in Congress: Their Effects on Senate Voting Behavior* (1974). *See also* A. Wildavsky, *The Politics of the Budgetary Process* 136–37, 168 (1974).
10. *See e.g.,* Altman *et al., supra* note 7, at 149–55; Altman, "The Politics of Health Care Regulation: The Case of the National

Health Planning and Resources Development Act," 2 *J. Health Pol., Pol'y & L.* 560, 573–76 (1978).

11. The questionnaire was circulated to all HSAs existing in the spring of 1977. It was not pretested, and responses were not necessarily representative.

12. Such "lobbying," which is entirely acceptable in a legislative setting but generally regarded as improper in a regulatory agency, can of course facilitate vote trading and the formation of coalitions in support of particular projects. The 1979 amendments to Public Health Service Act §1532(b) expressly prohibit ex parte contacts with decisionmakers at the state level, thus confirming the view that the state agency is a regulatory body whose processes must be protected from off-the-record influences. Significantly, however, the House-Senate conference committee dropped language in the Senate bill that would have applied the same stricture to HSA deliberations, S. Rep. No. 96-309, 96th Cong., 1st Sess. 79 (1979), thus confirming that HSAs are viewed as legislative rather than regulatory bodies.

13. Altman *et al., supra* note 7, at 155.

14. *See generally* J. Miller & B. Yandle, eds., *Benefit-Cost Analyses of Social Regulation: Case Studies from the Council on Wage and Price Stability* (1979).

15. *See* Havighurst & Blumstein, "Coping with Quality/Cost Tradeoffs in Medical Care: The Role of PSROs," 70 *Nw. U.L. Rev.* 6 (1975); Havighurst, Blumstein, & Bovbjerg, "Strategies in Underwriting the Costs of Catastrophic Disease," 40 *L. & Contemp. Prob.* 122, 150–53 (1976).

16. *See* Havighurst & Blumstein, *supra* note 15, at 33–35; Havighurst, Blumstein, & Bovbjerg, *supra* note 15, at 145–50.

17. *See* note 11, *supra.*

18. *See* Havighurst & Blumstein, *supra* note 15, at 17.

19. *See generally* Havighurst, Blumstein, & Bovbjerg, *supra* note 15, at 138–53.

20. H.R. 6575, 95th Cong., 1st Sess. (1977).

21. 42 Fed. Reg. 48,501 (1977). *See* " 'Numbers Game' by HEW Concerns Critics of Draft Guidelines for Health Planning," *Health Planning & Manpower Rep.* Nov. 28, 1977, at 2.

22. *See* R. Crossman, *A Politician's View of Health Service Planning* 26 (1972); Bosanquet, "Inequities in the Health Service," 17 *New Soc'y* 809, 912 (1974).

23. 42 C.F.R. §121 (1980).

24. *See, e.g.,* S. 1485, 96th Cong., 1st Sess. (1979) (Senator David Durenberger); S. 1590, 96th Cong., 1st Sess. (1979) (Senator Rich-

ard Schweiker); H.R. 7527, 96th Cong., 2d Sess. (1980) (Representative Richard Gephardt, Representative David Stockman); H.R. 7528, 96th Cong. 2d Sess. (1980) (Representative James Jones).

25. I. Kristol, *Two Cheers for Capitalism* 27–31 (1978).

26. Weaver, "Regulation, Social Policy, and Class Conflict," 50 *Pub. Interest* 45, 62 (1978).

27. *Id.* at 61.

28. *See* Altman *et al.*, *supra* note 7, at 151–55.

29. *See* Havighurst, "Reply to Stephen Weiner," *supra* note 1, at 251–52.

3 CERTIFICATION OF NEED
Theory and Experience

Health system planners and regulators will probably exert their greatest influence over the level and character of competition in the course of administering state certificate-of-need laws. These laws (in effect in all states but one by late 1980) require that a certificate of need be obtained from the state before certain capital investments in health facilities may be made or certain new health services may be instituted.[1] This requirement is similar to requirements for "certificates of public convenience and necessity" widely imposed in the public utility and transportation industries. Such entry controls are highly anticompetitive in concept, but their adoption in the health care industry was not challenged on this basis until about half the states had adopted them.[2] By that time, the conventional view of their desirability was so well established that Public Law 93–641's enactment in 1974 seemed a natural culmination. This chapter considers the grounds and consequences of these legislative developments.

Many states also perform certain health-planning services for the federal government pursuant to agreements under section 1122 of the Social Security Act.[3] Under an 1122 contract, a state conducts inquiries and makes recommendations to DHHS as to the need for proposed facilities and the appropriateness of reimbursing the interest and depreciation costs of such facilities under federal health care programs. This book concentrates on the certificate-of-need approach since it is likely to displace the 1122 program in due course. In any event, it is the more potent control mechanism because it directly prohibits the operation of unapproved facilities, not just reimbursement of their capital costs.

The discussion here looks at the purposes that certificate-of-need laws are supposed to serve and the limited evidence concerning their efficacy, which remains in some substantial doubt. Legislative matters, including the role of competition in such regulation and the appropriate coverage of certificate-of-need laws, are explored in Part II.

THE PURPOSE OF ENTRY AND INVESTMENT CONTROLS

Certificate-of-need laws were conceived to restrain the perceived impulse of health care institutions of all kinds to overinvest in unneeded facilities and to provide unneeded services. Because of the prevalence of largely unquestioning third-party payment, the competitive market provides an inadequate deterrent to the creation of overcapacity, making direct public control arguably necessary. In undistorted competitive markets, a firm would not add new capacity unless the market was in disequilibrium, with demand exceeding supply, or unless it thought that it could achieve economies enabling it to outlast inefficient competitors. In normal markets, therefore, free entry provides an important guarantee that consumers' unmet needs will be satisfied and that efficiency will be maintained. At the same time, however, market forces also assure that no more resources will be committed to the industry than are necessary to achieve these objectives. Moreover, the threat of possible new entry is thought to exert a beneficial influence on the behavior of the firms already in the market, who must take care not to invite competition from more efficient firms.

The reasons that capital investment in the health sector does not fit the free market model are reasonably clear.[4] However, third-party payment alone is not a sufficient explanation for regulation. Instead, the justification for intervention is provided by the common practice of paying on the basis of retrospective cost reimbursement (or on some other cost-related basis, including reimbursement of patients for bills incurred) and the payers' extreme deference toward physician decisions concerning utilization of services.[5] These market characteristics have frequently made it possible for institutional providers to add facilities and raise costs without significant risk that the facilities will not be used or that revenue from their use will fail to cover costs (as they will in competitive markets with excess capacity). Furthermore, nonprofit firms, such as predominate in the health sector, have peculiar incentives inclining them toward growth as a means of gratifying their managers and of reinvesting profits and other funds that, under the restrictions usually applicable to nonprofit corporations, are neither distributable as dividends nor applicable to non-health-related activities. A nonprofit monopoly also tends to grow by plowing its excess earnings into the provision of nonremunerative services, including not only indigent care but also marginally productive undertakings, thereby assuming burdens that make it vulnerable to "cream skimming" by new and possibly less efficient competitors. Moreover, nonprofit firms are relatively slow to leave an overcrowded market because their managers have an incentive to stay in business even if salvageable capital is being eroded. Finally, nonprice competition, focused on attracting both doctors and insured patients, is also a force compelling investments that would otherwise not be made.

The foregoing arguments for regulation of entry are somewhat stronger than the usual arguments for entry controls into potentially competitive industries. This does not mean, however, that certificate-of-need laws are necessarily the best answer that public policy might find to deal with the problems presented. That depends on how well they work in practice as well as on how well alternative approaches would work. In addition to the empirical question about whether this form of regulation works well or poorly or not at all, a serious question exists as to whether this is theoretically the soundest approach that might be taken. In fact, it appears to have been chosen without due regard for all the alternatives, bearing out Charles Schultze's observation that, "consistently, where social problems arise because of distorted private incentives, we try to impose a solution without remedying the incentive structure."[6] The following statement shows that certificate-of-need laws follow the Schultze formula and do not operate at a fundamental level but instead address the perceived problems in the way least likely to upset established interests and institutions:

> . . .[W]hatever their merits, certificate-of-need laws are an attempt to deal merely with symptoms rather than root causes. . . . The arguments for certificate-of-need laws—and indeed the foundations of health planning itself—imply the continued predominance of financing mechanisms which encourage inefficiency both by guaranteeing recovery of costs, no matter how great, and by externalizing the cost of doctors' and patients' consumption decisions. Such exclusive reliance on health insurance and other types of third-party payment is not inevitable, nor must its impact necessarily continue to be as pernicious as it has been under existing payment systems. Viewed in the light of possibilities for more fundamental changes in the market for insurance and health services, certificate-of-need laws may appear as conservative measures, designed to preserve the very institutions which create the problems to which they are addressed.[7]

Hospital rate setting by state agencies, a later and even less developed policy initiative, moves incrementally beyond the conservative approach of certification of need but is still not a radical measure, leaving institutions a reasonable expectation that their costs will be covered and their market position entrenched. On the other hand, the Carter administration's hospital cost-containment proposals were quite radical because they would have introduced arbitrary revenue limits and other features threatening to institutions.[8]

Certification of need and rate setting are major components in a public utility approach to health services and to hospitals in particular. There are, however, significant differences between hospital regulation and traditional public utility regulation that suggest the limitations of both regulation and the public utility analogy. Hospital regulation is aimed at achieving operational efficiency and nonmarket control over the quantity of resources devoted to health care and not just the profit control that utility regulation seeks to impose. Economist Alfred E. Kahn, in his book, *The Economics of Regulation,* notes the difficulties of achieving operating efficiency and lowered costs through regulatory oversight of public utilities:

Manifestly, the operating expenses and capital outlays of public utility companies are by far the most important component of their rate levels, on the one hand, and the efficiency with which they make use of society's resources on the other. Therefore, in terms of their quantitative importance, it would be reasonable to expect regulatory commissions to give these costs the major part of their attention. But in fact they have not done so; they have given their principal attention instead to the limitation of profits.

The reasons for this perverse distribution of effort illustrate once again the inherent limitations of regulation as an institution of effective social control of industry. Effective regulation of operating expenses and capital outlays would require a detailed, day-by-day, transaction-by-transaction, and decision-by-decision review of every aspect of the company's operation. Commissions could do so only if they were prepared completely to duplicate the role of management itself. This society has never been willing to have commissions fill the role of management and doubtless with good reason: it is difficult to see how any company could function under two separate, coequal managements, each with an equally pervasive role in its operations.[9]

The limitations of regulation as a tool for achieving goals of the kind set for it in the health sector lead Kahn to the following observation about how regulation must function:

Although efficient operation and continuous improvement therein are, quantitatively, the most important aspects of industrial performance, the principal reliance for securing these results cannot, in the nature of the case, be placed on the regulatory process itself. The major contribution that regulation can make, and it is a modest one, can only be the providing of incentives—or taking care not to remove incentives—for private managements to exert themselves continuously in this direction.[10]

Prospective hospital rate setting is currently seen in just this light, as a method for strengthening hospital incentives to control costs. Such regulation can perhaps be seen as improving incentives in the hospital industry—but only because it is starting from a system of retrospective cost reimbursement, a regulatory technique producing very nearly the worst possible incentives for cost containment. (Payment on the basis of cost plus a percentage of costs is the only method that is clearly worse.) Nevertheless, the probability that regulation may represent an improvement in this instance should not obscure the inadequacies of the regulatory tool. Significantly, the most farsighted hospital rate-setting authorities are actively engaged in looking at internal costs and operations and in using other hospitals as yardsticks in setting rates, thus playing in a limited way the role of a second management. Competition may also have an important role to play in stimulating both efficiency and responsiveness to consumers' true wants when regulation cannot do the whole job.

Discussion in Chapters 7, 8, 11, 12, and 13 will suggest considerations for determining the appropriateness of investment controls for different types of health care facilities. The goal there is to help legislators, planners, and regulators implement regulation that is attuned to the public's true needs and restricts competition no more than is necessary in the circumstances. The ensuing discussion of the theory underlying certification of need focuses primarily on hospitals, which present the most plausible need for regulation.

A MODEL OF THE CERTIFICATE-OF-NEED APPROACH

The perceived need for, and some of the consequences of, limiting the growth of hospitals are illustrated in Figure 3–1. The diagram presents a hypothetical nonprofit hospital's production possibility curve, showing the tradeoffs the hospital faces in deciding on the combination of quality and quantity of care it will offer to the public. The vertical axis (QL) measures the *quality* of care in terms of the quantity and cost of inputs employed to provide each service—that is, the content of each service and the intensity of care. The horizontal axis (QN) measures the *quantity* of services in terms of beds, facilities, and patient care capacity of the institution. The heavy curve links the various combinations of quality and quantity that could be achieved by the hospital with the resources available to it. If the hospital is operating on this production possibility frontier, it can increase the quantity of services rendered only by degrading quality and can improve quality only by reducing its capacity.

Let us assume, however, that our hospital is operating at point p_1. If it is operating off the production possibility curve because

Figure 3–1 Hypothetical Nonprofit Hospital's Production Possibility Curve

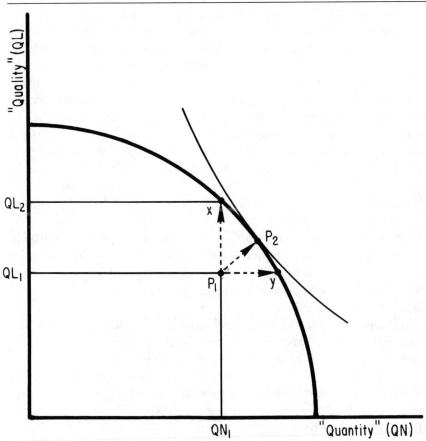

Notes:

The vertical axis *(QL)* measures the *quality* of care in terms of the quantity and cost of inputs employed to provide each service.

The horizontal axis *(QN)* measures the *quantity* of services in terms of beds, facilities, and patient care capacity of the institution.

The heavy curve links the various combinations of quality and quantity that could be achieved by the hospital with the resources available to it.

of managerial slack or inefficiency draining resources away from patient care, it would be likely to stay at that point. Let us therefore hypothesize that the hospital is operating off the curve only because the frontier has recently shifted outward as a result of some new development that has made additional resources available to it. A new infusion of philanthropy, a surplus from recent operations, or an expansion in health insurance or other third-party coverage available to the patients seeking treatment would all have this effect. In what direction would management move from point p_1 in putting its added resources to work? If it should wish to put all resources into improving the quality of care provided, it would move up the dotted line to point x, whereas it would move to point y if it should choose to keep quality constant and increase only the quantity of care provided. But probably it would prefer to improve in both directions and would therefore move to some point on the arc xy. (Any move outside the arc would mean reducing either QL or QN below present levels, implying that the original choice of point p_1 was a mistake.) Precisely where it will end up on the arc xy is a matter of management discretion.

Management preferences, which will in fact dictate the institution's choice of a strategy for spending the newly available resources, can be represented by an indifference curve linking combinations of quality and quantity that management regards as equally attractive. Although there is a series of nonintersecting curves that might be drawn for a given hospital (showing its preferences for allocating different quantities of resources), the indifference curve that interests us is the one shown, because it alone has a point of tangency with the production possibility curve, point p_2. At this point, hospital management would achieve the greatest possible gratification ("utility," as the economists call it) given the resources at the institution's disposal.

Because preferences ultimately explain a hospital management's growth strategy, those which dictate the shape of management's indifference curves have been at the heart of the argument for adopting certificate-of-need laws to constrain managerial discretion. Such laws are frequently said to be necessary because managers of nonprofit hospitals do not single-mindedly pursue the public good but instead seek the institutional and personal prestige and the managerial perquisites that come from growth, large size, and a reputation for medical excellence. In addition, management's indifference curve, or preference function, also necessarily reflects the hospital's need to compete with other hospitals on a nonprice basis for physicians' favor—and thus for patients—by providing the facilities and services that doctors need to practice their profession in the most satisfying and remunerative way. It is thus a combination of managerial and professional preferences that pushes hospitals to the "northeast" in the diagram in pursuit of both improved quality and expanded output of services rendered.

Certificate-of-need laws were adopted because it was perceived that the demand for beds and services was in part artificial, more a function of the availability of facilities and financing than of objective medical need. Demand, because it was heavily subsidized through insurance and subject to some manipulation by providers, appeared to be satiated only after the optimum level of services had long since been surpassed and substantial costs had been incurred without commensurate (or even demonstrable) benefit from the added services rendered. Controls on facilities growth were therefore thought to be desirable as a means of reducing the system's need and opportunity to create demand and revoking the invitation to expand without risk.

Despite the apparent logic of investment controls, a careful look at Figure 3–1 suggests that the expectation of benefit from certification of need for new facilities may have been misplaced. For even if we assume that a certificate-of-need law could be so effectively administered that it imposed an absolute moratorium on growth along the quantity axis, it does not follow that costs would be reduced or that the optimal level of spending and mix of services would be approached. From Figure 3–1, it should be obvious what happens when growth beyond QN_1 is constrained and management's desire to move to point p_2 is frustrated: The hospital moves to point x, since all other points on the arc xy are foreclosed; the "quality" of care is thus increased to QL_2. Although it is clear that real-world certificate-of-need laws may also constrain some growth on the QL axis, it is also clear that they leave many avenues for hospitals to grow without legal constraints, including many opportunities that would be reflected on the QN axis. Because controls are incomplete, their effectiveness is necessarily in doubt.

What has the certificate-of-need law achieved in our model? It has altered the allocation of resources by directing new spending into qualitative improvements instead of new beds, new capacity, and so forth. While this may be a desirable development, there is no basis for assuming that it is. After all, growth along the QL axis measures only the number and cost of inputs, not the change in the quality of outcomes, and there is some reason to doubt that marginal gains in patient benefit will be worth the cost incurred. (For example, one must wonder why patients were previously unwilling to pay for improvements in quality that were apparently attainable.) Moreover, the constraint imposed on growth has presumably prevented an increase in the number of patients treated, and the treatment benefits thus lost would have to be offset against any qualitative gains. The overriding point, however, is that there has been no saving in health care costs. The reason is, of course, that there has been no attempt to control the resources available to the hospital, only an attempt to control some (but not all) of the symptoms of the basic problem, which remains the hospital's ability to dispose of societal resources without accountability to those who ultimately pay the bills.

What if hospital rate regulation were introduced? The result would be indeterminate but somewhat more promising than with certification of need alone. Rate regulators can effectively influence the availability of resources to the hospital and thus the location of its production possibility curve. Thus, despite an increase in the insurance coverage of the population served by the hospital, the rate setters could prevent the institution from seizing the new growth opportunities presented, keeping it at point p_1. Whether a rate-setting agency would do this in fact is far from clear, of course, but, unlike the certificate-of-need agency, it at least would have the power to prevent growth along all dimensions. Nevertheless, pressures to permit (alleged) improvements in quality are hard to resist. Moreover, under customary cost-related rate-setting formulas, a hospital that incurs costs in excess of its revenues in one year will usually be allowed to raise its rates in the following year to cover the previously unrecognized costs. By this process, the hospital can expand with only a one-year lag in recoupment, which might prove no deterrent at all if it were allowed to amortize the debt incurred to finance any temporary loss.

An aggressive rate-setting agency might prevent its processes from being abused by setting an arbitrary maximum rate of increase in hospital revenues. Such a cap would have to be set fairly high, however, and would probably become a floor. Moreover, the cap might easily be deemed a violation of the hospital's constitutional rights if it were viewed as denying it a fair opportunity to recover its costs. Another strict approach would be to refuse cost-justified rate increases as a penalty for what the agency might identify as inefficiency, but few agencies would have the capacity to measure efficiency or the confidence to superimpose their judgments on those of management. Perhaps other rate-setting approaches, particularly the setting of a single rate for a group of comparable hospitals (which would be faced with having to collude in order to raise their average costs), would reduce the problem to manageable proportions and effectively alter hospital incentives. While the prospects for successful rate-setting initiatives are not particularly bright,[11] they are more promising than any realistic hope that certification of need will contain overall costs. Indeed, with rate setting in place, the certificate-of-need program is reduced to supplying the rate-setting agency with a basis for disallowing one of several categories of costs. Judging solely on the basis of its ability to encompass the true problem, the cost-containment potential of hospital rate setting is significantly greater than that of certification of need.

An important empirical study, next discussed, confirms that certification of need is of doubtful effectiveness in controlling costs because so many things escape the regulators' scrutiny and because hospitals appear to redirect their growth orientation when they are frustrated at one turn. Simply stated, the problem is that "inflationary pressures may, like a balloon, bulge out at another place even if growth in one direction is effectively prevented."[12]

ANALYTICAL AND DESCRIPTIVE STUDIES OF EXPERIENCE UNDER CERTIFICATE-OF-NEED LAWS[13]

Salkever and Bice have produced empirical evidence that early certificate-of-need laws imposed only a weak constraint on capital investment in health facilities. Although the growth of overall bed capacity was slowed, as certificate-of-need proponents desired, the growth rate of capital investment per bed rose so that there was essentially no effect at all on the growth of hospital investment generally. Furthermore, Salkever and Bice found that certificate-of-need programs did not have a significant effect on total hospital costs. Savings from the lower admission rates and total hospital days resulting from control over bed growth were offset by the higher per diem costs of upgrading the style of care.[14] These findings are consistent with the hypothesis that resource availability, as implied by the production possibility curve in Figure 3–1, is the essential issue and that all the energies expended in certification of need may be no more useful than rearranging the deck chairs on a sinking vessel.

The Salkever-Bice study was the most ambitious early effort to determine the actual impact of certification of need.[15] Looking at the period 1968–72, they examined both the changes in investment patterns attributable to the introduction of certificate-of-need laws and the differences in investment between states with and without such laws. Using standard statistical techniques, they controlled other variables and attempted to isolate differences attributable solely to certificate-of-need laws. Both analyses concluded that, while overall capital investment was unaffected, investment was redirected from beds to other uses. In a study updating Salkever and Bice's work through 1974, Wendling also found regulatory ineffectiveness.[16]

Salkever and Bice attributed the ineffectiveness of certificate-of-need agencies in controlling overall investment and per capita total costs to a combination of factors, including both (1) the planners' fascination with bed capacity and consequent neglect of other expenditures and (2) the limited jurisdiction of certificate-of-need agencies over smaller investments in capital equipment. On the basis of their findings, they speculated that "if the preferences of hospital administrators, trustees, and medical staffs cannot be satisfied by the addition of new beds, alternatives will be found among the less regulated options such as new equipment and services."[17] They also suggested that hospitals may have found the cost of financing growth to be lower because controls reduced competitive risks and perhaps also an institution's total borrowing.

Salkever and Bice warned against interpreting their findings as proof of the need for more extensive regulatory control. Although they attributed regulatory ineffectiveness in part to the availability of capital investment opportunities not subject to certificate-of-need requirements, Figure 3–1 reveals that the problem is much broader than the incompleteness of the regulators' jurisdiction over growth along the QN axis. Without opening up questions about regulators' effectiveness in exercising the powers they do possess, we have seen that growth along the QL axis, too, would have to be controlled if cost-control objectives are to be achieved. Thus, labor costs—both wage rates and the ratio of hospital personnel to beds—would have to be controlled along with all other noncapital inputs. In effect, the regulatory body would have to serve as a second hospital management sitting in judgment on the first. Kahn's observation of the limits of this approach, quoted previously, points toward the possibility that incentive-oriented regulation and competition may be preferable to giving regulators more direct powers and larger supervisory staffs.

Nevertheless, the Salkever-Bice study necessarily leaves many questions unanswered. For one thing, the possibility that improved quality and accessibility of services resulted from the redirection of investment must be recognized. The newly established planning process may also pay indirect, even intangible, dividends by stimulating awareness of community needs and strengthening institutional commitment to meeting them. In addition to being unable to take account of such unmeasurable benefits, Salkever and Bice were largely confined to using statewide data, leaving open the possibility that the effectiveness of a few good local planning programs—whose success, if recognized, might be replicable elsewhere—was lost in the aggregate data. Arguably, too, the study may have focused on certificate-of-need laws before the mechanism had been developed to its full potential; perhaps the organizational changes made pursuant to Public Law 93–641 would produce better, or different, results in time. Another possibility is that certification of need works better in conjunction with hospital rate setting and other controls.

Confirmation of the Salkever-Bice finding that certification of need has not affected total hospital investment is provided by Hellinger in a similar study, which concluded that any effect was statistically insignificant.[18] Hellinger did find, however, that hospital investments rose appreciably immediately prior to implementation of certificate-of-need programs, presumably as hospitals moved their plans ahead in order to escape the regulatory net. One might expect studies of certification of need to be confused by this acceleration of investment, since a decline in new investment immediately after implementation of the law would appear to be a corollary. The findings of Salkever and Bice may thus seem even more powerful in light of this distorting factor. A possible caveat is that experience immediately before and after enactment of a certificate-of-need law is so unreliable that a longer time horizon is needed.

In a comprehensive study of health sector regulation, Sloan and Steinwald confirmed the general findings of Salkever and Bice concerning certificate-of-need laws and concluded more generally that "as a group, regulatory programs did not meaningfully contain hospital costs during the first half of the 1970s."[19] In this study, data from 1,228 short-term general hospitals was analyzed over the six-year period from 1970 to 1975. In addition to using more recent data, Sloan and Steinwald compensated for several other limitations of the Salkever-Bice study in their methodology. In particular, the existence of other regulatory programs, such as hospital rate setting and utilization review, was also considered in the multivariate analysis, allowing both an assessment of various combinations of regulatory strategies and the detection of changes due principally to certificate-of-need programs.

Perhaps the most significant analytical improvement by Sloan and Steinwald was their multiple characterization of certificate-of-need laws. Where Salkever and Bice and Wendling had considered only whether a certificate-of-need law was in effect, Sloan and Steinwald included several variables to account for the various ways in which the age and structure of certificate-of-need programs might affect hospitals in various states. In addition to confirming Salkever and Bice's general finding that certification of need was ineffective, they were able, because of the completeness of their analysis, to conclude that all regulatory programs had failed to curb hospital costs during the period of their study.[20] They were also able to be more explicit than Salkever and Bice regarding the form of hospital compensatory spending when blocked by regulation. Whereas Salkever and Bice purported to detect alternative capital investments when some capital spending was thwarted by certificate-of-need laws, Sloan and Steinwald found a diversion of funds toward expansion and up-grading of the labor force; for example, demand for licensed practical nurses (LPNs) rose, and registered nurses increased in numbers relative to LPNs.[21] Noting this freedom to employ higher quality or more expensive labor, Sloan and Steinwald concluded that there are reasonable grounds for skepticism regarding industry claims that increases in expenses such as food, fuel, and insurance are the principal sources of hospital cost inflation.[22]

A marginally more optimistic conclusion about certificate-of-need regulation has been reached by Louise Russell, who has found that certificate-of-need laws have had some effect on the adoption of specific new hospital technologies.[23] Russell's analysis shows that in states with laws that went into effect between 1965 and 1969 (a class dominated by New York), certificate-of-need review held down the allocation of beds to intensive care and slowed the increase in the number of hospitals doing open-heart surgery. In states with laws effective between 1970 and 1973, the growth of cobalt therapy and open-heart surgery was reduced, although Russell adds that the latter finding is "statistically a bit shaky."[24] It should be noted that Russell's study does not address the question whether certificate-of-need laws have resulted in a net reduction in hospital costs or whether they only redirect investment toward technologies that are not so closely watched by reviewers. Russell observes, however, that to avoid such an evasive shift in investment patterns regulators must "watch everything at once—a near impossibility."[25]

In still another study, Rothenberg found no reason to be encouraged by New York's experience as the first state to adopt certification of need and the state with the longest experience.[26] Her method was to compare trends in twenty-five counties over the five-year periods before and after the establishment in 1966 of the certificate-of-need program. Although experience showed a reassuring improvement in the correlation between population change and bed-supply growth in seventeen smaller counties and in Rochester, Long Island, and northern metropolitan areas, overall experience was not so favorable: "The simple correlation between change in the number of general care beds and change in population size was weaker after 1965 in all counties, suggesting an undesired outcome. That is, general care beds were added in areas where either population change was negative or where it was relatively stable."[27] The results seem to have been dominated by hospital growth in New York City, where population was not increasing.

A more disturbing finding in the Rothenberg study was that health planners' specific projections of local bed needs did not seem to determine hospital growth any more after adoption of certification of need than before, even though it was thought that giving the planners sharper "teeth" would increase their influence over resource allocation. Although the desired reduction in the growth of the supply of short-term hospital beds was achieved, the correlation of growth patterns with planners' estimates of "needs" was weaker after 1965 than in the five years preceding.[28]

A similar finding was made by Lewin & Associates, Inc., in a study looking at a sample of states and areas:

> Nearly 75% of the sample states and areas (30 of 41) approved hospital beds in excess of 105% of their published need projection for five years hence. Fourteen of these began the period overbedded and approved additional beds; five others became overbedded during the period studied as a result of the projects they approved.
>
> Only five states and areas began the period with more than 105% of the projected need for long term care beds. However, all of these approved still more beds and six other jurisdictions approved additions to bed supply that made them overbedded.[29]

A striking aspect of the Lewin study, in contrast to Rothenberg's, is that Lewin gives New York the highest marks for its certificate-of-need program relative to other states, whereas Rothenberg finds reason to doubt the New York program's effectiveness. Rothenberg's findings related to a somewhat earlier period, before hospital rate setting took effect in New York, and may therefore be less pertinent as a guide to New York's overall regulatory success. Lewin, on the other hand, appears to have attributed to the certificate-of-need program the consequences of the squeeze put on New York hospitals by rate regulation. It does appear that Rothenberg looked more minutely at New York State's experience and found an unevenness in performance that the Lewin study necessarily missed. This unevenness casts at least some doubt on the proposition that certification of need worked well or accounted in any important way for the patterns of growth found in New York.

Rothenberg disputes findings in an unpublished study by Leavy[30] that attributed to the New York certificate-of-need law the substantial post-1965 increase in the average size (and presumed efficiency) of hospitals. Although the percentage of small hospitals and nursing homes did indeed decline sharply in New York State after 1965, Rothenberg shows that this trend was at least as pronounced in the five years before 1966.

The study of Lewin & Associates is more descriptive than analytical, though it purports to measure the effectiveness of the certificate-of-need process. Its general conclusion was as follows:

> In our view, it is clear from the evidence produced by this study that, as presently administered, [certificate-of-need] controls do not perform effectively in preventing unnecessary capital investment in health facilities and services and thus are not an effective means of containing health costs. In the first place, the effect of [certificate-of-need] proposals on health costs is seldom a major factor in area and state decisions on such proposals. Second, [certificate-of-need] controls do not appear to limit the creation of new beds and services to the pre-defined levels of need, which are generally conceded to be fairly generous. Finally, the types of investments that are permitted under [certifcate-of-need] controls do not presage the sorts of changes in the mix of health care facilities and services that are thought to be necessary to make the health care delivery system more cost-effective, nor is there any evidence that [certificate-of-need] decisions are made based on consideration of the trade-offs between various types of care.[31]

The Lewin study's evaluation of the program's ability to contain overall additions to hospital assets led to findings that were "relatively more encouraging than the findings with respect to [certificate-of-need] effects on bed supply.[32] This finding is directly contrary to the findings of the Salkever-Bice and Hellinger studies but, not being the result of an analytical study controlling for other variables, it probably can be discounted.

The most prominent feature of the Lewin study is its hopeful conclusion that the faults discovered can be overcome:

> When evaluating public policy ... it is essential to distinguish between the limitations that are inherent in the policy itself and those that result from the manner in which the policy is implemented. A

few states and areas have achieved at least relative success in limiting unneeded capital investment. Moreover, these states differ from the others in that they tend to have well developed need projections, review criteria and data resources. These factors can be replicated in other states and areas and presumably will lead to more effective [certificate-of-need] regulation once they are in place.[33]

It is notable that the New York program, whose success is disputed by Rothenberg, is the Lewin study's most prominent example of an effective certificate-of-need law.

Other essentially descriptive studies, like the Lewin study, have been substantially more positive than the analytical studies about what certification of need has achieved, and they are especially inclined to hold out hope for the future, as the Lewin study did. Thus, Bicknell and Walsh, examining the Massachusetts experience from their perspective as participants in the regulatory process in that state, compare applications with approvals and take credit for keeping the general hospital bed supply 468 beds below "what might have been."[34] A similar survey of experience in the state of Washington noted that "quantification of the impact of the program on cost containment is difficult," mostly because the program was thought to have discouraged many projects, which could not be counted, and to have had several intangible benefits. Its conclusion was that "by June 1973, total cost savings resulting from the program were estimated at over $25,000,000 (including denials, withdrawals, and modifications)."[35] Another application-counting exercise was reported as follows:

> The extent of savings in health-care costs that can be achieved by requiring certificates of need is indicated by a new study of Health Systems Agencies in a six-state Midwestern area. H.E.W. says that during a two-year period, H.S.A.s there saved nearly $690,000,000 on proposed construction projects for nursing homes and hospitals. About one project in four was downgraded, disapproved, or withdrawn. Taking into account the loan interest and depreciation that were avoided on the proposed facilities, total savings exceeded $2 billion.[36]

Finally, in 1973, the New York commissioner of health claimed that the state program "had disapproved construction of over 51,000 'hospital and nursing home' beds, saving approximately

$1.6 billion in capital costs and $738 million annually in operating costs.[37]

It should be obvious that these claims of cost savings based on application counting do not square well with the analytical studies cited above or with the continued virulence of health care cost escalation. There are several reasons why turn-down rates and totaling of the dollar value of applications denied do not present an accurate picture of the cost savings achieved. Sometimes several applications are mutually exclusive, so that granting one while turning down the other creates no saving. Applications may not be equally sincere, as indicated by the number of approvals that are not acted upon; perhaps the purpose of some applications is simply to preempt a possible competitor or to verify that no unexploited opportunity exists. Moreover, when regulators take credit for scaling down a proposal, they conveniently ignore the possibility that the applicant inflated its request in anticipation of the planners' desire to avoid seeming to rubber stamp it. Most important, rejection of an application may prompt the disappointed applicant to apply to expand in a different way; regulators, being human, may feel inclined to make up for their earlier action by approving the new venture if it seems any kind of improvement over the first. Under this scenario, several rejections could occur without affecting aggregate investment. Finally, it must be observed that none of the descriptive studies acknowledge the possibility, dramatized in Figure 3–1, that regulation has altered the character of health care expenditures without reducing them.

Because descriptive studies are nearly always undertaken or sponsored by persons with a stake in the regulatory process, their conclusions and air of hopefulness are suspect. While claiming questionable successes, they usually also note shortcomings in the regulatory effort and convey the impression that the regulators, though conscientious, have lacked the statutory powers, the legislative support, the public understanding, and the funds necessary for maximum effectiveness. In other words, the position adopted is that most commonly taken by advocates of regulation: cautious optimism in the face of obstacles limiting regulation's effectiveness, coupled with a determination to persevere.

The Lewin, Bicknell-Walsh, and other descriptive studies based on interviews with regulators and examination of gross statistics of regulatory performance are all premised on a belief that such regulation is here to stay. Under this assumption, participants and analysts perceive it to be their responsibility to identify the positive features of the regulatory process and to build the regulators' confidence, all with a view to making regulation as effective as possible. If the assumption of regulation's irrevocability is made explicit and if evidence is not distorted to support unwarranted claims, it is not irresponsible to accentuate the positive. But too frequently any appearance of effective administration is cited as vindicating the regulatory premise itself. Proponents of regulation also use any evidence of beneficial impact, however questionable, to validate their plea for more money and increased powers to raise the average level of performance. Small glimmers of success are thus used to turn findings of widespread regulatory ineffectiveness to the regulators' political advantage. One can only conclude that the persistent assumption of regulation's political irrevocability is self-serving, intended to divert discussion away from regulation's failures.

Two studies of certificate-of-need experience released in 1981 have also not succeeded in finally resolving the question of effectiveness. In the most ambitious study yet undertaken, Policy Analysis Inc. and Urban Systems Research and Engineering, Inc., concluded as follows:

> In toto, we found no strong statistical association between the presence of [certificate-of-need] regulation and variation in hospital investment behavior, hospital cost inflation, the distribution of hospital facilities, or the structure of the hospital industry. There may have been some subtle effects but, on balance, the evidence does not convince one of any really significant [certificate-of-need] effects.[38]

In releasing this study, DHHS's Health Resources Administration (HRA) noted that, although the study was more sensitive than earlier ones to differences between programs, it covered only data through 1976 and could not detect whether programs that had been in existence more than five years might be more effective than younger ones. In HRA's view, "seven-nine years is probably a more reasonable time to allow for assessing program impact."[39] It is beyond the scope of this discussion to evaluate this highly complex study or to do more than note HRA's exception to it. Certainly, nothing has been learned that would dilute the skepticism that theoretical analysis and earlier studies have induced.

In another recent study, Howell examined the Massachusetts certificate-of-need program[40] and offered reasons for preferring to use "measures of intermediate outcome" in evaluating its success. After offering some plausible reasons for not using actual capital investment through 1976 as a basis for evaluating a program enacted in 1972, Howell focuses primarily on describing and assessing process and program dynamics, concluding that, despite substantial improvement over time and success in some areas, "Certificate of Need has not established a binding constraint on hospital capital expenditures."[41] Howell's objective in her study was not primarily to assess the desirability of regulation, which she apparently regarded as a settled issue in Massachusetts, but to "improve regulatory performance."[42] In keeping with the usual regulator's view of competition, she minimizes its importance by strictly equating it with HMOs and treating all fee-for-service care as immune to reform by competition.

Perhaps the most that can be hoped for, in light of the analytical studies cited, is some recognition that regulation cannot be counted on to do the whole job and that more fundamental change, especially in the financing system, should not be neglected, even if one maintains faith that regulation can contain some of the system's distortions. Bicknell and Walsh, for example, admit that regulation alone is not enough,[43] though they do not appear to concede, or even recognize, the possibility that changes in health care financing and the introduction of competitive impulses could in any way obviate certification of need.

This survey of analytical and descriptive studies strongly suggests that certification of need so far has not been a significant success. Debate can still be launched on the effectiveness of particular programs, however, and on the prospects for greater effectiveness in the future. Moreover, the studies undertaken are not conclusive, and their methodology is inevitably subject to technical criticism. But enough seems to have been settled to raise serious doubts that certification of need should be relied on as an important cost-containment tool and to establish the substantial merit of earlier warnings that this kind of regulation could not, for a wide variety of reasons, do the job.[44] The Carter administration's 1977 proposal to put an arbitrary cap on new hospital investments nationwide constituted a dramatic public recognition of the weakness of the original certification-of-need concept, suggesting that patience with existing regulatory mechanisms was running out. Although the Carter proposal would have left HSAs and the state agencies the leading role in allocating the right to invest in hospital facilities, it would have changed fundamentally the nature of their function. Where previously it was thought that regulation could place appropriate and acceptable limits on health sector investments, it apparently was felt that only an arbitrary ceiling could achieve the desired goal. Another conclusion that might have been drawn is that competition and market incentives should be given a chance.

NOTES

1. For a compilation of state laws as of January 1978, see Medicine in the Public Interest, Inc., *Certificate of Need: An Expanding Regulatory Concept* (1978).
2. *See, e.g.,* Havighurst, "Regulation of Health Facilites and Services by 'Certificate of Need'," 59 *Va. L. Rev.* (1973); *Regulating Health Facilities Construction* (C. Havighurst ed. 1974); Noll, "The Consequences of Public Utility Regulation in Hospitals," in Institute of Medicine, *Controls on Health Care* 25 (1975).
3. 42 U.S.C. §1320a-1(b) (1976).
4. *See* Havighurst, "Certificate of Need," *supra* note 2, at 1155–69.
5. In turn, third-party payment practices may be traced to the tax laws, provider preferences, and government policy. *See generally* Chapter 4. *See also* Havighurst, "Controlling Health Care Costs: Strengthening the Private Sector's Hand," 1 *J. Health Pol., Pol'y & L.* 471 (1977).
6. C. Schultze, *The Public Use of Private Interest* 65 (1977).
7. Havighurst, "Certificate of Need," *supra* note 2, at 1155.
8. S. 1391 and H.R. 6575, 95th Cong., 1st Sess. (1977); S. 570 and H.R. 2626, 96th Cong., 1st Sess. (1979).
9. 1 A. Kahn, *The Economics of Regulation* 29 (1970).
10. *Id.* at 32.
11. *See generally* Bauer, "Hospital Rate Setting—This Way to Salvation?" 55 *Milbank Mem. Fund Q.* 117 (1977); Sloan & Steinwald, "Effects of Regulation on Hospital Costs and Use," 23 *J.L. & Econ.* 81 (1980). For some evidence that established rate-setting

programs have desirable effects, see Biles, Schramm, & Atkinson, "Hospital Cost Inflation under State Rate-Setting Programs," 303 *New Eng. J. Med.* 664 (1980); Sloan, "Regulation and the Rising Cost of Health Care" (1980) (unpublished paper).

12. Havighurst, "Certificate of Need," *supra* note 2, at 1148.

13. For an exhaustive literature review, see D. Cohodes, C. Cerf, & J. Cromwell, *A Review of the Research Literature on State Certificate of Need Programs* (March 1978) (unpublished study by Urban Systems Research and Engineering, Inc., and Policy Analysis, Inc.). For a less critical but more recent review, including some studies not evaluated here, see Statement of James R. Kimmey before the Task Force on Human Resources and Block Grants of the House Budget Committee, March 13, 1981.

14. D. Salkever & T. Bice, *Hospital Certificate-of-Need Controls* 75 (1979).

15. Their results were first published in Salkever & Bice, "The Impact of Certificate-of-Need Controls on Hospital Investment," 54 *Milbank Mem. Fund Q.* 185 (1976).

16. Wendling, "A Reexamination of the Impact of Certificate-of-Need Laws," in 1978 *Socioeconomic Issues of Health* 23 (J. Werner & J. Leopold eds.)

17. Salkever & Bice, *supra* note 14, at 22.

18. Hellinger, "The Effect of Certificate-of-Need Legislation on Hospital Investment," 13 *Inquiry* 187 (1976). Hellinger's methodology is criticized by Sloan & Steinwald, *supra* note 11, at 85.

19. Sloan & Steinwald, *supra* note 11, at 105.

20. *But see* Biles *et al., supra* note 11, and Sloan, *supra* note 11, both of which conclude that hospital rate-setting programs may have helped curb costs.

21. Sloan & Steinwald, *supra* note 11, at 106.

22. *Id.*

23. L. Russell, *Technology in Hospitals: Medical Advances and Their Diffusion* 162 (1979).

24. *Id.*

25. *Id.*

26. E. Rothenberg, *Regulation and Expansion of Health Facilities: The Certificate-of-Need Experience in New York State* 106 (1976).

27. *Id.* at 114.

28. *Id.* at 115. For a critique concluding that "the regression results add little to either the analysis or its presentation," *see* Bays, "Book Review," 12 *Health Services Research* 335, 336 (1977).

29. 1 Lewin & Associates, Inc., *Evaluation of the Efficiency and Effectiveness of the Section 1122 Review Process* ch. 1, at 13 (1975).

30. W. Leavy, "The Article 28 Story: New York State's National Leadership in Health Facility Planning" (1972) (unpublished mimeograph).
31. Lewin & Associates, *supra* note 29, ch. 1, at 25.
32. *Id.* ch. 4, at 20.
33. *Id.* ch. 4, at 25.
34. Bicknell & Walsh, "Certification-of-Need: The Massachusetts Experience," 292 *New Eng. J. Med.* 1054, 1056 (1975).
35. Health Policy Analysis Program, Univ. of Washington, Dep't of Health Services, *Certificate of Need in Washington: An Examination of Federal Requirements and State Options for Change* 48 (2d rev. ed. 1975).
36. *Med. Econ.* July 25, 1977, at 12. For a later recitation of "documented cost savings," based on a survey by the American Health Planning Association, see H. Rep. No. 96–190, 96th Cong., 1st Sess. 37–38 (1979).
37. Address by Hollis I. Ingraham before a panel of the National Health Forum, Chicago (March 20, 1973).
38. 1 Policy Analysis Inc. & Urban Systems Research and Engineering, Inc., *Evaluation of the Effects of Certificate of Need Programs* 21 (1981). The executive summary, comprehensive report, and analytic studies fill 947 pages.
39. Cover Note accompanying *id.* (Feb. 1981).
40. Howell, *Regulating Hospital Capital Investment: The Experience in Massachusetts* (National Center for Health Services Research, Research Summary Series 1981).
41. *Id.* at 18.
42. *Id.* at 20.
43. Bicknell & Walsh, *supra* note 34, at 1060.
44. P. O'Donoghue, *Evidence about the Effects of Health Care Regulation* (1974); Havighurst, "Certificate of Need," *supra* note 2; May, "The Planning and Licensing Agencies," in *Regulating Health Facilities Construction, supra* note 2, at 47; McClure, "The Medical Care System under National Health Insurance: Four Models," 1 *J. Health Pol., Pol'y & L.* 22 (1976); Newhouse & Acton, "Compulsory Health Planning Laws and National Health Insurance," in *Regulating Health Facilities Construction, supra* note 2, at 217; Noll, *supra* note 2; Posner, "Certificate of Need for Health Care Facilities: A Dissenting View," in *Regulating Health Facilities Construction, supra* note 2, at 113.

4 COMPETITION IN HEALTH CARE
A Constructive or Destructive
Force?

Whether competition can play a helpful role in stimulating improved performance in the health services industry is a much-debated question. Many discussions of health economics and health sector regulation have rather quickly dismissed the market as a mechanism for organizing the industry without giving serious attention to the possibilities for improving the market's ability to function or to the comparative advantages and disadvantages of the market and regulation. Medical care is frequently said to be a special kind of service that the market cannot be relied on to allocate and price efficiently. In a recent paper, however, economist Mark Pauly posed the question, "Is medical care different?" and answered it, "Yes, no, and maybe."[1] Specifically, he argued that competitive mechanisms have positive value in the provision and consumption of certain kinds of medical care, though perhaps not all kinds. This suggests that planners and regulators in the health care sector have a responsibility for deciding when competition can serve a useful purpose and when it cannot. The discussion here seeks to supply some of the perspective needed to make such judgments; it is not, however, a treatise on health economics.[2]

CONDITIONS MAKING COMPETITION A QUESTIONABLE MECHANISM OF SOCIAL CONTROL

The market for medical care does not closely resemble the textbook model of a perfect competitive market. That fact alone, however, does not make competition irrelevant to organizing and motivating health care providers. The large volume of literature dismissing the competitive market as a mechanism for controlling the health sector does so too quickly. Not only do regulation advocates neglect the possibilities for intervening to improve the market's functioning, but they usually overstate the difficulties that exist. While real, the departures from the textbook model are not so important or substantial as to be fatal to the effective use of competition.

✓Consumer Information Problems

Consumer ignorance is often singled out as the chief obstacle to the reliable functioning of the health services marketplace. Although uncertainty necessarily prevails about the effectiveness of many medical treatments and about the technical aspects of diagnosis, the essential problem is not the general limits of knowledge—from which providers as well as patients suffer—but the specific technical ignorance of consumers respecting the quality and probable utility of the care they receive. But consumers are also ignorant about many other things that they buy, and it is easy to overstate the problem as it arises in the health sector.

The health care consumer's primary problem is to identify a trustworthy and competent physician who can assist in making treatment decisions and in choosing a hospital and needed specialists. Perceiving the importance of a correct choice, the consumer can be expected to invest considerable time and effort in the search. The individual will employ such more or less reliable substitutes for actual knowledge of a physician's ability and trustworthiness as past experience in repeated dealings with that physician and others, a physician's general reputation, the advice and direct experience of others, and a variety of professional credentials that may serve to distinguish the more competent and reliable from the less competent and trustworthy.

Licensure itself presumably provides some assurance, and disciplinary mechanisms serve further to reduce the risks of dealing with providers in comparative ignorance. Indeed, one premise of regulation in the health care sector is that the existing minimal standards set by regulation make it reasonably safe to leave consumers free to make choices among licensed professionals. This is not to say that public controls are adequate or that great differences in professional skills do not exist, but only to suggest that the risk of serious error may have been reduced enough to alleviate some of the compunctions we might have about allowing consumers to use independent judgment.

The choice of a physician has other dimensions besides the quality of care received and the physician's honesty in dealings with the patient. In particular, fees for particular services may vary widely, yet the consumer is unlikely to be aware of market opportunities to obtain equivalent services for a lower price. Consumer ignorance thus gives each practitioner a significant degree of pricing discretion—that is, monopoly power. The question of precisely how this power is used has generated much discussion among economists because physicians do not appear to maximize their profits by charging all the market will bear. Instead, they are said to set fees below a profit-maximizing level in order to leave some excess demand, allowing them to choose the more interesting medical problems or the more congenial patients or to enjoy the prestige that comes from turning patients away.[3] Another theory speculates that individual physicians have a target income level they would like to achieve and that they voluntarily forgo additional available earnings, perhaps because they would feel guilty about getting any richer.[4]

These debatable explanations of physician pricing behavior relate only to the questions of what physicians do with their market power and do not undercut the conclusion that they possess it. A recent study by economists Mark Pauly and Mark Satterthwaite has added an interesting footnote to the notion that consumer ignorance underlies the individual doctor's monopoly power.[5] Contrary to the usual assumption that the presence of many producers in a market increases competition and will therefore reduce prices, Pauly and Satterthwaite show why just the opposite result may occur. They argue that a larger number of available physicians complicates the consumer's problem of getting and verifying information about any one physician. The larger number of practitioners means that one's acquaintances are less likely to have overlapping experiences, making comparisons difficult. Thus, in a community with only three physicians, nearly everyone would have an idea about the characteristics of each, whereas in a community with many doctors, such comparative evaluations would not be readily available. Pauly and Satterthwaite purport to show a significant statistical relationship between the level of physician fees and factors complicating consumer efforts to obtain comparative evaluations.

The consumer information problem cannot be resolved simply by relying on private producers of information to meet consumer needs. The nature of information as a public good, widely available without payment, causes a market failure arguably justifying public intervention. Despite the great value to consumers of information concerning medical care providers, it will be systematically underproduced in a private market because, once it is published, it can be widely shared and used by consumers who pay nothing toward the cost of its production. Although one must be wary of concluding that more information always justifies its cost, some collective action is clearly indicated, and indeed one finds that voluntary as well as some public action has been directed to the special problem of meeting consumer information needs. A number of consumer groups and some HSAs have taken steps to provide information for consumers' benefit.

Consumers' strong incentive to exercise care in buying medical services might be expected to cause them to combine their interests in some way, pooling information and employing experts to help them make choices that they feel ill equipped to make themselves. Although employment groups, particularly unions, have sometimes served this purpose, it has been more common to leave consumers to their own devices. Moreover, health insurers have rarely, if ever, taken steps to help consumers shop intelligently. One possible explanation is that consumers have in fact felt secure in their choices and have not demanded any assistance, but the more likely explanation is that most possibilities have been foreclosed by legal and professional restraints. Recent professional resistance to the compilation of physician directories, though now somewhat overcome,[6] is indicative of past obstacles. The profession's view has been that qualitative and price differences among its members are to be obscured, not broadcast. Health system planners and regulators could take steps to remove restrictions on, and even to stimulate, information flow. What must be recognized is that an unrestricted competitive market, by permitting consumers to act in concert in collecting and sharing information, could yield some valuable solutions to the problem of consumer ignorance.

The case for encouraging competing alternative delivery systems rests heavily on informational considerations. Group practices and HMOs are valued by consumers in part because they supply a degree of quality assurance, serving the consumer as what economist Milton Friedman has called "department stores of medicine"[7]—that is, as middlemen exercising expert judgment in the choice of physicians and other inputs. As such, they can earn a reputation that can be easily ascertained even in a large market such as Pauly and Satterthwaite found to contribute to ignorance and monopoly power. Moreover, many HMOs are consumer sponsored, a collective response to consumers' purchasing disabilities in the health services marketplace. Even where this is not the case, however, consumers may view an HMO, a group practice, or other "closed-panel" plan as a kind of agent, to be trusted because of the consumer allegiance it has earned and the perception that it is striving to maintain its reputation and position by serving consumers well.

Another way of looking at the problem of consumer ignorance regarding the quality of care is to focus on the incentives for providers to maintain quality since, if such incentives are reasonably well ordered, even the most ignorant consumer will benefit. Thus, in a competitive market, the average consumer's knowledge is not as important as that of marginal consumers, whom providers all compete to attract and who may be more knowledgeable than the customer who is generally content and not looking for an alternative. Although physicians of doubtful competence could probably dupe a number of patients, they might still have to strive for improved quality in order to maintain demand for their services at a level high enough to keep their appointment books filled and their charges up. The same is true of HMOs and other health plans, which must meet certain enrollment objectives and therefore must have broad appeal. In causing competitors to strive to keep old customers and attract new ones, competition induces efforts that usually benefit all customers, not just those who are most knowledgeable.

Incentives for maintaining good quality care are also strengthened by the threat of malpractice suits for serious mishaps. Potential tort liability thus compensates at least imperfectly for the patient's inability to assess accurately the quality of care he is about to receive. Although improvements in the tort system are needed, it would be unfortunate if desirable incentives were eliminated.[8] At present, liability laws, like licensure and professional discipline, supply a basic level of protection that might be regarded as sufficient to allow consumer choice to operate somewhat freely despite incomplete information.

Perhaps the most striking observation one can make about consumer ignorance in the health field is that it is enhanced rather than alleviated by the professional and regulatory controls that have been imposed on the system under a rationale largely founded on the prevalence of ignorance. Thus, state statutes, rules of regulatory boards, and professional ethics have long prohibited advertising ("solicitation") by professionals—sometimes even to the extent of preventing the disclosure of relevant credentials and many other objective facts, including prices. Regulation has thus not only neglected to correct the condition that is said to justify regulation in the first place, but it has made the problem appreciably worse.

It can be argued, of course, that a little knowledge is more dangerous than none at all and that patients are better off in the dependent state to which their ignorance condemns them. Indeed, if the consumer is given and can evaluate price information but cannot make judgments concerning quality, there is a legitimate basis for concern that quality will be excessively eroded. This would occur as less scrupulous providers perceived opportunities to attract patients without loss of income by imperceptibly reducing quality as well as lowering price, thereby forcing others to do so as well. But, despite the plausibility of the argument for suppressing price information if ignorance of quality cannot be overcome, the numerous existing quality assurance mechanisms may provide a floor that protects consumers against serious abuse.

In any event, such mechanisms would seem to be more appropriate ways of dealing with the quality problem than curbing price advertising, and they should probably be strengthened. Moreover, the option of suppressing information is no longer available, because the principle that information concerning professsional services must be freely available, for better or for worse, received recognition in 1977 by the U.S. Supreme Court as constitutional doctrine.[9] Whereas this case concerned state-imposed restraints on truthful advertising, the same laissez-faire approach toward the free flow of information is likely to prevail under the antitrust laws, which apply to private restraints. The Federal Trade Commission (FTC) has recently invoked antitrust principles to invalidate most of the American Medical Association (AMA) restrictions on physician advertising.[10] It seems clear that regulators in the health sector must now turn their attention away from restricting access to information and toward improving the reliability and completeness of the information available.

Third-Party Payment

Another problem with relying on the competitive market to allocate health resources is that consumers have elected to insure themselves against having to pay medical bills. The presence of insurance dispels cost consciousness at the point of consumption, and encourages even affluent patients to obtain more and better services than they would choose to purchase if they were spending their own money. Government programs for the elderly and the needy have been modeled on traditional insurance plans, thus extending to larger numbers the financial protection that has permitted costs to rise by reducing cost consciousness. The problem of third-party payment is perhaps the central complexity in health policy development and health sector regulation.

One detrimental effect of third-party payment is to make much of the competition that goes on in the health sector focus on factors other than price. To the extent of their insurance coverage, patients are not interested in the dollar cost of what they receive but only in whether it is valuable enough to them to warrant the inconvenience and possible discomfort involved. This has caused costs to rise dramatically as providers compete by seeking, not to become more efficient, but to confer new medical benefits—however small and without regard to cost—and to reduce inconvenience and discomfort.

In the hospital sector, competition has focused primarily on attracting physicians, who bring their insured patients with them to the hospital and do not themselves pay for use of the facility. Physicians value sophisticated equipment and high-quality services for both economic and noneconomic reasons. For this reason and because most patients have hospitalization insurance and do not have to worry substantially about costs, hospital competition has stimulated primary attention to acquiring the latest equipment and to increasing capacity to render more and better services. Similarly, physicians, competing among themselves to serve patients whose concerns about costs are reduced by the availability of third-party payment, often find themselves pressed to provide more and costlier services because patients expect them.

Competition that emphasizes the quantity and quality of services and systematically neglects price may easily be counterproductive, raising costs well above the level that would otherwise be incurred. While quality improvements are clearly desirable, there can be no assurance that they are worthwhile when they are adopted without anyone's having faced the true cost. Nonprice competition among hospitals has been compared with competition among regulated airlines, which were long prohibited from competing in price and therefore emphasized frills and unwise additions to capacity: "Hospitals, too, have a '747' problem arising from the absence of price competition—strong competitive pressure to invest excessively in the latest technology even though the market for it is thin."[11] In the context of automatic third-party cost reimbursement, therefore, competition can be an undesirable influence and has been one of the main reasons for adopting certificate-of-need laws governing capital investment and other regulatory programs.

As with consumer ignorance, it is possible to overstate the problem presented by the departure from the perfect competitive model that third-party payment represents.[12] Insurance need not be fatal to a functioning marketplace. Indeed, health services are only one among many services that are regularly purchased with insurers' money. While health services are unique among these insured services in the extent to which the presence of insurance can cause excessive spending, many forms of casualty insurance have had to cope with cost problems of exactly this type. In fact, the phenomenon of insurance-induced risks, flowing from alterations in private behavior that bring on insured events or that raise the cost of repairing losses once they have occurred, is so well recognized that it has been given a name by economists. "Moral hazard" is associated with most forms of insurance and is recognized as a problem that insurers must try to solve or minimize in designing coverage and administering claims.

Although the cost problem that health insurers face is not fundamentally different from that facing other casualty insurers, there are some special circumstances. For example, it appears that many consumers have special expectations where health care is at stake and may resist some forms of cost control that would be acceptable in other settings. Moreover, it is extremely difficult as a practical matter to draft policy language accurately specifying insured events or exclusions from coverage and to administer detailed specifications. Although there is no question that health care cost containment presents a complex challenge, the problem remains purely an administrative one, differing from moral hazard problems confronted in other types of insurance only in degree. For this reason, the questions raised about the compatibility of competition and third-party payment usually misrepresent the dimensions and nature of the problem. The key question is simply whether consumers are getting good service from insurers in the form of roughly the right blend of financial protection and cost containment. Are health services being paid for in the most cost-effective ways? Are insurers doing all they can for consumers? Do consumers have a full range of options available to them?

Recognition of moral hazard as a problem that financing plans should address as a service to their subscribers underscores the particular necessity for introducing competition at the point where the selection of a financing plan is made. Group practice HMOs are the most widely recognized competitive response to the third-party payment problem, which they address by essentially eliminating the passive third party, putting providers on a fixed budget, and limiting the facilities available for their use. But competition could also serve to stimulate traditional health insurers to address cost issues more aggressively. Thus, freely competing insurers might undertake to pay only fixed indemnities, to negotiate advantageous payment rates with individual providers, or to impose cost-containment measures of other kinds, perhaps limiting coverage to essential services and leaving more discretionary services to be bought without benefit of insurance. Because the mechanisms needed to limit subsidization to essential services could be costly to administer, insurers might gravitate toward using closed panels of cooperating providers.[13] A strikingly attractive model that an insurer might adopt is the so-called health care alliance, which is a cluster of providers, including a group of physicians (perhaps a multispecialty group practice) and one or more hospitals; because it would be separately rated for insurance purposes, an alliance could effectively market its efficiency and cost effectiveness in competition with HMOs and traditional insurance plans.[14]

Third-party payment as such, then, is not the problem, since it is possible for consumers to obtain financial protection without buying at the same time an unmitigated moral hazard. Instead of assuming that current financing methods are immutable, public policy must be concerned with whether the private sector has had the incentives and the opportunity to arrange health care financing on terms that best serve consumer needs and expectations. Unfortunately, in the health sector, the tax laws have stimulated overinsurance and discouraged private cost containment,[15] and providers have effectively resisted the development of cost-effective financing mechanisms.[16] Even with the tax law as it is, however, insurers have some incentive to control costs and may be expected to respond to their customers' increasing cost concerns.[17] In addition, antitrust enforcement, rapidly emerging as a potent force reducing the threat of professional retaliation against unwanted innovations, should soon allow consumer cost concerns to be better served.

It is fundamental to this analysis that the financing system, while the source of most of the system's current cost problems, is subject to fundamental reform through the operation of newly liberated market forces. Although the challenge of controlling costs without alienating insureds and individual providers is complex, the increasing cost consciousness of health insurance purchasers, particularly employers and unions, should be enough to stimulate insurers and other entities to compete actively to offer the best mix of coverage, cost containment, and administrative control. Consumer desire for financial protection does not, in itself, require regulation to control health care costs. Far from making competition untenable, it sets a challenge that might well be met more effectively under competition than otherwise. Government's primary role can be seen as one of maintaining, through antitrust enforcement and the design of public programs, market conditions that allow the competitive private sector to seek solutions to the cost escalation that naturally arises when a third party is introduced into the medical care transaction.

Physician Control of Demand

When consumer ignorance of the technical side of medicine, externalization of costs to third-party payers, and professional restraints on third-party cost-containment efforts are combined, physicians are left with great decisionmaking discretion. While many studies confirm that physicians exercise great control over the demand for their own and other health services, it must be recognized that this is not a discrete phenomenon but simply the way in which consumer ignorance and third-party payment manifest themselves. As expanding third-party payment has reduced apparent prices, the changes induced in consumption and cost have been interpreted by some observers to be the result of demand creation by physicians rather than a market response to lower prices. These observers would apparently fault physicians, as creators of demand, for not continuing to prescribe only those treatments that people would have chosen if they in fact faced the full cost. The effect of third-party payment is apparently not well distinguished in these observers' minds from the effect of consumer ignorance, which arguably permits physicians to defraud a patient by knowingly prescribing services whose value is less than the patient's net (after insurance) cost. The ultimate issue here is whether physicians can and do systematically violate their fiduciary responsibilities. While such breaches undoubtedly occur, it has not been shown to be a pervasive phenomenon.[18] One study compared the incidence of surgery in families of physicians and attorneys and found no significant difference, suggesting that the attorneys' physicians did not abuse their trust.[19]

For many observers, the bottom line in the argument over competition versus regulation is the perception that physicians, not patients, control demand. But even granting this argument some validity, it must be observed that it, too, can be overstated by ignoring the existence of numerous ways in which consumers can protect themselves in a competitive market against the specific market deficiency. Most critics of competitive strategies admit, for example, that HMOs succeed in altering provider incentives and thus eliminate the problem. They persist in their proregulation views, however, on the ground that fee-for-service providers cannot otherwise be curbed in their demand-creating behavior except through public regulation. Nevertheless, as suggested above, health insurers have unexercised power and unexplored opportunities to affect provider behavior; competition, both from HMOs and otherwise, should induce them to police not only fraudulent behavior but the effects of third-party financing. More selective insurance coverage, with limits and specific exclusions enforced through pretreatment authorization of payment, would put providers in a position of being accountable to patients for excess costs incurred and would alert patients to questionable prescriptions. Benefits could be limited to fixed amounts or offset by substantial copayments, thus placing a cost-containment burden on the consumer's cost consciousness and on the professional's fiduciary obligation to compare the cost and value to the patient of the treatments prescribed.[20] Closed-panel arrangements, excluding the free spenders or those not submitting to administrative checks, could impose other controls on physician discretion.[21]

Increased availability of the HMO and other closed-panel options and competitively induced changes in private insurance plans could thus substantially weaken the physician's power to create demand by giving consumers more ways to escape the hazard that their ignorance and need for financial protection create for them. If health system planners and regulators are alert to the possibilities for such private solutions to the cost-containment problems generated by third-party payment and consumer ignorance, they might facilitate insurers' and others' experimentation with different approaches and the imposition of cost-control measures even over the opposition of the medical profession. In the long run, physician control of demand may be substantially easier to contend with privately than publicly because the incentives to control costs and to challenge professional dominance are stronger.

ANTICOMPETITIVE TRADITIONS: PROFESSIONAL DOMINANCE AND GOVERNMENTAL INVOLVEMENT

Perhaps the greatest obstacle to introducing competition as an effective force in the health care sector is the simple fact that it has been absent so long, or at least has been so curtailed, constricted, and distorted as to make it an ineffectual control. Its credibility is therefore low, and experts tend to look elsewhere for solutions to the problems that are preceived. Nevertheless, the weak state of competition in the health sector is attributable to several specific factors, all of which are subject to change if policymakers attach priority to strengthening competition. Although health system planners and regulators can do many things to improve competition, some improvements can be achieved only by new (or the amendment of old) legislation.

Professional Dominance: Licensure and Self-Regulation

The first circumstance vitiating competition in the health sector is the dominant position of the medical profession. An important source of professional power is physician licensure, which drastically limits the inputs that may be employed in providing medical services. Although restrictions have been relaxed from time to time to permit many categories of nonphysician personnel to participate in treating patients, the medical profession has maintained most of its control. By virtue of their political influence, physicians have limited the extent of nonphysicians' gains, which usually take the form of narrow exceptions to the broad prohibition of unlicensed practice in state medical practice acts. Most ancillary health care personnel are required to function under the supervision or orders of a physician, and their education programs and employers are likely to be under the medical profession's control or influence. For the few categories allowed to practice independently, a variety of constraints prevent interprofessional competition from developing, except within narrow ambits. Moreover, other licensed occupations have learned to be as assiduous as doctors in protecting their territory against intrusions. Interprofessional issues are normally resolved by negotiations, often with the resulting treaties being ratified by the state legislature, rather than by submitting the matter to the vote of consumers in the competitive marketplace.

The breadth of the physician's legal authority is, of course, much greater than the scope allowed any other health professional. Indeed, it appears that the physician is licensed as more than a competent technician, since the range of dangerous tasks that the licensee is empowered to perform is much broader than any single individual could be expected to master. This unrealistically broad grant can be viewed as implying a special trust of the individuals licensed, who should at least know their own limits, and as a confession of the state's own inability to make more refined judgments concerning physicians' skills. The medical profession has itself moved into the vacuum thus left by the legislature and has purported to supplement limited state control by enforcing high ethical and other standards among its members. Consumers undoubtedly benefit in many respects from the profession's assumption of authority over matters relating to ethics and the quality of care, but the presence of private regulation is potentially inconsistent with competition.

The scope of private regulation by physicians is very broad. At the national level, physician organizations are tightly knit together through a maze of interlocking boards. Medical education, specialty certification, the training of allied health professionals, the accreditation of hospitals, and many other aspects of the system are substantially under professional control or influence. Although the bodies exercising power in these areas are allowed some freedom of action, they have little or no discretion to adopt or accept innovations that are at all out of keeping with the profession's economic interests or its prevailing values.

The situation is similar at the state and local levels, where organized professional interests dominate utilization review (PSROs) and "foundations for medical care," the extension of hospital staff privileges, and key elements of the health care financing system (most Blue Shield plans and many individual practice associations). The network of control relationships reaches even the individual practitioner, who stands to lose referrals, hospital privileges, the benefits of various professional associations, and even the respect and society of professional friends if their expectations are not needed. Thus, although medical practitioners appear to be independent entrepreneurs, their behavior is subject to controls and influences that sharply diminish the prospects for competition, which requires a capacity for independent action. To the extent that the profession can arrive at and publicize a consensus as to what "professional ethics" or "the quality of care" require of a practitioner, individual physicians are highly unlikely to deviate from the indicated line of conduct. Innovations not to the profession's liking will find the climate inhospitable in any event. If physicians pursue an innovative course that requires the cooperation of professional colleagues or access to resources under direct or indirect professional control, they may find it impossible to survive.

Another aspect of the medical profession's dominance is the solidarity that emanates from the tendency of physicians to think and act alike on matters of professional concern. While much of this tendency reflects the power relationships and available sanctions just described, there is also an ideological element that foreordains much parallel behavior. The controlled and highly uniform process of medical education, the licensure system, the hierarchical structure of the organized profession, and the various power relationships all contribute to inculcating a particular image of the physician and his responsibilities, a dominant value system, and a strong fraternal sense among the profession's members. An industry in which the members are bound by fraternal ties is unlikely to be intensely competitive and is apt to engage in anticompetitive concerted action whenever necessary to further collective interests. Thus, in many communities, local professionals have demonstrated their propensity to act in parallel fashion to ward off such competitive threats as HMOs. In recognition of the retaliatory power of professional groups, would-be innovators often seek approval from the county medical society before moving ahead. Health insurers in particular have usually felt compelled to touch that base before instituting even a mild cost-containment measure, such as a second-opinion plan designed to reduce the incidence of questionable surgery. The possibility that the antitrust laws can be employed to overcome professional solidarity in the face of threatened innovation is currently the subject of much interest.[22]

In addition to insisting on its right to approve or disapprove reforms that others might attempt, the medical profession frequently offers its own "reforms." When they have involved any economic sacrifice on the profession's part, such reforms have been forthcoming only when competitive or political pressures have reached such a threatening point that the profession is forced to choose between the lesser of two evils. The corollary is, of course, that the public receives the lesser of two "goods"—and frequently more the form of reform than its substance. Examples of this scenario are numerous: Blue Shield plans developed in response to the demand for health insurance; peer review of the reasonableness of fees developed in response to insurers' fee-screening efforts; foundations for medical care and individual practice associations developed in response to the threat of independent HMO development and governmental action on health care costs; and the much-vaunted "voluntary effort" to control hospital costs emerged in direct response to the Carter administration's proposed hospital cost-containment bill.

Among the hazards of such professional activities is the risk that they will preempt opportunities for competitively inspired change, establishing an entry-discouraging price level that is substantially less advantageous to the public than real competition would be. Another concern is the probability that the profession's dominance will be perpetuated by shoring up its political position and strengthening its claim of progressiveness. Each time the medical profession is allowed to establish a new line of defense, its solidarity in resisting more extensive change initiated by others is strengthened and seemingly legitimized. A great deal of attention is being paid to the antitrust status of professionally sponsored "reforms" that stand in the way of competitive developments.[23]

Governmental Interference with Competitive Developments

The health sector's anticompetitive traditions have also evolved in large measure from government's various interventions in the industry, first to assure the quality of care and later to improve access to care by providing financing for certain disadvantaged groups. As in the case of medical licensure, governmental interventions have frequently reflected the medical profession's exercise of political power to obtain legislative backing for its specific preferences and dominant status.[24] Indeed, even when legal steps have been taken without the profession's express approval, the profession's dominance is at least as likely to be confirmed as weakened. Thus, the Medicare law, which physicians largely opposed, was modeled after Blue Cross and Blue Shield, the financing mechanisms that least threatened provider interests. Subsequently, the PSRO law, designed to control costs and the quality of care under the Medicare and Medicaid programs, gave the profession new powers and responsibility, strengthening its legitimacy and even authorizing it for the first time to discipline such competitors of the traditional system as HMOs.[25]

State law is responsible for repressing many market developments that might, over time, have improved the health care industry's performance and averted some of the present difficulties. Licensure laws, enacted to assure quality, were parlayed into restrictions on advertising and strict professional control over medical schools, a power that was long used to limit the profession's numbers and to cultivate values that are not wholly those of the heterogeneous public that the profession serves. Another side effect of licensure laws was the express or implied prohibition against both the "corporate practice" of various health-related professions and the involvement of lay or proprietary interests in the provision of various services. The providers thus excluded from the industry were precisely those most likely to break ranks and compete aggressively for the consumer's dollar. These restrictions, together with others in the insurance laws, also prevented or greatly hampered the development of alternative delivery systems, such as HMOs. They also accorded to the provider-dominated prepayment plans, Blue Cross and Blue Shield, the dominant role in the financing of medical care. As the providers' chosen instruments, the "Blues" were the model of "ethical" insurer behavior and have for a long time effectively inhibited innovation in third-party payment mechanisms.[26]

Regulatory limitations on the supply of health facilities, described in Chapter 3, have long stood in sharp contrast to government policies on manpower. During the long period when the supply of hospitals was being expanded through the Hill-Burton program, the nation tolerated substantive restrictions on the supply of physicians imposed by organized medicine largely through control of the medical schools and accreditation programs. At about the time that excess hospital beds were beginning to be perceived as a problem, concerns about a doctor shortage induced the federal government to embark on heavy subsidization of growth in the number and size of medical and other health professional schools. Beginning with the Health Professions Educational Assistance Act of 1963, the government succeeded in doubling the number of medical school places, expanding the educational pipeline to the point that the physician manpower pool seems in danger of becoming a flood. Physician-population ratios are reliably expected to reach nearly 250 per 100,000 by 1990, up from 177 in 1975.[27] Like the Hill-Burton subsidies program before it, the policy of expanding the supply of physicians and other health professionals is now being regretted. Some policymakers, fearing physicians' demand-creating powers, are casting about for ways to reduce the flow of new manpower, but, with the schools already in being and no simple regulatory fix possible, it is proving difficult. Some consolation may be drawn, however, from the possibility that the increased physician supply will contribute in due course to competition's emergence.[28] This prospect depends not on the simple economic model in which any increase in supply lowers prices but on the probability that physicians, on the lookout for market opportunities, will be increasingly willing to undertake, participate in, or cooperate with competitive and cost-conscious innovations in financing and delivery. The increasing supply of physicians is already a dominant fact of the 1980s, and it bodes well for competition. With the 1979 health planning amendments, federal policies toward manpower and facilities are more nearly consistent with each other than ever before. They are also consistent with the principle of competition.

Another form of governmental intervention that has inhibited competitive developments over a long period is the tax subsidy for employer-purchased health benefits.[29] By making it possible to pay bills with untaxed dollars, this subsidy has encouraged the purchase of more comprehensive coverage with less cost sharing than consumers would otherwise choose. Reduced frequency and magnitude of out-of-pocket payments has meant less cost consciousness and less room for price competition to operate. Even the normal incentive of competing health care financing plans to keep their costs (and premiums) down is lessened where consumers must pay income and social security taxes on any savings realized and passed on in wages. Weakened cost consciousness has also reduced both political and market pressures to challenge professional dominance and to introduce innovative payment and delivery systems. Certain pending legislative proposals, billed as procompetitive, would change the tax treatment of employer-paid premiums, thus strengthening the economizing incentives needed to make competition focus more on price and cost considerations.

Hedged about, inhibited, and diluted in so many legal ways, competition has had practically no opportunity to demonstrate its potential in the health sector. The few HMOs that made it as competitors are simply the rare exceptions that prove the rule, succeeding against substantial legal and other professionally sponsored obstacles.[30] If the lessons of the past are understood, health system planners and regulators might be able not only to avoid using their regulatory powers to destroy useful competition, but also to influence state legislation and regulatory and enforcement decisions on particular matters so as to bring about helpful changes in the legal environment for competitive developments. With the appreciation of competition's prospects that this book seeks to instill, the planner-regulators may help to realize the potential for significant reform that is implicit in the expanding physician supply, new pressures for cost containment, increased freedom for innovation in financing and delivery, and any further federal and state legislative initiatives on behalf of competition that may follow in the wake of the 1979 health planning amendments.

Government Financing of Care

Government involvement in the health sector as a major third-party payer is a more recent development. Nevertheless, the Medicare program, in extending the Blue Cross and Blue Shield model of financing, largely perpetuated the defects of the non-competitive system that had developed, and its infusion of new subsidized demand, undermining cost consciousness still further, triggered a new round of cost escalation. Changes in the Medicare and Medicaid programs since their enactment have reflected a desire for a less complaisant payment system than that originally borrowed from the provider-dominated private sector and an increasing willingness to use government's buying power to change the system. But competition played no significant role under the approach employed. Moreover, when limited provision was made for HMOs to participate in Medicare in 1972, the law was structured so that there was little incentive for HMOs and federal beneficiaries to find each other.[31] Even though HMOs could serve Medicare patients much more cheaply than the traditional fee-for-service, cost-reimbursement system, Congress's unwillingness to open up meaningful competition left government in the position of supporting demonstrable inefficiency. Recently, renewed efforts have been made to allow both HMOs and Medicare eligibles to benefit from the latter's enrollment. Although technical problems are being encountered in giving Medicare beneficiaries the opportunity to make cost-conscious choices, competition may yet be given an opportunity to function usefully under federal programs.

It is sometimes argued that the large role played by government as a purchaser of health care precludes a role for competition in the industry. While it undeniably complicates determination of whether competition is useful or dysfunctional in particular circumstances, government's involvement does not necessarily make competition irrelevant. First of all, government's method of payment varies for particular services and in some cases does not prevent competition from serving as some constraint on price. Second, nonprice competition may be a beneficial force for quality assurance with respect to some services despite the earlier warning about its possible wastefulness. Third, government's utilization controls and benefit limits may serve to offset some of the problems associated with nonprice competition. Fourth, as in the case of the proposed Medicare amendments to accommodate HMOs, government can change its approach to payment in ways specifically designed to make competition work as an effective control where it does not do so now.[32]

Ethical Traditions and Impulses

Professional dominance and governmental policies in the health sector all appear to reflect some distrust of competition and free markets on ethical grounds. There persists, for example, some discrimination against proprietary institutions as participants in health care on the ground that they may expose the public to lower quality care, profiteering, and so forth.[33] It is also argued that advertising contributes to commercialism, a lowering of professional standards, and a weakening of trust between doctor and patient. More generally, it is thought that consumers cannot choose well and are better off, on balance, with less choice but with access to a profession with high ethical standards. The health planning effort long had the earmarks of a hospital cartel, which was tolerated out of a sense that competition would be undesirable. Professional dominance has its roots in similar sentiments.

While these arguments against meaningful competition in the health care industry are all plausible, they have been pushed rather far—being used historically, for example, to justify harassment of HMOs and other mechanisms through which consumers sought to express their concerns about costs. Not surprisingly, they have been advanced and advocated most strongly by those whose economic interests they serve. There are, however, strong ethical arguments on the other side of the debate as well, since consumers may be said to have a right not to be kept dependent and in ignorance,[34] a right to a wider range of choice, and a right to benefit personally from the economizing choices that they might make if they or their advisers were better informed about the limited benefits that medical science can confer in many circumstances. It is at least possible that the ethical foundations of anticompetitive policies in the health care sector are gradually being found shaky, self-serving, and elitist.

Perhaps the ultimate stumbling block in implementing a policy of encouraging price competition and consumer choice is an unarticulated but overriding sense that willingness to pay, which is in part a function of ability to pay, should have no place in determining consumption of health services. This egalitarian impulse, because it is not articulated, explained, or justified, is difficult to confine to the areas where valid social justice issues are indeed present. For example, its proponents have never fully adjusted their aspirations in light of the steadily increasing evidence and awareness that a great deal of medical care is of debatable and frequently negligible utility. One might have thought that the more realistic goal would be to make all essential care accessible to everyone but leave people free to choose, with professional or other expert advice, whether to purchase (or to insure against) those extra tests or procedures or hospital days, or whatever, that would not be clearly worth their cost in all or most cases. To insist on total equality throughout the medical care spectrum is to defy the reality of differences in people's tastes and preferences, to give the poor medical benefits when they would much rather have other things, and to carry symbolism very far. Nonetheless, the resistance to the use of competition and consumer choice as mechanisms of social control in this field is surely traceable to this symbolic impulse as much as to well-defined doubts about the strategy's practical efficacy. There should, however, be no doubt that it is possible to achieve reasonable equity goals without sacrificing competition. Indeed, the increased efficiency that competition yields should make it easier for society to meet its commitment to provide good care for its least advantaged citizens.

ANTITRUST AND THE HEALTH SECTOR

An important new source of pressure on the anticompetitive features of the health services industry is the federal antitrust laws. Indeed, the main reason why competition is currently weak in the industry is that antitrust long played a lesser role in health services financing and delivery than in other industries. Not only did the localized character of medical services appear to insulate local practices from the federal government's power over interstate commerce, but it was widely believed, until 1975, that the so-called learned professions were largely exempt from antitrust scrutiny. Although the courts had never squarely so held, it was thought that physicians, lawyers, and perhaps some other professionals were not engaged in "trade or commerce" and that professional activities, undertaken in the name of professional ethics and the quality of professional services, were fundamentally different from similar concerted activities carried out by industrial groups.

In 1975, in *Goldfarb v. Virginia State Bar*,[35] the Supreme Court made clear that the professions were not exempt from the antitrust laws, though the Court also indicated that certain disciplinary and other activities of the professions might be treated differently from similar activities in more commerical fields.[36] The full impact of the antitrust laws on the medical profession has yet to be finally determined, but the *Goldfarb* case triggered substantial interest on the part of the FTC and the Department of Justice in applying antitrust principles in the health sector. The cases to date suggest that any distinctions that may be drawn between professional and industrial activities will be narrow and will not unduly hamper efforts to introduce competition through antitrust enforcement.[37] Nevertheless, the localized nature of many restraints, their informal or hit-and-run character, and possible defenses based on alleged ethical and quality concerns may still make effective enforcement difficult. It remains to be seen whether clarification of the law will have deterrent effects significantly changing the competitive climate. Health system planners and regulators should be alert to what the antitrust agencies are doing, and may find opportunities to help in the enforcement effort, thereby strengthening competition in their communities.

The first antitrust targets in the health services industry after *Goldfarb* were selected by the enforcement agencies without any overall sense of purpose beyond giving the law its due effect. For this reason, the early initiatives gave neither the industry nor the wider public any clear signals about what benefits the enforcement effort hoped to achieve or how it could be reconciled with other health policies being forged in other parts of the government. Not many observers could see more than marginal practical value, for example, in the FTC's early and highly publicized attack on the AMA's code of ethics, with its restrictions on physician advertising.[38] Similarly, the FTC's challenge to the AMA's role in the Liaison Committee on Medical Education, which accredits medical schools, confused many people by seeming to rely on outdated evidence concerning professional control over physician supply;[39] in any event, it could hardly be expected to have an immediate or perceptible impact on industry performance. Furthermore, early complaints issued against professionally developed "relative value studies" have seemed misguided to many observers, who perceive no benefit and some inconvenience from the various consent orders and decrees obtained.[40] Finally, various signs from the FTC about possible antitrust issues presented by the traditional professional controls in the manpower area—specialty certification, hospital staff privileges, and restrictions on nonphysician practitioners—have caused consternation in professional circles[41] and have seemed to many others to represent only dangerous meddling in delicate matters affecting the quality of care.

A full appraisal of the foregoing enforcement initiatives would reveal that each was well justified, even though some of them may have been based at the outset on incomplete understanding of the industry or may not have been as wise a use of enforcement resources as some other undertaking in the industry. Since those early initiatives, however, the enforcement agencies have gained sophistication and acquired the insights needed to allocate their resources strategically and with a policy objective in view. Nevertheless, the early enforcement moves represent the larger part of what has so far met the public eye, and are still the basis on which the antitrust effort is judged by most observers. They have, in fact, become quite peripheral to the main enforcement mission, which has only just begun to take perceptible shape.[42]

A series of recent actions aimed at eliminating a set of closely interrelated restraints on the organization and operation of health services financing have become the main focus of the antitrust enforcement effort in the industry. Unlike the actions mentioned above, these represent a systematic campaign to change the industry's fundamental ground rules, which heretofore have been largely laid down by the organized medical profession, and to facilitate innovation responsive to the heretofore neglected interests of consumers.[43] The antitrust goal is to break down the barriers to competition at the crucial interface between health plans and physicians.

The FTC staff, with new sophistication and occasional help from the Justice Department's Antitrust Division, has identified a series of control mechanisms by which the organized medical profession has effectively manipulated its own economic environment, preventing third-party financing mechanisms from becoming aggressive purchasers of inputs needed by their beneficiaries and from embarking on the reorganization of health care delivery and its closer integration with financing. At this writing, a number of investigations and enforcement initiatives were nearing completion with the probable result that each of these several weapons, so reliable in the past, would eventually be blunted. The enforcement agenda now attaches paramount importance to the following types of restraints on the private financing system:

- *Direct control over Blue Shield plans.* Blue Shield plans were originated by, and in most areas are still directly or indirectly controlled by, organized medicine. The FTC staff proposed the issuance of a "trade regulation rule" that would terminate all formal relationships,[44] leaving Blue Shield plans in a position to serve as the consumer's rather than the profession's agent. The state of Ohio achieved a similar result through litigation with the state medical society.[45]
- *Direct control over other financing entities.* In recent years, state and local medical societies have established new types of financing and peer review programs that serve the profession much as Blue Shield did in an earlier era. The so-called foundations for medical care and individual practice associations (IPAs) are seen by many as reforms, since they may tighten control over the profession's "bad apples"—that is, those who overcharge or overutilize resources according to the profession's standards. The FTC staff proposed that the commission consider prohibiting all profession-dominated financing mechanisms, in recognition of their effect in perpetuating the profession's control over the processes of change.[46]
- *Boycotts and related restraints.* Where financing plans are independently operated, they nevertheless must fear organized medicine's power, which has been brought to bear from time to time by organized boycotts or other concerted refusals to deal.[47] A simple example of the phenomenon is the FTC's complaint against two dental societies that encouraged their members to withhold from dental insurers X-rays needed for cost-containment purposes.[48] A particularly egregious case involved a state medical society's solicitation of powers of attorney authorizing it to withdraw individual physicians as participating providers in an independent Blue Shield plan that had taken some unwanted initiatives.[49] Such coercive actions are flagrant violations of the Sherman Act.
- *Collective bargaining.* Medical societies have actively sought to negotiate with health insurers over their cost-containment initiatives and have usually been successful in doing so, with

the result that collectively asserted professional interests are always accommodated in the moves that are made. The threat of boycott and other profession-sponsored unpleasantness underlies all such negotiations, and antitrust prohibitions against such conduct might cause such collective bargaining to diminish in importance. But such negotiations are themselves independent violations of the law. In 1979 the FTC issued a complaint against the Michigan State Medical Society to bar it not only from engaging in concerted refusals to deal but also from negotiations with third-party payers.[50]

- *Professional prescription of third-party practices.* In a variety of ways, organized medicine has prescribed the reimbursement methods of third-party payers. The methods adopted by controlled Blue Shield plans, having the clear acceptance of the profession, have tended to become the industry norm, for reasons varying in subtlety from other third parties' fear of boycotts to "oligopolistic interdependence" or dominant-firm leadership in the insurance industry.[51] Specific professional actions that have also contributed to the suppression of independent action by competing financing plans include the promulgation of relative value studies (RVSs) and the sponsorship of peer review panels to mediate disputes over fees and other matters of economics. The antitrust campaign against RVSs makes excellent sense when seen in this context,[52] and peer review systems are being scrutinized in the same light.[53]

- *Restraints on physicians' sale of their services.* A major objective of several organized health professions has been to prevent bargaining between individual professionals and third-party intermediaries engaged in retailing their services.[54] While state-sponsored prohibitions of "corporate practice" are important restraints,[55] they are not sufficient in themselves to suppress competitive developments, and they have been supplemented by profession-developed ethical restrictions on "contract practice" and other efforts to maintain the fee-for-service mode of payment. The FTC's case against the AMA's code of ethics sought to invalidate provisions on these subjects as well as the restrictions on advertising.[56] Though little noticed, this aspect of the case may turn out to have the greater practical significance.

• *Restraints on HMOs.* In the original *AMA* case, decided in 1943,[57] the Supreme Court found a criminal conspiracy to suppress an HMO in Washington, D.C. Had it not been for this prosecution, it is unlikely that competition would have survived even as a vestige in the medical services industry. But, in spite of it, HMO development has been restrained in many ways by local medical groups. Antitrust enforcers have found it difficult to intervene at critical junctures to protect new HMOs, because such intervention is apt to harm the fledgling plan by causing resistance to harden and the HMO's foothold to disappear as otherwise cooperative physicians seek to avoid controversy. Thus, while several enforcement initiatives have been taken to help HMOs and severe penalties are likely to be sought when a violation is found, antitrust cannot be counted on to solve the many problems of HMOs.[58] This observation should strengthen the conviction that the marketplace must be opened up as much as possible to innovations of all kinds. Because HMOs are too readily identified as the profession's enemy, they cannot be counted on alone to change the competitive climate in very many places very soon. It is therefore imperative that change be encouraged on many fronts so that weakened, but still viable, professional defenses can be overwhelmed.

The antitrust laws' challenge to the traditional activities of the organized medical profession does not depend on identifying an anticompetitive purpose underlying professional conduct. On the contrary, it may be conceded that most of the physicians participating in the profession's reform and peer review efforts have been sincerely providing what in their view is a public service. Viewed within the inherited tradition that the profession has a responsibility to reform itself and to keep the quality of care high, these professionals' motives cannot easily be impugned. Nevertheless, the antitrust laws do not prohibit only concerted activities that are undertaken with specific anticompetitive intent. An anticompetitive effect is enough, and thus it may be that actions taken in the finest traditions of the medical profession may violate the law because they are inconsistent with competition. Antitrust doctrine, carefully evolved through long experience, embodies a presumption that competition will yield better economic performance than an industrywide combination of competitors.[59]

Antitrust law requires that physicians cease thinking of their profession, or of the dominant fee-for-service sector, as a single economic entity charged with making crucial economic decisions about medical care. Instead of trying to improve the economic performance of the profession as a whole, physician reformers must now concentrate their efforts on strengthening some competitive entrant in the market—that is, a group practice, an HMO, or some other entity that faces substantial competition and must therefore stand or fall on the basis of its ability to serve consumers. Only in a competitive context, where discrete plans establish their own standards of practice through internal peer review, careful selection of physicians, or otherwise, can consumers be assured that their interest in finding a satisfactory accommodation among conflicting quality, cost, and other factors is being protected.[60] While many useful professional activities can continue under an antitrust regime, a fundamental refocusing of professionalism and a withdrawal from the field of economics seem certain to be compelled.[61] Paradoxically, a group of reputable physicians could contribute more to the valid reform of the medical care system by breaking ranks with their fellow professionals and embarking on an entrepreneurial course than by working diligently in peer-review programs.

It can be seen that antitrust enforcement is a major new factor in the health services industry. Although its significance is still speculative, the potential for rapid and meaningful change exists where it previously did not, and, for this reason, all earlier pessimistic assessments of competition's prospects in the industry must be reexamined. Of course, a great deal hinges on how the law unfolds. Many issues have yet to be addressed before it can be known for certain whether antitrust can or cannot effectively deter anticompetitive activities in this industry and carry out the implications of procompetitive policies. While the stage is set for a revolution, it may yet be suppressed by law enforcers, judges, regulators, legislators, and interest groups that either cannot see, or see but choose to resist, what a procompetitive policy requires. The following paragraphs suggest a few of the legal obstacles to bringing antitrust to bear in the health care marketplace.

The antitrust laws have an uncertain effect in industries subject to extensive economic regulation and restrictive legislation at either the federal or the state level. In some circumstances, the antitrust laws will not apply to anticompetitive activities of regulated competitors that are authorized by a regulatory agency. In health sector regulation, however, the antitrust laws would still seem applicable (and not subject to abrogation by regulatory approval) in view of the absence of both an express statutory exemption and pervasive regulation clearly intended to displace market forces.[62] It would therefore appear that the nation's general policy favorable to competition is applicable to the health sector except insofar as specific statutory directives and clear legislative policy make it obviously inappropriate.

Where state laws are largely responsible for anticompetitive conditions, the antitrust laws may provide a vehicle for overcoming their more restrictive effects. The law in this area is unclear, but congressionally expressed federal policy may, under the supremacy clause of the Constitution, sometimes override state laws and regulatory schemes that are inconsistent with it. Nevertheless, states are entitled to adopt policies of their own, and the federal courts generally respect clearly articulated state policies, particularly if they provide some protection for consumer interests that might be adversely affected by the displacement of competition. Though some recent case law indicates deference to anticompetitive state policies,[63] it may still be possible to challenge state action where the federal policy of antipathy toward monopoly and concern for consumer welfare is not served. Thus, while a state is surely free to achieve its legitimate objectives by regulatory means, legislation seeming to serve special interests at the expense of the consuming public might well be struck down as inconsistent with overriding federal policy.[64] Even if federal antitrust policy is deemed too general to override specific state enactments, it is possible that the FTC can by rule declare impermissible a specific practice that is expressly permitted or required by state legislation.[65]

Another limitation on the scope of antitrust as a guarantor of competitive behavior in the health care sector has been the existence in the McCarran-Ferguson Act of an express exemption from the antitrust laws for "the business of insurance to the extent that such business is . . . regulated by state law."[66] Although some insurer practices remain subject to federal antitrust scrutiny, the industry is widely suspected of being inadequately competitive due to the sheltering effect of the McCarran-Ferguson Act and to state regulation that places greater emphasis on insurers' financial stability than on innovation. In health insurance in particular, certain special privileges enjoyed by Blue Cross and Blue Shield, particularly their special relationships with providers, have impaired commercial insurers' ability to compete.[67] A special issue raised under the McCarran-Ferguson Act is whether concerted actions of providers taken in cooperation with insurers enjoy an exemption;[68] it would be a serious blow to competition if such provider combinations were somehow shielded from antitrust attack.

Although the insurance industry may be somewhat lacking in imagination and initiative, pressure from sophisticated purchasers could be expected to induce innovation if other circumstances were conducive. To respond to these competitive pressures, insurers need antitrust protection against concerted professional resistance to their cost-containment initiatives. A 1979 case decided by the Supreme Court indicates that, even though they must be prepared to defend their practices under the antitrust laws, insurers are free to drive hard bargains with providers whose services they underwrite.[69] Though not resolving the antitrust issue, that case made clear that cost containment is a legitimate insurer activity and reported the Department of Justice's opinion that provider-insurer agreements on prices are not illegal in the absence of special circumstances.

THE ARGUABLE VIRTUES OF A COMPETITIVE MARKET FOR HEALTH SERVICES

Despite the many obstacles to competition in health services, there are no market or technological factors that make monopoly inevitable and competition impossible. To be sure, the circumstances of this industry are unusual, though not in a way that would necessarily prevent competition from functioning usefully. One should expect, however, that competition would take unusual forms as competitors actively seek ways to counteract the consumer's disadvantages as a purchaser of health services and to overcome the problems that insurance necessarily introduces. It is precisely these possibilities for innovation to solve the industry's special problems that make a significant effort to establish a competitive regime seem likely to pay significant dividends. Even the existing legal barriers to competition are not so pervasive that competition cannot function usefully, though some legal changes—particularly in the tax and insurance laws—would help greatly to foster needed change. Those barriers to change that are merely institutional or attitudinal could probably be overcome rather quickly once the first olive is out of the bottle and competitive pressures begin to build. Naturally, major reorganization of this complex industry will necessarily take time, but there are many signs that the process of education, experimentation, and change has already begun.[70]

A brief general statement of some of the virtues of relatively free markets may be useful as the final step in preparing the minds of health policymakers and health system planners and regulators to think in a balanced and constructive way about possible roles for competition in a regulated health services industry. The antitrust laws reflect in a general way Americans' appreciation of the value of competition and free markets, not only for their own sake as an expression of our commitment to individual freedom, but also on pragmatic grounds as, at least presumptively, the best guarantor of efficiency in the employment of limited resources and of consumer satisfaction and welfare.

The price system, when it is working well, conveys vast amounts of information in a readily understandable and usable form to guide the conduct of a multiplicity of private actors, both producers and consumers. Market prices relate all consumer goods and services, and all inputs into their production, to each other in terms of their cost of production and their relative scarcity. The price system forces individuals to "vote" with their dollars for the items they want produced and to express the strength of their preferences by their willingness to pay. In turn, it generates incentives to produce, and produce efficiently, those things, and only those things, that people value enough to make them willing to pay the cost of production. It also stimulates efforts to discover new products and services that will attract consumer support in the democratic marketplace.

A competitive economy will produce not only what the majority wants but also what individuals want badly enough to pay for, thus avoiding the tendency of political processes to serve only the preferences of the majority and highly organized minorities in the spending of revenues collected from everyone. While it is obvious that markets cater to people in proportion to the dollars they have to spend (and thus seem to favor the rich), even poor persons are served by the production of goods and services tailored to their needs and pocketbooks. Most important, reliance on free markets is not inconsistent with government programs to redistribute wealth from richer to poorer so as to improve the capacity of low-income citizens to obtain producers' attention to their wants.

At least as a paradigm, the price system for determining what goods and services will be produced, and by whom and by what means, is an admirable, even inspiring, mechanism. Economist Frank Knight once expressed his admiration for it as follows:

> One of the most conspicuous features of organization through exchange and free enterprise, and one most often commented upon, is the absence of conscious design or control. It is a social order, and one of unfathomable complexity, yet constructed and operated without social planning or direction, through selfish individual thought and motivation alone. No one ever worked out a plan for such a system, or willed its existence; there is no plan of it anywhere, either on paper or in anybody's mind, and no one directs its operations. Yet in a fairly tolerable way, "it works," and grows and changes. We have an amazingly elaborate division of labor, yet each person finds his own place in the scheme; we use a highly involved technology with minute specialization of industrial equipment, but this too is created, placed and directed by individuals, for individual ends, with little thought of larger social relations or any general social objective. Innumerable conflicts of interests are constantly resolved, and the bulk of the working population kept generally occupied, each person ministering to the wants of an unknown multitude and having his own wants satisfied by another multitude equally vast and unknown—not perfectly indeed, but tolerable on the whole, and vastly better than each could satisfy his wants by working directly for himself.[71]

It is this view that leads even liberal economists generally to favor use of incentives and prices rather than central control as the primary instrument for shaping an industry's performance.

Even where market failures are discovered—and they turn up with great regularity—economists are usually reluctant to scrap the market mechanism altogether, preferring to fix it in some manner so that it serves the public better.

Charles L. Schultze, in his 1976 Godkin Lectures at Harvard,[72] examined several grounds on which markets provide an attractive alternative to central direction through regulatory "command-and-control modules." First, he emphasized that markets operate on the basis of consent, and do not depend either on coercing compliance with centrally dictated norms or on inspiring people to act against self-interest out of a concern for collective welfare. "Indignant tirades about social responsibility," he said, "can't hold a candle to schemes which reduce the profits of firms who pollute."[73] The point also has relevance in medical care, where appeals to physicians to "do better" are not likely to avail much. Indeed, we have already observed how nonprice competition leaves health care providers little alternative to behaving as they do. Moreover, to eradicate such dysfunctional competition by regulation would be difficult and would involve additional costs in limiting consumers' opportunities to express their varying preferences. Furthermore, health care providers value their independence and would vigorously resist the control measures that would be needed to curb the influence of nonprice competition. On the other hand, revitalization of the competitive market, with renewed focus on price, is an attractive objective precisely because it preserves the doctor-patient relationship and, paradoxically, both the independence and the accountability of providers.

Schultze also observed that reliance on the market "reduces the need for hard-to-get information."[74] Emphasizing the complexity of issues that regulators must confront, he argued that "where feasible, building some freedom of choice into social programs does provide substantial advantages, either in generating explicit information for policymakers about the desirability of alternative outcomes or in bypassing the need for certain types of information altogether."[75] The information needed to regulate the medical care system well, making allowances for widely varying circumstances, is practically unattainable, since it includes detailed facts about both the medical condition and the personal preferences of each individual patient. Without correct incentives, the system cannot be counted on to address correctly the countless minor but cumulatively significant tradeoffs between costs and benefits that exist in each encounter between doctor and patient.

Another virtue of the market observed by Schultze is its ability to stimulate inventive activity and direct it toward socially desirable goals.[76] By the same token, innovation can be greatly distorted by the incorrect signals generated when markets are not working well. Regulation in the health sector is designed to control malfunctioning of precisely this kind, and later chapters consider when market conditions are such that incentives for innovation can safely be allowed to operate and when they should be frustrated. Absent a thoroughgoing overhaul of the financing system, regulation is an essential feature of the health care system, but competition may still serve as a vehicle for reforming private financing mechanisms as well as the delivery system itself.

Schultze's last argument for relying on markets whenever possible was paradoxical in a society as accustomed as ours to intense political bargaining as the precursor and vehicle of change. Pointing out that "efficient use of resources requires constant change,"[77] Schultze observed how uncomfortable government is with any alteration in the status quo that harms any interest group appreciably. On the other hand, markets, when they are working well, are neither sentimental nor responsive to interests solely on the basis of their possession of power and influence. They can therefore generate rapid, even revolutionary, change whenever it is called for by shifts in consumer tastes, the appearance of new technology or cost-saving innovations, and so forth. Schultze commented at some length on how, when political mechanisms are employed, efficiency is likely to be sacrificed. Because inefficiency imposes hidden and widely distributed costs, it is politically preferable to a visible cost borne by an identifiable interest group, even though the magnitude of the former cost might be very much greater. Schultze's observation that governmental mechanisms attach the highest priority to doing "no direct harm" has serious implications for attempts to solve the health sector's problems by regulatory means.

If anything, Schultze may have understated the problem of government's resistance to change and its use of regulation to curb and control it. Certainly not everyone would share his faith in "a steady maturing of both the electorate and political leaders"[78] to halt the creeping inefficiency brought about by government's assertion of ever-widening responsibility. But it must be admitted that recent deregulatory moves in previously regulated industries and in the health care industry itself may be a reward to Schultze's hope.[79]

CONCLUSION: THE POTENTIAL SCOPE OF COMPETITION IN THE MEDICAL CARE INDUSTRY

Even though advocates of competition in the health services industry have had considerable success lately in opening up the health policy debate, their efforts have not yet succeeded in communicating fully and clearly how competition would address the key problems that bedevil health policy, particularly the problem of health care costs. "Competition" has become a widely used watchword, but it has not been fully appreciated as a dynamic concept of general applicability. Instead, it is usually understood simply as a code word for HMOs and for their wider development as a competitive alternative to traditional fee-for-service medicine. But the HMO concept, however defined, is only one of the possible manifestations of competition, and it is important to recognize that the HMO experience, while revealing competition's possibilities, does not exhaust them. The discussion here seeks to convey the essentials of competition as a strategy in health policy and to show why, properly understood, it is potentially applicable to all medical care, even including that which is paid for on a fee-for-service basis with third-party financial assistance.

Why Competition's General Applicability Goes Unrecognized

A combination of factors accounts for the limited appreciation of competition's potential scope and for the unfortunate equation of the market strategy with HMO development. The chief problem has been simply the difficulty of communicating complex ideas to a large audience that is unsophisticated about competition and about how private actors in competitive markets might strive to help consumers solve the problems they confront in a complex world. Most of the chief advocates of competition have been handicapped in their efforts to maintain the idea of competition as a broad and dynamic, rather than a narrow and static, concept by their own close identification with the HMO movement. Moreover, because people have difficulty in visualizing how changed incentives and strengthened competition might work in health services, market advocates have found it necessary to minimize theoretical discussion and to reify the idea of competition by stressing the tangible successes of the HMO movement. Even though they have striven to emphasize the possibilities for expanding the definition of HMO to encompass a much wider range of alternative financing and delivery arrangements,[80] they have not yet succeeded in overcoming their audience's reluctance to accept the proposition that, if consumers would in fact find more speculative possibilities desirable, those possibilities would be realized in a market-oriented system. There is also great resistance to the idea that the competitive process, if it works reasonably well, validates the outcome. Many observers want to be told in advance what the result of competition would be so that they can decide whether they approve.

There are other important reasons besides nonacceptance of the market's legitimacy as a democratic instrument why market advocates have had trouble generalizing their message. One reason is that their main opponents, the advocates of regulation, have largely embraced the HMO concept and have used it to discredit the dominant fee-for-service system. They contend that the latter must be regulated precisely because it lacks the specific features—provider prepayment, for example—that make the HMO an effective allocator of resources. To these observers, the HMO is the exception that proves the rule that the traditional sector cannot be controlled by market forces, and they refuse to concede the possibility that lessons concerning competition's broader potential can be drawn from HMO experience. By making competition a synonym for HMO development, regulation advocates have successfully confined the concept to encompass only a limited (and heavily regulated) component of the market, thus preserving the larger system as regulation's natural province. Moreover, because HMOs have been the object of federal promotion and subsidies since 1973, the interventionists have tended to see them as a successful government program rather than as a success of the free market. Having embraced, even co-opted, the HMO concept as a liberal reform, they can claim that they, too, support competition, even as their regulatory endeavors proceed resolutely on the assumption that competition is not and could never be relevant to the system as a whole.

Providers, too, have found it possible to accept competition in at least a tentative way as long as it is kept synonymous with HMO development. While not unthreatening to providers, HMOs are something they can "live with" without too much discomfort, since HMOs are often ineffectual competitors. Closed-panel HMOs are hard to start, tend to grow slowly, and are often dependent on the goodwill of the dominant system for essential resources (e.g., specialist care and hospital beds). Moreover, the concept can be co-opted to some extent by organizing profession-sponsored HMOs of the IPA variety. Thus, while providers have largely accepted the HMO idea as a fait accompli, organized medicine has striven to confine this one competitive breakthrough so that market forces will do as little damage as possible. Indeed, the medical profession uses the presence of some competition, in the form of an occasional HMO, as part of its argument to legitimize the traditional system and thereby hold off the regulators.

The overriding irony is, of course, that providers share with the advocates of regulation a motive to confine the idea of competition and to suppress the fact of its relevance to the dominant fee-for-service sector. The conventional view of competition is also shared by the private health insurance industry and the Blue Cross and Blue Shield systems, who also find it convenient to define competition so that it contemplates no changes other than those that fit under the HMO rubric. Even the HMOs themselves are not anxious for the secret to get out that they are not the only vehicle whereby competition can be imported into the industry, since they might lose the special privileges they now enjoy or, worse, be faced with the necessity for competing in a truly competitive market. A full understanding of the health services industry and of competition's place in it cannot be gained from listening only to the diagnoses of those who have a stake in minimizing its potential.

Health Plans and Health Providers: The Need
for Competition at the Interface

The thesis of this book is that the policy of competition has general applicability and that the economic performance of the entire health services industry is in question only because of the absence of robust competition. This chapter, though not purporting to be a full analysis, has said enough to allow us to identify both the precise point where the market has failed consumers and the basic causes of that market failure. It is the remediability of these causes that supplies the basis for hopefulness concerning competition's future prospects.

Because a good deal of competition does exist in health services and health services financing, it is hard to recognize that there is practically no competition whatsoever where it matters most—namely, at the interface between the providers of care and health care financing plans. Although providers do compete among themselves in many ways, costs are not adequately controlled by such competition. The reasons why such competition as exists is not, on balance, a beneficial force are familiar: consumers are ignorant of prices and other relevant matters; third-party payment eliminates cost consciousness; and providers, freed of a fiduciary responsibility for costs, heavily influence demand. Similarly, although private health plans other than HMOs do face each other in a competitive market, they do not compete appreciably in cost containment. Indeed, the problem is precisely that third-party payers are just that and nothing more—payers, not purchasers of services. They do not compete in seeking to buy needed inputs—providers' services—at reasonable prices and on reasonable terms. Providers are thus spared the necessity of competing among themselves either on the basis of price (except to the limited, though nonnegligible, extent that consumers retain some residual cost consciousness) or on the basis of their willingness to cooperate with insurers' efforts to control the impact on utilization of insurance-induced distortions in consumers' and providers' incentives. It should not take much imagination to see that, if health plans did compete in the purchase of the inputs needed to meet their subscribers' expectations, providers would have to compete meaningfully among themselves in the sale of those services.

The noncompetitiveness of the market in question is neither accidental nor the result of revealed consumer preferences. The existing third-party payment system, characterized by passivity and complaisance and not by aggressive purchasing, is the result not of free consumer choice but of careful nurturing by organized providers, who have adamantly demanded that third parties not act as purchasing agents for their subscribers. The various practices by which provider organizations have dictated the conduct of third-party payers are listed earlier in this chapter as restraints of trade currently targeted for antitrust enforcement. That antitrust "hit list," revealing actual instances of suppression of independent actions by third parties seeking to control their costs, suggests that, in the absence of restraints, things would be quite different.

Although specific instances of overt restraint do appear, one does not have any overall sense that third parties are straining to compete in the purchase of providers' services. Indeed, far from seeking greater freedom, most insurers claim to be doing all they can reasonably be expected to do to control costs, and they have been highly receptive to increasing regulatory control.[81] The unpleasant fact is, however, that the private third parties, even though they are subject to pressure to conform to providers' preferences, cannot be absolved of complicity both with the providers and with each other in the suppression of competition. Some major third-party payers (e.g., Blue Shield plans) are, of course, actually under direct provider control, but most others, to the extent that they deal directly with providers at all, approach them as a collectivity, not as competitors, and deal either with the hospital association or with the medical society on questions involving cost containment.[82] While there is always a question whether another approach is possible given the likelihood of boycott or other retaliation by providers, the third parties have appeared to welcome provider dictation more than they struggled against it. It can be assumed, moreover, that insurers have been quite happy not to compete in the demanding and largely uncertain business of controlling moral hazard. Certainly it is much more convenient and profitable for commercial insurers and the Blues to serve as pass-through mechanisms for an increasing volume of dollars.[83]

It would be asking a lot to expect the health insurance industry to resist rather than to encourage the perception that it is primarily the government's responsibility to solve the cost problem. Nevertheless, it is surprising that the current proregulation stance of the health insurance industry has triggered so little suspicion that government is threatening once more to spare a major industry the necessity of having to be competitive. Once again, it must be remembered that one cannot discover the potential benefits of competition by asking those who would prefer the status quo. The fact is that regulation is a highly questionable remedy for the lack of competition at the plan-provider interface if that lack of competition results from avoidable conduct of the plans and providers in question. Thus, if reluctance on the part of health insurers to compete in the purchase of inputs arises from oligopolistic behavior, it may be fairly asked why the regulators should intervene to control costs on the insurers' behalf, reducing rather than increasing the pressure on them to break ranks. On the other hand, if the explanation is not a tacit conspiracy among insurers but the simple fact that any plan wishing to drive hard bargains would be stonewalled by the providers, one may wonder at encouraging regulation that would prevent entry by new and more competitive providers. Later chapters argue for regulatory and nonregulatory strategies to break up such overt or tacit conspiracies as may account for competing health plans' inadequate pressures on providers.

Finally, it must be noted that the success of closed-panel HMOs results in large part simply from their buying professional and hospital services in a competitive market. Because they have had relative freedom to move their patients to hospitals of their own choosing, they have frequently been able, despite conspiracies to prevent it, to obtain price and other concessions. Physicians' services are also purchased on a competitive basis, though the noncompetitiveness of the larger market makes it necessary to pay high wages. Utilization is kept under control either by selecting efficient physicians in the competitive market or by inducing physicians to accept the plan's cost-conscious oversight and administrative arrangements. The HMO model thus illustrates the value of competition at the plan-provider interface, where competitive pressures to keep health plan premiums low can be transmitted to providers, thus triggering meaningful competition among them both over the prices to be paid and over the administrative checks needed to cope with moral hazard.

The key insight here is that nothing in the HMOs' success absolutely limits the availability of the same tools to non-HMO health plans. By using provider participation agreements and any of a variety of possible modifications of the closed-panel model, any health insurer could give its insureds the benefits of competition. With the antitrust laws to restrain provider retaliation, health plans can and should begin, at long last, to assume their proper role as the consumer's purchasing agents. Although competition will not be popular with either providers or insurers, absent conspiracy it should take hold.

NOTES

1. Pauly, "Is Medical Care Different?" in Federal Trade Commission, Bureau of Competition, *Competition in the Health Care Sector: Past, Present and Future* 19 (W. Greenberg ed. 1978).

2. For a more rigorous application of economic theory to health policy issues, see J. Newhouse, *The Economics of Medical Care: A Policy Perspective* (1978); *see also Competition in the Health Care Sector, supra* note 1.

3. Feldstein, "The Rising Price of Physicians' Services," 52 *Rev. Econ. & Statistics* 121 (1970).

4. U.S. Department of Health, Education and Welfare, Health Resources Administration, *The Target Income Hypothesis and Related Issues in Health Manpower Policy* (1980).

5. Pauly & Satterthwaite, "The Effect of Provider Supply on Price," in *id.* at 26.

6. *Cf.* Health Systems Agency v. Virginia State Bd. of Medicine, 424 F. Supp. 267 (E.D. Va. 1976).

7. M. Friedman, *Capitalism and Freedom* 159 (1962).

8. *See* Schwartz & Komesar, "Doctors, Damages, and Deterrence: An Economic View of Medical Malpractice," 298 *New Eng. J. Med.* 1282 (1978); Havighurst, " 'Medical Adversity Insurance'—Has Its Time Come?" 1975 *Duke L.J.* 1233, 1241–52.

9. Bates v. State Bar, 433 U.S. 350 (1977). *See also* Virginia State Bd. of Pharmacy v. Virginia Citizens' Consumer Council, 425 U.S. 748 (1976); Health Systems Agency v. Virginia State Bd. of Medicine, 424 F. Supp. 267 (E.D. Va. 1976).

10. American Medical Ass'n v. FTC, 638 F.2d 443 (2d Cir. 1980), *cert. granted,* 49 U.S.L.W. 3946 (1981).

11. Havighurst, "Regulation of Health Facilities and Services by 'Certificate of Need,'" 59 *Va. L. Rev.* 1143, 1162–63 (1973).

12. For a typically simplistic analysis, see U.S. Department of Health, Education and Welfare, *Tentative National Health Plan* §II.E (Staff Draft, 1979).

13. Havighurst & Hackbarth, "Private Cost Containment," 300 *New Eng. J. Med.* 1298 (1979).

14. Reynolds, "A New Scheme to Force You to Compete for Patients," 54 *Med. Econ.* 23 (March 21, 1977).

15. Feldstein & Friedman, "Tax Subsidies, the Rational Demand for Insurance and the Health Care Crisis," 7 *J. Pub. Econ.* 155 (1977). *See* Chapter 14 for a full discussion.

16. Havighurst, "Professional Restraints on Innovation in Health Care Financing," 1978 *Duke L.J.* 303.

17. Havighurst & Hackbarth, *supra* note 13.

18. Some deviation from perfect fiduciary performance is unavoidable and is not a justification for intervention. *See* Darby & Karni, "Free Competition and the Optimal Amount of Fraud," 16 *J. L. & Econ.* 67 (1973). It is notable that the medical profession's claim of stewardship over the standards of medical practice—through profession-sponsored peer review mechanisms—is subject to challenge under conflict-of-interest principles, which to an important degree underlie the antitrust prohibition of monopoly. The critical distinction is that, under competition, consumers' ability to choose among competing providers and delivery systems gives fee-for-service providers a strong incentive to act as consumer agents.

19. Bunker & Brown, "The Physician-Patient as an Informed Consumer of Surgical Services," 290 *New Eng. J. Med.* 1051 (1974).

20. *See* Havighurst, "The Role of Competition in Cost Containment," in *Competition in the Health Care Sector, supra* note 1, at 359.

21. For fuller expositions of potential cost containment techniques in the private sector, see Havighurst & Hackbarth, *supra* note 13; Havighurst, "Private Cost Containment: Medical Practice under Competition," in 1979 *Socioeconomic Issues of Health* 41 (G. Misek ed.).

22. *See* Havighurst, *supra* note 16. *See also* discussion *infra.*

23. For example, the so-called "voluntary effort" by the medical profession and the hospital industry to control hospital costs was denied clearance by the Antitrust Division of the Department of Justice. "Justice Declines to Take Antitrust Position on Hospital

Cost Containment," *Antitrust & Trade Reg. Rep. (BNA)* No. 869 (June 22, 1978), at A-17. Moreover, the Federal Trade Commission's Bureau of Competition has been investigating the competitive effect of the profession's control of medical prepayment plans, including Blue Shield plans, individual practice associations, and foundations for medical care. Federal Trade Commission, Bureau of Competition, *Medical Participation in Control of Blue Shield and Certain Other Open-Panel Medical Prepayment Plans* (Staff Report to the Commission and Proposed Trade Regulation Rule, April 1979).

24.   *See* P. Feldstein, *Health Associations and the Demand for Legislation: The Political Economy of Health* (1977).

25.   Havighurst & Bovbjerg, "Professional Standards Review Organizations and Health Maintenance Organizations: Are They Compatible?" 1975 *Utah L. Rev.* 381, 389–93, 401–11.

26.   *See* Goldberg & Greenberg, "The Effect of Physician-Controlled Health Insurance: U.S. v. Oregon State Medical Society," 2 *J. Health Pol., Pol'y & L.* 48 (1977).

27.   U.S. Department of Health, Education and Welfare, Health Resources Administration, *A Report to the President and Congress on the Status of Health Professions Personnel in the United States* ch. 4, at 3 (1978).

28.   *Cf.* Sloan & Feldman, "Competition among Physicians," in *Competition in the Health Care Sector, supra* note 1, at 57.

29.   For a more complete discussion, see Chapter 14.

30.   *See* Note, "The Role of Prepaid Group Practice in Relieving the Medical Care Crisis," 84 *Harv. L. Rev.* 887 (1971).

31.   *See* Social Security Amendments of 1972, Pub. L. No. 92-603, §226, 86 Stat. 1396, 42 U.S.C. §1395mm (1976).

32.   *See, e.g.,* A. Enthoven, *Health Plan* (1980); Enthoven, "Consumer-Choice Health Plan" (pts. 1 & 2), 298 *New Eng. J. Med.* 650, 709 (1978). *See also* Chapter 14.

33.   Clark, "Does the Nonprofit Form Fit the Hospital Industry?" 93 *Harv. L. Rev.* 1417 (1980).

34.   *See* cases cited in note 9 *supra.*

35.   421 U.S. 773 (1975).

36.   421 U.S. at 787, n.17.

37.   *See, e.g.,* National Soc'y of Professional Eng'rs v. United States, 435 U.S. 679 (1978).

38.   *See* American Medical Ass'n v. FTC, 638 F.2d 443 (2d Cir., 1980), *cert. granted,* 49 U.S.L.W. 3946 (1981).

39.   *See* Statement of Daniel C. Schwartz, Acting Director, Bureau of Competition, Federal Trade Commission, before the Advisory

Comm. on Accreditation and Institutional Eligibility, U.S. Office of Education, March 24, 1977, Washington, D.C.

40. *Cf.* Havighurst & Kissam, "The Antitrust Implications of Relative Value Studies in Medicine," 4 *J. Health Pol., Pol'y & L.* 48 (1979).

41. *See, e.g.,* Avellone & Moore, "The Federal Trade Commission Enters a New Arena: Health Services," 299 *New Eng. J. Med.* 478 (1978); Randall, "The FTC and the Plastic Surgeons," 299 *New Eng. J. Med.* 1199 (1978).

42. For a fuller exposition of this thesis, see Havighurst, "Antitrust Enforcement in the Medical Services Industry—What Does It All Mean?" 58 *Milbank Mem. Fund Q.* 89 (1980).

43. *See* Havighurst, *supra* note 16.

44. *See* Federal Trade Commission, *supra* note 23. The commission subsequently decided to pursue the matter on a case-by-case basis rather than through rulemaking. 46 Fed. Reg. 27,768 (1981).

45. *See* Settlement Agreement, Ohio v. Ohio Medical Indemnity, Inc., Civ. No. C-2-75-473 (S.D. Ohio, filed March 22, 1979).

46. Federal Trade Commission, *supra* note 23, at 273–307. *See* Havighurst & Hackbarth, "Enforcing the Rules of Free Enterprise in an Imperfect Market: The Case of Individual Practice Associations," in *A New Approach to the Economics of Health Care* (M. Olson ed.) (in press).

47. *See* Havighurst, *supra* note 16.

48. Indiana Dental Ass'n, Consent Order (FTC File No. 781-0023, Nov. 15, 1978); Indiana Fed'n Dentists, No. 9118 (FTC, March 25, 1980) (initial decision).

49. Michigan State Med. Soc'y, No. 9129 (FTC, June 19, 1981) (initial decision).

50. *Id.* Physicians who are independent entrepreneurs, not employees of a hospital or other organization, are not protected by the antitrust exemption granted for collective bargaining by labor organizations. *See, e.g.,* Columbia River Packers Ass'n v. Hinton, 315 U.S. 143 (1942).

51. *See* Goldberg & Greenberg, *supra* note 26.

52. *See* Havighurst & Kissam, *supra* note 40, at 58–61. *But see* United States v. American Soc'y of Anesthesiologists, 473 F. Supp. 147 (S.D.N.Y. 1979).

53. *Cf.* Arizona v. Maricopa County Medical Society, 643 F.2d 553 (9th Cir. 1980), *cert. granted,* 49 U.S.L.W. 3663 (1981); Pireno v. New York State Chiropractic Ass'n, 1981–1 Trade Cases (CCH) ¶64,047 (2d Cir. 1981).

54. *Cf.* Gibson v. Berryhill, 411 U.S. 564 (1973) (optometrists' opposition to salaried practice); Group Life & Health Ins. Co. v. Royal

Drug Co., 440 U.S. 205 (1979) (pharmacists' suit against insurer); Indiana Dental Ass'n, Consent Order (FTC File No. 781-0023, Nov. 15, 1978) (barring dentists from refusing to provide X-rays for insurer's use in utilization review).

55. *See, e.g.,* North Dakota Bd. of Pharmacies v. Snyder's Drug Store, 414 U.S. 156 (1973) (upholding state law on corporate practice).

56. American Medical Ass'n v. FTC, 638 F.2d 443 (2d Cir. 1980), *cert. granted,* 49 U.S.L.W. 3946 (1981).

57. American Medical Ass'n v. United States, 317 U.S. 519 (1943). *See also* Group Health Coop. v. King County Medical Soc'y, 39 Wash. 2d 586, 237 P.2d 737 (1951).

58. *See* Kissam, "Health Maintenance Organizations and the Role of Antitrust Law," 1978 *Duke L.J.* 487.

59. *See, e.g.,* United States v. Socony-Vacuum Oil Co., Inc., 310 U.S. 150 (1940).

60. *See* note 18 *supra.*

61. *See* Kissam, "Antitrust Law, the First Amendment, and Professional Self Regulation of Technical Quality," in *Regulating the Professions* (R. Blair & S. Rubin, eds. 1980).

62. *See* discussion in Chapters 5 and 6.

63. *See, e.g.,* New Motor Vehicle Bd. v. Orrin W. Fox Co., 439 U.S. 96 (1978).

64. *See* California Retail Liquor Dealers Ass'n v. Midcal Aluminum, Inc., 445 U.S. 97 (1980); United States v. Texas State Bd. of Accountancy, 1979 Trade Cases (CCH) ¶62,546 (5th Cir. 1979).

65. *See* American Optometric Ass'n v. FTC, 626 F.2d 896 (D.C. Cir. 1980).

66. 15 U.S.C. §1012(b) (1976).

67. *See* Goldberg & Greenberg, *supra* note 26.

68. *Compare* Pireno v. New York State Chiropractic Ass'n, 1981–1 Trade Cases (CCH) ¶64,047 (2d Cir. 1981) *with* Bartholomew v. Virginia Chiropractors Ass'n, 612 F.2d 812 (4th Cir. 1979), *cert. denied,* 446 U.S. 938 (1980).

69. Group Life & Health Ins. Co. v. Royal Drug Co., 440 U.S. 205, 210 n.5, 214 (1979).

70. *See,* e.g., Council on Wage and Price Stability, Executive Office of the President, *The Complex Puzzle of Rising Health Care Costs: Can the Private Sector Fit It Together?* (1977); National Chamber Foundation, *A National Health Care Strategy* (1978) (a five-part series on business involvement with health); S. Caulfield & P. Haynes, *Health Care Costs: Private Initiatives for Containment* (1981).

71. F. Knight, *The Economic Organization* 31–32 (1951).

72. C. Schultze, *The Public Use of Private Interest* (1977). Quotations in the following discussion are taken from the shorter version in *Harper's,* May 1977, at 43.

73. *Id.* at 45.

74. *Id.* at 46.

75. *Id.*

76. *Id.* at 47.

77. *Id.* at 46.

78. *Id.* at 62.

79. *E.g.,* Airline Deregulation Act of 1978, Pub. L. No. 95–504, 92 Stat. 1705 (codified in scattered sections of 49 U.S.C. (Supp. III 1979)); Motor Carrier Act of 1980, Pub. L. No. 96–296, 94 Stat. 793 (to be codified in scattered sections of 49 U.S.C.); Staggers Rail Act of 1980, Pub. L. No. 96–448, 94 Stat. 1895 (to be codified in scattered sections of 49 U.S.C.).

80. *See, e.g.,* McClure, "On Broadening the Definition of and Removing Regulatory Barriers to a Competitive Health Care System," 3 *J. Health Pol., Pol'y & L.* 303 (1978); Havighurst & Hackbarth, *supra* note 13.

81. *See, e.g.,* Froehlke, "Promising Approaches to Cost Containment: The Health Insurance View," 56 *Bull. N.Y. Acad. Med.* 152 (1980).

82. *See, e.g.,* Metropolitan Life Insurance Company, Cost Containment at Metropolitan, at 8, 11 (no date).

83. For a fuller discussion of insurer attitudes toward competition, see Havighurst, *supra* note 16, at 336–42. This source rejects the insurance industry's desire for an antitrust exemption to enable collective bargaining with providers. Clearly such an exemption would be incompatible with the kind of competition looked for here.

II DRAFTING HEALTH PLANNING AND CERTIFICATE-OF-NEED LEGISLATION TO FOSTER COMPETITION

5 CHARGING THE PLANNER-REGULATORS TO WEIGH COMPETITIVE VALUES

A certificate-of-need law is anticompetitive by definition, since it restricts market entry by new firms and competitive initiatives by incumbents in the market. Similarly, the usual conception of health planning implies the substitution of a single central decisionmaker in the place of market forces as the dominant influence in allocating resources to and within the health care system. Nevertheless, a certificate-of-need law need not be administered to stifle all competition, and planners charged with designing a desirable health care delivery system need not dispense with competition altogether. Indeed, planner-regulators might elect to supplant competition only where it is clearly dysfunctional and actively promote it wherever its benefits are reasonably expected to exceed its costs. This chapter addresses the legal mandate given to the planner-regulators under both federal and state law. It is primarily concerned with elaborating and assessing the significance of the procompetition language that Congress introduced into Public Law 93–641 by Public Law 96–79, the National Health Planning and Resources Development Amendments of 1979.

Skillful drafting of health planners' and regulators' statutory mandate may not alone offset the strong anticompetitive biases that regulators bring to most endeavors. As a class, regulators are highly receptive to arguments that market forces are an unrelia-ble guide compared to their own judgment. Moreover, in addition to perceiving market pressures as unruly and frequently unfair vehicles of change, regulators usually find that reducing competi-tion is an excellent way of earning the cooperation of the regulat-ed firms. Given the anticompetitive propensities of regulators that flow from these perceptions, it would be difficult to write a certificate-of-need law that imposes on the legislative grant of power to curb competition just those conditions that are needed to assure that power's judicious use. Thus, adherence to the procompetitive legislative specifications in this chapter cannot guarantee that competition would not be inappropriately elimi-nated or prevented on many occasions by agencies whose discre-tion would necessarily remain broad. Probably the most that can be hoped for as the result of the 1979 changes in federal law, which largely embraced the approach suggested here, is that a substantial minority of HSAs and state agencies will take serious-ly their new responsibility for harnessing rather than destroying competitive forces. Part III provides a fuller estimate of the legal and political significance of the 1979 amendments for regulatory performance. The focus in Part II is on legislative policy.

Perhaps the most important prerequisite for maintaining com-petition in a regulated industry is strong political support for the idea of competition and the values that it represents. Such politi-cal support was critical to the initiatives by which the Civil Aero-nautics Board (CAB) substantially deregulated the airline industry prior to the enactment of deregulatory legislation, which mostly ratified the new procompetitive policy. Similarly, the procompetitive efforts of the Interstate Commerce Commission (ICC) and the Federal Communications Commission (FCC) re-flect a political environment that is increasingly attuned to the consumer's interest in lower prices and better service and that is increasingly skeptical of government's ability to achieve laudable statutory objectives without unduly sacrificing economic efficien-cy. Just as a favorable political environment enabled the CAB, the ICC, and the FCC to promote competition without special legislative instructions, an explicit legislative mandate to main-tain competition in the health services industry would probably have little effect on regulatory outcomes in the absence of strong political support for the procompetitive strategy. The political consensus would have to be clear enough that agencies indulging their anticompetitive proclivities would risk losing power and resources. Even an activist judiciary willing to enforce a procompetitive approach would be incapable of altering the basic tone of a regulatory program that felt no political pressure to foster competition.

COMPETITION IN HEALTH LEGISLATION BEFORE THE 1979 AMENDMENTS

Prior to 1979, there was very little political and statutory support for a procompetitive approach to health sector regulation. While federal policy looked in more than one direction, the dominant view contemplated a centrally planned system and acknowledged no role at all for competition. The year 1979 saw substantial changes in federal policy. A review of the legislation in effect prior to the 1979 amendments indicates how far Congress and other policymakers have had to come in order to embrace competition as a potentially constructive feature of the health services industry.

Federal Legislation

Public Law 93–641, which added Titles XV and XVI to the Public Health Service Act, was practically devoid of language that could be construed as charging the planner-regulators with a responsibility to consider competition in their deliberations. The legislative history of Public Law 93–641 confirms the impression that the act was conceived as creating a planning system that, as to all matters within the planner-regulators' broad jurisdiction, would totally displace market forces as an allocator of resources. The Senate committee report revealed congressional acquiescence in the prevailing conventional wisdom concerning the efficacy of competition in the health services industry:

> The need for strengthened and coordinated planning for personal health services is growing more apparent each day. In the view of the Committee the health care industry does not respond to classic mar-

ketplace forces. The highly technical nature of medical services together with the growth of third party reimbursement mechanisms act
to attenuate the usual forces influencing the behavior of consumers
with respect to personal health services. For the most part, the doctor
makes purchasing decisions on behalf of the patient and the services
are frequently reimbursed under health insurance programs, thus reducing the patient's immediate incentive to contain expenditures.[1]

The validity of such blanket assertions as these is questioned in
Chapter 4, but the relevant congressional committees and their
staffs seem to have acted on the premise that the competitive
marketplace, because it was part of the problem, could not be
part of the solution.

Only in dealing with HMOs did federal health legislation prior
to 1979 acknowledge some role for competition.[2] Even here, however, competition was far from a prominent consideration.
Neither the HMO Act of 1973, which actively supported HMO
development, nor Public Law 93–641, which made some special
provision for encouraging HMOs, provided any real indication
that HMOs were valued as anything more than a desirable alternative. Although there was practically no indication in the laws
or their legislative history that Congress appreciated the competitive stimulus that HMOs could supply in the system, the initiatives taken on behalf of HMOs reflected a preference for a policy
that was procompetitive in fact. Moreover, by supplying some
protection for HMOs against discrimination by the health system's planner-regulators, federal law signified a lack of confidence
that planner-regulators would consistently view this type of competitive initiative solely on its merits. Unfortunately, singling out
HMOs qualified under the federal HMO Act for such special
treatment appeared to confirm the view that such HMOs are the
only procompetitive initiatives in the health care sector deserving
recognition. While this view is patently wrong, federal health legislation prior to 1979 failed to recognize any other role for
competition.

While the architects of federal health legislation were blind to
competition's possible benefits, the antitrust laws remained in
place as an expression of a general federal policy presumptively
favorable to reliance on decentralized private decisionmaking and
consumer choice to allocate an industry's resources. The antitrust
laws apply to the health care industry as long as explicit federal

or state health legislation does not set them aside. Their increasingly aggressive enforcement in the health sector beginning in the mid-1970s, while leaving overall federal policy somewhat inconsistent and unclear, indicated that competition had not been finally ruled out as a desirable force in the industry.

State Law

Despite the neglect of competition in the original federal health planning legislation and other enactments, there would still have been room for competition to operate in local health services markets if state law or the state and local planner-regulators had been inclined to permit it. Nevertheless, no state gave competition even an honorable mention until the state of Utah enacted its Pro-competitive Certificate of Need Act in March 1979.[3] Though literally a contradiction in terms, that official title and the new law's substance put Utah unequivocally on record in favor of maintaining a market-oriented health care system under regulatory oversight administered in compliance with Public Law 93–641. Competition-related provisions of the Utah law (as amended in 1981) are set forth in Appendix A.

The unique features of the Utah law resulted from a combination of factors. Resistance to pressures from the federal level to adopt a traditional certificate-of-need law led the Utah legislature to commission Lewin & Associates, Inc., a consulting firm, to conduct a major investigation of health care costs in Utah and alternative methods of controlling them. The idea of introducing procompetitive principles into certification of need, which was drawn from early drafts of this book, provided the basis for discussions that ultimately led to the embodiment of those principles in the proposed legislation.

THE CONTEXT IN WHICH COMPETITION ISSUES WERE ADDRESSED IN THE 1979 AMENDMENTS

Whereas competition was almost totally excluded from federal health policy prior to 1979, the 1979 amendments have now largely redressed this balance insofar as health planning is concerned. Before examining those amendments specifically, this discussion sets forth some of the context in which they were developed. It also sets forth some specific drafting proposals that were made available to congressional draftsmen and thus helped to shape congressional thinking.

The 1978 Proposed Amendments

Despite what looked like a broad consensus supporting their enactment, proposed amendments to Public Law 93–641 failed to pass in the final days of the Ninety-fifth Congress.[4] Those amendments would not have advanced the cause of competition. Although HMO prospects would have been materially improved, the main thrust of the amendments was to tighten the planning system's grip on developments and to narrow the room for planners to conclude that competition could assist in identifying and promoting the public interest. A number of proposed additions to the legislative findings and purpose, to the law's "national health priorities," and to the required decisionmaking criteria all proceeded from the same central-planning impulse, making competition seem more obviously irrelevant to Congress's thinking than ever before. Also ominous for competition was the requirement in the bill passed by the Senate that state health plans specify as targets or quotas "the number and type" of a wide range of facilities and services; such particularity was called for even with respect to several noninstitutional services (such as home health care) that would not have had to be covered by state certificate-of-need requirements. The thrust here toward centralized decisionmaking was underscored by the proposed requirement that state certificate-of-need programs provide that only services or facilities that are "consistent . . . with the State health plan" shall be offered in the state. Although a state plan might still have declared that competition would be allowed to operate with respect to some facilities and services, such a procompetitive element would have been largely gratuitous and might well have been objected to at the federal level.

It was fortunate for competition that the 1978 amendments failed to pass, thus allowing the Ninety-sixth Congress to reconsider their basic thrust toward command-and-control regulation. In many respects, the 1978 amendments would have represented further nails in the coffin of competition, except insofar as they would have benefited a limited class of HMOs. Moreover, they would have presented severe problems for states (such as Utah) and state or local planner-regulators who wished to submit fewer matters to governmental control and to leave more to market forces. Significantly, the Ninety-sixth Congress reexamined the premises of the original law and the proposed 1978 amendments. As the next section shows, events changed somewhat the nature of the problems that the amendments had to address, thus creating the opportunity for giving competition the recognition it had previously lacked.

A Conflict Between Health Planning and the Antitrust Laws

In late 1978, the Antitrust Division of the Department of Justice had pending before it a request by the Central Virginia HSA (CVHSA) for a "business review letter" indicating a favorable opinion from an antitrust standpoint of certain HSA activities. The primary issue concerned the HSA's efforts to gain providers' voluntary compliance with certain of the planning agency's recommendations for the closing, conversion, and consolidation of services. Because these efforts involved the HSA in negotiations with competing providers and the possibility of the providers' mutual withdrawal from competition under tacit or even explicit anticompetitive agreements, a severe antitrust problem was presented. Although the Antitrust Division has no power to grant immunity from all kinds of antitrust attack, the CVHSA apparently hoped that, by declaring its intention not to sue to terminate questionable activities undertaken in the name of health planning, the division could significantly reduce the risks attending legal uncertainty.

Despite a certain sympathy with the planners' objectives, the Antitrust Division was reluctant to issue a favorable ruling. In due course, the issue was brought to the attention of congressional staff members working on the health planning amendments and served, more than any other single thing, to prompt serious consideration of competition's role in the industry and in the planning and regulatory process. Both for this reason and because the legal and policy questions remain controversial at this writing, the antitrust issue is elaborated at some length here. However, the following discussion examines the issue as of the time that the amendments were being considered, leaving the current controvery for discussion in Chapter 6.

The Antitrust Division would have been justified if it had refused in early 1979 to give its blanket approval to CVHSA's implementation activities insofar as they might lead to concerted action by competing hospitals and other providers with respect to consolidation, closing, conversion, or sharing of services. The legal argument was complex but addressed the question whether the original Public Law 93–641 provided a statutory basis for finding an implied exemption from the usual antitrust rules governing agreements among competitors to reduce output or divide markets. The involvement of the HSA as a quasi-public overseer of the process obviously made the case different from a typical cartel agreement, but this difference would not amount to a decisive legal distinction unless Congress had adequately revealed an intention to authorize an HSA to approve, or broker, agreements that would otherwise violate antitrust principles. Because Public Law 93–641 specified no explicit exemption from the antitrust laws, congressional intent had to be ascertained by inference, and it is a settled principle of statutory construction that exemptions from the antitrust laws are not "lightly" attributed to Congress.[5] An implied repeal of antitrust principles will normally be found only where there is a "clear repugnancy" between the regulatory scheme and antitrust doctrine—that is, where the exemption is necessary to make the regulatory program work in accordance with Congress's declared intention.[6] The courts will also look for signs that Congress assigned to the regulatory agency the task of weighing competition.[7] Without evidence that the HSAs were appointed to safeguard the values that underlie antitrust doctrine, the courts would presumably be less likely to conclude that Congress intended to remove questions of competition from the jurisdiction of the antitrust enforcement agencies and the courts.

Public Law 93–641 was quite vague as to how excess capacity in the health care system was to be handled. While the provisions for "appropriateness review" of existing institutions were obvi-

ously pregnant with the desire to identify and eliminate unneeded beds or facilities, the law was conspicuously silent as to what
would happen once a condition of excess had been discovered. It
was the lack of a statutory mandate to proceed to remedy such a
condition that originally prompted the CVHSA to inquire
whether its efforts to close unneeded obstetrical beds by obtaining voluntary cooperation and mutual withdrawal by competitors created antitrust problems either for the HSA itself or for
the cooperating providers.

It seems clear that an antitrust problem arises, if at all, only
with respect to efforts to bring about the consolidation, sharing,
conversion, or closing of services. Other HSA activities undertak-
en pursuant to Public Law 93–641 were spelled out sufficiently in
the original statute to prevent serious antitrust issues from being
raised. Obviously, HSAs must be careful not to act beyond their
statutory powers or without due process in restricting competition or private actors' market opportunities.

Public Law 93–641 and its legislative history did contain numerous indications that Congress wished the HSAs to do something about industry overcapacity. For example, in section 1502
the law identified a number of objectives deserving "priority consideration" in health planning activities, including "the development of multi-institutional systems for coordination or
consolidation of institutional health services (including obstetric,
pediatric, emergency medical, intensive and coronary care, and
radiation therapy services)." Moreover, provisions on appropriateness review [sections 1513(g) and 1523(a) (6)] and the development of local and state health plans contemplated establishment
of numerical objectives for the system, and several provisions of
the original enactment indicated Congress's desire that these
goals, once determined, be implemented by local efforts. Thus,
the HSAs' basic mandate [section 1513(a)] included a direction to
"reduce documented inefficiencies, and implement the health
plans of the agency." Specific directions with respect to plan implementation include [section 1513(c)] a direction to "seek, to the
extent practicable, to implement its HSP and AIP with the assistance of individuals and public and private entities in its health
service area."

While some statutory language thus might have been deemed
to constitute authority to seek the cooperation of providers in

closing facilities or curtailing services, the legislative history of Public Law 93–641 revealed that the conference committee specifically eliminated language that would have directed the HSA, upon finding in an appropriateness review that a service or facility was unneeded, to "work with the provider of the service or with the facility, the state agency, and other appropriate persons for the ... elimination ... of such service or facility." [8] Because of both this significant omission and the lack of language specifically contemplating anticompetitive agreements among competitors, the statute could only be read as insufficiently specific concerning the methods by which an unneeded facility could be eliminated to warrant finding an exemption from the usual antitrust prohibitions for any explicit or tacit anticompetitive agreements that an HSA might work out between competitors. Moreover, the lack of a specific directive to consider the possible benefits of competition would have weighed against inferring an exemption.

Other technical arguments might also have been advanced to protect the HSA and providers working with it from antitrust liability. For example, an HSA could have claimed that it was a government instrumentality and was therefore entitled to a "state-action" exemption. [9] Similarly, providers dealing with the HSA might have claimed to be exempt on the ground that they were merely petitioning a governmental body and that the antitrust laws cannot prohibit competitors' conferring over proposals to be duly submitted to the HSA for approval and incorporation in the agency's health plans. [10] Even if the HSA were viewed as a private agency, the HSA and the providers could have claimed that they were acting jointly to advise the state agency in performing a quasi-legislative function. Nevertheless, all of these arguments would ultimately founder on the lack of HSA or state agency power to bless anticompetitive agreements to comply with the health plans and appropriateness reviews once they were duly promulgated. Even if all cartel activity leading to specific health plans and to explicit recommendations for closure or consolidation were protected under the foregoing doctrines, anticompetitive concerted action in the implementation of such plans and recommendations would still have lacked even a colorable defense.

Thus, while an HSA might have made recommendations concerning desirable closings, conversions, and consolidations and embodied them in its health plans, it could not, without running antitrust risks, do more than persuade individual hospitals (or other providers) unilaterally to conform to its wishes. The difficulty of avoiding carrying messages between competitors and participating in exchanges of assurances among them would have made the HSA's activities in these areas highly dangerous[11] unless and until the antitrust issue was clarified. This sharp conflict between substantial federal policies received early attention as the Ninety-sixth Congress turned it attention to the unfinished business of amending Public Law 93–641. As noted above, this issue was the key that first opened the door to explicit consideration of the role of competition in a planned and regulated health care system.

The easy, but not the most responsible, way for Congress to resolve the emergent conflict between health planning and the antitrust laws would have been simply to enact an explicit exemption from the antitrust laws for all participants in efforts to implement consolidations, conversions, and closings indicated by a state health plan. There were several reasons, however, why Congress would probably not adopt this direct approach to resolving the issue raised by the CVHSA. First, such an explicit exemption would have run against a rising tide of concern about existing antitrust exemptions, most of which are widely suspected of doing much mischief.[12] Second, a bill providing for an explicit exemption would probably have been referred to the antitrust subcommittees of Congress, which might be less sympathetic to the perceived need for an exemption than the committees that authored Public Law 93–641; the health subcommittees would probably prefer to solve the problem in a way that preserves their own jurisdiction. Third, a blanket exemption would undoubtedly have been opposed by the Antitrust Division of the Justice Department and the FTC, which nevertheless might not have resisted a proposal giving competition adequate and explicit recognition in the regulatory process. Finally, solving the problem simply by enacting an express exemption would have given broad powers to the health agencies without any responsibility even to consider the consequences of eliminating competition; while Congress had shown no concern over this matter in the past, neither had it faced the issue as directly as it would have been forced to do by a proposed antitrust exemption.

For these reasons, Congress might have been expected to perceive that the more politic, as well as the more sensible, approach to conferring antitrust immunity on voluntary agreements would be to amend the planning law so that it would support the finding of an *implied* exemption. Moreover, continued reliance on voluntary compliance with planners' recommendations was probable because Congress was unlikely to give the planner-regulators the outright power to consolidate, convert, or close unneeded facilities by regulatory fiat. The stage therefore appeared to be set in early 1979 for Congress to lay a statutory foundation for inferring an antitrust exemption for plan implementation efforts. As earlier discussion shows, however, an exemption would be inferrable only if there were a clear statutory statement that HSA-sponsored negotiations among competing providers were contemplated and that the resulting agreements to reduce output and allocate markets were deemed acceptable despite their anticompetitive character. Achieving complete clarity on this point would require that the regulators be explicitly charged with weighing the costs of sacrificing competition along with other factors in making and implementing their health plans. Only if a court in an antitrust case were satisfied that Congress viewed the HSAs as performing the function of guarding competitive values could it be counted on to foreswear the courts' jurisdiction to prevent competition's inappropriate sacrifice. Thus, in order to lay a firm foundation for an implied exemption from the antitrust laws, Public Law 93–641 would have had to be amended to make competition an explicit value in regulatory and planning decisions.

As it turned out, the 1979 health planning amendments did nothing to extend the planners' regulatory power to implement closings, conversions, and consolidations. Congress was apparently unwilling either to give the planners the power to accomplish such changes by fiat or to confer explicit or implied antitrust immunity on private anticompetitive agreements that the planners might negotiate. Instead, the amendments approached the matter altogether differently by giving the planners some power to use federal money to buy out identified excess capacity.[13] As Chapter 6 shows, this solution left the antitrust laws not only firmly in place but with new support in the legislative history, which expressly affirms their potentially positive contribution to the industry's performance.[14] Most important, although Congress declined the opportunity to resolve the particular conflict between antitrust policy and regulation by expanding the regulators' power to eliminate competition, it nevertheless did adopt the proposal to assign them an explicit responsibility for weighing competition's possible value in carrying out their general regulatory responsibilities. It is quite possible that, if the antitrust specter had not been raised by the CVHSA, the idea of incorporating competition as a new desideratum in the planning legislation would not have taken hold.

Specific Proposals for Incorporating a Role for Competition in Public Law 93–641

There were, in early 1979, several reasons why the Ninety-sixth Congress might consider introducing competition as an explicit consideration in regulatory decisionmaking in the health care sector. In addition to the specific need, discussed above, for a clarification of whether Congress contemplated exclusive jurisdiction by the health agencies over antitrust-type questions, there was a more general need to redress Public Law 93–641's total neglect of both competition's current value as a mechanism of social control over some elements of the complex health care industry and its potential for a wider and more effective role in the future. Furthermore, the then-pending proposal for hospital cost-containment legislation, featuring a new set of heavy-handed regulatory controls, seemed to call for a reassessment of the drift toward regulation. As events turned out, Congress became in 1979 a receptive audience for procompetitive proposals.

In the course of discussions of the antitrust issue and of the cost-containment legislation, an early draft of this chapter was made available to congressional committees and their staffs. That draft identified a number of points at which competitive considerations might be introduced into Public Law 93–641 in an effort to restore appropriate balance to health planning-cum-regulation. Several specific amendments were suggested that would simply have added references to competition as a means of supplying the dimension so conspicuously absent in the law as written. One proposal was that Congress's stated "findings and purpose" in section 2(a) of the orginal enactment[15] should be amended to convey that the failings of the financing system necessitating regulation might be temporary and did not necessarily disable the market for all purposes. Another suggestion was that the "national health priorities" declared in the planning law (section 1502) should include the following new item for "priority consideration": "The strengthening of competitive forces in the health services industry wherever competition and consumer choice can constructively serve to advance the purposes of quality assurance, cost containment, and responsiveness to consumers' preferences." The reference to "strengthening competitive forces" was borrowed from President Carter's recommended principles for national health insurance. It was believed that the clause, which is similar to that finally adopted, would not be controversial because it contemplates competition only where it serves the public well. Another such noncontroversial proposal was that, as a fifth essential purpose enumerated in section 1513(a), HSAs should be charged with "promoting constructive competition in local markets for health services."

Beyond these more or less hortatory provisions, it was suggested that there were a number of substantive matters and requirements that would have to be addressed if Public Law 93–641 were to be at all effective in bringing competition into the picture. In the long run, the real key to the HSAs' and state agencies' functioning, both in controlling health system growth through certification of need and in eliminating excess capacity through implementation of the findings of appropriateness reviews, is the health plans themselves. In recognition of the federal government's eagerness to make state health plans, health systems plans (HSPs), and annual implementation plans (AIPs) definitive prescriptions of the type, number, and location of the health facilities and services that an area needs, it was proposed that the planners be required to address specifically the scope to be allowed competition in the state or community. In particular, it was suggested that HSPs be required to indicate which specific types of services and facilities would be of greater benefit to consumers, having regard to quality, cost, convenience, and other factors, if offered under competitive conditions without regulatory restraint on aggregate supply.

Another critical point in the original legislation was section 1532(c), which prescribed nine explicit decisionmaking criteria to be employed by HSAs and state agencies in reviewing specific projects for certification of need or other purposes. While these criteria could have been supplemented by the states or the agencies, federal law should not so obviously leave competition out of the calculus. Accordingly, it was proposed that a new criterion be added that would cause the decisionmakers to consider in each case the possibility that new market entry or expanded supply would yield net benefits, either in lowering prices or in improving service quality.

Finally, it was suggested that new statutory language was required to resolve the specific antitrust issue raised by the CVHSA in its approach to the Justice Department. This language would have appeared in connection with the provisions for appropriateness review in section 1513(g) and required that, before recommendations for closures, consolidations, or conversions were implemented, they must be made institution-specific and incorporated either in an AIP or in an amendment to the HSP or state health plan. This requirement would have formalized the HSA's actions and provided the occasion for an explanation and justification of their anticompetitive impact. It was further suggested that the law should state that, once the appropriate procedures had been followed and the requisite findings made, the HSA was authorized to sponsor explicit agreements among competitors that would bring about compliance with the plan and the elimination of excess capacity. While these specifications would have required a substantial redrafting of the provisions for appropriateness review, adherence to them would have laid a solid foundation for courts to infer that Congress wished to confer an antitrust exemption.

The legislative changes thus proposed were not thought to be unduly controversial. In many respects, they would simply have brought the health planners' statutory charter into conformity with the thinking of many enlightened planners, who were willing to acknowledge that competition is often preferable to monopoly and that certification of need has often neglected this fact, unnecessarily strengthening the strong providers and narrowing the range of options in the system. For example, the American Health Planning Association, in connection with the CVHSA's application, had indicated a desire to meet with the Antitrust Division staff "to consider how in their planning activities, HSAs and [state agencies] might take into account the fostering of competition."[16] It would have been peculiar indeed if Congress had turned out to be more reluctant to acknowledge the legitimacy of competition as a consideration in regulatory decisionmaking than were the planners themselves.

Congress's Increasing Receptivity to Competition in Health Services

The foregoing proposals were made as Congress was becoming more receptive than ever before to the idea of competition in health services. The reasons for the emergence of this new interest in nonregulatory strategies included not only the effective advocacy of several spokespersons for competition outside of government but also increasing evidence that competition can indeed change providers' behavior. In particular, experience in the Twin Cities was viewed as a demonstration that competition could increase efficiency in fact as well as theory.[17] Furthermore, with the FTC's involvement in health services, competition had gained for the first time an influential advocate within the federal bureaucracy itself, one with good credentials as a consumer advocate. Moreover, the FTC's work in antitrust enforcement added credibility to the idea of competition, both by improving understanding of why the market had performed badly in the past and by increasing appreciation of the market's potential for stimulating major market-induced innovations in financing and delivery.

Perhaps the main factor triggering new congressional interest in a nonregulatory health policy was the Carter administration's hospital cost containment bill, first introduced in 1977 and defeated in late 1979. This proposal would have launched a new era of federal cost-containment regulation whose implications were highly troubling to many legislators. The arbitrariness of the bill's formula for restraining hospital revenue increases was palpable and represented a major departure from regulation based on need and other criteria that were ostensibly objective and sensitive to the values at stake. Indeed, the bill appeared to signify both a major escalation in the war with the private sector and an acknowledgment that the forms of regulation with which Congress had previously been comfortable had failed to produce adequate results. Thus given a glimpse of the road ahead if Congress continued to pursue regulation, some members recoiled and began seeking other routes to the desired destination. Witnesses were invited to "debate" the relative merits of regulation and competition before the relevant subcommittees, and several congressional leaders in the fight against the administration bill subsequently sponsored procompetitive bills.[18] These proposals, together with the enactment of procompetition language in the health planning amendments, show unmistakably that 1979 and the Ninety-sixth Congress marked a significant turning point in congressional attitudes toward competition in health services financing and delivery.[19]

The Relevance of the Larger Deregulation Movement

In addition to reflecting specific developments in health policy thinking and experience, Congress's increasing receptivity to competition as an alternative to regulation in health services also reflected the growing national discontent with governmental regulation in general. Indeed, the emphasis that the health planning amendments place on competition can probably be understood only in light of the strong movement for regulatory reform and even for deregulation of certain major industries, something long thought to be politically impossible. Because of the new national mood and new sophistication concerning regulation's systematic failings, even legislators who may doubt the wisdom of extensive deregulation have begun to support regulatory reforms designed to reduce the anticompetitive effect of economic regulation.

The suggested amendments to Public Law 93–641 would have resulted, not in deregulation, but in a regulatory pattern similar to that long prevailing in other federally regulated industries, such as trucking, communications, and natural gas transmission. In those industries, the agencies in charge possessed broad powers to restrict entry, foster monopoly, and condone mergers, consolidations, and agreements among competitors that would otherwise violate the antitrust laws. However, the courts have read the agencies' mandates to pursue the "public interest" to mean that they may not sacrifice competition without expressly weighing its benefits against the benefits to be gained by alternative policies.[20] By the same token, the courts do not allow an agency to forgo regulation in favor of competition without findings of competition's value in the specific circumstances.[21] This pattern of agency accountability for the fate of competition in a regulated industry is no guarantee that regulators will not inappropriately sacrifice competition or the public interest; the range of regulatory discretion remains broad. Nevertheless, this pattern was the product of a long evolution, and its explicit adoption in the health care industry would be a strong signal to the regulators. Moreover, a strengthening of this pattern and of the procompetition signal had been embodied in various ways in several important proposals for regulatory reform. Thus, there seemed to be a good warrant for its explicit adoption in the health care sector through legislative changes making competition a value for which the regulators are responsible. The proposal was hardly a radical one.

Regulators in other industries have rarely been accused by objective observers of promoting too much competition. Adding accountability for competitive values to the health planning statute was not expected therefore to do more than somewhat reduce the persistent hazard of anticompetitive regulatory abuses. The hope was that, at least, it might keep options open by maintaining flexibility and allowing deregulation arguments a hearing. With regulation being undertaken at the state and local level, it was hoped that experience using different strategies could be compared and that, in the long run, the optimal mix of regulation and competition might be discoverable. As things turned out, Congress agreed that, by 1979, it was clearly time for explicit legislative recognition of the possibility that market forces could help as well as hinder the process of allocating health resources.

THE 1979 AMENDMENTS' PROCOMPETITION LANGUAGE: CONGRESS DECLARES A NEW VIEW OF COMPETITION

The 1979 amendments to Public Law 93–641 generally adopted the principles, though not always the language, embodied in the specific proposals set forth above. The committee staffs that drafted both the Senate and the House bills had an early draft of this chapter before them in their work. In addition, the House draftsmen were briefed on the antitrust problems arising out of the Central Virginia HSA application and on the Utah certificate-of-need law, which was enacted during the drafting of the bills. In neither the House nor the Senate were amendments to increase the sensitivity of planner-regulators to competitive factors regarded as controversial or as partisan issues. In the Senate subcommittee, the specific amendments were proposed by the Republican minority, but the chairman, Senator Kennedy—a leading advocate of regulatory reform and of competition and deregulation in the airlines and trucking industries—was apparently receptive to the general principles. In the House, the staff of the Democratic majority took the initiative. Although the two houses proceeded independently, each produced a bill that gave competition not only due recognition but a prominence totally unprecedented in health legislation. Despite wide differences in language, their independent arrival at agreement on the general objective of restoring competition as a candidate for a role in allocating health resources indicates an unusual degree of consensus and clarity on an important change in the premises of national health policy.

The procompetition changes in Title XV of the Public Health Service Act (enacted in Public Law 93–641) all appeared in section 103 of Public Law 96–79, under the heading, "The Role of Competition in the Allocation of Health Services." The committee reports are of particular interest and are referred to at several points. Because the House Committee's extensive statement of congressional purpose is particularly instructive, it is set forth in Appendix B.

The key provision for ascertaining Congress's purpose is section 1502(b) of the amended Public Health Service Act, which provides extensive findings concerning competition's role in allocating health care resources. Each of the substantive provisions touching on competition, which are discussed below, has specific reference to section 1502(b). Adapted from language in the House bill, it provides as follows:

(1) The Congress finds that the effect of competition on decisions of providers respecting the supply of health services and facilities is di-

minished. The primary source of the lessening of such effect is the prevailing methods of paying for health services by public and private health insurers, particularly for inpatient health services and other institutional health services. As a result, there is duplication and excess supply of certain health services and facilities, particularly in the case of inpatient health services.

(2) For health services, such as inpatient health services and other institutional health services, for which competition does not or will not appropriately allocate supply consistent with health systems plans and State health plans, health systems agencies and State health planning and development agencies should in the exercise of their functions under this title take actions (where appropriate to advance the purposes of quality assurance, cost effectiveness and access and the other purposes of this title) to allocate the supply of such services.

(3) For the health services for which competition appropriately allocates supply consistent with health systems plans and State health plans, health systems agencies and State health planning and development agencies should in the performance of their functions under this title give priority (where appropriate to advance the purposes of quality assurance, cost effectiveness, and access) to actions which would strengthen the effect of competition on the supply of such services.

Far from being a ringing general endorsement of competition in health services, section 1502(b) is instead a carefully drafted clarification of the concept of regulation embodied in the planning act. Its essential message is that health services should be divided by the planner-regulators into two categories, those "for which competition does not or will not appropriately allocate supply" and those for which competition is a reliable allocative mechanism. In general, command-and-control regulation should be employed to allocate resources used in rendering services in the former category, whereas market forces should be allowed to function with respect to the latter, unless to do so would undercut some countervailing statutory purpose. Thus, the planner-regulators are no longer entitled simply to assume the appropriateness of command-and-control intervention with respect to all services under their jurisdiction. Instead, they must make a threshold determination concerning the market's efficacy, and, in the absence of an explicit finding of market failure or some other extraordinary circumstance, they must not substitute their own judgment for that of the marketplace. Part III gives a detailed discussion of how planner-regulators should carry out this new mandate.

Section 1502(b) also serves the salutary purpose of advancing understanding of why competition has not been an effective mechanism in the past, specifically identifying the financing system as the source of the problem. More importantly, the reference to *"prevailing* methods of paying for health services by public and private health insurers" (emphasis added) implies the possibility that different payment methods might exist in the future and permit competition a larger role. Similarly, the reference, in paragraph (2), to services "for which competition does not *or will not* appropriately allocate supply" (emphasis added) suggests that in the future competition's role might be enlarged. These nuances should serve as a signal to the regulators that they should not assume that what needs regulation today will necessarily need regulation tomorrow. The House committee report was particularly explicit on this point, declaring that

> If . . . an innovative financing, reimbursement or service delivery arrangement affecting institutional health services, were designed so that the method of payment by patients (1) created incentives for patients to respond to prices charged and (2) placed the providers at financial risk for unnecessary or excessive services, the committee would expect that planning agencies would, in awarding certificates of need, consider whether the effect of that new arrangement will be to properly allocate the supply of those services.[22]

Paragraph (2) of section 1502(b) appears to identify "inpatient health services and other institutional health services" (the latter a defined term including significant outpatient services provided by institutional providers) as being among those "for which competition does not or will not allocate supply" and which therefore must be allocated by regulatory means. The previously quoted sentence from the House report makes it clear, however, that paragraph (2) was not intended to declare such services subject to command-and-control regulation for all time and under all circumstances. It is argued at another point[23] that Congress was simply stating its assumption that, due to the current extent of third-party coverage of such services, regulation is probably required. What comes through clearly is that, in accordance with the common view that regulation is to be employed only where an irremediable market failure exists, Congress wants the regulators to adopt a command-and-control posture only where it is necessary and not to do so where it is not. In section 1502(b) and its legislative history, Congress has called attention in at least a general way to the kind of market failures that warrant intervention.

The Senate committee report on the planning amendments supplies an especially dramatic demonstration that Congress has indeed arrived at a new perception concerning the permanence of the need for regulation. The 1979 report restates some crucial language from its 1974 report on the original planning law, repeating it almost *in haec verba* but with an amendment that reveals an altogether different conclusion about competition's future place. Whereas in its earlier report, in a much-quoted statement, the committee had stated its view that "the health care industry does not respond to classic marketplace forces,"[24] it has now restated that proposition as follows: "In the view of the committee the health care industry *has not responded* to classic marketplace forces" (emphasis added).[25] Underscoring its new perception, the committee immediately repeats and amplifies that thought and goes on as follows:

> Despite the fact that the health care industry has not *to date* responded to classic marketplace forces, the committee believes that the planning process—at the Federal, State, and local level—should encourage competitive forces in the health services industry wherever competition and consumer choice can constructively serve to advance the purposes of quality assurance and cost effectiveness.[26] (Emphasis added.)

At another point, the Senate committee states its view that health sector regulation has been unduly neglectful of competition and declares its desire that the regulators avoid the vices of regulators in other industries:

> The Committee realizes that since initiation of the Act, the orientation of the planning process has become increasingly centralized, threatening to leave out competition altogether. With these provisions, the Committee introduces into the health planning law the recognition that planning agencies at all levels have as important a responsibility to promote competition among health care providers as

the obligation to encourage cost containment, facility closure or shared services. The experience with other public regulatory authorities has been one of creating industry cartels which emphasize market stability rather than innovation and consumer preference. The Committee intends to protect against such tendencies in health sector regulation.[27]

Another amendment of the nonsubstantive portions of the planning law reveals even more clearly congressional expectations about competition's potential place. To the act's already long list of "national health priorities" in section 1502(a), which previously was notable for the absence of even an oblique reference to competition, the amendments add the following new priority, drawn from the Senate bill and echoing language from the Senate committee report and from the proposals described earlier: "The strengthening of competitive forces in the health services industry wherever competition and consumer choice can constructively serve, in accordance with [section 1502(b)], to advance the purposes of quality assurance, cost effectiveness, and access." In keeping with this theme but on a more substantive level, the amendments assign HSAs a new function in section 1513(a)(5)—namely,"preserving and improving, in accordance with section 1502(b), competition in the health service area." This new affirmative duty to strengthen competition could serve as a mandate to HSAs to participate actively in the reform of the financing system, which would in turn permit less command-and-control regulation.

The amendments' other substantive provisions bearing on competition take the form of two additional criteria that certificate-of-need agencies are to employ in their decisionmaking. The first new criterion [section 1532(c)(11)] requires them to weigh, "in accordance with section 1502(b), the factors which affect the effect of competition on the supply of the health services being reviewed." Here the message is that the ability of the market to allocate resources of the type in question must be considered with care. If competition works reasonably well, the market should probably be left the allocative task.

The other new criterion [section 1532(c)(12)], which was drawn from the Senate bill, requires that the regulators consider "improvements or innovations in the financing and delivery of health services which foster competition, in accordance with section

1502(b), and serve to advance the purposes of quality assurance and cost effectiveness." Again, it appears that Congress wants the planner-regulators to consider the possibility that changes in the financing and delivery system will allow the demand side of the market to discipline the supply side more effectively, thus reducing the need for regulatory allocation of resources. These new criteria, together with Congress's stated preference for relying on market forces where they serve the public interest in "quality assurance, cost-effectiveness, and access," confirm the clear message of section 1502(b): Before embarking on command-and-control regulation in a particular case, health system regulators must address the threshold issue of whether a market failure in fact exists.

The new procompetition language added to Public Law 93–641 by the 1979 amendments and summarized here significantly shifts the focus of health planning and certification of need and has important implications both for the planner-regulators themselves and for the health care industry as a whole. This discussion has been confined to an appraisal of the legislation itself and leaves to Part III a full exploration of the practical significance of the change in the planners' and regulators' statutory mandate. Likewise, the concern here is with the amendments' general meaning and underlying concept. Issues surrounding the precise interpretation and construction of the new statutory language are left for later discussion. One legal issue that deserves discussion here, however, involves something that the 1979 amendments did not do—namely, remove the antitrust laws as a check on the attempts by health planners to rationalize the provision of services in local markets. Because this aspect of the 1979 amendments also has substantial implications for the nature of health planning and the role of competition in health services and also because the conflict between the antitrust laws and the planning enterprise remains a controversial matter, an extended discussion is provided in Chapter 6.

BUILDING PROCOMPETITIVE FEATURES INTO STATE LAW

With the 1979 amendments, the federal statute is specific enough that amendment of state certificate-of-need laws could add very little to the clarity of the planner-regulators' legal mandate to give competition due weight in formulating their plans and making regulatory decisions. Nevertheless, some changes in state laws will be required to bring them into compliance with the federal legislation. It would be desirable if those changes reflected not only the letter of, but also the same spirit as, the federal statute. The addition of independently conceived procompetition language to a state law would reinforce the planners' political mandate and improve the chances that the new emphasis on competition would be taken seriously. The establishment of an independent procompetitive policy in a state would go far toward weakening the hope of providers and regulators alike that the federal legislation does not portend or require any real change in regulatory philosophy.

The discussion here sets forth some specifications for state certificate-of-need legislation. Although some procedural changes might further improve the prospects for competition-sensitive regulation, adoption of the specifications herein would complete the substantive framework for a procompetitive regulatory strategy.

The first step in redrafting a state law to make competition a significant factor in planning and regulatory decisions is to state as clearly as possible in legislative findings the legislature's intent, including its understanding of the precise policy problem that it seeks to solve by enacting a certificate-of-need law. This should be done without overstating the case for regulation and in such a manner as to leave it clear that competition also has a constructive role to play. The following language is suggested:

The legislature hereby makes the following findings as its predicate for the enactment of this law and as a guide to its implementation and interpretation:

1. That regulation of the growth and development of the health services industry is needed to correct for distortions caused by the currently prevailing system of public and other third-party payment for health care

2. That, in view of the currently prevailing system of public and other third-party payment for health care, development in this state of a facility for the provision of health services may be affected with a public interest and may therefore be not a right but a privilege, to be granted only on an affirmative demonstration not just of the desira-

bility of such facility and the services rendered therein but of their economic appropriateness

3. That health planning and regulation should displace market forces as the operative mechanisms for guiding the growth and development of the health services industry only where competition and consumer choice cannot constructively serve to advance the purposes of quality assurance, cost effectiveness, and responsiveness to consumer preferences

The foregoing legislative findings state only the narrow rationale for regulatory intervention in the private development of health facilities and services. They avoid sweeping statements, such as are found in several states' laws, to the effect that the health care system does not respond to ordinary market forces. Such language is, of course, an invitation wholly to ignore competition's potential and to extend regulation well beyond the need for it. While the suggested findings embrace competition, they do so only as a complement to regulation and make it clear that competition is to be fostered only when it has positive benefits. It is hard to think that these findings could be objected to on principle. The legislative findings contained in the Utah law are of interest here. Though adapted from an early draft of the language set forth above, those findings (section 26–22–2 in Appendix A) are more explicit on several points.

A subtle feature of the suggested findings is the reference in both paragraphs (1) and (2) to the failings of the "currently prevailing" system of payment. The stress on the problem of current payment mechanisms is meant to keep open the possibility that future changes in the financing system would be recognized as perhaps narrowing the necessary scope of regulation. This point is meant to anticipate discussion in Part III of the need to focus on developments on the demand side of the market in making regulatory policy with respect to the supply side. If the state law were one that undertook to specify HSA functions, it might include a mandate for HSAs actively to stimulate change in the financing system so that market forces could effectively discipline a greater portion of the industry. The original Utah law was explicit on this point, but the provision was dropped in 1981, perhaps because the new federal law expressly assigns HSAs the new task of "preserving and improving ... competition in the health service area."[28]

One aspect of the federal mandate that a state statute might usefully expand upon and clarify is the substance and development of the state health plan. The 1979 amendments make the state health plan (SHP) a definitive rather than an advisory document[29] and charge the statewide health coordinating council (SHCC), now an official state instrumentality,[30] with finalizing it. It would appear that, in most states, statutes will have to be amended to formalize the SHCC's new status and provide for the SHP's preparation and completion. These amendments should be drafted in light of the discussion elsewhere[31] of the importance of allowing parties in certificate-of-need proceedings to challenge conclusions concerning the amenability of particular services and markets to competition, conclusions which, once they are embodied in the SHP, are required to be given conclusive effect in regulatory decisions. It would also be desirable if state law made clear, as the federal statute fails to do, that the SHP should address competition issues explicitly.[32] The following language is suggested:

> The SHP shall specify for each type of health service dealt with therein (giving reasons for the conclusions reached) whether or not consumers would enjoy a net benefit, having regard to the quality, accessibility, and actual cost of such service and to the system's responsiveness to consumer preferences, if competition were allowed to operate or were encouraged. The SHP shall also describe the financing systems currently prevailing in the state, specifying in particular the deficiencies therein that adversely affect consumers and necessitate regulation by diminishing the benefits and feasibility of competition.

State law may also supplement the decisionmaking criteria in the amended Public Law 93–641, which states in section 1532(c) that certificate-of-need review and SHP development "shall include *at least*" the criteria listed (emphasis added). Although the federal criteria relating to competition are reasonably clear and might simply be adopted *in haec verba* to show the state's concurrence, it might also be desirable for state law to adopt procompetitive criteria that are expressed somewhat differently. The following criteria are suggested for use in SHP development, certificate-of-need decisions, appropriateness reviews, and other decisions:

1. The effect of additional facilities or services of the particular type in question on the maintenance of competitive conditions in the local market for health services and for health services financing and prepayment

2. The value of competition and consumer choice in constructively advancing, with respect to services of the type in question, the purposes of quality assurance, cost effectiveness, and responsiveness to consumers' preferences

3. The ability of individual third-party payers to introduce, and administer at reasonable cost, coverage limitations, contractual arrangements with providers, fee schedules, or other administrative controls over the price and utilization of services of the type in question.

Paragraphs (1) and (2) track language in the earlier legislative findings, thus making it as clear as possible that these criteria lie at the heart of the statutory scheme. Paragraph (3) reflects the important idea, which is developed at length in Chapters 11 and 12, that the planner-regulators should allow entry and new investment without a specific finding of need if strategies available to third-party payers might reasonably be expected to prevent inappropriate utilization and noncompetitive pricing. Thus, existing practices of health insurers or government programs need not be the only guide as to what is possible or desirable, and a responsible regulator might sometimes seek to put pressure on third parties to negotiate charges and curb artificially created demand by permitting new competition and investment even when the third parties and others might prefer to have them restricted.

Because competition is frequently sacrificed by regulators in order to protect existing firms, it might be deemed desirable for state law to clarify that competition is to be promoted without regard to such impacts. One way in which this principle might be implemented is by language excluding as a legitimate criterion "the competitive impact of a proposed service on an existing provider or on the ability of an existing provider to continue to offer services of the same or another type." This language addresses not only protectionism that might flow from political influence or from an unduly close relationship between the regulators and existing providers but also efforts by regulators to protect a provider's monopoly revenues that are being used to subsidize some arguably desirable activity. Because its effect would be to rule out completely the claim of "cream skimming" as a justification for excluding a competing entrant from the market, it would probably be read to conflict with an amended criterion in the federal law [section 1532(c)(9)], which requires consideration of a new construction project's effect "on the costs and charges to the public of providing health services by other persons." For this reason, a different approach would have to be adopted. There is much to recommend Utah's creative handling of the problem [section 26–22–12(1)(f) in Appendix A] which requires, first, a finding that the service being subsidized meets an "overriding public need" and, second, a quantification of the subsidy. Chapter 10 discusses at some length the circumstances that might occasionally warrant the adoption of a protectionist stance, indicating that the Utah approach might be the best way of balancing the possible public need for internal subsidies against the policy of promoting competition. Whatever the approach adopted, it should be clear that exclusionary regulation is justified to assure quality-of-care objectives, such as where an underutilized service could reasonably be expected to have poorer outcomes.[33]

CONCLUSION: THE POLICY SIGNIFICANCE OF THE NEW FEDERAL REGULATORY MANDATE

Taken together, the 1979 procompetition amendments to Public Law 93–641 fundamentally alter the character and thrust of health planning and certification of need. Whereas the command-and-control mentality and the idea of allocating resources through central planning previously supplied the act's sole foundation, the law now embraces a mix of strategies and gives clear instructions to the planners and regulators that allocation by market forces is to be preferred if it can reasonably be expected to serve the public well.

The legal and policy significance of the new regulatory mandate can perhaps be most fully appreciated in light of more general developments in regulatory reform. Recent regulatory reform proposals at the federal level reflect policies toward regulation and competition that are quite similar to those embodied in the health planning amendments. The latter amendments may be seen, for example, as bearing a similarity both to President Carter's 1978 executive order directing executive-branch agencies to weigh the economic impact of regulatory initiatives[34] and to several legislative proposals to extend similar regulatory analysis requirements to independent regulatory agencies.[35] Though similar to these initiatives, the health planning amendments seem even better calculated to make a real difference in regulatory outcomes. Because those other measures were triggered in large part by concern over the high compliance costs occasioned by controls to protect health, safety, and the environment, they less clearly establish that the restoration of competition is also a paramount regulatory objective. Moreover, because the mandates in those measures are not industry-specific, the regulators will find it easy to conclude that the message was intended for someone else. Finally, there has been some reluctance to allow the courts to review specific regulatory actions in light of these new instructions, and thus the message is largely hortatory, depending for its effectiveness solely on what it may convey to the agencies about the attitudes of their political overseers. The health planning amendments, on the other hand, being industry-specific and enforceable in court and reflecting an emerging seriousness in Congress about competition in the health sector, would seem to be of a substantially different order. Indeed, Congress appears to have departed very far from its customary practice of leaving the regulators' mandate vague and internally inconsistent, thus forcing them and the courts to make the hard policy choices.

Although many regulatory reform proposals have been addressed primarily to the need for benefit-cost analysis in health and safety and environmental regulation, there has also been explicit recognition of a need to assure that regulation does not suppress competition any more than is necessary. This theme first appeared prominently in a bill sponsored by Senator Kennedy and was subsequently carried over into a new bill that was offered in late 1979 with such widespread bipartisan support that its eventual passage seemed a reasonable prospect. This bill (S. 2147), entitled the Regulatory Flexibility and Administrative Reform Act, would have required federal agencies, before adopting a policy or rule, to consider its "effects on competition" and to make "a finding that the policy or rule is the least anticompetitive alternative legally and practically available to the agency to achieve its statutory goals." This latter mandatory finding would have been subject to judicial review. The new requirements to maintain competition would have been specifically directed to agencies that are engaged in economic, as opposed to social, regulation.

Although S. 2147 would not have applied, by its terms, to the health-planning and regulatory agencies contemplated in Public Law 93–641, its mandate was essentially the same as that already incorporated, according to the foregoing analysis, in the 1979 amendments. The requirement that health planners and regulators assess, with respect to each particular service, the market's efficacy as a resource allocator corresponds directly to the reformers' proposal to require that "economic regulatory agencies . . . choose the least anticompetitive alternative when issuing a major rule or policy." Two proposed legislative findings incorporated in S. 2147 stated the same general presumption favorable to competition that is reflected in the health planning amendments:

(9) in the normal course of events, the free market is the appropriate means for allocating goods and services and has proved to be the most effective means of regulating the economy;

(10) to encourage competition and innovation, government regulations should not impose needless entry barriers to the marketplace.

At the time the 1979 health planning amendments were adopted, there was no other federal regulatory statute—with the possible exception of recent airline legislation[36]—that was as explicit and compelling in its mandate to promote competition as the health planning legislation. Indeed, given this state of the deregulation art and the extraordinary difficulty of introducing competition in health services, it appears that Congress took just about the longest step it could possibly have taken toward the goal of deregulation of the health sector. While it remains to be seen how far toward that goal it will be possible to go, the law is surprisingly clear. Nevertheless, it is by no means certain that a change in the statutory formulation of the regulatory mandate can make much practical difference. Indeed, the practical significance of the procompetition language in the 1979 amendments depends ultimately on many other matters, including the willingness of planner-regulators to honor its intent, the true potential of competition as an allocator of resources in the health sector, and the willingness of Congress to take additional steps to improve competition's efficacy.

NOTES

1. S. Rep. No. 93–1285, 93d Cong., 2d Sess. (1974), *reprinted in* 1974 *U.S. Code Cong. & Ad. News* 7842, 7878.
2. *See* Chapter 8 for discussion of legislation affecting HMOs.
3. 1979 Utah Laws ch. 95.
4. H.R. 11488 and S. 2410, 95th Cong., 2d Sess. (1978).
5. California v. FPC, 369 U.S. 482, 485 (1961); United States v. Philadelphia Nat'l Bank, 374 U.S. 321, 348 (1963).
6. United States v. Philadelphia Nat'l Bank, 374 U.S. 321, 351 (1963); Silver v. New York Stock Exchange, 373 U.S. 341, 357 (1963).
7. *See* United States v. Radio Corp. of America, 358 U.S. 334 (1959); 1 P. Areeda & D. Turner, *Antitrust Law* ¶224, at 145 (1978).
8. H.R. Rep. No. 93–1640, 93d Cong., 2d Sess. (1974), *reprinted in* 1974 *U.S. Code Cong. & Ad. News* 7842, 7983.
9. *See* Parker v. Brown, 317 U.S. 341 (1943); Cantor v. Detroit Edison Co., 428 U.S. 579 (1976).
10. *See* Eastern R.R. Presidents Conf. v. Noerr Motor Freight, Inc., 365 U.S. 127 (1961); UMW v. Pennington, 381 U.S. 657 (1965) Huron Valley Hosp., Inc. v. City of Pontiac, 466 F. Supp. 1301 (E.D. Mich. 1979).
11. *Cf.* Interstate Circuit, Inc. v. United States, 306 U.S. 208 (1939).
12. *See* National Comm'n for the Review of Antitrust Laws and Procedures, *Report to the President and the Attorney General* 177–95 (1979).
13. Pub. L. No. 96–79, §301, *adding* Public Health Service Act §§1641–43.
14. *See* H.R. Rep. No. 96–190, 96th Cong., 1st Sess. 54 (1979).
15. 42 U.S.C. §300k(a) (1976).
16. Letter from Anthony T. Mott, president of the American Health Planning Association, to John H. Shenefield, assistant U.S. attorney general, November 13, 1978.
17. *See* Christianson & McClure, "Competition in the Delivery of Medical Care," 301 *New Eng. J. Med.* 812 (1979); Iglehart, "HMOs Are Alive and Well in the Twin Cities Region," 10 *Nat'l J.* 1160 (1978).

18. *E.g.*, S. 1485, and S. 1590, 96th Cong., 1st Sess. (1979); H.R. 7527 and H.R. 7528, 96th Cong., 2d Sess. (1980).

19. Even Senator Edward Kennedy, long one of the leading proponents of the regulatory approach to controlling health care costs, has carved out a substantial role for competition in his latest national health insurance proposal. *See* Starr, "Kennedy's Conservative Health Plan," *New Republic*, June 9, 1979, at 18.

20. *See, e.g.*, McLean Trucking Co. v. United States, 321 U.S. 67 (1944).

21. FCC v. RCA Communications, Inc., 346 U.S. 86 (1953); Hawaiian Tel. Co. v. FCC, 498 F.2d 771 (D.C. Cir. 1974).

22. H.R. Rep. No. 96–190, *supra* note 14, at 53–54.

23. *See* Chapter 10.

24. S. Rep. No. 93–1285, *supra* note 1, at 7878.

25. S. Rep. No. 96–96, 96th Cong., 1st Sess. 52 (1979).

26. *Id.* at 53.

27. *Id.* at 85.

28. Pub. L. No. 96–79, §103(c), *amending* Public Health Service Act §1513(a). *See* Utah Code Ann. §26-33-8 (Supp. 1979), *repealed by* 1981 Utah Laws ch. 126, §1.

29. Pub. L. No. 96–79, §117(a), *adding* Public Health Service Act §1527(a)(5).

30. The planning law does not refer to the SHCC as a "state instrumentality," but contemplates that the governor will (1) appoint the members of the SHCC (although at least 60 percent of the members are chosen from lists of nominees submitted by the state's HSAs); (2) select the SHCC's chairman with the advice and consent of the state Senate; and (3) exercise a veto over any draft SHP that he "determines does not effectively meet the statewide health needs of the State as determined by" the state certificate-of-need agency. Public Health Service Act §1524, *as amended*.

31. *See* Chapter 10.

32. In comments on the regulations implementing the certificate-of-need provisions of the 1979 amendments, DHHS emphasizes that "it is through the development of plans that planning agencies should determine whether a specific health service responds to competitive forces, not through individual determinations as applications [for certificates of need] are being reviewed." 45 Fed. Reg. 69,771 (1980).

33. *See* Luft, Bunker, & Enthoven, "Should Operations Be Regionalized? The Empirical Relation between Surgical Volume and Mortality," 301 *New Eng. J. Med.* 1364 (1979).

34. *See* Exec. Order No. 12,044, 3 C.F.R. 152 (1978 Compilation).
35. *See, e.g.,* S. 262, S. 755, and H.R. 77, 96th Cong., 1st Sess. (1979).
36. Airline Deregulation Act of 1978, Pub. L. 95–504, 92 Stat. 1705 (codified in scattered sections of 49 U.S.C. (Supp. III 1979)).

6 THE ANTITRUST LAWS AND HEALTH PLANNING FOLLOWING THE 1979 AMENDMENTS

One of the more surprising things about the 1979 health planning amendments is that they did not, after all, address the specific antitrust issue raised by the Central Virginia HSA (CVHSA) in its application to the Justice Department, described in Chapter 5. One view of the significance of Congress's silence on the question might be that the amendments left the legal question in the same unresolved posture as before. Another interpretation might be that, by failing to override what it knew to be the Justice Department's view, Congress accepted it. This chapter analyzes the legislation and some significant subsequent developments in an attempt to resolve the conflict between antitrust policy and the health planning community.

The conclusion expressed herein is that the 1979 amendments, if anything, reinforced the view developed in Chapter 5 that the federal planning act does not authorize planning agencies to immunize private anticompetitive arrangements from scrutiny under the antitrust laws. Furthermore, recent judicial decisions should not be read to alter this conclusion. Finally, the view is expressed that it would be bad policy as well as bad law to grant exempting powers to health system planners or regulators.

WHAT CONGRESS DID

As noted in Chapter 5, congressional staff members were aware of the impasse that had developed between the Antitrust Division and the CVHSA and of the underlying question of statutory interpretation. Whereas the Senate bill and the accompanying committee report were nevertheless entirely silent on the matter, the House subcommittee staff did consider it. The House committee report devotes several paragraphs (set forth in Appendix B) to the antitrust exposure of the agencies themselves. It does not, however, mention explicitly the more difficult and practically troublesome problem of the antitrust status of HSA-sponsored agreements between competitors to consolidate, share, convert, or eliminate services or facilities. Nevertheless, it says enough to indicate that the committee accepted the consequences of the doctrine that antitrust exemptions will not be "lightly" inferred or inferred at all in the absence of a "clear repugnancy" between a regulatory scheme and antitrust doctrine.[1]

Because the amendments added nothing to the scope of the agencies' regulatory power over anticompetitive agreements among competitors, the statute still fails to satisfy the minimum requirements for inferring that Congress intended to give the agencies the power to insulate such transactions from antitrust laws. Revealing an awareness of this requirement and its significance, the House committee report notes that, although the agencies were required to perform certain functions, including appropriateness reviews, "agency acts which are not necessary to carry out such functions or which are outside the scope of Title XV are not authorized and therefore not immune from the application of the antitrust laws." The report also lists the specific functions of HSAs that the antitrust laws should not be construed to inhibit, conspicuously omitting the brokering of anticompetitive agreements. Because the House committee was specifically aware of the opportunity for resolving the CVHSA problem by widening the regulators' power to approve anticompetitive agreements, decisive significance can be attached to the failure to grant that authority and even to allude to such agreements as a desirable way of rationalizing the system. Not only does the 1979 legislative history clarify antitrust's prospective applicability, but it casts helpful light on the intent of the 1974

Congress, revealing perfectly why it is dangerous for courts to impute to Congress an intention to set aside the antitrust laws when such an intention has been neither declared nor revealed by specific action. Viewed in light of the committee's familiarity with the problem, the House committee report clearly expected and intended that the antitrust laws would be given their normal effect of requiring competition except where an exemption was necessary to avoid a specific conflict.

The House committee report also endorsed antitrust as a general policy in the health care industry. Although it also noted that "unfettered competition could further aggravate health system problems" and that "a practical and realistic analysis of the health care industry argues for exceptions to the rule," the discussion made clear that antitrust principles were set aside only to the extent that regulation was specifically substituted. In keeping with established doctrine, the committee report did not invite the courts to consider whether competition is a desirable influence in particular circumstances or to decide the extent to which it should be enforced in any situation where Congress had neither stated its intention to set the antitrust laws aside nor established a regulatory scheme that could not work in the absence of an exemption. Because health planning agencies do not have the statutory power to immunize agreements among competitors, all such agreements for merger, consolidation, sharing, conversion, or elimination of competing services would seem, under traditional doctrine, to remain fully subject to the rules of antitrust following the 1979 amendments.

LEGAL DEVELOPMENTS

Two recent cases in the federal courts deal with the relationship between the antitrust laws and the health planning effort. In the *Huron Valley Hospital* case,[2] a Michigan district court held that denial of a certificate of need for construction of a new hospital could not be an antitrust violation, even if irregularities were involved, and that the antitrust laws do not prohibit competing hospitals from engaging in concerted action to influence a certificate-of-need decision. This holding was clearly correct since the decisionmakers were carrying out explicit statutory duties and the private defendants' actions clearly fell within the so-called *Noerr-Pennington* doctrine,[3] which holds that the antitrust laws were not intended to reach political action or efforts to influence public policy. The court's opinion included, however, some imprecise language that, while unnecessary to the decision, was read by many as a sweeping repeal of antitrust principles insofar as agency activities are concerned.

A more important case is *National Gerimedical Hospital and Gerontology Center v. Blue Cross*, in which the lower courts' recognition of a sweeping implied exemption[4] was reversed by the Supreme Court in June 1981.[5] In the absence of a state certificate-of-need law, a Blue Cross plan had refused, as a cost-containment measure, to enter into a reimbursement contract with a new hospital built without the approval of the local HSA. The hospital sued Blue Cross, claiming that the antitrust laws required it to deal with any hospital that would like to have its services offered on favorable terms as part of the Blue Cross package. Instead of addressing the validity of this claim—which, incidentally, is highly questionable[6]—, the district court held that, by virtue of Public Law 93–641, "the antitrust laws were not intended to apply to members of the health care industry, clearly acting within the scope of the Act."[7] This conclusion, like the dictum of the *Huron Valley* court, was based on Public Law 93–641's implicit rejection of competition and market forces as a constructive force in the industry. The court of appeals in *National Gerimedical* affirmed this reasoning of the lower court, quoting at length from its opinion.

The Supreme Court unanimously reversed the lower courts in *National Gerimedical* on the ground that antitrust scrutiny of Blue Cross's conduct would not conflict with the operation of any federal or state regulatory scheme. The Court simply applied the established principle, ignored by the lower courts, that the Sherman Act is to be reconciled with the specific mandates of regulatory statutes and not swept aside altogether in the presence of regulation.[8] It thus easily rejected the claim that Congress had created "a 'pervasive' repeal of the antitrust laws as applied to every action taken in response to the health planning process."[9] Unfortunately, in deciding the easy case before it, the Court appeared to attach weight to several factors whose absence or presence in a later, harder case might be taken as indicating that an implied exemption should be found. In general, Justice Powell's opinion indicated a possible willingness, in a future case, to accept emanations from a statute and its legislative history as a basis for inferring an exemption and thus not to require a specific conflict between statutory regimes before setting antitrust law aside. The discussion below of a more difficult case—the problem raised by the CVHSA ruling request—demonstrates the need to confine the *National Gerimedical* decision to its facts and the issues actually litigated.

The Justice Department's Letter to the Central Virginia HSA

The contention has been made that the only defensible reading of Public Law 93–641, as amended, is that Congress meant to leave the antitrust laws in place as a check on anticompetitive arrangements and activities not expressly contemplated in federal or state law. In May 1980, the Antitrust Division of the Justice Department declared its support for this view in finally responding to the CVHSA's request for a ruling concerning its plan implementation activities.[10] The department's letter refused to grant a blanket clearance to HSA-sponsored agreements among competitors, even agreements effectuating the configuration of services embodied in a state or local health plan.

The department's advisory letter stated, first, that it would not challenge any agency activity that was required by the planning law in connection with certificate-of-need review, federal grant review, and appropriateness review. The department refused, however, to foreswear possible challenges to a fourth category of agency activities, namely efforts "to implement its Health Systems Plan and Annual Implementation Plan with the assistance of individuals and public and private entities." The letter observed that some such activities might give rise to violations of the antitrust rules governing agreements not to compete and were "not necessarily authorized or even contemplated by the Act." As an example, the department went somewhat out of its way to single out a provision in an earlier CVHSA plan encouraging hospitals offering obstetric services "to explore the feasibility of cooperative assessments that will result in joint action to adjust the number of beds, physicians and allied health manpower, and the division of services." The department then noted with approval that CVHSA had stated in its revised ruling request that it would not engage in implementation activities involving concerted action by providers.

The Justice Department's letter does not state the full legal basis for its conclusion, but the following paragraph reveals that its analysis is essentially that set forth in Chapter 5:

> In essence we do not believe that the Health Planning Act creates a complete antitrust exemption for all efforts by HSAs, and private parties working with HSAs, to implement health plans. An antitrust exemption protecting all activities which arguably furthered the general statutory goals is not, in our view, justified. The legislative history of the Act reveals no congressional intent to restrict the operation of the antitrust laws to such an extent. Moreover, that interpretation would clearly conflict with the well-established principle that implied repeal of the antitrust laws is disfavored and that antitrust exemptions should be construed narrowly.

After stating this view of the law, the department then indicated that it would exercise its prosecutorial discretion with a view to broader policy considerations. As a result, planning agencies and institutions cooperating with them in plan implementation probably run no serious risk of antitrust prosecution as long as their activities are undertaken in good faith and with recognition of competition's possible benefits. The conclusion of risklessness would not hold, however, if the actions taken should adversely affect private parties who are in a position to bring a private antitrust action; the courts do not have discretion comparable to that of government prosecutors in deciding whether to give effect to the law's requirements.

Technical peculiarities in legal doctrine give rise to the somewhat striking anomaly that, while it may be illegal for hospitals to agree among themselves to abide by an HSA health plan once it is adopted, it is clearly permissible for them to act in concert in helping to develop the plan. This latter result flows from the judicial view (the *Noerr-Pennington* doctrine[11]) that the antitrust laws were not intended to prevent collective petitioning of government such as is involved in developing a health plan that is eventually to be approved or adopted by the state. Because there is an ultimate political check on the plan development process, there is arguably no need for antitrust courts to scrutinize private activity that precedes the promulgation of the plan. But, even though the plan may appear to derive political legitimacy from the participatory process by which it is developed, the health-planning legislation fails to give it any explicit legal or other effect except in the certificate-of-need process. The courts, in deciding what effect to give the plan in light of the antitrust laws, must take their cue from Congress, and Congress has not seen fit to give the agencies any power to implement the plan directly. Indeed, Congress has been ambivalent from the beginning concerning the legal effect of health plans and the wisdom of granting plan-implementing powers. Under all the circumstances, the Justice Department's ruling seems to have been correct.

Having said all this, it must be noted that an unrelated technical change made in the 1979 amendments might be construed to allow providers positioned as in the CVHSA situation to claim the *Noerr-Pennington* defense for their agreements to propose the closing of facilities. Under regulations implementing a new definition added to the law without comment by the congressional committees, any capital expenditures involved in closing beds or services must now apparently be subjected to a certificate-of-need requirement.[12] Thus, the agencies may in a given case have the final word on whether the agreed-upon closings will in fact occur and can, if they will, consider whether competition is inappropriately impaired. If the providers' anticompetitive agreement is not implementable without agency action and can be seen as a petition for such action, it can be persuasively argued that the antitrust laws do not apply. While the agencies have no power to approve the anticompetitive agreement itself and the *Noerr-Pennington* defense would not, as a technical matter, apply to an agreement to carry out the closures once approved, the argument for recognizing an exemption of sorts—not the same implied exemption found by the lower courts in *National Gerimedical* or considered in the Justice Department letter, it will be noted—is fairly strong. It would be ironic indeed if a statutory technical amendment made almost inadvertently should be held to have given rise to an antitrust exemption that Congress carefully chose not to confer. Perhaps this observation is the best argument for either strictly construing the statutory language in question[13] or refusing to apply the *Noerr-Pennington* defense where Congress's intent is so unclear.

The Justice Department has had a subsequent opportunity to pronounce on an anticompetitive agreement among providers that had the effect of restraining system growth.[14] In settling certain litigation, two hospitals agreed that one of them would not compete with the other in certain lines of business and sought the Antitrust Division's approval. In a business review letter denying the requested blessing, the department noted that the agreement, in addition to being a clear restraint, would deprive the planning and regulatory agencies of certificate-of-need applications. It also seemed to stress the absence of regulatory or HSA authorization and the fact that the agreement had not been "addressed by the health systems agency plan." Although the department had no occasion to state whether endorsement of such an agreement by the local HSA would confer an implied exemption, it seemed slightly more inclined toward that conclusion than in its CVHSA letter. Perhaps political pressures were beginning to have an effect.

Implications of the *National Gerimedical* Case for the CVHSA Problem

A footnote in the Supreme Court's opinion in the *National Gerimedical* case will undoubtedly be cited by some as resolving in the health planners' favor the various problems raised by the CVHSA's ruling request.[15] This claim, which will be made even though those issues were not before the Court and were not fully explored or argued, depends, paradoxically, on the Court's attempt to narrow the scope of its decision by emphasizing that "our holding does not foreclose future claims of antitrust immunity in other factual contexts." By signifying the Court's possibly different view of a situation "where . . . an HSA has expressly advocated a form of cost-saving cooperation among providers," Justice Powell's opinion implies that he, at least, would accept the argument that the antitrust laws do not apply to HSA-inspired joint ventures and might even hold a naked market-division agreement to be exempt if ratified by an HSA.[16] Though far from being definitive or binding, this implied legal conclusion would be wrong and would probably not be reached if the Court heard fuller argument.

The Court's erroneous dictum on CVHSA-type issues may have resulted from trying to sense Congress's intentions concerning plan implementation by interpolating from vaguely revealed purposes rather than by reading the statute. Like both of the lower courts and the district court in the *Huron Valley* case, Justice Powell gave particular weight to Congressman Paul Rogers's 1978 assertion on the floor of the House (apropos of no pending legislation) that, if the antitrust laws were applied to curb competitor collaboration supportive of planning, "Public Law 93–641 simply could not be implemented."[17] The widespread acceptance of this crucial statement of fact is surprising, to say the least, since it is not supportable in any literal sense. The antitrust laws do not prohibit all collective actions that competitors might take[18] and do not apply at all to voluntary compliance with plans by individual providers or to compliance that is coerced by the force of public opinion or by a felt need to curry favor with the regulators. More generally, the antitrust laws could not prevent achievement of the act's main objective, which was to induce state adoption of federally approved certificate-of-need laws governing new investment.

What Congressman Rogers apparently meant by his indefensible statement—and the idea that must have caused the Supreme Court to cite that statement as the basis for suggesting a "clear repugnancy" between the planning act and the antitrust laws— was that Congress must have intended to supply some specific means of rationalizing the delivery system and of eliminating unneeded health facilities from the market. These were, after all, results that Congress certainly seemed to desire. Because it was unclear how, other than by voluntary compliance, actual rationalizations or reductions in services could occur without an antitrust exemption, Congressman Rogers wanted—and the Supreme Court felt called upon to supply—such an exemption for private entities who might collaborate to further these purposes.

The Supreme Court's urge to provide plan implementation tools that Congress had not itself supplied might make sense if Congress were always logical and consistent. But one cannot assume that Congress always intends to supply the means to achieve its stated aspirations. Indeed, the legislative history of

Public Law 93–641, particularly the appropriateness review provisions, reveals that Congress consciously withheld from the planner-regulators the specific powers needed to implement cutbacks in services.[19] Despite all the rhetoric, the congressional committees had real policy doubts about implementing such plans and political doubts about extending the regulators' power. Moreover, as noted in Chapter 5, Congress dropped language specifically contemplating informal HSA efforts to implement findings of excess capacity.[20] Given this history, the idea that Congress must have intended an antitrust exemption does not stand scrutiny. Congress might easily have expected that its desire to reduce capacity, though expressed, would go unrealized unless and until it was implemented either in later amendments, for which currently stated aspirations might pave the way, or by the states.

In light of these observations, it is particularly significant that, in writing the 1979 amendments with specific knowledge of the CVHSA issue and the planners' frustration, Congress was still unwilling to grant to HSAs this new implementation power and wrote legislative history accepting the antitrust consequences. Instead of laying the basis for an implied antitrust exemption, as it was invited to do, Congress authorized funds for the purpose of buying out excess capacity,[21] thereby pursuing the goal of system reduction and rationalization by a totally different means. Thus was Congressman Rogers's minor premise also invalidated. Obviously, the reintroduction of competition as a positive value in the industry must also weigh in favor of leaving antitrust its accustomed role in the absence of a specific conflict.

One can perhaps sympathize with the courts' difficulties in trying to assess congressional intentions, particularly if they cannot perceive the possibility of inconsistencies between declared ends and legislated means. Precisely because Congress frequently obfuscates when it can settle on no corporate intent, it must be concluded that considerable wisdom underlies the customary rule that a congressional intention to create an antitrust exemption should not "lightly" be inferred. The only sensible allocation of decisionmaking authority is one in which the courts hold Congress to a high standard of clarity and refuse to supply powers and authorities (and antitrust exemptions) that have not been expressly granted. If Congress wants to confer an exemption, it is always free to do so, and the existence of a clear rule puts Congress on notice that it must face issues, not evade them in the hope that the courts will do the job assigned to Congress by the Constitution.

Because there was no real conflict, let alone "clear repugnancy," between Public Law 93–641 and the antitrust laws, Justice Powell's receptiveness to an antitrust exemption for CVHSA-type agreements appears to rest on a different, seemingly unprecedented ground. This new ground is the existence in a statute or its legislative history of a general congressional finding that competition does not work well in the industry in question. All of the cited opinions on the conflict between health planning and antitrust, including the Supreme Court's, referred to the previously cited Senate report finding of 1974 that "the health services industry does not respond to classic marketplace forces." Unlike the lower courts, however, the Supreme Court refused to base a blanket exemption on this language, finding that the planning act "is not so incompatible with antitrust concerns as to create a 'pervasive' repeal."[22] Nevertheless, the Court did place substantial weight on the language in section 1502(b), added by the 1979 amendments, which indicates Congress's view that competition is not always a desirable force in the health care industry, particularly with respect to "inpatient . . . and other institutional health services."[23] The Court appears to have read this language as calling for some relaxation of the antitrust laws even in the absence of a specific conflict with the regulatory scheme. This approach would be a substantial departure from past doctrine.

The most obvious problem that the Court would face in applying such a novel doctrine would be in knowing how and where to relax the law. For example, would an HSA's approval of an anticompetitive agreement be sufficient to exempt it even in the absence of judicial or state agency review of that approval? (The Court implied elsewhere in its opinion that the HSA in Missouri, as a private rather than a governmental body, could not have conferred immunity on Blue Cross even if it had instructed Blue Cross to act as it did.[24]) Would a possibly unreviewable[25] finding in a state health plan of competition's inappropriateness with respect to all hospital care confer immunity on a hospital monopolist? Would such a finding insulate all or only certain types of anticompetitive agreements among hospitals? Suggesting that exemptions might cover some but not all otherwise questionable

conduct, the Court stated that "cooperation among providers"—
does this include a naked CVHSA-type market-division agreement?[26]—differs substantially from Blue Cross's refusal to deal.[27]
Antitrust law provides no doctrinal basis, however, for exempting
one of these forms of conduct and not the other. Indeed, contrary
to the Court's implication, competitor agreements are usually regarded with greater suspicion than unilateral refusals to deal,
which are probably not unlawful at all.[28]

In view of the impossibility of knowing what specific implications to draw from some congressionally expressed doubt about
competition's current value in a particular setting, the Court
should adhere to its traditional insistence that Congress alone
must declare those implications. If the Court instead undertakes
to make its own judgments about when an exemption is or is not
appropriate, it will have "set sail on a sea of doubt"[29] which nine-
ty years of antitrust jurisprudence should have taught it to
avoid.[30] The wisdom of the "clear repugnancy" test is revealed by
the difficulty and subjective artificiality of trying first to guess
what was in the back of Congress's collective mind and then to
fashion a different, milder antitrust regime to fit a situation
where competition has been declared a mixed blessing.

THE POLICY ISSUE: SHOULD PLANNER-
REGULATORS BE EMPOWERED TO GRANT
ANTITRUST IMMUNITY?

The legal conclusion that the antitrust laws apply to HSA plan
implementation activities does not, of course, foreclose discussion
of the policy question of whether such activities should enjoy an
antitrust exemption. Even though Congress appears to have given
its answer to this question by not enacting an express or implied
exemption in the 1979 amendments, the Justice Department's
CVHSA letter sparked many complaints in the planning community, which appeared to perceive it as a policy determination
rather than as a legal opinion. The controversy seemed likely to
trigger appeals by the planners to Congress for authority to continue fostering cooperation among local providers as a primary
means of achieving goals set through the planning process. Also,
there is always a danger that the Justice Department will waffle

on its CVHSA position, perhaps in the belief that the Court has spoken in the *National Gerimedical* footnote. A brief discussion of the policy issue in light of the 1979 amendments should therefore be helpful. Moreover, a policy discussion will be particularly illuminating since the new statutory emphasis on competition, like antitrust doctrine, represents a direct challenge to planners' preference for collaboration as a way of life.

The Health Industry's Tradition of Centralized Decisionmaking

Local health planning has always had some of the earmarks of a cartel. Planning agencies originally developed at the local level to serve a variety of functions, including both the establishment of priorities for using philanthropic and governmental (Hill-Burton) funds and the allocation of service and geographic markets among hospitals anxious to minimize competition.[31] Eventually, with the growth of health insurance and public financing, the agencies were no longer greatly concerned about curbing competition for limited funds and for price-sensitive customers. Increasingly, the agencies were expected by the public to limit the system's exploitation of open-ended financing sources and to curb emerging nonprice competition, which was driving the system to incur unjustified costs. Reducing competition, originally undertaken voluntarily by providers for their own benefit, had become a goal of public policy.

As regulatory powers were increasingly conferred on the health-planning agencies, nonprovider interests, some of them antagonistic to providers, were required to be given a voice in the planning process. Introducing consumer interests in this way can be viewed as an attempt to democratize the cartel. Nevertheless, Congress did not see fit to extend full regulatory (plan implementation) powers to the local agencies, even with their new participatory processes and the political accountability supplied by state agency oversight. In its reluctance to embrace finally and completely the idea that a provider cartel could be made democratic and accountable enough to define and serve the public interest, Congress revealed the same distrust of private power in which the antitrust tradition is rooted. Moreover, the emerging

national distrust of economic regulation, which has so often
served private rather than public interests, is also evident in Congress's hesitance to embrace centralized decisionmaking.

In addition to being consistent with broad policy traditions
and trends, the new antitrust threat to the health planners' free-
lance efforts to broker anticompetitive agreements appears to
have served the salutary purpose of calling attention to the broad
implications of relying too heavily on cartel-like private cooperation to allocate health resources. In particular, the Justice Department's legal position put Congress squarely in the position in
1979 of having to face head-on the hard policy questions on which
it had been less than explicit in the past: Did it really want to
invest the planning agencies—with their cartel-like features—with
plenary powers? What additional safeguards in the nature of regulatory oversight and procedural openness and due process should
be introduced before granting these agencies the power to confer
antitrust immunity on private arrangements? Is there an alternative to relying on regulation and on "benign" cartels to allocate
resources in this industry? Should competition have an active
role? Should competition to be placed wholly at the mercy of the
planners and regulators and allowed to function only with their
concurrence? It seems clear that Congress was not prepared to go
along with the planners' view on these matters.

The Temptations of Short-run Expediency

The problem with relying on competition is, of course, that, as
things are currently organized and paid for, it very often produces
perverse effects. Yet, the current state of affairs is not inevitable
and could change, making more services amenable to effective discipline by market forces in the consumer interest. Planning and
regulation that are carried out solely on the basis of the perception that the financing system is currently dysfunctional may
serve strongly to confirm and reinforce the system's dysfunctional
features. Thus, for example, acceptance of even a modified cartel
form of organization may discourage a third-party payer from
making an effort to force providers to compete among themselves
for the opportunity to treat its subscribers, and, even if it should
undertake such efforts, the market's cartel characteristics will re-

duce the prospects for their success. Thus, if health planners are authorized to foster cartel behavior, the competitive strategy could easily be frustrated.

On the other hand, frustration of the planners' plan implementation efforts could easily impose significant short-run costs on the public because of the way in which the system is currently financed. A major policy dilemma is thus posed between expediently pursuing a questionable, but arguably second-best, strategy in the hope of procuring some short-run gain and resolutely pursuing a long-run policy that, though it promises much, may prove to be not only somewhat costly in the short run but unachievable in the long run. As Part III seeks to demonstrate, the 1979 amendments have given the planner-regulators both the responsibility and the opportunity to address this dilemma directly with respect to each discrete service in each discrete market, preserving the opportunities for, and encouraging, change in payment and purchasing mechanisms while also preventing excessive growth and cost escalation where market forces are not yet reliable. The specific question here, however, is whether the statutory framework created by the 1979 amendments can and should be adapted so as to give the planner-regulators an additional tool to curb arguable excesses where the market is thought to impose inadequate constraints on spending.

Earlier discussion outlined a proposal to resolve the antitrust problem that was made to the House health subcommittee staff during the debate on the 1979 amendments. This proposal is still technically viable. It would involve formalizing the process for approving anticompetitive agreements and requiring the agencies expressly to weigh the costs of such agreements—the competitive benefits forgone—against the gains from implementing the agency's plans, including gains from weakening dysfunctional nonprice competition. The theoretical merits of this proposed solution can hardly be denied, but the arguments against it, which apparently influenced the Ninety-sixth Congress not to adopt it in the 1979 amendments, are quite strong. Ultimately, they reduce to whether the agencies can be trusted—or, alternatively, can be effectively bound by an express statutory directive—to give competition appropriate weight in their calculations. The answer to this empirical question, which Chapter 15 considers in a necessarily inconclusive way, is so doubtful that Congress or the Justice Department could well decide that the danger of undue sacrifice of competition is too great to justify granting or conceding to the agencies any antitrust-exempting powers. Certainly Congress and the Antitrust Division could reasonably conclude that more evidence of the agencies' willingness to accept and of their ability to carry out the new procompetition mandate is needed before any powers to curb competition are recognized.

Breaking the Tradition

Perhaps the best reason for denying the agencies the power to broker anticompetitive agreements among competitors is the apparent need for a sharp break with the health care industry's tradition of relying on cooperation rather than competition to solve any problem that is identified either by the providers themselves or by an aroused public. The antitrust laws are now being invoked to break down the traditional power of organized providers,[32] and the procompetition language in the 1979 amendments represents another challenge to the health planning tradition of centralized decisionmaking and cooperation. These developments should be causing a widespread reexamination of established practices and assumptions, but, judging from the dismay expressed in the planning community over the Antitrust Division's letter, there is some reason to think that the message has not gotten through. Congress would be well advised to seize any opportunity to reiterate its desire to redirect the planners' efforts by denying them the power they seek to set aside the rules of competition. Given the deep-seated tradition of suppressing competition in the name of planning, the signal to the agencies that their emphasis should be placed elsewhere must be very clear.

The antitrust enforcers have again performed the useful service of alerting the world to the coziness of would-be competitors in the health care sector. It would almost certainly be a significant setback for the idea of competition in this industry if Congress were now to intervene to give the planners an apparent victory over the Antitrust Division or if the Antitrust Division should modify its stand. Even if Congress or the Justice Department should act in a way that kept the policy preference for competition (where it works) technically paramount, the planners would undoubtedly perceive their new authority primarily as a rebuke to the advocates of competition. The harm to competition's fragile status in the health care sector in general and in the planning community in particular could easily outweigh any cost savings that agencies might achieve through encouraging competitors to divide markets and to collaborate in other legally questionable ways.

The conclusion that Congress should adhere to the choice it made in the 1979 amendments and that the Antitrust Division should not recede from its position is reached despite an awareness that some real economies could be gained through competitor collaboration and might be frustrated by uncertainties concerning the legality of particular arrangements. Theoretically, antitrust law does not seek to discourage efficiency-generating collaboration by competitors. Nevertheless, because the law faces great difficulty in distinguishing procompetitive from anticompetitive activity, serious legal uncertainty can often exist about particular joint ventures. Moreover, the law often must be arbitrary in dealing with cases in the large gray area where consequences are unpredictable. (Merger law, which turns largely on market share percentages, is the best example.) Under such arbitrary standards, there is a real risk that arrangements that are actually efficient would be found unlawful. Because these circumstances, plus the threat of treble damages, may deter a significant amount of valid and desirable integration, it is tempting to allow a regulatory body to immunize arrangements that it deems to be efficient. If such an agency were instructed to maintain competition to the maximum extent that efficiency considerations permit, there would be no departure from the substantive objective of the antitrust laws, only somewhat greater room for employing the "rule of reason" approach.

Despite these beguiling arguments for regulatory rather than judicial enforcement of antitrust principles in the health care industry, the case has not been made. For one thing, the claims of frustrated efficiency are not documented. Moreover, there is every reason to think that they are exaggerated both by industry interests, who may be seeking relief from competition rather than legal uncertainty, and by planners, who may be unsympathetic to competition and seeking expanded functions for themselves. Although the law's uncertainty and occasional arbitrariness may be a real barrier to needed integration in the highly concentrated hospital sector, it would appear simply too difficult, at the moment at least, to assure that any attempt to ameliorate that problem would not result in a change in the substantive commitment to competition and a return to business as usual in the planning agencies. Given the currently paramount need to wean the health care industry once and for all from its noncompetitive habits, the antitrust laws should be left in place as a useful check on HSAs' undue encouragement of cartel behavior and providers' undue preference for collaboration when competition would serve the public better.

NOTES

1. California v. FPC, 369 U.S. 482 (1961); United States v. Philadelphia Nat'l Bank, 374 U.S. 321 (1963); Silver v. New York Stock Exchange, 373 U.S. 341 (1963). *But see* United States v. National Ass'n of Securities Dealers, 422 U.S. 694 (1975) (arguably relaxing the requirement of "clear repugnancy" by inferring exemption solely on the basis of a general and unexercised oversight power possessed by the agency).

2. Huron Valley Hosp., Inc., v. City of Pontiac, 466 F. Supp. 1301 (E.D. Mich. 1979).

3. Eastern R.R. Presidents Conf. v. Noerr Motor Freight, Inc., 365 U.S. 127 (1961); UMW v. Pennington, 381 U.S. 657 (1965).

4. National Gerimedical Hosp. and Gerontology Center v. Blue Cross, 628 F.2d 1050 (8th Cir. 1980), *affirming* 479 F. Supp. 1012 (W.D. Mo. 1979).

5. 49 U.S.L.W. 4672 (1981).

6. *See id.* at 4676 n.19. Except in unusual circumstances, antitrust law does not impose on one party a duty to deal with another party or require justifications for refusals to deal. *E.g.,* United States v. Colgate & Co., 250 U.S. 300 (1919). Indeed, freedom to deal or not is the essence of competition. Though having finally won on the immunity point, the plaintiff in this case is almost certain to fail on the merits unless it can establish that Blue Cross, rather than being an independent actor and agent of consumers, was controlled by or in a conspiracy with plaintiff's hospital competitors. Competitors' control of a dominant financing entity with the power to fix prices and exclude competitors presents some distinct antitrust problems. *See* Virginia Academy of Clinical Psychologists v.

Blue Shield, 624 F.2d 476 (4th Cir. 1980); Federal Trade Commission, *Staff Report on Medical Participation in Control of Blue Shield and Certain Other Open-Panel Medical Prepayment Plans* (1979).

7. National Gerimedical Hosp. and Gerontology Center v. Blue Cross, 479 F. Supp. 1012, 1021 (W.D. Mo. 1979).

8. Silver v. New York Stock Exchange, 373 U.S. 341, 357 (1963).

9. 49 U.S.L.W. at 4676.

10. Letter from Sanford M. Litvack, assistant attorney general, Antitrust Division, U.S. Department of Justice, in the matter of Central Virginia Health Systems Agency, May 6, 1980.

11. *See* note 3 *supra* and accompanying text.

12. 45 Fed Reg. 69,746–47 (1980) (to be codified in 42 C.F.R. §123.404(a)(2), (3)). The cited regulations implement Pub. L. No. 96–79, §117(b), *adding* Public Health Service Act §1531(6). Discussion in Chapter 7 argues that Congress did not intend to require certification of need for closing services and that the regulations should be withdrawn.

13. *See* note 12 *supra*.

14. Letter from Sanford M. Litvack, assistant attorney general, Antitrust Division, U.S. Department of Justice, in the matter of Westlake Health Campus Association and Lakewood Hospital, August 27, 1980.

15. 49 U.S.L.W. at 4676 n.18. This footnote reads in its entirety as follows:

Nevertheless, because Congress has remained convinced that competition does not operate effectively in some parts of the health care industry, *e.g.,* 42 U.S.C. §300k-2(b), we emphasize that our holding does not foreclose future claims of antitrust immunity in other factual contexts. Although favoring a reversal in this case, the United States as *amicus curiae* asserts that "there are some activities that must, by implication, be immune from antitrust attack if HSAs and State Agencies are to exercise their authorized powers." Brief for the United States as Amicus Curiae 16, n. 11. Where, for example, an HSA has expressly advocated a form of cost-saving cooperation among providers, it may be that antitrust immunity is "necessary to make the [NHPRDA] work." *Silver v. New York Stock Exchange,* 373 U.S. 341, 357 (1963). See 124 Cong. Rec. H11,963 (daily ed. Oct. 10, 1978) (Rep. Rogers) ("The intent of Congress was that HSA's and providers who voluntarily work with them in carrying out the HSA's statutory mandate should not be subject to the antitrust laws. If they were, Public Law 93–

641 simply could not be implemented.") Such a case would differ
substantially from the present one, where the conduct at issue is
not cooperation among providers, but an insurer's refusal to deal
with a provider that failed to heed the advice of an HSA.

16. The language used ("cost-saving cooperation") might not cover a
     naked restraint such as was considered in the CVHSA ruling. For a
     case in which Justice Powell, writing for the majority in a 5–4
     decision, found an implied exemption without the usual direct con-
     flict betwen statutory regimes, see United States v. National Ass'n
     of Securities Dealers, 422 U.S. 694 (1975). *See* note 1 *supra.*

17. 124 Cong. Rec. H11,963 (daily ed. Oct. 10, 1978). *See* note 15
     supra.

18. This is not the place to elaborate the relevant legal principles
     (which are not always easy to apply), but it is important to ob-
     serve that, even under the antitrust analysis favored here, planners
     may still broker efficiency-enhancing agreements among competi-
     tors that do not unduly threaten to undercut competition in the
     wider market. There remains, then, ample room for HSAs to en-
     courage multi-institutional arrangements and shared services, even
     if no antitrust exemption is inferred. The planning act's support
     for multi-institutional and shared services is thus entirely consis-
     tent with the recommended analysis and in no way supports the
     argument that Congress intended an antitrust exemption.

19. *See* 44 Fed. Reg. 71,754 (1979) (DHEW recounts the legislative his-
     tory of the appropriateness review provisions in its comments on
     the final regulations). Appropriateness reviews, which HSAs were
     required to undertake periodically, involve assessment of the cur-
     rent need for existing facilities. Although a finding that a facility
     or service was in oversupply or that a particular provider was un-
     needed was pregnant with termination possibilities, Congress, hav-
     ing considered providing for decertification, left it at that.

20. *See* Chapter 5, note 8 and accompanying text.

21. *See* Pub. L. No. 96–79, §301, *adding* Public Health Service Act
     §§1641–43.

22. 49 U.S.L.W. at 4676.

23. *Id.* at 4676 n.18 (quoted at note 15 *supra*), 4675 n.13. The construc-
     tion of this provision, in particular whether it creates a conclusive
     or some other presumption of competition's destructiveness, is an
     important issue for the thesis of this book and is explored at
     length in Chapter 10.

24. 49 U.S.L.W. at 4676.

25. The reviewability of findings on competition in state health plans is explored in Chapter 10. The importance of reviewability by a government agency or a court is suggested by *Silver v. New York Stock Exchange,* 373 U.S. 341, 357–61 (1963).

26. *See* note 16 *supra.*

27. 49 U.S.L.W. at 4676 n.18 (quoted in note 15 *supra*).

28. *See* note 6 *supra.*

29. United States v. Addyston Pipe & Steel Co., 85 Fed. 271, 284 (6th Cir. 1898). This opinion by Judge (later Chief Justice) William Howard Taft is the classic expression in antitrust law of the need to focus on competition alone and not to balance it against other supposed values.

30. *See* National Soc'y of Professional Eng'rs v. United States, 435 U.S. 679 (1978).

31. *See* Havighurst, "Regulation of Health Facilities and Services by 'Certificate of Need'," 59 *Va. L. Rev.* 1143, 1148–50 (1973).

32. For discussion of another situation involving a temptation to relax antitrust requirements in pursuit of short-run cost savings, see Havighurst & Hackbarth, "Enforcing the Rules of Free Enterprise in an Imperfect Market: The Case of Individual Practice Associations," in *A New Approach to the Economics of Health Care* (M. Olson ed.) (in press).

7 COVERAGE OF A CERTIFICATE-OF-NEED LAW

Some types of health care resources are more subject than others to efficient allocation by market forces and are therefore less appropriate for regulation by certification of need. As a result, legislative decisions concerning the types of facilities and services that are to be covered by a state certificate-of-need law focus attention directly on the ability of competition to yield net benefits to consumers. This chapter addresses some general themes as well as some specific issues encountered in deciding whether to impose certificate-of-need requirements for particular types of investments and new service offerings.

While coverage of a certificate-of-need law should ideally be determined on the basis of which mechanism—regulation or competition—has the comparative advantage in allocating particular types of resources efficiently, coverage issues have usually not been defined in this way. Indeed, many observers have appeared to believe that the extension of health planning and entry controls to encompass new areas of responsibility is always desirable. Although the original enactment of certificate-of-need laws required rebuttal of the customary presumption against interference with private decisionmaking and investments, that rebuttal was apparently accomplished so effectively that, for a while at least, the presumption appeared to run the other way—in favor of collective decisions on all aspects of the delivery system. Planners found it possible to rest their case for expanded powers on the premise that central planning is good in itself, confidently asserting that comprehensive jurisdiction was necessary to permit planning to achieve its full and undoubted potential.

Although arguments against central planning were sometimes advanced by interests that wished to avoid regulation, the strength of opposition was often diluted by the desire of some established providers to enjoy the protection against new competition that regulation could supply. To a large extent, coverage issues tended to be resolved on the basis of the relative political strengths of the antagonists—the purveyors and potential beneficiaries of regulation, on the one hand, and the potential losers from regulation, on the other. As is usual in political settings, competition lacked a significant constituency of its own. Thus, the merits of the policy choice—that is, the existence or nonexistence of a true market failure whose adverse effects could be effectively overcome by regulatory intervention—have had little to do with legislative outcomes on coverage questions in the past.

Legislative decisions on the coverage of certificate-of-need laws occur at both the state and federal levels. Fortunately for competition, recent developments at the federal level indicate that coverage issues are henceforth more apt to be faced with an eye to the utility of market forces. This chapter, after considering generally the role that coverage limitations—exemptions or exclusions—should play in a competition-sensitive regulatory framework, will discuss the federal requirements concerning coverage of state certificate-of-need laws and particularly the significance of the 1979 amendments to Public Law 93–641. It will then examine briefly several of the particular coverage choices remaining to the states under federal law. But, before addressing specific legislative issues, it is appropriate to consider just how crucial coverage issues are for the maintenance of competition.

STATUTORY EXEMPTIONS VERSUS REGULATORY DISCRETION

Now that the 1979 amendments have given planner-regulators a clear mandate to foster competition, it might be supposed that the coverage of a certificate-of-need law is largely inconsequential for competition. And, indeed, if the statutory regime works as intended, applicants for certificates of need will, by hypothesis, never be excluded from the market if competition could adequately allocate resources in their sector of the industry. Unfortunately, however, giving regulators a statutory directive to weigh competitive values is alone not a sufficient step to guarantee that competition will be given its due. Moreover, the administrative costs of regulation—to both government and private actors—are far from negligible and should be avoided by imposing jurisdictional limits whenever regulation's benefits are less than certain. Thus, there are good reasons why the regulators' power should not extend to a particular type of service unless a specific need for their intervention can be convincingly identified.

McClure's Exemption Strategy

Walter McClure has presented a lengthy and well-reasoned argument for employing explicit statutory exemptions as the crucial element in a mixed market and regulatory strategy.[1] His argument begins by elaborating the deficiencies of regulation in what he calls a "structure-incentive analysis." This insightful analysis, focusing on the political economy of regulation, apparently despairs of ever overcoming the influence of numerous perverse incentives that seem to cause politically exposed regulators systematically to prefer command-and-control methods over procompetitive strategies and to further the interests of incumbent providers at the expense of the taxpayer-consumer's ultimate interest in efficiency. McClure's recitation of the distortions arising both from regulation's political environment and from the technical intractability of regulatory problems is a sobering reminder, comparable to that in Chapters 1 and 2, that raising regulators' competition consciousness in ways such as those discussed in Chapter 5 could easily fail to improve the quality of regulation materially.

From his survey of regulation's shortcomings, McClure concludes that market forces must be allowed to operate—where they can operate advantageously—without the threat of regulatory suppression. He opts for "a combined market-regulatory strategy" in which statutory exemptions sharply distinguish those health care providers who are subject to effective market control from those who are not. In his view, providers would have a choice in submitting to discipline either by market forces or by regulation but would be denied the option of continuing to operate without appreciable external control or only under self-regulation.

McClure specifies at length the conditions that would have to be met in order to qualify for exemption.[2] In general, he has sought to define and exempt those nonmonopolistic health care plans that integrate the delivery and financing of care to a degree that is sufficient, in his judgment, to warrant a conclusive presumption that they not only face, but are organized to respond to, market pressures to contain costs. In McClure's view, the paramount objective should be to expand the definition of market-sensitive health care plans to encompass more than HMOs. The progress to date in creating such statutory exemptions from certificate-of-need requirements is explored in Chapter 8, which deals with HMO experience with health planning and regulation and describes the limitations of the 1979 amendments on the coverage of HMOs by state laws.

McClure's approach to promoting competition, while attractive, might have been thought too categorical to have any hope of success. A strong legislative bias exists, as McClure observes, in favor of treating all competitors uniformly, even if they differ in ways that would justify subjecting them to different regulatory regimes. Exempting some providers from regulatory controls would thus be viewed by many legislators as favoritism and an unfair handicapping of the regulated competitors. Even if these legislators could be persuaded to grant seemingly preferred status to certain providers, they would be inclined to delineate the exempt category by an extensive technical definition, thereby imposing burdensome new regulatory requirements such as appeared in the original federal HMO legislation. This inclination to impose new regulation as the price of "exemption" flows not only from a desire to appear fair by clarifying the grounds for granting the exemption, but also from a political need to avert criticism if some exempt and seemingly preferred plan should prove less than an ideal entrant in the marketplace.

Another reason why legislators might be slow to grant broad exemptions is that an unregulated competitive sector can be expected to erode the revenues of the regulated sector. The competing firms could do this by engaging in what are pejoratively called "cream-skimming" tactics—that is, attracting healthier, paying patients and leaving the poor risks and the less affluent to be treated by others. The potential impact of competition on the regulated firms' financial stability and their capacity for cross-subsidization will thus weigh decisively against exemption with many legislators, particularly those under the influence of regulated constituents and the beneficiaries of internal subsidies. Moreover, most of McClure's unregulated health plans would necessarily have many dealings with regulated providers, making it difficult both to maintain a clear line between the exempt and nonexempt sectors and to give the exempt providers the freedom in acquiring inputs that their exposure to effective market forces would seem to justify. In short, the legislature, in considering an exemption proposal, would face all the same pressures, temptations, and technical arguments that regulators face when they are asked to tolerate competition and its implications. Furthermore, as the conclusion to Chapter 8 shows, a residual need for regulation of capital investments by any organized health plan can be demonstrated as long as the dominant financing system remains in its current state of severe market failure. For all these reasons, the exemption strategy, while appealing, may never be quite as clean as McClure seems to think or realized as fully as he seems to hope. While the 1979 amendments went surprisingly far in exempting HMOs, Congress apparently did not think that that step was a sufficient vindication of competition, for it also adopted the procompetition language reviewed in Chapter 5.

The Parallel Strategy of Encouraging Procompetitive Regulation

Without disputing McClure's belief in the desirability of a broad exemption from regulation for those health care plans whose organization and market environment indicate that market forces can control their performance, one can insist on the parallel importance of requiring the regulators to have due regard for competition. Indeed, if the legislature were clear in its desire to promote competition, it should be able to achieve comparable procompetitive results by either stratagem. Thus, if the political consensus favorable to competition were strong enough to permit McClure's broad exemption strategy to be adopted, that same political support for competition could reasonably be expected to yield procompetitive regulation in response to an express mandate. Even if many state agencies and HSAs continue to follow their anticompetitive instincts under the new procompetitive mandate of the 1979 amendments, other agencies may embrace the procompetitive policy wholeheartedly, yielding local experimentation and dynamism and perhaps the successes and new ideas needed to invigorate the wider market. Thus, holding out for McClure's broad exemption might well sacrifice possibilities for promoting competition. The reciprocal risk is, of course, that the strategy of Chapter 5 may result in nothing more than lip service being given to competition, establishing the form of procompetitive regulation without necessarily delivering its substance.

While a legislature might lack the single-mindedness and self-confidence needed to adopt McClure's strategy without compromise, it still might be presuaded to adopt the less definitive approach of charging the regulators to promote competition wherever feasible as ultimately the preferable allocator of health care resources. Such an approach shifts the hard technical decisions to the regulators and spares the legislators the necessity of offending any powerful interest directly. Inevitably, some regulators, sensing the legislature's ambivalence, would feel safe from political repercussions in ignoring the mandate, and the courts could not be relied on to enforce it except in the clearest cases. But other regulators and a few courts might take it seriously, supplying the impetus needed to open competitive loopholes in the regulated system.

These observations demonstrate the dilemma faced by a competition advocate like McClure in choosing a line of argument. Whereas insisting on a broad exemption runs the risk that the best will prove the enemy of the good, endorsement of the milder strategy runs the opposite risk that it will be chosen in lieu of an exemption approach on the assumption that the regulators, properly instructed, will define the proper role for competition. Moreover, building an ostensible procompetitive dimension into regulation might simply entrench the regulators more strongly by enhancing their legitimacy without significantly changing their performance. The very fact that the policies suggested in Chapter 5 have not proved overly controversial and have been received favorably by many planner-regulators and defenders of regulation should increase concern that the competition idea would be strangled rather than embraced by the regulators. On the other hand, preliminary impressions from the state of Utah suggest that a working political consensus favorable to affirmative efforts to improve the functioning of market forces coalesced around the principles expressed in that state's new procompetitive certificate-of-need law. While choice of a political strategy remains difficult for market advocates, it seems likely that, in some milieus at least, more progress can be made by working with the planner-regulators than by trying to work around them.

Putting aside the interesting matter of political strategy, the ideal legislative strategy is, rather obviously, to write a certificate-of-need law embodying both principles. This is precisely what Congress, with surprising skill and farsightedness, did in the 1979 amendments by exempting HMOs, on the one hand, and altering the planner-regulators' mandate, on the other. States could adopt the same general approach in their certificate-of-need laws. Thus, a state law should have coverage provisions no broader than needed to satisfy federal requirements and to deal with documented market malfunctions and should include a strong mandate to the planner-regulators to concern themselves not only with suppressing the symptoms of market failure but also with remedying the market failure itself, thus reducing the need for their services in the future. These two approaches to enhancing competition address somewhat different problems and should therefore be seen not as mutually exclusive but as complementary. Whereas an exemption or exclusion from coverage creates, in effect, a conclusive presumption that regulation is not needed, inclusion of a particular type of facility or service under a certificate-of-need requirement should not create a conclusive presumption to the opposite effect. Instead, coverage can be seen as creating a rebuttable presumption of some kind. Depending on the drafting, the presumption might run in favor of or against the need for exclusionary regulation, requiring either that the applicant show that market forces are reasonably effective or that the agency, to justify a bar to entry, show that they are not. Where a conclusive presumption—that is, an exemption or exclusion—is not warranted, local market conditions, the characteristics of financing mechanisms and the service in question, and the actual or potential availability of alternative public and private cost-control strategies all become relevant to the planner-regulators' decisions on whether to exercise their exclusionary powers. Exemptions and exclusions thus have great value in reducing the scope of inquiry (and the related costs) and in eliminating both uncertainty and the risk of regulatory excess.

Just as adoption of the statutory mandate strategy of Chapter 5 would not obviate concern about the nominal scope of regulation, McClure's exemption strategy, by itself, would not be a complete procompetitive policy. In seeming to conceive of the problem of regulation in all-or-nothing terms, McClure appears to write off the traditional sector altogether as hopelessly incapable of evolution toward competitive status. Also, McClure's total reliance on exemptions may be based on too categorical a denial that regulators can play a role in promoting competition, ignoring the possibility that in some markets the regulators could be the decisive influence in moving the traditional system in new, competitive directions. Finally, the McClure approach obscures the continuity of issues surrounding the choices between regulation and no regulation. Thus, the same mode of analysis that leads McClure to exclude certain competitive health care plans from the regulators' jurisdiction might lead the legislature to exempt other types of providers, services, or facilities from certificate-of-need requirements. Indeed, the considerations developed in Part III for regulators' use in making policy toward entry in different submarkets of the health services industry are equally relevant in legislative decisions on the coverage of regulatory laws.

For these reasons, the optimal feasible strategy is the dual one of mandating procompetitive regulation, as advocated in Chapter 5, while simultaneously exempting from regulation or excluding from coverage those providers who are adequately disciplined by market forces. An approach similar to McClure's idea of exempting comprehensive health plans that meet certain criteria assuring their accountability in the marketplace is specifically examined in Chapter 8, dealing with HMOs, the prototype of Mc-

Clure's favored mechanisms. Latter portions of this chapter are concerned with other specific coverage limitations that are suggested by the analytical approaches employed by McClure and explored in depth in Part III.

FEDERAL COVERAGE REQUIREMENTS

Public Law 93–641, as amended in 1979, substantially limits state discretion with respect to the coverage of certificate-of-need laws. The basic federal requirement, which is contained in Public Health Service Act section 1523(a)(4)(B) and enforced by the threat of denial of federal funds for other Public Health Service Act programs,[3] is that the state agency "administer a State certificate of need program which applies to the obligation of *capital expenditures* within the State and the offering within the State of *new institutional health services* and the acquisition of *major medical equipment*" (emphasis added). The emphasized terms are all defined at length in the act.[4] Regulation of "capital expenditures" and "new institutional health services" is required only insofar as they are undertaken by a "health care facility," which term is defined under DHHS's regulations to mean "hospitals, skilled nursing facilities, kidney disease treatment centers (including free standing hemodialysis units), intermediate care facilities, rehabilitation facilities, and ambulatory surgical facilities."[5] All these terms except "kidney disease treatment centers" are defined in detail but none in such a way as to include private physicians' offices.

In most cases, the federal statute requires state review only where a minimum number of dollars is involved. These dollar minimums were substantially increased in the Omnibus Budget Reconciliation Act of 1981, which, in reducing federal financial support for planning and regulation, also sought to reduce the agencies' mandatory burdens. A "health care facility" (HCF) must now be subjected to regulation with respect to any capital expenditure made by it or on its behalf, for any purpose, in excess of $600,000 (as adjusted for inflation).[6] Small capital investments by an HCF are subject to approval if they affect the HCF's bed capacity by as much as 10 percent or ten beds[7] or if they would add a new service or terminate one previously offered; indeed, initiation of any new service entailing more than $250,000 (as adjusted) per year in operating expenses must be regulated whether or not a capital investment is involved.[8] As later discussion shows, the acquisition of certain major medical equipment (costing more than $400,000, as adjusted) must be approved whether made by an HCF or some other provider.

Although most of the foregoing requirements are minimum ones allowing states to go further if they so choose, the 1979 amendments expressly limited the right of states to impose more than the required restrictions on HMOs.[9] As to state coverage of HMOs, therefore, the rule is essentially the converse of that prevailing in T. H. White's imaginary ant kingdom, where "everything not forbidden is compulsory."[10] Whereas the original Public Law 93–641 had made extensive coverage of HMOs mandatory, the 1979 amendments, in an important procompetitive move discussed in Chapter 8, reversed the previous policy by prohibiting all but a limited form of regulation.

Service Terminations and Bed Reductions

A surprising and little noticed feature of the 1979 amendments was language seemingly extending mandatory certificate-of-need requirements to any capital expenditure associated with an HCF's termination of a particular service or a substantial reduction in its complement of beds. Even though the rationale for regulating service and bed reductions must be profoundly different from the cost-containment rationale for covering new investments and services, the congressional committees did not discuss that rationale. Nor did they explain or even explicitly recognize that the language chosen—the state must cover any capital expenditure that "substantially changes" the bed capacity or the services of an HCF[11]—could logically encompass service cutbacks as well as expansions.

Although the main reason for subjecting service and bed reductions to certificate-of-need requirements is to assure availability of services,[12] it is not clear, legally, that an HCF can be required by law to maintain a service that is losing money. Although regulated utilities have comparable service obligations, utilities are legally guaranteed the right to charge rates on their overall business that should yield a fair return on total investment.[13] Because HCFs have no such guarantee and are routinely denied the right to recoup losses by allocating costs to government financing programs, the constitutional question surrounding service obligations seems substantial. Moreover, the policy of meeting needs through "involuntary servitude" also seems wrong in principle. For one thing, institutions burdened with money-losing services that they cannot terminate would have to be protected by regulation against competition eroding the excess revenues from other services out of which they subsidize the loss operations.[14] As Chapter 10 discusses, such protectionism for internal subsidies might occasionally be justified, but this further manifestation of the public utility franchising approach to the provision of institutional services should be eradicated.

It seems probable that DHHS could readily resolve these serious policy and constitutional problems by revising its regulations. The act is easily subject to a different interpretation, particularly in the absence of any legislative history signifying a congressional desire to give regulation this new and questionable dimension. Moreover, the new congressional goal of reducing the agencies' mandatory responsibilities would be served by a reinterpretation. Finally, it is a canon of statutory construction that one should adopt a narrow reading if significant constitutional issues can thereby be avoided. In general, it may be said that DHHS bent the regulatory scheme out of shape when it twisted a few statutory references to "access" into an unauthorized system of hidden subsidies to finance health care for certain social groups.

A Typology of Coverage Issues

As described in Chapter 5, the great contribution of the 1979 amendments to Public Law 93–641 was to clarify that certificate-of-need laws enacted by the states do not obviate a role for competition with respect to everything encompassed therein. The interrelationships among mandatory coverage, the new procompetition mandate to the planner-regulators, and the new HMO exemption indicate that federal law now recognizes the following categories of facilities and services:

1. Those so unlikely to be allocated appropriately by competition that their regulation by the state should be mandatory. (As to facilities and services in this category, the planner-regulators are not to presume that competition is irrelevant but are to make findings as to competition's allocative capacity.)
2. Those so likely to be subject to effective competition that entry and investment regulation by the states on the basis of need should be prohibited. (HMOs, as prepaid providers subject to a fair market test, represent the only service currently in this category of exempt services.)
3. Those not clearly one way or the other, so that the states can make their own judgments concerning coverage. (Again, however, the planner-regulators themselves must weigh competitive factors in deciding on specific policies toward regulated services.)

The remainder of this chapter is primarily concerned with state legislative decisions exercising the discretion left them under federal law with respect to facilities and services in category (3). Whereas this and the following chapter on HMOs deal primarily with legislative questions, Part III is concerned with how to regulate both facilities and services in category (1) and those in category (3) that the states elect to subject to regulation. To a significant extent, such regulation requires the agencies to make at a local level the same kinds of judgments concerning the efficaciousness of competition that are treated as legislative choices here.

The discussion here does not undertake to challenge Congress's judgments about the minimum scope of certificate-of-need requirements—that is, its allocation of particular facilities and services to category (1). Serious questions might be raised, of course, in specific instances about relying on entry controls rather than on changes in reimbursement practices to deal with the problems that exist. Nevertheless, with the 1979 amendments, federal law now contemplates that planner-regulators will be attuned to demand-side factors and changes and will not be concerned solely with limiting supply under outmoded assumptions. Thus, all questions that might be raised concerning the coverage of legislation can be taken up in considering the regulatory stance to be taken with respect to a particular type of facility or service. Conversely, the analysis in Part III could easily be employed in considering coverage issues at the federal and state levels. For example, Chapter 13, though not addressing coverage issues as such, reveals that coverage of ambulatory surgical facilities and nursing homes does not so obviously serve the public interest that it should not be reconsidered.

COVERAGE OF HOME HEALTH CARE BY CERTIFICATE-OF-NEED REQUIREMENTS

An interesting example of a coverage issue having implications for competition is provided by home health care. Although DHHS's early regulations under section 1122 originally covered home health agencies within the definition of a regulated health care facility, its regulations under Public Law 93–641 amended the 1122 definition in such a way as not to require the states to subject home health services to certification of need.[15] In the 1979 amendments, Congress confirmed the view that coverage of home health care should not be mandatory by rejecting new proposals that would have made it so.[16]

Under federal law, the states remain free to impose a certificate-of-need requirement for new home health services if they so choose. More than thirty states have elected to impose such regulation—including, it may be noted, the state of Utah in its otherwise "pro-competitive" law. In deciding whether to enact or to continue need-oriented exclusionary regulation of home health agencies, the state legislatures must consider whether such regulation suppresses desirable competition and whether such weakening of competition as would occur would be offset by any benefits that could not be achieved by less restrictive means. Similar questions must be confronted by HSAs and state agencies in exercising such authority as they may be given over home health agencies. Thus, the considerations developed here are equally relevant to the development of regulatory policy once regulation has been imposed. This discussion of the legislative issues may be viewed as a tentative application of the principles proposed in Chapters 11 and 12 for regulators' use.

Home Health Care Described

Home health care, which includes a wide variety of professional services delivered in the patient's home, is an increasingly significant feature of the health services system. Some significant facts, particularly its relative importance in federal health care programs, appear in the following quotation from a 1979 research publication of the Health Care Financing Administration (HCFA):

> Although the level of spending for these services is relatively low, its recent and continuing growth makes it particularly noteworthy. The basic services provided by home health agencies are home visits by nurses, aides and other nonphysician health professionals. These services are considered, in part, substitutes for the more expensive institutional care. In 1972 about $280 million was spent for such home health services, about a third of which was funded by the Medicare and Medicaid programs. By 1978 the level of total expenditures had risen to about $845 million, about 80 percent of which was funded by Medicare or Medicaid. Thus, most of the growth in spending for home health agencies was financed by HCFA programs. This growth was due mainly to the increase in number of persons using such services. In 1972 home health visits were provided to about 250,000 persons under Medicare and 113,000 under Medicaid. By 1977, nearly 700,000 Medicare recipients and about 300,000 Medicaid recipients were receiving home health care.
>
> About 8 percent of home health agency expenditures are provided by hospital-based agencies .... [17]

In 1980, Congress expanded Medicare coverage of home health care by dropping both the previous requirement of three days of hospitalization and the limit to one hundred home visits. [18]

Home health care has been controversial in large part because it is paid for on a cost reimbursement basis by the Medicare program, opening the door to high costs. In the Medicare-Medicaid Anti-Fraud and Abuse Act of 1977, Congress directed DHEW to study home health care and to make legislative recommendations concerning it. When finally submitted, DHEW's report was rejected as inadequate by congressional committees. [19] A concurrent study by the General Accounting Office (GAO) identified a need to tighten certain reimbursement practices to prevent profiteering, sometimes through the use of not-for-profit agencies whose management contracts and other transactions with for-profit affiliates artificially inflate their costs.[20] Because of the prevalence of cost reimbursement, competition's place in the industry has been less obvious than it might otherwise be. Neither DHEW (DHHS) nor the GAO has yet paid appreciable attention to competition as a force for fostering either quality or economy in home health care.

Rationales for Controlling Entry by Home Care Agencies

The usual rationales for certification of need do not apply to home health care. Thus, cost-escalating overutilization induced by unquestioning third-party payment has not been shown to be a problem. Indeed, it seems reasonable to expect that most users of expanded services will represent cost savings to the system rather than higher costs, since their most likely alternative is more expensive inpatient care. Unlike many elements of the health care system whose growth has been deemed to require restraint by certificate-of-need requirements, home health care has not been accused of growing too fast or of being overly abundant. Indeed, as of a recent date, the United States had only one homemaker for every 5,000 people, as compared to ratios of 1 to 121 in Sweden and 1 to 726 in the United Kingdom,[21] and there are 603 U.S. counties without any home health service.[22] With an aging population and a desire to reduce institutionalization, the need for home health services would hardly seem debatable. Because certificate-of-need laws were expressly designed to inhibit growth, it seems undesirable to impose them on elements of the system that should be rapidly expanded.

Need-focused entry regulation also seems substantially less warranted or necessary where significant capital investments are not involved. Certificate-of-need laws in the health sector have focused primarily on capital outlays, which have been seen as entailing future public obligations to pay. As long as the prospects for major change in the methods of financing health care are limited, this perception may be correct, but it has no bearing on home health services, which, because they involve negligible capital expenditures, remain free to expand or contract as needed in the future and impose no obstacle to change and no commitment of future resources. The significance of capital investment as a justification for regulation is developed at greater length in Chapter 11.

Lacking the usual justifications for controlling entry in the health care sector, advocates of certification of need for home health agencies have fallen back on other rationales that are much less convincing. Their arguments are in fact quite general, reflecting a broad faith in central planning and regulation and an undiscriminating distrust of competitive developments. Indeed, the thrust of these claims is not much more precise than the simplistic, yet widely accepted and beguiling, argument that, if some regulation and planning are good, more must be better. DHEW in its comments explaining its 1977 decision not to require coverage of certain freestanding outpatient services, summarized the arguments presented to it on the point as follows:

> The commenters felt that the definition of facilities covered should remain as inclusive as possible, and they argued that there is need both to plan and to regulate the entire range of "health care facilities" providing health services. Further, they saw improved standards of care, integrated system-wide planning, the prevention of overdevelopment and duplication of effort in the health care industry, and an evenhanded approach to both institution-based and freestanding providers of home health care, outpatient physical therapy, and ambulatory care services as by-products of certificate of need reviews.[23]

There is good reason to think that such arguments often originate with interest groups that wish to see competition kept to a minimum. In the home health care field, the proponents of entry controls are frequently existing providers who profess to advocate orderly development but actually seek protection against competition. In particular, nonprofit organizations that have become active in the field seek to exclude proprietary firms, which threaten to grow rapidly and which frequently provide services at lower cost.[24] Hospitals and nursing homes may also wish to see the home care option develop slowly and under tight control so that fewer of their patients will have occasion to select it.

Even though, as revealed in questionnaire responses received in connection with this study, the vast majority of health planners favor covering home health services, the lessons from other regulated industries suggest that regulators are not usually the best judges of the value of or the need for their own regulatory services. Indeed, in this case it appears that the planner-regulators are reaching for authority that they do not know how to exercise. Health planners have developed no methods or criteria for assessing the need for home care in particular markets.[25] This lack of standards would leave certificate-of-need applicants, who bear the burden of proving need, largely at the mercy of agency discretion. Moreover, the certificate-of-need agencies may be heavily oriented to the importance of inpatient care. They may also be biased against certain types of provider—particularly for-profit ones—and, even if they are not strongly influenced by established interests, they will not be able to ignore competitive impacts on incumbent providers in reaching their judgments. Finally, in order to assure "coordination" and "cooperation," regulators have commonly expected that new applicants will have established contractual arrangements with existing providers. This requirement leaves the latter with an ultimate veto power over new entrants and perpetuates their control.

A review of home health care regulation by Gary, Hyman, and Spiegel, who appear generally sympathetic to the health-planning and regulation effort, concludes as follows with respect to the certificate-of-need agencies' ability to discharge their responsibilities in the area: "Unless vested interests are held in check, competition will be restricted, the benefits of pluralism will be limited to the older established groups, and innovation may well be squelched."[26] The recommendation of this careful analysis is that certificate-of-need requirements not be extended to home health services.

Appraising Competition's Value

While the states that elected in the past to cover home health care in their certificate-of-need laws cannot be faulted for failing to resist the trend then implicit in federal law and policy, the 1979 amendments to Public Law 93–641 require a fundamental reappraisal. Moreover, the federal mandate is sufficiently changed that competition's value in this sector of the industry can no longer be ignored. The House committee report on the 1979 amendments strongly indicates that regulation should have a better rationale than is reflected in the arguments usually advanced for covering home health care:

> The committee's decision to not include home health services ... in the title XV requirements for coverage by State certificate of need programs ... was based partially ... on the committee's belief that the supply of those services would not be excessive if they were not regulated and that market forces of supply and demand may appropriately allocate them.[27]

Even though market forces may not always be capable of allocating home health resources consistently to the best advantage, there is little doubt that competition in home health services will produce enough positive benefits that no possibility of its regulatory suppression should be permitted. The discussion below, in arguing for this conclusion, indicates some of the problems associated with competition in this field as well as its benefits. The overriding point is that market forces need not work perfectly before they can be the mechanism of choice for allocating particular types of health resources.

Third-party payment for home care is increasing largely as a result of recognition of the need to reduce the preference for third-party financed institutional care over uninsured home services. Even where third-party payment is available for home services, however, it is not likely to cover as many of the patient's expenses as are covered for institutional care—food, for example. Because home health services will not usually compete on an equal basis with institutions for the consumer's patronage, one cannot count on competition to assure optimal patient placement. Still, allowing competition and relatively free market entry is more likely to reduce overall costs than to increase them, since most of the patients receiving such care would probably be institutionalized if it were not available. Moreover, competitive innovation in the home health field should make that option increasingly attractive to patients and physicians, thus eliminating some of the main obstacles to discharging patients from hospital and nursing home beds.

Although home health services are an obvious and frequently desirable substitute for inpatient services, the cost saving over inpatient care may sometimes be more apparent than real. As indicated, it may reflect only a shifting of housekeeping expenses to the patient or his family. Moreover, skilled manpower utilization may be less efficient in home care. For example, the patient may need attention only for short periods, or at unpredictable times, yet the health worker may be precluded by distance from performing other skilled tasks when not needed by the patient; inpatient care, by contrast, allows a single worker to serve several patients simultaneously. Although the proper placement of a patient is a function of many complex medical and practical factors, the pressure for home treatment, particularly in public programs, may sometimes be based more on a desire to reduce program costs than on medical or efficiency considerations. These problems have little to do with the appropriateness of free market entry, however, and should be dealt with by other means, such as utilization controls designed to assure that patients get both the care that they need and the financial protection that they are entitled to either under law or under private health plan contracts.

Even if costly overutilization might eventually become a hazard with third-party financed home health services, it is far from clear that entry regulation would be the correct social response. Using utilization review techniques, public and private third parties should be able to deny continued coverage where medical and other factors do not indicate a need. Federal programs have established PSROs for this purpose, and social service agencies, attuned to nonmedical problems, may play a role as well. Both public and private third parties should find it easy to negotiate with competing home health agencies to procure standing contracts under which remuneration, scope of services, and effective implementation of utilization controls would be provided for. Given these long-run possibilities for controlling possible abuse of the financing system's coverage of home care, the need for regulatory controls over aggregate supply seems obviated. Indeed, health planners could probably do much more to improve the system's performance by encouraging public and private financing programs to obtain home health services under provider participation agreements dealing with utilization controls as well as price.

Even though traditional forms of third-party payment have invited escalation in unit costs as well as utilization abuses, it is doubtful that entry regulation, even if coupled with rate regulation, could match the effectiveness of active competition among home health agencies in containing the cost of home services. Some patients still pay all or some of the cost of home care themselves, and they and their physicians and other advisors will be cost conscious in selecting a provider. Moreover, third parties could use competitive bidding techniques to identify high-cost providers, whose services could then be excluded from coverage, or could fix a flat per-visit payment, thereby keeping their own costs down and cost differentials visible to patients. Some competition, at least, will therefore focus on the price of home care as well as quality—as competition so often fails to do in health services. Prices prevailing in the cost-conscious sector of the market will help other third-party payers determine how much to pay, and competition based on price should promote efficiency and hold down personnel costs. Thus, even the Medicare program, which pays for home health services on a cost-reimbursement basis but which can employ maximum cost limits by type of home visit,[28] would benefit from competition in the larger market. State Medicaid programs also fix flat rates of payment for home care,[29] and the adequacy of these rates could be judged better if a competitive market existed.

Many of the arguments for certification of need appear to focus on concern about the quality of services that might be provided in an unregulated market, and this would appear to be a legitimate concern. But, while certification of need may serve in some respects to maintain quality, quality assurance is also achievable by licensure, certification, and registration and inspection systems. Because they do not focus on need, these forms of quality regulation should be significantly less prone to suppress desirable competition. Moreover, quality gains from need-oriented regulation may often come at a high cost as protected incumbents allow costs to rise in the name of quality, knowing that consumers will be denied lower cost options of adequate quality that would appear if entry were not artificially restricted. Certificate-of-need laws and agencies were not designed for quality assurance and should not be used as such if their basic service of limiting supply is not required.

It it not clear, moreover, that competition cannot help to maintain the quality of care provided. It is obvious that some patients will lack the information, knowledge, and opportunity for repeated dealings that are ordinarily thought to be necessary to make competition work well. But, in this case, the patient's physician and other advisors, including other family members and social service personnel, will serve as knowledgeable purchasing agents, creating competitive pressures that should keep home health agencies up to the mark. On the other hand, supply restrictions may work to limit choice and thus prevent competitive pressures from operating to raise quality. Moreover, competition would seem a valuable complement to public quality-assurance efforts, which can only set minimum standards and cannot foster constant striving for quality improvements throughout the industry. Public regulation might also adopt such large margins for error— unnecessary credential requirements, for example—that costs would be raised well beyond the point yielding commensurate benefits. Though quality-related regulation would not be obviated by competition, it might be more flexible and realistic if market forces also operated and it were not the sole source of quality assurance.

Preventing the Extension of Hospital Monopoly

Though uncontrolled market entry for competent providers would foster desirable competition, there may be a significant danger that hospitals would develop home health services of their own and thereby monopolize the posthospital care of their former inpatients. It would seem that, rather than having hospitals simply extend their services in this manner, a system of referrals by physicians and hospitals to competing private agencies would offer significant quality assurance and cost advantages. This suggests a possible rationale for a certificate-of-need law covering institutionally based home care services and not freestanding ones. If this rationale were adhered to, a satisfactory blend of regulation and competition might emerge: Hospitals would be restricted in their ability to extend their monopoly into their patients' homes by vertical integration, but hospital entry into home health services could be permitted if a need appeared and if services were made available in the manner least restrictive of competition. Thus, if need were established by a showing of inadequate competition, inferior quality, excessive cost, or specific efficiencies achievable as a result of the hospital connection, an institution's entry into the provision of home health services could perhaps be permitted on the condition that it establish referral procedures assuring the maintenance of meaningful competition. If these procompetitive principles were adhered to, health sector regulation might usefully promote competition rather than curtail it. Even if complete coverage of home health care was provided for in certificate-of-need legislation, the administering agencies should confine themselves to addressing such competition-related issues.

A hazard of regulating only institutionally based home health services is that institutions would press for eliminating what they would allege to be discrimination in favor of freestanding agencies. They might easily be successful in getting the law's coverage expanded, leading to the enfranchisement of a few protected services, with their portions of the market staked out by the regulators and competition greatly curbed. An alternative, nonregulatory policy for dealing with the threat of institutional monopoly over home health services might be to rely on antitrust principles. General principles could be employed by federal or state courts to prevent vertical integration[30] and "tying" arrangements[31] whereby hospitals monopolized home care for their former inpatients. If these legal principles were clear, competing home health agencies and the local HSA might be perceived as a threat to enforce the principle of free consumer choice. Indeed, it might be possible under antitrust principles to force hospitals to spin off their existing home health services or to make other adjustments to assure effective competition.

A Strong Conclusion

This review of home health services compels the conclusion that regulation of home health services by certificate of need is most unlikely to be in the public interest. The attempt to push regulation into this area where it is not needed provides as convincing a demonstration as we have of the thinness of the regulation advocates' arguments and of the strong element of self-interest that frequently underlies ostensible distrust of market forces.

CLINICAL LABORATORY EQUIPMENT

In enacting the 1979 health planning amendments, Congress rejected proposals that would have added independent clinical laboratories to the list of providers whose capital investments the states are required to regulate by certification of need. In requiring the regulation of "major medical equipment" acquired for use in serving inpatients, Congress defined the term to exclude equipment purchased by independent laboratories that are certified under the Medicare program.[32] Thus, laboratories not associated with a hospital or a physician's office are free from federally mandated regulation. Nevertheless, they may be subjected to certificate-of-need requirements by state law if such requirements are enacted prior to September 30, 1982. After that date, federal law will bar the states from broadening their coverage of "major medical equipment."[33] States must therefore examine their coverage of such equipment purchases by an early date.

The impetus for the movement to regulate clinical laboratories is supplied by the rapid rise in the use of clinical tests and the large dollar costs involved. Clinical testing represents about 10 percent of the nation's health bill, and its total cost has been increasing at a rate of about 15 percent a year, faster than overall health care costs.[34] Innocent explanations for these cost and utilization trends include increasingly attractive opportunities to substitute tests for valuable physician time, the development of more efficient equipment whose lower costs justify more testing, and the increasing sophistication of medical care, which enhances the value of tests in diagnosis and treatment. On the other hand, much testing is alleged to be of marginal utility, and indeed there are a number of substantial reasons why utilization abuses could be expected to occur. Hospital cost accounting methods and cost reimbursement financing systems, coupled with the declining average cost of tests due to scale economies, have made in-house testing highly profitable for hospitals, leading them to encourage an increase in the use of such ancillary services. Moreover, with third-party financing in its present form, hospitals enjoy a captive and cost-oblivious market for such services, limiting the value of competition from independent laboratories.[35] Physicians also find testing profitable and may step up in-office testing in response to constraints on their allowable fees.[36] Physicians are also alleged to exploit payers' passivity by ordering tests solely to reduce their problems in defending possible malpractice suits. In addition, there have been instances of outright fraud and kickbacks whereby laboratories and physicians have conspired to exploit public and private financing programs.

Disentangling and assigning weights to these various causes of the increasing utilization and price of laboratory services would obviously be extremely difficult. Nevertheless, it is hard to see how need-oriented regulation of entry and investment by independent laboratories would solve any important problem. Independent laboratories would seem to represent efficient and highly desirable competitive alternatives and to be less prone to some of the observed abuses than the captive laboratories with which they compete. Paid on the basis of charges rather than costs and operating in a competitive environment where at least some cost consciousness prevails, they would seem to be a desirable feature of a competitive marketplace. Moreover, as financing mechanisms change and increasingly insist that providers economize in the use of ancillary services, the availability of low-cost independent laboratories, both as alternative providers and as yardsticks for evaluating other laboratory charges, should assist third parties in containing costs. Finally, many independent laboratories serve large, even nationwide, markets and would not be amenable to local health planning.

A full investigation of the clinical laboratory industry with all of its diverse components is currently being undertaken by the Rand Corporation. Preliminary results reveal no basis for contemplating their regulation by certification of need.[37] Although concern has been expressed about undue concentration in the industry,[38] that is not a problem that entry regulation can do anything about. Indeed, the ease of entering the market is such that competition is likely to operate quite effectively even with small numbers, unless regulatory controls inhibit entry. On balance, the House committee would seem to have been correct in its judgment that "the inclusion of major medical equipment purchases by independent laboratories [under state certificate-of-need laws] does not appear to be necessary at this time,"[39] and in its belief that "market forces of supply and demand may appropriately allocate" the supply of clinical laboratory services.[40]

SOME CANDIDATES FOR EXPANDED COVERAGE

In some instances, the states might be well advised to go further in regulation than Public Law 93–641, as amended, requires. For example, a strong case can be made for more extensive regulation of acquisitions of capital equipment such as computed tomography (CT) scanners by physicians for their private offices. Moreover, it will be seen that the logic of regulating the location of physicians' offices—that is, the supply of physicians in an area—is difficult to dispute if one accepts the basic rationale of certificate-of-need laws.

A case can also be made for more extensive coverage of hospital investments than is required by federal law. The Salkever-Bice study, discussed in Chapter 3, suggests that, cumulatively, hospital capital investments in amounts below statutory thresholds may represent a significant problem, and this problem may have been exacerbated by 1981 increases in the federally mandated thresholds. Because investments below the current thresholds may be regarded as a loophole, a state might wish to assert jurisdiction over some of them. To limit the administrative burden resulting from a larger number of applications, the state agency might be encouraged to define categories of investment, such as housekeeping equipment and replacements, that do not require explicit approval. Short-form applications might be provided for investments less likely to be controversial. By thus focusing regulatory effort where it is most needed, expansion of the capacity of hospital pathology and radiology services could be controlled, and the appropriateness of utilization of these profitable services could be scrutinized.

The suggestion that certification of need might be expanded beyond minimal federal requirements is made on the assumption that the states would also, at the same time, introduce strong procompetition language to assure that the expanded regulatory powers are employed selectively and invoked only where market forces are not working well. In fact, such expanded regulatory powers could be used constructively by a market-oriented agency to speed the introduction of private sector cost controls. For example, Chapter 12 argues that control over capital investments could be relaxed for any provider who had contracted on a long-term basis with an independent financing plan concerning the price and utilization of the service to be offered. If regulation were relaxed for such providers and used only to limit entry and investment by providers who remain unaccountable to consumers or their purchasing agents, the pressure on providers to submit to contractual controls would be very great, and the financing plans' bargaining power, and thus the efficacy of market forces, would be significantly enhanced.

Ambulatory Care Facilities

In recognition of "serious definitional difficulties," DHEW decided in 1977 not to require the states to impose certificate-of-need requirements on ambulatory care facilities other than "kidney disease treatment centers, including freestanding hemodialysis units," and "ambulatory surgical facilities."[41] The regulations' definition of the latter term expressly excluded "the offices of private physicians or dentists, whether for individual or group practice."[42] The states were encouraged, however, "to undertake various approaches" toward dealing with "organized ambulatory health care facilities."[43] These same terms and requirements were incorporated in the definition of "health care facility" in the regulations implementing the 1979 planning amendments.[44] On the other hand, the amendments extended regulation to acquisitions of certain major medical equipment located in ambulatory settings such as a private physician's office. The mandate to regulate major medical equipment extends, however, only to equipment costing $400,000 (after 1981 amendments) and only to "equipment that will be used to provide services for inpatients of a hospital." Prior to September 30, 1982, a state may elect to regulate therapeutic and diagnostic equipment that is used to serve only outpatients.

Putting aside the definitional complexities of achieving appropriate regulation, the case for covering some outpatient care is quite credible. Precisely because institutions may be barred under certificate-of-need laws from overinvesting in sophisticated medical equipment, a market opportunity may be opened for physicians or other unregulated providers to invest in the same equipment and to offer its use on an outpatient basis. The CT scanner has become something of a cause célèbre for just this reason,[45] and considerable pressure has been generated to control the proliferation of such machines by extending regulatory power to doctors' offices. Because third-party payers widely cover such outpatient diagnostic tests and because scanners, while immensely valuable as diagnostic tools, are subject to overutilization, a strong case for their regulatory control has been stated. Thus, Congress's reluctance to mandate more extensive regulation in the 1979 amendments may have been more a political concession to the medical profession than a policy conclusion that the market works well enough with respect to outpatient services of this kind to obviate regulatory oversight. The legislative history did, however, suggest that market failure is more substantial for inpatient care than for ambulatory services.[46] Though not universally true, this observation is generally correct both because third-party payment of inpatient care is more extensive and more often based on cost and because an institutionalized patient is a captive of the institution and unable to shop (with his physician's help) for needed services. Nonetheless, it does not appear that a careful assessment of the market for ambulatory services has been made. Congress, for political reasons, seems to have left that assessment to the states.

Before extending regulation to capital-intensive outpatient services, alternatives to regulation need to be evaluated. It may be quite practical and effective for a third-party payer to undertake cost controls of its own with respect to such services rather than relying on regulation-induced restrictions on the service's availability to limit its exposure. For example, a third-party insurer might control costs of outpatient CT scans in various ways, including refusing to pay for scans under any or all of the following conditions: (1) where the equipment, though not subject to regulation, has not been given planners' approval; (2) where the scan was not indicated under specific medical criteria, which might be promulgated by the planners, by the local medical society or PSRO (although the doctors' possible conflict of interests should be recognized), or by the third party itself; (3) where the third party's medical consultant had not approved the scan for payment in advance; or (4) where the provider had not entered into an agreement with the plan specifying the terms on which services would be provided to plan subscribers.

As Chapter 15 suggests, HSAs could well assist private insurers in establishing such private cost controls, thereby greatly reducing providers' incentive and opportunity to circumvent certificate-of-need requirements imposed on institutions. Particularly in view of the high cost and political difficulty of imposing effective regulatory control on diagnostic and therapeutic equipment in doctors' offices, attention should certainly be given to strengthening market disincentives to unwanted investments. In the long run, this approach to the problem is probably preferable to expanding regulation.

A number of states have imposed certificate-of-need requirements on large capital investments in equipment to be installed in physicians' private offices without regard to whether the equipment will be used to treat inpatients or outpatients.[47] Although it is hard to object to these regulatory extensions on the ground that the market allocates these resources well enough, it is regrettable that the easy course of expanding regulation is so often taken without exploring fully the possibility that third-party payers could protect themselves and their premium payers against price and utilization abuses, thereby obviating regulation. Regulation has so far not been so outstandingly effective that its extension is clearly the best solution to every leak detected in the present regulatory framework. The so-called tar-baby effect has again and again produced regulatory extensions in other regulated industries that, though seemingly expedient at the time and in the circumstances, ultimately stifled initiative and innovation. Moreover, regulators frequently expend more energy in seeking the power to do more things than in doing well the things that they are already charged with doing.

Obviously, the ideal solution to dealing with the weakness of market controls over capital-intensive outpatient services would be to impose regulation of the procompetitive kind advocated herein, leaving the planner-regulators to judge local conditions, stimulate the emergence of market forces, and deregulate specific services as soon as possible. Equally obviously, there remain serious questions whether the planner-regulators will accept this definition of their function and carry it out in good faith. In view of this uncertainty, the states might be better advised to limit regulation's scope and hope for spontaneous and planner-assisted market developments.

Regulating the Location of Physicians' Practices

The theoretical case for regulating the location of physicians' practices under certificate-of-need laws is quite strong, raising the interesting question of why the emphasis has been primarily on institutions. Just as the argument for regulating hospital growth is based on Roemer's law that the hospital bed supply and the supply of other capital resources create their own demand, a convincing case for using regulation to distribute physicians can be based on findings that physicians also create demand for their services. For example, Fuchs and Kramer and others have found demand for medical services to be more strongly correlated with the physician supply than with the population's health status,[48] and warnings against the cost implications of an impending oversupply of physicians are now being heard in many quarters. Moreover, expanding the physician supply has been seen by many as an inadequate response to the maldistribution of physicians, because physicians tend to congregate in urban areas and suburbs, and it is feared that even heavy concentration in those areas will not produce price competition intense enough to drive some of them to underdoctored areas. Although recent signs suggest that maldistribution is ameliorating,[49] it probably cannot be concluded that market forces are now fully capable of allocating the physician supply efficiently.

If one had to distinguish between physical and human capital with respect to the likelihood of demand creation and the potential for abuse of third-party financing mechanisms, one would have to conclude that physicians represent a greater potential drain on societal resources than institutions. Even though they are subject to fiduciary responsibilities to their patients and competitive pressure not to violate these responsibilities, physicians exercise substantial discretionary spending power. Moreover, physicians collectively possess many ways of legitimizing large expenditures on marginally productive services. Thus, PSROs are asked by federal law to define medical necessity; the law of medical malpractice deters economizing by demanding adherence to a community standard of care whose benefit/cost ratios are unsubstantiated; and profession-sponsored peer review systems and ethical norms purport to speak for the public on such crucial matters as the reasonableness of fees and utilization practices. As long as financing programs remain essentially passive in accepting prices and utilization practices, the case for regulation remains strong. Although it is true that a larger proportion of outpatient services than of inpatient services is paid for out of pocket, that proportion is below 40 percent and falling as insurance becomes more comprehensive. If certificate-of-need regulation makes sense at all—and it is reasonable to believe that it does not—then it makes sense to use it to limit the supply of physician services available in a given place in order that some rationing of services will ensue.

In these circumstances, then, a state might reasonably believe that it could improve the access of its underserved citizens to physicians and could control overall costs by limiting the freedom of physicians to open a practice wherever, whenever, and in whatever specialty they wish.[50] Nevertheless, this discussion is not intended seriously to propose extension of certificate-of-need requirements to allocate the supply of physicians' services.[51] Its purpose is mostly to illustrate once again the vast implications of certificate-of-need regulation and the very limited extent to which present regulation addresses the source of the problem. In order to be significantly effective, certification of need must go much further than it has so far, yet the political obstacles to making it effective in this way are exceedingly great. Perhaps the health planners' long-term agenda includes closing this loophole and others, as the political power of physicians is eroded, but that will obviously take a long time. There would seem to be little doubt that encouraging competitive developments and changes in health care financing would pay dividends long before the political influence of the health planners is sufficient to offset that of physicians and allow them to extend their sway to all the resources requiring control if this technique of cost containment is to succeed. Once they recognize the inadequacy of their power to contain costs by imposing all of the supply constraints needed to be effective, health planners and regulators should finally see the wisdom of redirecting their efforts toward reforming the demand side of the market.

NOTES

1.   W. McClure, *Comprehensive Market and Regulatory Strategies for Medical Care* 391–427 (InterStudy 1979).

2. McClure, "On Broadening the Definition of and Removing Regulatory Barriers to a Competitive Health Care System," 3 *J. Health Pol., Pol'y & L.* 303 (1978).

3. Public Health Service Act §1521(d), *as amended*; *see* North Carolina *ex rel.* Morrow v. Califano, 445 F. Supp. 532 (E.D.N.C. 1977), *aff'd mem.*, 435 U.S. 962 (1981).

4. Public Health Service Act §§1531(5), (6), and (7), *as amended*.

5. 45 Fed. Reg. 69,745 (1980) (to be codified in 42 C.F.R. §123.401).

6. Public Health Service Act §§1527(a)(1)(B) and 1531(6), *as amended*.

7. *Id.*; 45 Fed. Reg. 69,747 (1980) (to be codified in 42 C.F.R. §123.404(a)(2)).

8. Public Health Service Act §§1527(a)(1)(A) and 1531(5), *as amended*; 45 Fed. Reg. 69,747 (1980) (to be codified in 42 C.F.R. §123.404(a)(3)).

9. Public Health Service Act §1527(b), *as amended*.

10. T. H. White, *The Once and Future King* 122 (Berkley ed. 1966).

11. Pub. L. No. 96-79, §117(b), *adding* Public Health Service Act §1531(6).

12. 45 Fed Reg. 69,752 (1980) to be codified in 42 C.F.R. §123.412(5)(ii)); *see also* Havighurst, "Regulation of Health Facilities and Services by 'Certificate of Need'," 59 *Va. L. Rev.* 1143, 1166 (1973).

13. *Cf.* Blanchette v. Connecticut General Ins. Corp., 419 U.S. 102 (1974).

14. Havighurst, *supra* note 12, at 1164–65, 1188–94.

15. 42 C.F.R. §100.102(e) (1980).

16. H.R. Rep. No. 96-190, 96th Cong., 1st Sess. 53 (1979).

17. Gibson, "National Health Expenditures, 1978," *Health Care Financing Rev.*, Summer 1979, at 12.

18. "Omnibus Reconciliation Bill Passed; 53 Medicare-Medicaid Changes OK'd," *Health Services Information*, Dec. 8, 1980, at 3.

19. Demkovich, "In Treating the Problems of the Elderly, There May Be No Place Like Home," 11 *Nat'l J.* 2154 (1979).

20. U.S. General Accounting Office, *Home Health Care Services— Tighter Fiscal Controls Needed* (1979).

21. L. Gary, H. Hyman, & A. Spiegel, *Home Health Care Regulation: Issues and Opportunities* 4 (Hunter College of the City of New York, Urban Research Center 1977).

22. *Hearings on the Labor-HEW Appropriations Bill for Fiscal Year 1981 before the Subcomm. on the Departments of Labor and Health, Education, and Welfare of the House Comm. on Appropriations*, 96th Cong., 2d Sess. 356 (1980).

23. 42 Fed. Reg. 4002, 4006 (1977).

24. *E.g.*, Gary, Hyman, & Spiegel, *supra* note 21, at 6–7.

25. *Id.* at 7.
26. *Id.* at 9.
27. H.R. Rep. No. 96-190, *supra* note 16, at 53.
28. 42 U.S.C. §1395x(v)(1) (1976); 42 C.F.R. §405.460 (1980).
29. 3 *CCH Medicare and Medicaid Guide* ¶15,550 *et seq.*
30. *See, e.g.,* Otter Tail Power Co. v. United States, 410 U.S. 366 (1973).
31. *See, e.g.,* International Salt Co. v. United States, 332 U.S. 392 (1947).
32. Public Health Service Act §1531(7), *as amended.*
33. Public Health Service Act §1527(e)(1)(B), *as amended.*
34. Conn, "Clinical Laboratories," 298 *New Eng. J. Med.* 422 (1978).
35. *Id.* at 422–23.
36. P. Munch, *Economic Factors in the Use of Laboratory Tests by Office-Based Physicians* 61–62 (Rand Corp. 1980).
37. *Id.* at 61–64.
38. *See* Bailey, "From Professional Monopoly to Corporate Oligopoly: The Clinical Laboratory Industry in Transition," 15 *Med. Care* 129 (1977).
39. H.R. Rep. No. 96-190, *supra* note 16, at 75.
40. *Id.* at 53.
41. 42 Fed. Reg. 4002, 4006 (1977).
42. *Id.* at 4024.
43. *Id.* at 4006.
44. 45 Fed. Reg. 69,745 (1980) (to be codified in 42 C.F.R. § 123.401).
45. *See* Iglehart, "The Cost and Regulation of Medical Technology: Future Policy Directions," 55 *Milbank Mem. Fund Q.* 25, 30–35 (1977).
46. H.R. Rep. No. 96-190, *supra* note 16, at 52–53.
47. *E.g.,* Hawaii, Minnesota, Nebraska, and New Hampshire.
48. V. Fuchs & M. Kramer, *Determinants of Expenditures for Physicians' Services in the United States 1948-68* (Department of Health, Education and Welfare Pub. No. HSM 73–3013, 1972).
49. *E.g.,* Schwartz, Newhouse, Bennett, & Williams, "The Changing Geographic Distribution of Board-Certified Physicians," 303 *New Eng. J. Med.* 1032 (1980).
50. *See* Fein, "On Achieving Access and Equity in Health Care," in *Economic Aspects of Health Care* 23, 44 (J. McKinlay ed. 1975).
51. For such a proposal, see Tierney, Waters, & Williams, "Controlling Physician Supply through Certificate of Need," 6 *Am. J.L. & Med.* 335 (1980).

8 HMOs AND THE HEALTH PLANNERS
A Case Study in Regulatory Protectionism and Its Eradication[1]

Appearing in health policy discussions for the first time around 1970,[2] the HMO concept has been a recurrent theme ever since. Although this theme has never been altogether harmonious with the parallel theme of health planning, the clash of policies became audible only when HMOs began to encounter difficulties in obtaining certificates of need from the health care system's planner-regulators. These discordant notes, echoing in the halls of Congress, led in turn to the inclusion in the 1979 amendments to Public Law 93–641 of provisions that significantly limited the planner-regulators' authority over HMOs.[3] This chapter examines the conflict that developed between HMOs, as important vehicles for introducing competition in the health services industry, and the health planning and regulatory movement, which has tended to view competition only as a problem, not as a solution. This study of anticompetitive regulation will be helpful in understanding two problems that the 1979 amendments sought to overcome—first, the particular difficulties that HMOs encountered and, second, the general problem of regulation that gives inadequate weight to competition as a value.

HMOs contract with consumers to provide, as needed and for a fixed premium paid in advance, a defined, comprehensive set of medical and hospital services. They are deemed to have many

213

advantages over traditional fee-for-service medicine, particularly as it is currently paid for by third-party insurers, service plans, and government.[4] Many observers, including the draftsmen of the federal Health Maintenance Organization Act of 1973,[5] have viewed the HMO as a model system for efficiently financing and delivering health care that government should promote for its own sake.[6] An increasing number of other observers view HMOs, not as a necessarily better organizational mode, but as the most tangible and familiar vehicle for introducing meaningful competition into the health care industry and for putting pressure on traditional financing and delivery mechanisms to be more cost-effective.[7] It is this view of HMOs that is relevant to this discussion of anticompetitive regulation. Not all entities generally classified as HMOs are equally promising from the competition advocates' viewpoint, however. The discussion here focuses on HMOs that are independent of the dominant provider interests in their respective markets and thus embody a competitive threat to, rather than a defensive reaction by,[8] established providers.

HMO EXPERIENCE UNDER CERTIFICATE-OF-NEED LAWS

Whereas HMOs are vehicles of change in the health care system, certificate-of-need laws were conceived primarily to retard change, which was thought to be too haphazard, too uncontrolled, and, above all, too costly. Although not intended to stop all change, the regulatory mechanisms employed to administer certificate-of-need laws may not be fully capable of distinguishing between those changes that are desirable and those that are not. One possibility is that the political environment may cause regulatory and planning decisions to reflect special interests, particularly the interests of established providers fearful of competition. But even without domination by provider interests, regulators may have other reasons for being reluctant to admit innovative providers of a service to a market or to grant them the right to grow in their own way.

Why Regulators Might Resist HMO Initiatives[9]

HMO initiatives usually pose problems for incumbent providers, and these problems could easily induce sympathy on the part of the regulatory authorities. As happens with new entrants in other regulated industries, HMO competition can jeopardize the financial stability of existing providers, particularly hospitals. Because HMOs use hospitals less intensively than fee-for-service providers, an immediate effect on hospital occupancy rates could be anticipated. If a hospital is not financially secure, the threat could be quite substantial, and a convincing case could frequently be made for excluding the HMO altogether or tailoring its operation in such a way as to reduce its competitive impact.

Even if the planner-regulators feel no attachment for the institution as such, they might feel an obligation to the population it serves. Only if the community is clearly "overbedded" will the planners be comfortable in allowing an HMO to drive an existing hospital into bankruptcy, and, even then, strong community interests represented on the HSA board might support the institution and combine with provider interests to defeat, delay, or frustrate the HMO application. With such pressures at work, planner-regulators would be tempted to accommodate them by imposing conditions on the HMO's entry. For example, the HMO might be forced to reach an agreement to use the threatened hospital's beds and to pay an excessive rate, reducing the HMO's competitive impact and denying it the chance to negotiate a better deal or to obtain more satisfactory hospital services elsewhere.

Another set of expedient arguments for minimizing the competitive impact of a new HMO would be brought into play by the charge that the HMO is "cream skimming." By diverting insured patients from hospitals to outpatient care, the HMO removes an important source of the revenue needed by hospitals to provide unremunerative services to groups not covered by the HMO. Because internal cross-subsidization is common in hospitals, some valued services might have to be discontinued if revenue sources are eroded. If so, there would certainly be sentiment in the community for excluding the HMO, requiring it to replace the hospital's lost revenues, or compelling it to serve at a loss the underinsured population whose needs the hospital was meeting. Again, protectionist destruction of the HMO's competitiveness would seem justified to many, though some of those advancing the arguments would have other reasons for wishing to see the HMO's impact curbed.

While the foregoing grounds for preventing or limiting competition are essentially the same justifications that have been offered for similar anti-innovation policies in other regulated industries, another consideration seemingly justifying protectionism is peculiar to the health care sector. This is the so-called Roemer effect, the alleged tendency of the medical community to make use of available hospital beds even if the hospitalized patients could be treated equally well and at a lower cost as outpatients.[10] An HMO's appearance in a community could spread fear of the Roemer effect among health sector planner-regulators, who might easily see the HMO's primary strength—its ability to substitute outpatient for inpatient care—as creating a cost-escalating vacuum in the fee-for-service sector's beds. Hospitals might well be induced to make up for HMO-induced revenue losses by increasing the volume of services, and regulators, fearing this effect, might feel justified in penalizing the HMO for the fundamental defects in the fee-for-service system that permit the Roemer effect to occur. If so, they could perpetrate a colossal catch 22, treating the HMO's greatest strength as the fault warranting either its exclusion from the market or the extraction of its competitive teeth.

The problems that HMOs could expect to encounter in applying for a certificate of need are apparent in the planner-regulators' common perception that it is discriminatory to approve an HMO application in circumstances where a fee-for-service provider's similar application would be denied. This perception results in large part from the planners' fixation on the supply of beds or other facilities or equipment and the planners' inability to value the HMO for its different incentives and for the dynamic impact that it might have. No clearer example could be found of the high value that regulators place on appearing evenhanded in their dealings with regulated interests, even when evenhandedness requires that they shrink from distinctions based on efficiency and on differential ability to serve the public.

Beguiling arguments for curbing HMO competition might, of course, be resisted by health system planners and regulators out of a clear-sighted recognition that the short-run costs of HMOs will be outweighed by their long-run advantages.[11] But regulators of other industries have not been dependably clear-sighted in comparable circumstances, and the arguments that can be advanced against competition are not palpably foolish. Indeed, they have a potentially strong appeal to planners, who as a group tend to seek certainty and tight control over events and to abhor the unpredictable and uncontrolled processes of working markets. Moreover, the arguments would supply a superficially plausible rationalization for yielding to powerful interests.

It bears added emphasis that regulatory discrimination against HMOs may take forms other than outright denial of a certificate of need. Probably the more realistic concern is that conditions imposed on an HMO to protect existing interests against its full competitive impact would deprive the HMO of some of its market opportunities and competitive effectiveness. Regulators might see their function as mediating the terms of HMO entry into the market—a form of regulatory protectionism that has often appeared in other industries.

The Evidence Concerning Regulatory Discrimination Against HMOs

Evidence of actual regulatory obstructions to HMO development prior to the 1979 amendments has confirmed to some extent the predictions based on other regulatory experience. Although many health system planners and regulators have been receptive to HMOs, it appears that some HMOs have encountered significant problems. No attempt has been made here to collect and verify all the anecdotal evidence, but congressional hearings in 1978 provided glimpses into the difficulties that some HMOs have faced. More recent studies confirm the impression that regulatory obstacles to HMO development have been significant.

Congressional testimony by the AFL-CIO revealed twelve examples of HMOs that were blocked at least temporarily by local planning agencies.[12] The several case studies briefly presented in the congressional hearing suggested that providers used the HSA as a forum for opposing HMOs and spreading misinformation about them. HSA consumer members and staff appeared not to provide an effective counterbalance to the provider bias, since the consumer members and staff were frequently ignorant or had an agenda of their own. Thus, one plan was rejected because it would not locate close to a needy low-income population, reflecting both the HSA's desire to use the plan as a vehicle for cross-subsidization of services and its disinterest in encouraging competition for the right to serve self-supporting consumers.[13] In one instance where the possibility of having two HMOs in a single area was presented, the HSA was reported to have rejected the idea automatically, turning down the second HMO applicant on the ground of duplication without regard to the possible desirability of competition. These examples revealed not only the difficulty of getting HSA members to see HMOs as infusing needed competition but also the futility of HSA review itself, which lacked penetration, reflected biases more than facts, and appeared to serve no useful purpose.

The AFL-CIO testimony listed, without details, four HMOs that encountered difficulty in the planning process and never became operational.[14] The other HMOs whose experience was recounted succeeded in getting the requisite approvals in due course. Similarly, the Kaiser Foundation Health Plan, Inc., the largest and most experienced HMO, was never ultimately turned down in any of its projects. Nevertheless, Kaiser and other plans argue that delays and interruptions in scheduled expansions were costly and increased the uncertainties they faced. The fact that most HMOs and their projects were approved in the end may seem to make the HMOs' complaint less serious, but it also suggests that the trouble, delay, and costs incurred by both the HMOs and the planning agencies themselves were all for nought. Kaiser officials did not admit that their plans were significantly altered by the necessity for obtaining a certificate of need or other approval, and the AFL-CIO case studies revealed no constructive changes resulting from the planners' input.[15]

A few other examples of the ill effects of planning on HMO development can be cited. Even the respected certificate-of-need program in Massachusetts, which appears to have escaped provider influence, for a long time allowed its antipathy toward hospital growth to curb the ambition of the Harvard Community Health Plan to have its own hospital.[16] Unable to treat the HMO as a distinguishable case, the regulators put the plan in the position of having to use expensive university hospitals because community hospitals, under pressure from their medical staffs, would not grant admitting privileges to the HMO doctors. In this instance, the HMO's difficulties arose with the state agency and could not be overcome by appeal to a higher authority. This example best illustrates the problem with regulating hospital construction by HMOs. Older history of HMO hospital regulation reveals close votes or reversals of earlier turn-downs, confirming the fear that HMOs do indeed face at least harassment, delays, and higher costs.[17]

A questionnaire distributed in 1977 to HSA directors by the author also elicited evidence of HMO-HSA conflict, indicating that significant problems existed.[18] Of the twenty-six responding HSAs that had encountered applications of some kind from HMOs, seven reported recommending that the HMO application be denied and five of these indicated that their state agencies or other higher authority had concurred. Brief statements of reasons were requested, yielding evidence that in four cases lack of provider support was a factor, confirming concern that incumbent providers exert significant influence.

Questionnaire respondents were also asked whether the HSA (or its predecessor) had ever caused an application to be modified or imposed conditions on its approval. Thirteen of the twenty-six that had seen HMO applications answered yes, giving explanations that suggested accommodations with the interests of existing providers and that implied higher costs for the HMO.

A 1979 study by Brandon, Lee, and Segal (BLS)[19] reviewed two sets of survey data on the interaction between HMOs and planning agencies: their own data on closed-panel HMOs' perceptions of planning-agency impediments to their development of hospital resources and a major study by Analysis, Management and Planning, Inc. (AMPI)[20] of all regulatory responses to HMO proposals during a three-and-half-year period ending in 1978. The BLS data showed little more than that HMOs were apprehensive about planners' receptivity to their hospital-related proposals. This is a relevant fact if one proceeds from the assumption that, because HMO investments must pass a market test, any regulatory obstacle at all is unnecessary and a reflection of protectionist impulses. Since the ultimate issue is really the validity of this assumption, it should be no surprise that different observers arrive at different interpretations of the same data. In light of this chapter's conclusion that regulation of HMO investments serves a valid, though extremely limited, purpose, the findings of BLS are hard to evaluate. They do seem, however, to be cause for some concern.

The most interesting thing about the BLS paper is that the authors interpret the AMPI data differently than did AMPI itself. Discussing their different reading of the AMPI data, BLS stated that they "read the AMPI data to support the market reform arguments, whereas the AMPI researchers, who depended on health planners and regulators for their information, tend to downplay the hardship of regulation on HMOs. Perspectives differ . . . ."[21] Thus, the planning community, whose views AMPI would seem to reflect, would naturally accept the costs of regulation as a necessary evil and see the remedy for any unnecessary costs in better regulation, not in deregulation. The market advocate, on the other hand, is inclined to see so little value in erecting a barrier to HMO entry and investment that he perceives the AMPI finding that burdens were imposed on 30 percent of HMOs as evidence both that a large and avoidable cost is being incurred and that the true social cost of regulation, including its effect in discouraging entry and competitive aggressiveness, is considerably higher.

An unpublished study by Goldberg and Greenberg[22] used multivariate regression analysis of market data to determine that the development and growth of HMOs has not been correlated with the presence or absence of certificate-of-need laws. Given the necessarily small sample, the large number of variables affecting HMO growth, and the difficulty of controlling for all of them, one probably should not place much weight on this finding. Among the complicating factors that would render such a study unreliable is the probability that, before the federal requirement that HMOs be covered by state certificate-of-need laws was enacted, such coverage was most likely to exist in those states that had a greater potential for HMO development. Because the political pressure for such regulation would increase with the magnitude of the competitive threat, regulation and HMO growth could easily be found to coexist. In such circumstances, anecdotal and survey evidence seems more reliable than statistical analyses.

Another place to look for discrimination against HMOs or for systematic neglect of their competitive potential is in the state health plans that have emerged from the planning process. Prior to the 1979 planning amendments, few state health plans indicated any significant planning or regulatory commitment to HMO development or growth, let alone to the idea of competition. The AMPI study, collecting evidence as of 1978, reports that 41 percent of the HSAs had not addressed HMOs at all in their plans. Only 19 percent had assigned HMO development a high short-term priority.[23] Representatives of the Kaiser Foundation Health Plan have reported a surprising lack of interest in HMOs among California HSAs, despite the relatively large market share of HMOs in the state. Although the HSA for Orange County, California, wrote a chapter on HMOs in its plan and projected HMO enrollment growth, that plan was atypical. "The HSA staffs in the San Francisco Bay area had little desire to include the utilization data, costs, or experiences with planning offered by Kaiser."[24]

Elsewhere, the 1979 State Health Plan for Massachusetts was quite favorably disposed to HMO development[25] and even included language suggesting an openness to innovation that, despite countervailing considerations, might permit approval of HMO hospital construction.[26] Perhaps a more typical plan was the October 1978 draft of the HSA of Northern Virginia, widely regarded as an active and consumer-oriented agency. That draft had only a handful of references to HMOs in its 700 pages, mostly concerned with how the possible growth of plans in suburban Washington would affect utilization.[27] While the Northern Virginia HSA did not directly express interest in encouraging independent HMO growth, it did declare its intention to cooperate with local medical societies and physicians in developing IPAs.[28] In general, then, health planners and regulators, accustomed to perceiving their task as one of planning the dominant system, have been slow to adopt a favorable view of HMOs. Even when they have embraced HMOs, they have usually done so in terms assuring that HMOs will gain entry only insofar as they fit the plan and serve the planners' purposes. The idea that the market should be governed by consumer choice rather than the preferences of planners has yet to appear prominently in planning documents.

As the foregoing studies reveal, full evaluation of HMO experience with health planning-cum-regulation is difficult. Although useful information has been obtained by surveying existing HMOs, a complete view would also require information on HMOs that never got started due to regulation. One would also have to identify and assess the costs and benefits of changes in HMO behavior induced by the planner-regulators. Although only an intuitive assessment is possible, it would seem that some of the blame for the disappointingly slow development of HMOs should be assigned to certificate-of-need regulation that, if nothing else, substantially increased the number of bases that an HMO had to touch and the number of opposing interests that it had to satisfy. It remains to be seen whether the 1979 amendments relieving HMOs of some certificate-of-need requirements will improve their prospects.

FEDERAL LEGISLATION GOVERNING HMO DEVELOPMENT

Disregarding early warnings that regulating the market entry of HMOs might stifle their development and was in any event unnecessary, Congress decisively included HMOs within the ambit of its early regulatory moves. Indeed, HMOs were subjected to more extensive controls than fee-for-service providers. Although financing plans and provider organizations of other kinds could be established without government approval, establishment of an HMO was subject to planning agency review. Similarly, HMO outpatient facilities and services required certificates of need, even where comparable fee-for-service facilities did not. The history of subsequent legislation, however, has been one of gradual erosion of the planner-regulators' authority over HMOs. That history culminated in the 1979 planning amendments, which introduced certain exemptions for HMOs and recast the remaining regulation in a form that should prevent protectionism while serving other public objectives that have not previously been recognized as being at stake in HMO development.

The Law Prior to the 1979 Amendments

Health planner-regulators have exercised several types of authority over HMOs. Certificate-of-need authority, the main concern here, is exercised under state law, but Public Law 93–641, when it was adopted in 1974, bound the states to assert extensive regulatory power over HMOs. Throughout the rest of the 1970s until the 1979 amendments, the states were bringing their programs into line with this mandate. Section 1513(e) of Public Law 93–641 also charged HSAs with reviewing proposed uses of federal funds in their respective areas, and the advice of HSAs and state agencies to DHHS has presumably been influential in determining the flow of federal funds and loan guarantees to HMOs. Section 1122 of the Social Security Act, adopted in 1972, was the first federal law subjecting HMOs to the attention of planners.

In granting these powers, Congress indicated in several ways its desire that HMOs be favorably regarded by the planner-regulators. Section 1532(c)(8) of Public Law 93–641 directed planner-regulators to weigh "the special needs and circumstances" of HMOs qualified under the federal HMO Act. It also made development of HMOs, including those not so qualified, a "priority consideration." Likewise, section 1122 directed the secretary of DHEW to ignore a negative decision by a state planning agency and to allow Medicare or other federal reimbursement of HMO capital costs, if he believed that denial of reimbursement "would discourage the operation of . . . any [HMO, including an HMO not qualified under the federal act,] which has demonstrated to his satisfaction proof of capability to provide comprehensive health care services . . . efficiently, effectively and economically."

Later legislation put increasing emphasis on the planner-regulators' duty to foster HMO development and, in particular, on their responsibility not to indulge their protectionist proclivities. Thus, the 1976 amendments to the HMO Act of 1973 amended section 1532(c) of the planning law so as to insulate federally qualified HMOs from local prejudice by transferring from the state agencies and the HSAs to DHEW the primary responsibility for developing the criteria used in reviewing HMO applications. This same action also had the effect of transferring general responsibility for HMO criteria from the health planning program in DHEW to the more sympathetic HMO program. The conference committee report on this amendment stated that planning decisions should be made "on the basis of the need for HMOs and the need for their services for their enrolled members and reasonably anticipated new members and not on the need for the services in general if proposed by non-HMO providers."[29] It also underscored that cost and convenience to the HMO were the primary criteria to be used in weighing HMO applications for new facilities and services.

Subsequently, regulations under both the HMO Act[30] and the planning legislation, as amended,[31] and regulations governing reviews of proposed uses of federal funds[32] gave effect to the foregoing congressional concerns by requiring the state agencies and HSAs to consider only the needs of the HMO (in being or proposed) and its members (present or "reasonably anticipated"). Where the issue was whether an HMO should use available community resources in lieu of building its own, the only allowable considerations would be whether a five-year contract was available, whether the HMO could conveniently use its own personnel, and whether arrangements would be "administratively feasible" for the HMO and would "cost no more." The stated intention was that HMO applications not be judged "on the need for the services in general if proposed by non-HMO providers." Furthermore, HMO proposals were not to be rejected solely because another HMO already existed in the community. Although these regulations were clear in depriving the planner-regulators of available grounds for practicing protectionism at the expense of HMOs, they have benefited only those HMOs meeting the many detailed requirements of the federal HMO Act. Other HMOs apparently have been left to fend for themselves in a sometimes unfriendly environment.

The regulatory controls over HMOs were also relaxed under the 1122 program. Regulations under section 1122 included as a criterion for decisionmaking "whether the project will foster cost containment or improved quality of care ... through increased competition between different health services delivery systems."[33] The 1978 amendments to the HMO Act withdrew the special reference to HMOs in section 1122 and left HMOs subject to the same oversight as fee-for-service providers.[34] This meant that HMO establishments were no longer covered nor were HMO investments in outpatient facilities.

The 1979 Amendments

The main thrust of the foregoing legislative and regulatory changes was to curtail the discretion of planner-regulators with respect to HMO applications, not to limit their jurisdiction over HMOs. In 1979, however, Congress adopted a partial exemption strategy, eliminating state authority over some HMOs and limiting it over others. As to the planner-regulators' exercise of their remaining powers, Congress forcefully underscored the policy that had gradually emerged in the measures cited above—namely, that the agencies were not under any circumstances to reject HMO initiatives on protectionist grounds but were to confine themselves to another and much narrower set of concerns.

Congress's perception of HMO experience under planning and regulation was summed up in the Senate committee report on the 1979 amendments:

> The committee views with great concern a growing body of evidence that the planning process has seriously handicapped HMO development. Among the original purposes of the Health Planning Act was the encouragement of cost containment in the fee-for-service system through more efficient allocation and management of health care resources. In contrast to the fee-for-service system, health maintenance organizations contain internal cost containment incentives and have proved their ability to reduce health care costs. Despite this exceptional capacity to serve the overall goals of the planning process when allowed to operate properly, testimony before the committee revealed repeated instances of misunderstanding of the HMO concept and discrimination against HMO certificate-of-need applications at the HSA and State Agency levels. This evidence indicates that HMOs, because they compete with the fee-for-service system, are frequently given unobjective appraisals of CON applications by provider-dominated HSAs. This situation occurs particularly because HMOs are usually new entrants into an area and do not enjoy the presumptions benefitting the status quo under the planning process.
>
> The CON has been used to protect the status quo and thwart HMO development.[35]

Despite this strong statement, the Senate bill did not include a broad HMO exemption; instead, it would merely have limited the factors that planner-regulators could weigh in passing on HMO applications. In order to make the coverage of certificate-of-need laws consistent with section 1122 and to relieve HMOs of regulation where their fee-for-service counterparts are unregulated, the Senate bill would have prohibited the states from imposing certificate-of-need requirements on the establishment of new HMOs and on their introduction of certain new services and construction of outpatient facilities. As to HMO inpatient facilities and therapeutic and diagnostic equipment, the Senate bill would have provided special and highly favorable review criteria for HMOs qualified under the federal HMO legislation. The committee indicated, however, that it did "not intend to restrict HSAs and SHPDAs in their ability to give special CON consideration to other types of HMO's."[36]

The House bill went considerably further than the Senate bill in the direction of providing outright exemptions and indeed would have prohibited the states from imposing any significant certificate-of-need requirements on HMOs. Moreover, not only did the House bill make no distinction between federally qualified HMOs and other HMOs, it would have extended the exemption to any prepaid health plan whether or not included within any formal definition of HMO. The bill would also have exempted a proposed new facility or service of a non-HMO provider if an HMO or other prepaid plan had agreed to use the proposed facility or service for its subscribers and would provide at least 75 percent of the revenues from its use. The operative presumption was apparently that, because the prepaid plans were forced by competition to be responsive to consumer needs and cost concerns, their judgments of need, as reflected in their contracts with providers, could be accepted as an adequate demonstration of a true need. In an unprecedented statement of congressional acceptance of competition as a valuable force not limited to HMOs as traditionally defined, the House committee said:

> The committee in adopting this amendment intends to encourage organizations, groups, and individual providers providing a range of ambulatory and inpatient services on a prepaid basis. The development of such groups should offer consumers a choice between prepaid care and fee for service care and the committee wishes to encourage the competition between those systems of care that will develop.[37]

The far-reaching exemption in the House bill first appeared in what was called the "Gramm amendment," named after Representative Phil Gramm of Texas, an advocate of deregulation and of the introduction of market forces in the health care sector. The Gramm amendment took a firm position, consistent with the McClure exemption strategy discussed in Chapter 7, of exempting any new investment seemingly validated by the demand side of the market. Regulatory oversight would be dispensed with wherever an explicit and prospective purchasing decision was made by a financing entity serving a defined group of cost-conscious consumers who had chosen the plan in a competitive environment.

The Gramm amendment did not survive the House-Senate conference. The resulting legislation still retained, however, a broad HMO exemption. A total exemption from certificate-of-need requirements was provided for all HMOs having at least 50,000 subscribers, thus permitting such HMOs to construct hospital and other institutional facilities and to acquire diagnostic and therapeutic equipment without restraint. To qualify for the exemption, an HMO had only to establish that it met the membership requirement, (which is to be dropped in 1982), that its facility would be conveniently located for its members, and that 75 percent of the population to be served by the facility could reasonably be expected to be enrollees of the HMO.[38] An HMO could be exempt even if it was not federally qualified, and the applicable definition of HMO provided in section 1531(8) of the Public Health Service Act, as amended, was a broad one. The exemption also extends to facilities proposed by a non-HMO provider who has entered into a fifteen-year lease with an HMO for the use of the proposed facility.[39]

As to HMOs that are not exempt, states are to regulate only their acquisition of certain "major medical equipment" and certain capital expenditures undertaken by or on behalf of an HMO-owned inpatient facility.[40] The establishment of HMOs and their outpatient facilities is thus essentially exempt from coverage. Most important, planners and regulators are to apply special criteria when regulating nonexempt HMO services. These special criteria, drawn largely from the Senate bill and reflecting the earlier trend toward narrowed agency discretion, require the agencies to consult only the needs of the HMO subscribers (including new subscribers that the HMO can reasonably be expected to enroll), not to consider the effect of the HMO on incumbent providers, and to approve the proposal unless existing providers are willing to provide the needed services and facilities on reasonable terms.[41] The regulators oversight of even nonexempt HMO investments is thus sharply narrowed. The concluding section of this chapter looks in greater depth at their residual authority and the rationale for it.

Current Status of the 1122 Program and PUFF Reviews

The 1979 amendments affect only certificate-of-need regulation and leave unchanged section 1122 and agency review of proposed uses of federal funds—affectionately known as PUFF. In states having 1122 programs, HMOs must therefore still submit for review many expenditures that would be exempt from certificate-of-need requirements, and HMOs seeking startup funds under the HMO Act must submit to PUFF reviews, even though the establishment of the HMO per se is otherwise unregulated. Because DHHS, which is generally pro-HMO in its approach, must ultimately decide whether to accept agency recommendations based on both types of review, the urgency of reducing the agencies' role in reviewing HMOs for these purposes is perhaps not so great. Nevertheless, the cost and delay involved in presenting applications are not irrelevant considerations, and, if there is no need for certification of need, it is hard to see any necessity for the 1122 or PUFF review. Certainly the 1122 program and certification of need are so closely related and so parallel in their goals that the former's scope should be brought into line with the 1979 amendments. Indeed, this step is necessary to make the latter's exemption for HMOs meaningful in 1122 states.

PUFF reviews may often provide an occasion for rallying provider opposition to a fledgling HMO. Because it is not an antitrust violation for competitors to act collectively to influence governmental action in ways detrimental to a competitor, a PUFF review may easily serve as an umbrella for organizing opposition to the HMO, thus decreasing its prospects for obtaining needed cooperation from local providers. In general, it is hard to see any benefit from PUFF reviews of HMO funding, and some harms seem possible from turning federal funding for an HMO into a local political issue. Of course, the issue here is independent of the question whether government subsidies for HMOs are appropriate at all.[42]

REGULATORY POLICY TOWARD HMOs FOLLOWING THE 1979 AMENDMENTS

In the 1979 amendments, Congress went quite far toward exempting HMOs from certificate-of-need regulation and thus vindicating HMOs in their struggle against overregulation. Whereas Congress originally mandated that HMOs be covered by state certificate-of-need laws, it has now moved, in a substantial reversal, to grant a total exemption for the creation of new HMOs, for HMO construction of outpatient facilities, and for some other capital investments by HMOs. Such regulation as the states are required to retain over nonexempt HMO construction of inpatient facilities and aquisition of certain diagnostic and therapeutic equipment (such as CT scanners) is to be exercised in such a way that the HMO cannot be denied facilities that its members need. The remainder of this chapter attempts to capture the significance of these changes.

The End of Protectionism

Following the 1979 health planning amendments, every sign points to the conclusion that protectionism in the regulation of HMOs is illegitimate. Legally, Congress has left no room whatever for planner-regulators to restrain the development and growth of HMOs because of their probable impact on other providers or on costs in the fee-for-service sector (via the Roemer effect or otherwise). The message to the planner-regulators is that HMO competition, as such, must not be restrained for any reason, and the signal is clear enough that courts can be expected to enforce it. Thus, any suggestion of protectionism should be grounds for overturning a decision to deny a certificate of need to an HMO. The protectionist element need not be blatant nor the result of undue influence by established providers. Traditional planning dogma incorporates anticompetitive principles, and, though useful in regulating a failing market, these principles henceforth have no place in the regulation of HMOs.

An example of the protectionist outlook that should not be tolerated under the 1979 amendments appears in a 1976 study of ICF, Incorporated, entitled *Selected Use of Competition by Health Systems Agencies*.[43] Purporting to embody a liberal approach toward HMOs and competition, this study attempted to provide a quantitative rule of thumb for HSAs and state agencies to use in ruling on HMO applications for certificates of need. Recognizing the temptation for HSAs to be more concerned with short-term costs of "duplication" than with long-term benefits of competition, it proposed a standard whereby HSAs could determine when the latter outweighed the former. Because the ICF study is likely to be heavily relied on by planner-regulators seeking to comply with the procompetitive thrust of the 1979 amendments and because it is an inappropriate guide to such compliance, extended comment is required.

Although it was meant to show the value of HMO competition, the ICF study's quantification effort was essentially misleading since, in attempting to make an irrefutable case, it adopted conservative measures of benefits and costs and thus understated the probable value of HMOs. In addition to passing over the possibility that HMO competition would stimulate cost containment in the fee-for-service sector, the study overstated short-run costs of duplication by assuming that all the costs of obsolete capital investments would be borne by the public, not privately. Moreover, assumptions about the minimum efficient size of HMOs were based on arbitrarily restrictive conceptions, primarily the conception in the federal HMO Act. In general, the study did not present the strongest case for allowing HMO competition to develop without regulatory restraint. It could even have harmed the cause of HMOs and competition if those HSAs and state agencies that were already favorably inclined to HMOs accepted the implied invitation to require them to justify themselves in quantitative terms before they could be admitted to the market.

Although the ICF study was a somewhat progressive effort when it was undertaken in 1976, its regulatory approach would be forbidden under the 1979 amendments. Those amendments absolutely bar planner-regulators from weighing the impact of HMO competition on the system as a whole and from balancing the system's interests against the interests of HMOs and their subscribers. Since such weighing and balancing were the whole point of the ICF exercise, any reliance on that study today would be misplaced. Like the salutary antitrust principle requiring courts to refrain from making the essentially legislative judgment whether a particular restraint of trade has had good or bad effects, the new regulatory rule on HMOs would appear to be that their competition should be fostered, for better or for worse. That Congress has embraced competition so wholeheartedly in this context and rejected protectionism so totally is another crucial sign that the entire thrust of health sector regulation has been redirected.

The End of Regulation

The question then remains: Why regulate HMOs at all? An answer to this question and a set of principles for carrying out such regulation in the future can be gleaned from the legislative history of the HMO exemption and the abortive Gramm amendment. The exemption itself reveals congressional acceptance of the argument that market forces can be relied on to allocate resources where patients are choosing in a competitive setting with all the costs in view and providers are at risk for creating excess capacity. This crucial principle has potentially wider application—to any discrete service, not just to delivery systems like HMOs—and is, as Part III shows, the key to market-oriented regulation under the new procompetition language in the 1979 amendments. As innovation in financing plans (not only in the form of HMOs but in third-party plans as well) and increasing competition among such plans permit the demand side of the market to discipline the supply side and discourage inappropriate investments, the appropriateness of command-and-control regulation will diminish. The HMO exemption in the 1979 amendments reflects a congressional judgment that certain plans under certain circumstances can be conclusively presumed to satisfy the conditions necessary for the market to function. As to all other health services, no such presumption is possible. Nevertheless, under the procompetition language the planner-regulators are to judge the market's ability to allocate particular types of resources by assessing demand-side cost consciousness and the degree of risk borne by providers.

It might be argued that the rejection of the far-reaching Gramm amendment, which would have exempted all investments made by, or under contracts with, prepaid providers, signifies a less than total willingness on the part of Congress to embrace the ideal of unregulated competition among market-sensitive health plans. Close examination of the Gramm amendment's legislative history reveals, however, that Congress curtailed the sweeping exemption for another reason, not because of any reluctance to accept market forces as the ultimate regulator of supply. The specific concern that prompted the conference revision appears to have been that the Gramm amendment could have been used as a loophole whereby a sham HMO, by entering into a contract with a party wishing to build a hospital, could confer an exemption on that party, even though the HMO would not in fact be able to follow through on its contract and actually use the hospital to the extent contemplated. The concern was a valid one, for, once a hospital was built under the exemption and turned out to serve few HMO subscribers, it would be available for use by the remainder of the community, thus possibly contributing to an excess of hospital beds and further cost escalation. The draftsmen's solution was to add the requirement that an HMO qualifying for the exemption have at least 50,000 subscribers, thus assuring that it was bona fide and could be relied on to use the facility in question. That this was the concern that prompted the backing off from the Gramm amendment appears in Senator Kennedy's stated concern that, "if you're going to call it a duck, it really is a duck."[44]

The conference committee, in trying to close the loophole, appears to have identified a true market failure that warrants precisely the form of regulation that it preserved in cutting back the Gramm amendment. The problem is essentially the one that the conference committee identified, though it is broader than the concern that a sham or conscious evasion might sometimes be involved. The true problem is that HMO managers are unlikely to be sufficiently deterred by market forces from creating excess physical capacity. This possible tendency to overbuild, though not as pronounced as that of their fee-for-service counterparts, occurs for precisely the same reason: because their risks of loss are reduced by the prospect that any facilities that prove unnecessary to the HMO can always be marketed on a fee-for-service basis to patients having dysfunctional third-party coverage. In short, the same rationale that currently justifies supply-side entry and investment controls over fee-for-service providers applies. Government can be legitimately concerned that facilities installed, even in good faith, by an HMO today may become a burden on the public in the future.

It is therefore possible to question the House committee's justification for the broad Gramm exemption—namely, its "belief that the supply of [HMO] services would not be excessive if they were not regulated and that market forces of supply and demand may appropriately allocate them."[45] This statement is unsound insofar as it refers to the physical assets of HMOs since it neglects the limited extent to which the usual rationale for certificate-of-need laws applies to HMO investments in such facilities. It is true that, unlike nonprofit hospital managements, HMO administrators usually do not regard facility growth as a means of gaining prestige or as an end in itself. Furthermore, they usually will not be under pressure from physicians to expand facilities beyond the needs of patients. Nevertheless, HMO managements, in planning their capital facilities, may be too optimistic about the growth potential of their plans or their staying power. Not only might their natural enthusiasm and ideological commitment incline them this way, but the availability of subsidies and the nonprofit character of the typical plan may make them inadequately concerned about conserving capital. When these factors are combined with the serious weakness of the market sanction for overexpanding, it can be seen that HMO managers lack the appropriate incentives to be cautious in making their projections. Thus, although the rationale for regulation of physical growth and capital investment is significantly weaker than the rationale for supply-side controls in the fee-for-service sector, there would appear to be a legitimate need for regulatory oversight in defense of those who would bear the capital costs if the HMO overextended itself.

Regulation of HMOs under the 1979 amendments was designed precisely to address just this market failure. The basic exemption is conditioned on the receipt of assurances that HMO enrollees will comprise no less than 75 percent of the patients treated by the proposed facility—a hospital, for example. As to HMOs not qualifying for this exemption, the regulators' inquiry is likewise confined to assessing the risk that the facility will become a burden on the third-party financing system. The first criterion is whether the proposed facility "is required to meet the needs of the [HMO's] members and of the new members which [it] can reasonably be expected to enroll."[46] The statutory purpose here is by no means to place the planner-regulators in the position of second guessing the HMO management or to protect the HMO against managerial mistakes. Instead, the planner-regulators have been assigned the important, but distinctly limited, job of assuring that the HMO's management is not implicitly relying on the dysfunctional third-party payment system to bail it out in case its rosy enrollment projections are not achieved.[47] In this narrow respect—and only in this respect—the public has a legitimate stake in HMO decisions, and it will continue to have such a stake as long as—but only as long as—payment mechanisms in the third-party-financed system invite rather than deter excessive investment.

The only other criterion that Congress will permit planners and regulators to use in reviewing HMO certificate-of-need applications is whether the HMO can contract for the desired services or facilities in the fee-for-service sector. The planner-regulators are authorized to turn down the HMO application if the HMO can obtain the needed services (1) on a long-term basis, (2) using its own personnel, and (3) "in a reasonable and cost-effective manner which is consistent with [its] basic method of operation."[48] In general, the planner-regulators should approach this issue in the manner indicated in the earlier regulations; that is, their inquiry should be confined to whether a five-year contract is available and whether certain other conditions involving cost and convenience to the HMO are satisfied. The purpose here is simply to discourage an HMO from building new facilities that might ultimately burden the public when a satisfactory arrangement entailing no new capital investment could be made with the fee-for-service sector. While it may be seen as an additional advantage of this requirement that facilities that would otherwise be unused will find a use, this should be regarded as an incidental benefit, not as the primary objective. The sole regulatory focus should be on the HMO's convenience and needs and on whether its preference for developing its own facilities depends on the weak market sanction for any mistakes it might make in projecting its needs. Systemwide considerations have been excluded, except to the limited extent that the HMO can be fairly asked not to expose the system to potential burdens if the added cost to it of buying in the exisiting market is not appreciable.

Granting HMOs a broad right to build new facilities, subject to only limited regulatory control, has important and revealing implications. Take, for example, the effect of eliminating or liberalizing the restrictions on an HMO's right to build its own hospital. Planner-regulators have previously regarded HMO applications for hospitals with great suspicion. They have been concerned not only about the Roemer effect's driving up utilization in the fee-for-service sector as patients are transferred to the HMO's "unneeded" hospital, but also about the costs of obsolete fee-for-service capacity being borne, under various reimbursement formulas, by the public and not by the affected institutions. These concerns, which amounted to penalizing HMOs for the faults of the fee-for-service system, have always been questionable because they lead to protectionist regulation. The wisdom of the new approach is fully apparent, however, only if one appreciates the dynamics of a market in which such protectionist concerns cannot be implemented and more efficient competitors are thus allowed to grow at the expense of the less efficient. Some thoughts on these dynamics should be illuminating.

With liberal entry and investment regulation, an HMO's own presence as a viable competitor capable of rapid growth will itself supply a check on the fee-for-service sector's ability to generate new costs, since higher costs will drive more patients to the HMO. The strengthening of the HMO's capacity to compete thus supplies a strong incentive for third parties to institute, and for providers to accept, such competition-stimulating reforms as fee schedules, provider participation agreements, and effective utilization review. These potential benefits of removing systemwide considerations as a basis for restraints on HMO growth are difficult to quantify, but they are at the heart of the emerging market-oriented reform strategy.

On a less speculative level, the potential benefits of allowing HMOs freedom to invest can be seen in its predictable effect on interactions between HMOs and the fee-for-service sector. With a virtually unrestricted option to build its own facility, an HMO should find its bargaining power vis-a-vis existing hospitals enhanced, as the latter suddenly confront potential competition that they had previously counted on the planner-regulators to suppress. Thus, by virtue of its new ability to integrate backward into the hospital field, an HMO could reasonably hope to obtain concessions from a monopolistic hospital, or to break down a hospital or physician conspiracy formed to prevent the HMO from negotiating favorable terms, or to persuade a marginal institution to sell its facility to the HMO. It is a striking, and crucially important, paradox that granting HMOs a virtual exemption to create new capital facilities is likely to produce, not new construction, but better and more efficient use of existing facilities. In short, the power to provide one's own resources confers the power to negotiate effectively with the existing institutions and is thus the key to stimulating price and cost-saving competition at the crucial interface between competing health plans and providers.

In the last analysis, the market strategy requires that providers be forced ultimately into selling their services on a competitive basis to competing health plans, and HMOs can serve as the entering wedge in breaking down the barriers to establishing contractual relationships between plans and providers—physicians, hospitals, and others. Chapter 12 proposes a regulatory strategy, relying on the dynamic quality of the exemption approach examined here, to achieve this restoration of competition throughout the fee-for-service sector and to give third-party payers and new types of service-benefit plans, at long last, the chance to act effectively as their subscribers' purchasing agents and not as passive conduits through which consumer money flows to providers.

The full significance of the HMO exemption in the 1979 amendments can be appreciated only be recognizing that Congress did not stop with that procompetition step. Instead, it also went out of its way to charge the planner-regulators to exercise their regulatory powers in the rest of the market with a procompetitive and deregulatory thrust. Perhaps the best model we have for the regulatory approach that Congress wants the planner-regulators to adopt is that which Congress itself employed in addressing HMOs.

NOTES

1. Major portions of this chapter are adapted from Havighurst, "Health Maintenance Organizations and the Health Planners," 1978 *Utah L. Rev.* 123. Some material and documentation in that article are omitted or summarized here.
2. *See* P. Ellwood *et al.*, *The Health Maintenance Strategy* (Institute for Interdisciplinary Studies 1970).
3. Pub. L. No. 96–79, §117(a), *adding* Public Health Service Act §1527(b).
4. *See, e.g.*, Institute of Medicine, *Health Maintenance Organizations: Toward a Fair Market Test* 8–14 (1974); Luft, "How Do Health Maintenance Organizations Achieve Their 'Savings'?" 298 *New Eng. J. Med.* 1336 (1978); Luft, "HMOs, Competition, Cost Containment, and National Health Insurance," in *National Health*

Insurance: What Now, What Later, What Never? 283 (M. Pauly ed. 1980).

5. 42 U.S.C. §300e *et seq.* (Supp. III 1979).

6. The HMO Act's extensive regulatory provisions reflected a predominant focus on HMOs as an ideal instrumentality. *See* Havighurst, *supra* note 1, at 130–31; Institute of Medicine, *supra* note 4. The law disappointed expectations partly because of this orientation. *See* Starr, "The Undelivered Health System," 42 *Pub. Interest* 66 (1976).

7. *E.g.,* L. Goldberg & W. Greenberg, *The Health Maintenance Organization and Its Effects on Competition* (Federal Trade Commission, 1977); Enthoven, "Competition of Alternative Health Care Delivery Systems," in Federal Trade Commission, Bureau of Economics, *Competition in the Health Care Sector: Past, Present, and Future* 322, 335–36 (W. Greenberg ed. 1978); Christianson & McClure, "Competition in the Delivery of Medical Care," 301 *New Eng. J. Med.* 812 (1979); Havighurst & Bovbjerg, "Professional Standards Review Organizations and Health Maintenance Organizations: Are They Compatible?" 1975 *Utah L. Rev.* 381, 411.

8. Antitrust questions have been raised with respect to profession-controlled "individual practice associations," which are a component of one variety of HMO. *See* Federal Trade Commission, Bureau of Competition, *Medical Participation in Control of Blue Shield and Certain Other Open-Panel Medical Prepayment Plans* 273–307 (1979); Havighurst & Hackbarth, "Enforcing the Rules of Free Enterprise in an Imperfect Market: The Case of Individual Practice Associations," in *A New Approach to the Economics of Health Care* (M. Olson ed.) (in press).

9. *See* Havighurst, "Regulation of Health Facilities and Services by 'Certificate of Need'," 59 *Va. L. Rev.* 1143, 1204–15 (1973). This reference develops in somewhat greater detail the arguments set forth here.

10. The responsiveness of the demand for hospital services to bed supply was first noted in M. Roemer & M. Shain, *Hospital Utilization under Insurance* (AHA Hospital Monograph Series No. 6, 1959); *see also* Roemer & Shain, "Hospital Costs Relate to the Supply of Beds," *Modern Hospital,* April 1959, at 71.

11. *See, e.g.,* ICF, Inc., *Selected Use of Competition by Health Systems Agencies* (1976).

12. *Hearings on S. 2534 before the Subcomm. on Health and Scientific Research of the Senate Comm. on Human Resources,* 95th Cong., 2d Sess. (1978) (statement of the AFL-CIO). Brief case studies were included covering the experience of HMOs in Prince Georges

County, Md.; New Brunswick, N.J.; Lincoln, Neb.; Baton Rouge, La.; El Paso, Tex.; Greendale, Wis.; Amherst, Mass.; and Buffalo, N.Y. On the New Brunswick experience, revealing in depth the physicians' opposition and its effectiveness, see Kirchner, "Where Fee-For-Service Is under the Gun," *Med. Econ.*, Aug. 8, 1977, at 230.

13.   One HMO director was quoted as saying that consumer members had a "strong social agenda of their own. They could not accept any intrinsic value in an organization that valued fiscal solvency or saw its role as different from serving the poor as its top priority." *Hearings, supra* note 12.

14.   The HMOs were located at Windsor, Conn.; Pascagoula, Miss.; San Antonio, Tex.; and Miles City, Mont. *Id.*

15.   Kaiser's testimony in favor of limiting HSA jurisdiction over HMOs did not dwell on its own experience. *See id.* (statment by James A. Lane, vice president and counsel, Kaiser Foundation Health Plan, Inc.)

16.   Based on the author's conversations with officials of the plan and the Massachusetts Department of Public Health.

17.   *See* Havighurst, *supra* note 9, at 1209 n.217.

18.   All 198 HSAs then in existence were sent questionnaires; sixty-three questionnaires were returned. The survey was not scientifically designed or pretested. For the specific results, see Havighurst, *supra* note 1, at 145–47.

19.   Brandon, Lee, & Segal, "Testing the Anti-Regulatory Arguments of the Market Reformers: New Data on the HMO-HSA Relationship," 2 *J. Health & Human Resources Admin.* 391 (1980).

20.   Analysis, Management & Planning, Inc., "Executive Summary—Evaluation of the Impact of Planning Agency Review Actions and Decisions on Health Maintenance Organization Development" (unpublished paper, July 9, 1979).

21.   Brandon *et al., supra* note 19, at 422.

22.   L. Goldberg & W. Greenberg, "The Determinants of HMO Enrollment and Growth" (unpublished paper, 1979).

23.   Analysis, Management & Planning, Inc., *supra* note 20, at 4–5.

24.   Harm, "HMOs and HSAs," in *Management and Policy Issues in HMO Development* 55, 56 (Group Health Institute, 1979).

25.   Office of State Health Planning, Massachusetts Dep't of Public Health, *1979 State Health Plan* 286–89, 365–67 (1979).

26.   *Id.* at 419.

27.   Health Systems Agency of Northern Virginia, *Draft Health Systems Plan/Annual Implementation Plan* (1978).

28.   *Id.* at 231.

29. H.R. Rep. No. 94–1513, 94th Cong., 2d Sess. 37 (1976).

30. 42 C.F.R. §110.204(a) (1980).

31. 42 C.F.R. §122.310(b) (1980) (HSA review of new institutional health services); 42 C.F.R. §123.411(b) (1980) (state agency review of new institutional health services).

32. 42 C.F.R. §122.412(a)(10) (1980).

33. 42 C.F.R. §100.107(d) (1980).

34. Pub. L. No. 95–559, §14(b), 92 Stat. 2141 (1978) (codified in 42 U.S.C. §1320a-1 (Supp. III 1979)).

35. S. Rep. No. 96–96, 96th Cong., 2d Sess. 79–80 (1979).

36. *Id.* at 81.

37. H.R. Rep. No. 96–190, 96th Cong., 1st Sess. 81 (1979).

38. Pub. L. No. 96–79, §117(a), *adding* Public Health Service Act §1527(b)(1)(A). Legislation in 1981 provided for lifting the 50,000-subscriber requirement on October 1, 1982. Pub. L. No. 97–35, §949(c), (d), 95 Stat. 578 (1981), *amending* Public Health Service Act §1527(b)(1). This change went far toward adopting the substance of the Gramm amendment.

39. Pub. L. No. 96–79, §117(a), *adding* Public Health Service Act §1527(b)(1)(C).

40. Pub. L. No. 96–79, §117(a), *adding* Public Health Service Act §1527(b)(4).

41. Pub. L. No. 96–79, §117(a), *adding* Public Health Service Act §1527(b)(5).

42. The Omnibus Budget Reconciliation Act of 1981, Pub. L. No. 97–35, §§934(b), 941, 95 Stat. 571, 572–73 (to be codified in part in 42 U.S.C. §300e), reduced federal HMO subsidies and permitted waiver of HSA responsibility for reviewing proposed uses of federal funds.

43. *Supra* note 11.

44. "Health Planning Bill Awaits Final Congressional Action," 37 *Cong. Q.* 1920 (1979).

45. H.R. Rep. No. 96–190, *supra* note 37, at 53.

46. Pub. L. No. 96–79, §117(a), *adding* Public Health Service Act §1527(b)(5)(1).

47. Facilities built and equipment acquired under this special dispensation or pursuant to an exemption may not be sold or leased without obtaining a certificate of need or qualifying for an exemption. Pub. L. No. 96–79, §117(a), *adding* Public Health Service Act §1527(b)(3), (5).

48. Pub. L. No. 96–79, §117(a), *adding* Public Health Service Act §1527(b)(5)(2).

III COMPETITION ISSUES IN HEALTH PLANNING AND CERTIFICATION OF NEED

9 KEEPING COMPETITION IN VIEW IN PLANNING AND REGULATORY DECISIONS

However certificate-of-need laws are drafted and whatever their coverage, the administration of such laws has fateful implications for competition. Freedom of market entry is regarded by most economists as the best protection against the depredations of monopolists and cartels. Not only do new entrants into the market frequently bring with them innovative products, services, and organizational forms, but the threat of their appearance stimulates incumbent firms to serve consumers well and to anticipate their future needs. On the other hand, many of the worst regulatory misdeeds have involved protectionist restrictions on the development of new and more efficient services. No student of the regulated industries can view certificate-of-need laws—even Utah's "procompetitive" one—as anything but an invitation to eliminate useful competition.

The 1979 procompetition amendments to Public Law 93–641 represented a significant attempt to counter the anticompetitive tendencies of certificate-of-need regulation by clarifying the federal mandate to local health planners and state regulators. Nevertheless, the revised statutory directive is by no means a complete guarantee against abuse of regulatory powers, both because it can be narrowly interpreted and because regulators' behavior is hard to change in any event. It is thus necessary to hope that at least some planners and regulators will voluntarily pass up their numerous opportunities to suppress competition that they might usefully encourage. Part III is an appeal to planner-regulators to bear competitive principles in mind in their decisionmaking on specific health services. The general concepts expounded in this and the following three chapters are applied in a tentative analysis of particular services in Chapter 13. The principles developed and applied are, however, quite similar to those already employed in analyzing coverage issues in Chapters 7 and 8.

THE REGULATORY CHOICE BETWEEN LETTING THE MARKET DECIDE AND THE COMMAND-AND-CONTROL APPROACH

The thesis of Part III is that the health care system's planner-regulators, before exercising their jurisdiction to limit entry and restrict competition in a particular category of health services, should assess the affected market's actual and potential ability to allocate resources of the particular type involved. If competition appears to be a reasonably reliable social control mechanism under the circumstances, then regulation should foster rather than supplant it by command-and-control intervention. Wholehearted acceptance of this simple conceptualization of the regulators' task would greatly affect the regulatory agenda, the nature of health planning, the substance of many regulatory decisions, and, in the long run, the nature of the health care system. Whereas it is argued that the planner-regulators are now under a statutory duty to adopt this approach, this discussion is as much concerned with persuading planners of the approach's logic as with telling them how to fulfill their legal responsibilities.

In the administration of a health-planning and certificate-of-need program, judgments on the market's efficacy must, under current law, be explicit and supported by evidence and reasoned findings.[1] Such judgments may be reached either in a rule-making-type proceeding leading to the promulgation of a health systems plan (or state health plan) or on a case-by-case basis as particular services come up for detailed consideration. In either event, applicants for certificates of need and other interested parties should be given an opportunity to learn and to challenge the factual and other premises of these determinations. Because the public has a much greater stake in the fate of competition than in the fate of any single applicant, the issue is not simply the due process accorded the parties but the fullness of the consideration given to competitive values. While some courts may insist that competition be given a proper hearing under the new statutory mandate,[2] it will be unfortunate if the planner-regulators accept no more responsibility for competition than the courts force them to bear. Legal process, with its focus on the immediate parties and on their specific interests and self-serving arguments, cannot substitute for, and may even undercut, farsighted, imaginative planning in the public interest.

The natural tendency of many agencies, faced with this new statement of their regulatory function, will be to continue business as usual, claiming that they have always had due regard for competition's potential but have found it minimal in most instances. This chapter is meant to overcome this tendency both by challenging the conventional analysis that has caused command-and-control regulation generally to prosper at competition's expense and by explicating the 1979 amendments' requirement that competition be given a fair hearing. The overriding goal is to show the wisdom and the practical and legal significance of Congress's new signals to the planner-regulators.

Existing Market Forces as a Factor in Need Certification

An immediate issue in every decision concerning certification of need is, or should be, whether market forces sufficiently discourage, or do not unduly encourage, inappropriate investments and unneeded services. If market forces do not operate badly in these respects, then the certificate of need can usually be granted without further consideration, because competition and new market entry can reasonably be expected to induce efficiency, quality-of-care improvements, and responsiveness to consumer needs and preferences without seriously misallocating resources. Once competition is found to be efficacious, there are few countervailing factors strong enough to warrant its regulatory preemption.

While this analytical approach to certificate-of-need decisions is sound, the step of assessing the workability of competition has usually been omitted in the past. Presumably this has occurred because of an implicit assumption that the competitive market is universally incapable of determining need for any of the facilities or services covered by a certificate-of-need law. Nevertheless, although need is usually thought of as a function of medical, demographic, and geographic factors, a new facility or service might also be needed as a new competitive force in a particular market without regard to other circumstances. Nothing in the existing state statutes precludes interpreting the mandate of the certificate-of-need agencies to include an assessment of the need not for the facility or service as such but for competition. The 1979 amendments to Public Law 93–641 explicitly require such an assessment, and the congressional committee reports make clear that subjecting a new facility or service to a certificate-of-need requirement creates nothing stronger than a presumption, rebuttable in specific circumstances, that the market is not generally capable of allocating that category of resources efficiently.

Competition is, of course, too frequently used as a talisman in public debate, the suggestion being that anything curbing competition is automatically objectionable and that anything that goes on in free markets is ipso facto desirable. On the other hand, competition is also often passed over too quickly for a role in the future health care system on the basis that the health sector is a special case not following the textbook model or that the choice has been made to rely totally on regulation and to forget competition, which has been tried and has failed. But competition, properly understood, is a tool, not a talisman, and may indeed serve usefully in the structuring and operation of particular local markets for particular health services. Although health planners are now generally unaware of the part that competition can play, they can learn to recognize where competition can help, why it sometimes goes wrong, how it can be assisted to do what it can, and when it requires displacement.

The discussion in Chapter 4 established that competition is neither wholly good nor universally bad as a motivating and organizing force in the health services industry. Much turns on the specific circumstances affecting a particular service. Local factors will frequently have a substantial bearing on the state of competition and the feasibility of improving it. Some value judgments are also involved, and HSAs and state agencies may vary in their perceptions about the ethical and social implications of increased reliance on market forces, in their estimates of risks and benefits, and in their faith in alternative approaches. Despite the new federal mandates, the state and local agencies will continue to have fairly wide discretion in choosing a policy toward competition and may still be free, in some circumstances, to give it short shrift. Nevertheless, responsible regulators will make their choices on the basis of an open-minded analysis of market conditions. Chapters 11 and 12 are intended to suggest in some detail the techniques of such an analysis and the inputs it requires.

Can Regulators Face Competition Questions on Their Merits?

Successful regulation of entry in the health care sector requires a mixture of toughness and liberality. Toughness is required in saying no to proposals for desirable facilities and services that, even though they would survive and be heavily used in an unreliably competitive marketplace, seem unlikely to add more than a little to the quality or benefits of medical care—not enough to be worth their cost. On the other hand, liberality is required where, even though duplication of services seems a danger and apparent needs are already being met, a satisfactorily competitive market exists and incentives are not too badly distorted. But, while the need for these regulatory postures is clear, there is good reason to fear that politically exposed regulators in the health care sector will adopt precisely the opposite stance, being liberal toward new investments in unreliably competitive circumstances and tough in excluding promising competitive developments.

It should be obvious why, in a political world, regulation is more likely to restrain competition where it is helpful than where it is dysfunctional: Quite simply, prestigious institutions and established provider interests can be appeased by such policies and would be offended by any other. Thus, unless competition significantly threatens provider interests, political support for its suppression will be weak. Moreover, where third-party financing and cost reimbursement make it possible to gratify existing providers' natural growth impulses without causing appreciable harm to their competitors, the claims of "quality," "need," and "fairness" will be difficult for a few cost-conscious voices to contest. Unable in many cases to resist these claims and protectionist pressures, planner-regulators will be inclined to demonstrate their backbone and effectiveness by stamping out duplication where competition is most threatening to providers, perhaps precisely because it is likely to serve the public well. And, even if some successes are achieved in curbing investments by existing institutions, the hardships thus imposed can be compensated for by curbing competition from outsiders. Experience in other regulated industries underscores these fears, revealing the fundamental truth that protection from competition is the currency with which regulators purchase cooperation and peace from the regulated interests. In the cooperative and highly political enterprise that is health planning, the likelihood that this experience will be repeated seems great.

Of course, some of the reasons why regulatory agencies in other industries have frequently sacrificed desirable competition may have been, or can be, eliminated or ameliorated in structuring regulation of the health care industry. For example, steps can be taken to address the excessively political climate of decisionmaking, the regulators' special responsiveness and protectiveness toward their regulated constituency, the lack of consumer representation and cost consciousness in the regulatory process, the weakness of the planning component in the agencies, and the lack of precision in statutory mandates. But despite these possibilities for overcoming regulation's chronic insensitivity to competition's value, it is still far from certain that competition will receive a fair hearing or be viewed by health planner-regulators as a constructive instrument. Nevertheless, for purposes of this discussion, doubts on this score are set aside, and it is assumed that the planners and regulators are totally objective and that the sole obstacle to competition-sensitive regulation is their ignorance of how competition works or might work in this complex industry. The premise of the 1979 amendments would seem to be the same. It should not be forgotten, however, that this assumption of regulatory objectivity, while adopted *arguendo* here, is highly debatable and will remain so until regulatory experience reveals that health planners and regulators have developed a consistent capacity to help rather than hinder competition's emergence, wherever possible, as the ultimate regulator of health care costs and allocator of health resources.

The procompetition strategy should certainly not be based on the unrealistic hope that everyone in the health planning community can be persuaded or successfully instructed by law to change their belief that political decisions in which they participate are always better than private ones under the discipline of market forces. Instead, the expectation should be more modest, namely that at least a substantial minority of planning and regulatory agencies will recognize the greater potential of market forces for stimulating rapid and meaningful change and that, out of this minority's creative efforts to make the market function, will come new ways of organizing and paying for health services that will then be available for use in other markets and in public programs.

Deciding to Defer to Market Forces

If one adopts an ideal view of regulation, it is easy to see it as inevitably superior to the competitive marketplace. Regulation advocates can argue that the planner-regulators can avoid many of the adverse effects that poor information, ignorance, and income differentials inevitably bring about in unregulated markets. Nevertheless, regulators' supposed strengths are often illusory. In fact, the immense difficulty of implementing an ideal model of regulatory responsibility in a political milieu, of obtaining the data necessary to make the model work, and of making sound judgments on the myriad factual issues and value choices presented makes the regulatory ideal as irrelevant for practical purposes as the textbook model of the free market.

Regulators must learn to limit their interventions on pragmatic grounds. Such an approach would dictate that decisions should be left to the marketplace unless there is some substantial reason to expect market forces to miss the mark consistently and by a wide margin and to provide no incentives to correct any misallocations. The crucial judgment that the regulators must make in every case, with as much realism and objectivity as they can bring to bear, is whether their own processes or those of the market are more likely to have the comparative advantage in allocating resources of a particular kind. In making this judgment, they must strive to avoid the perennial trap of observing only the market's deficiencies in declaring that command-and-control regulation is required. Reference should be had not only to the economic theory of market failure but also to the accumulating and increasingly sophisticated literature on regulatory failure.[3]

Besides sometimes deferring to market forces on the basis of a careful assessment of the comparative advantages of an imperfect market and imperfect regulation, an agency might also sometimes decline to assume a command-and-control role simply because it has better things to do. Even believing that it might have something useful to contribute, the agency might still conclude that its limited resources would be better expended in other regulatory or nonregulatory activities than in making time-consuming but ultimately unreliable regulatory judgments on the need for some specific service. For example, nonregulatory efforts to strengthen the market's performance might be deemed a more productive use of agency energies than detailed review and comment on a certain set of inconsequential certificate-of-need applications.

If the analytical approach of comparing the ultimate allocative abilities of regulation and competition were carried to its logical conclusion, liberality toward entry by certain types of provider might sometimes be deemed desirable precisely because of the cost-escalating threat that such entry would pose. Such a threat of higher costs could sometimes be reasonably expected to stimulate consumers, employers, private health insurers, and others to take protective action against a proliferation of expensive overutilized services and could therefore be viewed as a desirable stimulus to innovation and the emergence of competitive forces. Some planner-regulators might construe their new legislative mandate as a charge not only to let such pressures build but also to undertake educational and other efforts to assure that the private sector will respond to them in appropriate ways. The private cost-containment actions thus stimulated would strengthen the market pressures bearing both on the providers of the service in question and on other private insurers, who would also have to take steps to address the cost problem. Even public programs could be regarded as capable of protecting themselves against pricing and utilization abuses by various means. Later discussion, particularly in Chapter 12, argues that planner-regulators should regard stimulation of reforms in the financing system by such strategies as an important responsibility. While controversial, this redefinition of the regulators' role opens up a pathway to measured introduction of market forces and to deregulation of local markets for health services. Whereas regulation usually inhibits change, this "market-forcing" strategy would stimulate it.

Thus, not only is it unnecessary that a regulatory decision to let the market allocate resources be based on a finding that market forces work infallibly, but it is not even necessary that the market have already demonstrated its capability to allocate the resources in question. It is enough that, considering the ultimate potential of both mechanisms of social control and the prospects for realizing these respective potentials in the health service area in a reasonable period of time with the resources available, the market seems the allocative mechanism of choice. Preconceptions of the market's potential based on how health care has been bought and paid for in the past must be reexamined in the light of new possibilities. The result to be avoided is regulatory intervention, designed in good faith to cure the symptoms of a past market failure, which has the inadvertent effect of preempting private sector developments that would address the problem more directly and with the benefit of the checks and balances that a working competitive market supplies.

THINKING CONCRETELY ABOUT MARKET FAILURE AS A RATIONALE FOR COMMAND-AND-CONTROL INTERVENTION

Certificate-of-need requirements are primarily a response to the distortions of the demand for medical care that are perceived to flow from the availability of third-party payment. While this general rationale has substantial validity, it does not finally establish the necessity for quantitative determinations of need with respect to every facility or service within the regulators' jurisdiction. In fact, many different circumstances surrounding a particular service and its financing may reduce the need for such command-and-control regulation, particularly if an adjustment for regulation's own shortcomings is made in the proregulation side of the regulatory balance. Before looking (in Chapter 11) at the specific characteristics of health services and their financing that affect the need for command-and-control regulation, it is important that the market failure to which regulation is ostensibly addressed be carefully examined.

The Problem: Not Third-Party Payment Itself, But Inadequacies in Its Design

There is a pervasive assumption that third-party payment is itself the market failure that necessitates governmental intervention and that, because third-party financing of some health care is inevitable, so is regulation. The underlying premise is that health insurance, though clearly needed to protect people against unpredictable costs, is so destructive of cost consciousness at the point of consumption that price competition becomes impossible, leaving only cost-escalating nonprice competition to operate. If the analysis stops here—with the recognition of what economists call "moral hazard," a costly phenomenon that is associated with insurance of all kinds—the case for intervention seems strong. But this is the point where analysis should begin, not end. Some brief observations concerning the forms that private cost containment might take will prepare the health system's planner-regulators to carry out their new task of determining whether operative incentives and the financing system in place with respect to particular services do or do not in fact foreclose useful competition among providers. This exposition of how the market's demand side could discipline the supply side may also guide health planners' efforts to strengthen market forces.[4]

Precisely because the moral hazard raises the cost of insuring against health care costs, one could reasonably expect that price competition would inspire cost-conscious health insurers to take countermeasures to limit in some way the discretion of providers and consumers to make contracts that commit the insurer's funds. Cost containment in an insurance plan is thus essentially an administrative problem to be solved in a competitive market by somehow accommodating all of the conflicting interests involved. As a conceptual matter, an insurance plan is not in the business of providing health services and can deal with costs only by varying its coverage—that is, its contractual commitment to pay particular expenses. By limiting its liability, the plan puts patients in the position of paying some of their own bills, thus restoring the usual market check on spending decisions. Although an ignorant patient must rely on his physician to consider his pocketbook in prescribing treatment, there is good reason to believe that physicians would indeed economize when to do so would be to the patient's advantage.[5] This results not only because of professional ethical behavior in a fiduciary capacity but also because, when the patient is paying the bills himself, competition induces intelligent economizing. In contrast, competition in the presence of unlimited third-party liability creates pressure for physicians to help patients take maximum advantage of the insurance fund. The overriding point is that market forces can operate without undue distortions even in the presence of third-party payment, simply by inducing selective coverage provisions in the insurance contract.

An insurer can design more cost-effective coverage by departing from automatic cost reimbursement either of providers for incurred operating costs or of insured patients for incurred charges. One way to do this is by drawing dollar lines. Approaches include imposing copayments and deductibles, establishing fixed benefits for certain services, and setting limits on what the insurer will pay in particular circumstances. In varying degrees, these approaches leave consumers conscious of the fees charged and the costs incurred. They thus provide some constraint on cost escalation without involving the insurer in direct oversight of medical decisions to incur costs.

As an alternative or additional strategy, a plan can limit its obligation to pay for particular services. A service might be excluded from coverage altogether because it is highly discretionary in particular cases and thus so prone to the effects of moral hazard that to insure against the need for it would be too costly. Yet another way of curbing patient-provider discretion would be for the insurer to agree to pay for a service only if certain conditions are met; one condition that might be imposed would be a requirement that the plan be given an opportunity to determine and advise the patient in advance of the extent of its contractual responsibility to pay for the hospitalization or treatment recommended. A plan might also use partial exclusions from coverage in the form of special cost-sharing requirements; these would make sense where the treatment's cost was high enough that some financial protection was needed but where the service was discretionary enough in some cases that a substantial financial deterrent was also desirable.

The strategies available to insurers would present administrative difficulties, and the costs of overcoming them would, in a competitive climate, be relevant to the decision to adopt particular measures. Nevertheless, where such techniques could be introduced at reasonable cost, consumers might find the lower premium to be advantageous even though it was coupled with greater exposure to certain risks. In order to make self-insurance of such risks more manageable and to prevent the patient's credit rating from standing in the way of treatment, an insurer could advance the needed funds, subject to repayment. In a competitive market, one would expect to find experimentation with cost-containment techniques and efforts to minimize the disadvantages of those techniques. As is regrettably not necessarily the case in government programs, ideas that do not satisfy consumer and provider needs and preferences will be dropped.

Explicit limitations of insurance coverage would often be difficult to administer without provider cooperation, and insurers could therefore be expected to enter into contractual understandings with providers. Under such participation agreements, providers might become obligated to disclose potential costs prospectively to the patient and to submit certain cases for predetermination of benefits. In a competitive world, some providers would accept such agreements, others would not. All providers would have a competitive incentive to accept such obligations, however, because they would thereby become more attractive to the plan's beneficiaries. An insurer might exclude services provided by nonparticipating physicians and hospitals from coverage altogether, or it might simply pay for their services on a less advantageous basis, perhaps reflecting the higher costs that their uncooperativeness creates for the plan as a whole.

The other generic type of cost-containment strategy that may be adopted in the private sector is the organization of alternative delivery systems. Instead of explicitly excluding certain services from coverage, a health plan might cover only services that were obtained from a closed panel of providers, such as a prepaid group practice, an individual practice association (IPA), or a health care alliance. Such alternative delivery systems integrate financing and delivery and obtain providers' economizing behavior through various internal management arrangements, such as direct employment, participation agreements governing prices and administrative requirements, internal peer review, or carefully designed incentive schemes. Without expressly limiting the services that will be paid for, such plans can achieve implicit coverage limitations by including in the closed panel only providers who accept the plan's controls and thus do not render or prescribe services that are perceived not to be worth their cost. Because decisions are made internally, consumers in such plans would never be confronted with hard choices about whether to spend their own money. Some consumers would regard this as a benefit, whereas others would undoubtedly prefer not to give up their freedom to choose their provider or to decide for themselves how much to spend on a specific health need. Thus, a competitive market is likely to feature health care plans of both basic types. Hybrid forms are also likely.

Like the use of explicit exclusions from coverage, use of the closed-panel model would be greatly facilitated by the use of provider participation agreements. Indeed, it would appear that such agreements are very nearly an essential feature of any health care plan that incorporates cost-containment measures. They are thus the sine qua non of a competitive system in which organized plans, competing among themselves to keep factor prices low, force providers into unwonted competition. It is possible, however, that an insurer, having identified a group of preferred providers—for example, a multispecialty group practice whose charges, efficiency, or style of practice give assurance of lower costs—might offer individual insureds a lower premium if they agree to confine their patronage to such providers. In this way, providers might be put at risk and forced into competition even without their consent. Perhaps other creative techniques might be developed, either for achieving cost containment without providers' voluntary participation or for inducing providers to cooperate even though they would prefer to go on as in the past.

While a sharp conceptual distinction can be drawn between insurance plans' manipulation of their benefit packages, on the one hand, and the close integration of financing and delivery in alternative delivery systems, on the other, the practical differences between these two approaches to cost containment are much less sharp. Thus, it is better to conceive of potential innovations in financing and delivery as lying along a spectrum between traditional insurance and service-benefit plans, on the one hand, and group-practice HMOs, on the other. Although nearly all types of cost-effective plans depend ultimately on provider cooperation and involvement, approaches vary in the degree to which the physician remains independent and accountable to the individual patient rather than the plan, the patient's chosen agent. There is no single mechanism that is clearly preferable to all others, and thus competition should be thought of simply as a dynamic process by which a variety of approaches are given a chance to show their worth. Despite the common propensity, it is a mistake to equate competition with any one organizational alternative, such as the HMO.

Competition among health plans is not a sufficient, though it is a necessary, condition for relying on competition to allocate resources in the public interest. The more problematical requirement is the existence of effective direct or indirect checks on providers' pricing and spending discretion, and this requirement can be met only if there is active bargaining over the terms on which provider cooperation and participation will be obtained. The crucial condition, then, is active competition in the bargaining arena at the interface between individual health plans and individual providers. Only if providers are forced by plans of various types into meaningful competition in selling their services, often on terms that they would not collectively agree to, can the market effectively translate consumer preferences into provider behavior. The ultimate key to establishing market forces as a mechanism of social control is thus provider competition focusing on price and acceptance of cost-containment responsibilities.

Because of the great potential for meaningful, competition-promoting change in private financing mechanisms, the presence of third-party payment in the market is not, by itself, a sufficient justification for maintaining regulation. As Chapters 11 and 12 discuss, the nature and scope of actual and potential financing arrangements must be carefully assessed to determine whether competition is or may be an effective and beneficial force with respect to particular services.

Identifying the True Causes of Market Failure

The conclusion that third-party payment alone does not justify regulation is not offered here as an argument for regulation's immediate repeal. The point is not that there is no market failure requiring policymakers' attention but, rather, that its nature is considerably different from what is commonly understood. Thus, a market failure cannot be assumed, and its causes, where it exists, must be looked for at a deeper level so that the prospects for its rectification can be more readily appreciated.[6]

As the previous discussion implies, the market for health services and the market for health insurance or other forms of financial protection cannot work well—and in particular cannot achieve the needed closer integration of financing and consumption or of financing and delivery—unless certain fundamental conditions are satisfied. First, consumers must have a strong incentive to choose health plans that effectively control costs. Second, health insurers must be free to design coverage and administrative arrangements in the interest of the consumer. And, third, alternative delivery systems must have unrestricted market opportunities so that they can be organized to supply any lacks in the third-party system. It is the failure of the market to satisfy these conditions in the past that accounts for the felt need for regulation. By the same token, the increasingly strong possibility that these conditions are beginning to be satisfied in a few markets, and will be satisfied more fully and in more markets in the future, makes it imperative that the health care system's planner-regulators consider closely whether their regulatory services are in fact needed in specific circumstances.

The stated prerequisites for efficient market performance have not been met in the past for essentially three reasons, which together account for the market failure that has occurred. First, federal tax law has strongly biased consumers toward buying comprehensive "first-dollar" coverage and discouraged insurer cost-containment efforts. As a tax-free fringe benefit, employer-purchased health insurance permits employee health care expenses to be paid with untaxed dollars, providing a strong incentive to buy more than the optimal amount of insurance coverage.

Second, most decisions on insurance coverage are made not by the consumer but by employers and unions, whose own interest in maintaining a beneficent image in the employees' eyes may cause them to act against the employees' true interests. Thus, in facing the tradeoff between more insurance coverage and more take-home pay, an employer or union leader may act either politically, emphasizing to the rank and file the visible benefits and obscuring the hidden costs, or paternalistically. Either way, the effect is likely to be that the decisionmaker places a higher value on comprehensive, hassle-free coverage than would the employee if he were offered a chance to economize.

The third significant cause of the insurance market's failure to respond to consumers' cost concerns is the effectiveness of privately imposed restraints of trade that have inhibited the market's performance from the beginning. As noted in Chapter 4, the medical profession and the hospital industry have effectively shaped private third parties' methods of doing business, preventing them from becoming aggressive purchasers of services and thus from triggering provider competition based on price, efficiency, and willingness to cooperate in cost containment. Moreover, the provider community in most markets has prevented various alternative delivery systems from having easy access to the market. Because of the restraints imposed, the market has been unreceptive to innovations addressed to the cost and moral hazard problems. As related in Chapter 4, current efforts to enforce the antitrust laws in the health care industry may shortly break down the most substantial barriers to competition. While much remains to be done in clarifying the law and bringing providers to account, the greater problem may now lie in overcoming the inertia of purchasers and insurers.

What needs to be observed here is that the market failures that have prevented the health insurance market from meeting consumer needs are all remediable. The antitrust enforcement effort has already begun to eliminate the most clear-cut professional abuses, and Chapters 14 and 15 discuss the other measures needed to make market forces operate constructively. Even though these measures have yet to be taken, there are already several markets in which alternative delivery systems are well enough established and consumers have enough competitive options that the need for any entry regulation at all is perhaps open to question.[7] Although one could argue that command-and-control regulation must predominate as long as the tax law is not changed and consumer choice remains restricted in some employment settings, the legislative choice not to change those competition-limiting conditions need not be deemed to render market forces wholly unreliable. As long as private restraints are curbed, the private market can function reasonably well even if the tax law continues to distort incentives and somewhat affects the equilibrium that market forces seek.

The implication of these observations for regulation is that market conditions can no longer be presumed to require command-and-control interventions in all cases. In keeping with their new congressional mandate, the planner-regulators must consider much more than merely whether third-party payment exists. They must also ask whether it still takes forms that fail to protect consumers from moral hazard, whether innovation in the financing system is still restrained, whether it is unreasonable to expect third parties to address a specific cost problem, and whether consumers have enough alternatives available to constrain effectively the performance of the third-party payers and the providers whose costs they underwrite. More generally, they must ask themselves whether, given the new opportunities for evolution toward more cost-effective types of insurance coverage and alternative financing and delivery mechanisms, it is right for regulation to retard that desirable evolution by intervening to shield inefficient insurers (and their customers) against the consequences of their failure to innovate. As argued more fully in Chapter 12, the most responsible regulatory policy will sometimes be to withdraw such protection, allowing competitive and cost pressures to induce insurers and consumers to seek new forms of insurance coverage or alternative delivery arrangements. It should be clear that regulation could easily become—and should strive to avoid becoming—the dominant remaining source of market failure, shoring up obsolete, dysfunctional financing mechanisms and barricading the avenues of change.

CONCLUSION

This chapter poses for health care planners and regulators the new challenge to foster competition in their regulatory decisions. Not only are they required by law, following the 1979 amendments, to give competition weight in their decisions, but sound logic should also lead them to permit competition to perform a constructive role in this industry. The following chapters are intended to establish the statutory basis and provide the analytical tools for structuring decisions on whether market forces can "appropriately allocate" health services of a particular type in a particular market.

Whether the procompetition language of the 1979 amendments, despite its surprising clarity in comparison with other regulatory legislation, will make an appreciable difference in regulatory behavior remains to be seen. What is perhaps most worrisome is not that the agencies will ignore the new statutory mandate altogether but that they will impose an unrealistic burden of persuasion on the advocates of competition and will produce simplistic analyses and thin conclusions in their effort to establish simultaneously the market's limitations and their own regulatory authority. Nevertheless, if the idea of competition is to be given a fair market test, it must be hoped that some agencies, at least a significant minority, will address these matters forthrightly, viewing both regulation and competition in the same harsh light and with greater sophistication concerning the industry and its problems. It is simply not enough anymore to be satisfied by pallid recitations of how the textbook model of a competitive market does not fit the health care industry. Congress knew that—and said as much—but still it legislated that competitive forces should be allowed to operate and strengthened wherever they can have a beneficial influence.

NOTES

1. Public Health Service Act §1532(b)(6), *as amended*, requires that HSAs, state agencies, and statewide health coordinating councils make written findings explaining the basis for all their decisions and recommendations under the planning act.
2. From time to time the courts have intervened to prevent regulators in other industries from selling out competition too quickly. *E.g.*, Continental Air Lines, Inc. v. CAB, 519 F.2d 944 (D.C. Cir. 1975); Northern Natural Gas Co. v. FPC, 399 F.2d 953 (D.C. Cir. 1968).

3. *E.g.*, Breyer, "Analyzing Regulatory Failure: Mismatches, Less Restrictive Alternatives, and Reform," 92 *Harv. L. Rev.* 549 (1979); Wolf, "A Theory of Nonmarket Failure: Framework for Implementation Analysis," 22 *J. L. & Econ.* 107 (1979); Schuck, "Regulation: Asking the Right Questions," 11 *Nat'l J.* 711 (1979).

4. For a more detailed discussion of the forms private cost containment might take, see Havighurst & Hackbarth, "Private Cost Containment," 300 *New Eng. J. Med.* 1298 (1979); Havighurst, "Private Cost Containment—Medical Practice under Competition," in 1979 *Socioeconomic Issues of Health* 41 (G. Misek ed.).

5. *E.g., Hearings on H.R. 5740 before the Subcomm. on Health of the House Comm. on Ways and Means,* 96th Cong., 2d Sess. 162, 165 (1980) (statement of William B. Schwartz, M.D.).

6. The reasons for the often poor performance of the health care market are also discussed in Chapters 4 and 14.

7. *Cf.* Christianson, "The Impact of HMOs: Evidence and Research Issues," 5 *J. Health Pol., Pol'y & L.* 354 (1980) (discussing the Minneapolis-St. Paul, Hawaii, and Denver-Boulder markets); Christianson & McClure, "Competition in the Delivery of Medical Care," 301 *New Eng. J. Med.* 812 (1979) (discussing Minneapolis-St. Paul).

10 DECISIONMAKING ON COMPETITION ISSUES UNDER THE 1979 AMENDMENTS

The new mandate to planners and regulators that was set forth in Chapter 5 must now be discussed in more practical terms as a help to those who must be guided by it. The law imposes on the planner-regulators a duty to consider, with respect to particular services in particular markets, whether competitive forces can serve the public interest well enough to obviate entry and investment controls. Before reaching the technical issues raised by this requirement, it is necessary to sketch the new decisionmaking framework and to address certain legal questions that arise in interpreting and giving effect to the new statutory directive.

CATEGORIZING SERVICES ACCORDING TO THEIR AMENABILITY TO MARKET FORCES

Section 1502(b), added to Public Law 93–641 by Public Law 96–79, instructs the planner-regulators to determine at the outset whether market conditions governing a particular health service are such that "competition does not or will not appropriately allocate supply" of that service. As the following chapters show, this threshold judgment will frequently be difficult, but it appears to be mandatory. One guide to knowing whether supply is "appropriately" allocated would appear to be provided by the new "national health priority" appearing in section 1502(a)(17), which specifies the desirability of competition "wherever competition and consumer choice can constructively serve to advance the purposes of quality assurance, cost effectiveness, and access." Reference to these same three objectives also appears in section 1502(b)(3), which instructs the planner-regulators to favor competition "where appropriate to advance [such] purposes." These three statutory goals, though seemingly conflicting, are nevertheless precisely the kinds of things that smoothly functioning markets effectively balance and reconcile through the process of letting consumers choose where and what they will buy and how much they are willing to spend. Indeed, one of the strengths of a free market system is its ability to deal with complex tradeoffs among competing desiderata by submitting them to consumer "votes" in discrete transactions. Some independent discussion of these three statutory objectives seems likely to be helpful in identifying those situations in which competition could safely be relied on to serve the public.

"Quality assurance," while profoundly important, is not an exclusive objective of health policy. Indeed, insurance-induced non-price competition, focusing on quality and amenities with price being no object, has supplied an important impetus for cost escalation in the industry. At the outset, it is essential to acknowledge the possibility that, because of the existence of perverse consumption incentives, prevailing levels of "quality" might sometimes be too high when judged with the cost of marginal increments in view. While competition can frequently motivate providers to maintain and improve quality, there will often be good reasons for not allowing competition to operate unless the cost-escalation hazard is under control.

"Cost effectiveness," while not synonymous with efficiency, has much in common with that goal. Nevertheless, in its most technical usage, cost effectiveness directs attention, not to the question implicit in the efficiency concept of what objectives are worth achieving, but to the choice of the cheapest means of achieving an agreed-upon objective. Although some significance might be attached to the use of cost effectiveness instead of efficiency as a policy objective here, Congress in fact substituted "cost effectiveness" in this context not for "efficiency" but for the term "cost containment."[1] Probably this choice of terms was intended to clarify that saving money was not an objective to be pursued irrespective of other values. It seems likely that Congress's main purpose was simply to juxtapose its cost and quality concerns in order to show that it did not wish competition to operate under circumstances where either variable would be maximized while the other was neglected.

The reference to "access" as a value that might be furthered by competition calls attention to the importance of service availability and convenience and to the market's responsiveness to new demand; again, however, access is not an absolute value and should not be weighed heavily if cost considerations are lost sight of in the marketplace. Sometimes, of course, the term "access" is used as shorthand for an equity objective, such as the availability of a service to low-income persons and their ability to pay. But, because competition can do nothing to improve ability to pay or assure the continued availability of services that are not self-supporting, the reference to access as a goal that competition might constructively serve cannot be read exclusively as a reference to equity goals. On the other hand, competition by so-called cream skimmers can sometimes reduce the availability of cross-subsidized services, and this adverse effect on access might, under section 1502(b)(3), occasionally warrant excluding an otherwise desirable competitor. In general, however, "access" should probably be read in this statutory context to refer primarily to the fact that competition can often improve the availability of services. As discussed later in this chapter, it should not be seized on to provide a general warrant for protectionist regulation that regularly sacrifices the benefits of competition to preserve services supportable only by internal subsidies.

The statutory reference to these three competing factors should be viewed primarily as a sign of Congress's awareness of the difficult tradeoffs that must somehow be accommodated before the resulting allocation of resources can reasonably be called consistent with the public interest. Because third-party payers have so often failed to act as agents for consumers either in purchasing providers' services or in policing expenditures from the insurance fund, the cost factor has been excluded in providers' and patients' decisions, thus causing competition to be a doubtful force for promoting overall consumer welfare. Nevertheless, it would appear that the planner-regulators must still determine in the light of all the circumstances, including any regulatory cost controls that may exist, the actual extent of the adverse effects that the absence of cost considerations in consumer choices might cause. Likewise, concern that consumers cannot appraise quality should not warrant automatic suppression of price competition if quality is subject to controls of other kinds. In other words, the listing of three statutory desiderata should not imply that the market's inability to take all three into account automatically invalidates reliance on competition. Judgment must still be exercised on the question of whether the market can "appropriately allocate" the services in question. Chapter 11 sets forth factors that are relevant in making such assessments.

As on all applications for certificates of need, the applicant bears the burden of proof on whether market forces "appropriately allocate" resources. Burdens of proof have substantive significance only when the evidence on the issue in question is declared inconclusive. Given the difficulty that will frequently be encountered in answering the question posed in the statute, some agencies may find this a convenient way of resolving the issue against the applicant and thus against competition. Nevertheless, the statute appears to mandate an explicit finding one way or the other on the issue of the market's efficaciousness. As the next paragraph demonstrates, the strength or weakness of the conclusion reached on this issue may still affect the ultimate outcome since the various statutory criteria must still be weighed against each other.

Under section 1502(b), a threshold determination that a service is not amenable to being "appropriately allocate[d]" by market forces necessitates command-and-control regulation of entry and new investment. A contrary finding that market allocation *would* work does not end the matter, however, since section 1502(b) says only that the planner-regulators in that event "should in the performance of their functions under this title give priority (where appropriate to advance the purposes of quality assurance, cost effectiveness, and access) to actions which would strengthen the effect of competition on the supply of such services." Presumably, one such action would be to permit free entry by all competent would-be providers of such services, but this result is not compelled. Instead, the regulators are apparently expected to apply all the various criteria of section 1532(c). In so doing, they must incorporate in their calculus the evidence bearing on the competition-related criteria of subsections 1532(c)(11) and (12). If that evidence was not strong, it could be outweighed by other factors. On the other hand, if the market seemed rather clearly capable of allocating resources efficiently, the "national health priority" of section 1502(a)(17) and the direction to "give priority" to actions strengthening competition would seem to create a clear presumption in favor of granting certificates of need. Arguably, only a very powerful counterargument, such as the need to preserve a truly vital internal subsidy,[2] could warrant suppressing competition in such a case.

This formulation of the decision process leaves a great deal to the agencies' judgment and thus to their discretion. Nevertheless, the steps in the decisionmaking process are reasonably clear and at least guarantee that competition will not be lost sight of through inadvertence.

CATEGORIZING INPATIENT AND OTHER INSTITUTIONAL HEALTH SERVICES

In deciding which services are amenable to allocation by market forces, health planners and regulators may be influenced by a distinction seemingly drawn in section 1502(b) and in the House committee report between "inpatient ... and other institutional health services," on the one hand, and noninstitutional services, on the other. The term "institutional health services" is a statutory term [section 1531(5)] incorporating some significant outpatient services provided by institutions. The language and legislative history of the 1979 amendments suggest that Congress may have intended to create a presumption that "inpatient ... and other institutional health services," because of the way they are paid for, are not capable at the present time of being appropriately allocated by market forces. An important issue of statutory construction is raised by some observers' belief that Congress intended for this presumption to be conclusive, relieving the planner-regulators of any duty to justify with reasoned findings their exercise of command-and-control authority over any service falling within the definition. DHHS appears to have adopted this construction of Congress's intent, stating in its commentary on regulations implementing the 1979 amendments that "Congress has stated that market forces do not or will not appropriately allocate supply for inpatient health services."[3]

The specific argument is that section 1502(b)(2) puts "inpatient ... and other institutional health services" permanently on the agenda for command-and-control regulation. That section expresses Congress's expectation that, "for health services, such as inpatient health services and other institutional health services, for which competition does not or will not appropriately allocate supply," the agencies will assume regulatory control. Despite the argument that this language characterizes institutional services in a way that absolutely precludes a regulatory decision that such services can be allocated by market forces, a full reading of the law and the committee reports rules out giving such conclusive effect to what must be read as a merely illustrative reference to such services. While the new law does embody a strong assumption that institutional services currently require regulation, it still requires a finding of market failure as a predicate to command-and-control regulation of any service. This reading can be strongly documented, as the following paragraph shows.

The House committee report on the 1979 amendments, which went far out of its way to emphasize that inpatient and other institutional services currently require regulation, clearly stated the regulators' responsibility to recognize that future evolution in the financing and delivery system might someday obviate command-and-control regulation for such services:

> If ... an innovative financing, reimbursement or service delivery arrangement affecting institutional health services were designed so that the method of payment by patients (1) created incentives for patients to respond to prices charged and (2) placed the providers at financial risk for unnecessary or excessive services [,] the committee would expect that planning agencies would, in awarding certificates of need, consider whether the effect of that new arrangement will be to properly allocate the supply of services.

Consistent with this recognition of the possibility of change, the specific cause of the current market failure stated in section 1502(b)(1)—namely, "the *prevailing* methods of paying for health services ..., particularly for inpatient health services and other institutional health services" (emphasis added)—must be read as contemplating that significant reform in the financing system might present a new question. Similarly, section 1502(b)(2) itself refers to "services ... for which competition does not *or will not* appropriately allocate supply" (emphasis added); the use of the disjunctive supports the possibility of changed market circumstances. Furthermore, both of the new decisionmaking criteria added by the procompetition amendments to section 1532(c) also embody the idea that command-and-control regulation is appropriate only where there is a demonstrated market failure and that specific market circumstances must be evaluated to establish that this precondition is satisfied; thus, the agencies are charged with considering (1) any "factors which affect the effect of competition" and (2) any "improvements or innovations in the financing and delivery of health services which foster competition." Finally, the new "national health priority" in section 1502(a)(17), echoing language in the Senate committee report, embraces competition "*wherever* competition and consumer choice can constructively serve" the public interest (emphasis added).

Although Congress is frequently obscure, in this case it has been reasonably clear, both in embracing the concept that regulation of the command-and-control variety must be justified in specific circumstances and in stating its view that, as things now stand, inpatient and other institutional services probably require regulation. There seems to be no basis, however, for reading the law to state anything stronger than a rebuttable presumption of the need for regulation of such services. This presumption—if indeed that is not too strong a word for a weakly specified expectation—would certainly be overcome by a showing of specific circumstances in a particular market that make that market reasonably effective and constructive as an allocator of the service and resources in question. A somewhat harder question would be whether arguments premised solely on the value of nonprice competition could also be offered. Although Congress left no doubt that it did not value competition that had cost-escalating tendencies (and indeed regarded such competition to be a major source of the problem to which regulation is addressed), the statutory scheme appears to permit all arguments to be made. The agencies should, of course, be vigilant about letting applicants assert the benefits of competition without also recognizing its possible costs.

Chapter 11 attempts to put the nonprice competition issue in proper perspective.

The reading of section 1502(b)(2) advocated here is consistent not only with the statutory language and legislative history but also with sound regulatory theory and common sense. Thus, the diagnosis of the market failure set forth in Chapter 9 indicates that there is no policy basis for making a conclusive distinction between institutional and noninstitutional services, particularly as those services are defined in the law. On the contrary, the current market failure is attributable to prevailing payment methods, which, even though they may apply more pervasively to some inpatient services, are applicable to services of all types. The House committee report, while emphasizing problems in the payment system, did not purport to analyze the wide variety of "institutional" services even though there are some obviously relevant distinctions among them. For example, as Chapter 13 illustrates, the case for regulating entry into the nursing home market is not nearly as convincing as the case that can currently be made for controlling the hospital bed supply. Furthermore, some noninstitutional services, such as office-based therapeutic and diagnostic equipment, seem much better candidates for regulatory control than some of the outpatient services offered by institutional providers that are covered by the term "institutional health services."

For these reasons, it does not appear that Congress intended to give more than general guidance as to the particular services likely to require command-and-control regulation now or in the future. On the contrary, the amended health-planning law is surprisingly consistent in its adherence to the basic principle that the regulators should regulate only where regulation is necessary and that, even though no statutory exemption is warranted for a particular service, the necessity for its command-and-control regulation cannot be taken for granted for all time or under all circumstances. Thus, Congress's emphasis on the probable need for entry controls over institutional services should be read simply as an effort to assure that the regulators do not abdicate where their services are in fact required and where the long-term adverse consequences of permitting unnecessary capital investments could be considerable. Above all, the statute provides a mandate to adapt future regulation to recognize, and perhaps even to foster, hoped-for changes in health care financing that will finally permit reliance on market forces. For these reasons, the distinction between institutional and noninstitutional services is of only limited value in advancing the analysis.

STATE AND LOCAL HEALTH PLANS AND COMPETITION

The 1979 amendments were not entirely clear on how Congress's new interest in competition is to affect the development, nature, and status of state and local health plans. The suggestion had been made[4] that the agencies should be expressly instructed to specify in such plans the appropriate role of competition with respect to particular services; the object of this proposal was to clarify that health plans should not focus exclusively on dictating the type, number, and location of health resources, and should recognize that competition is an alternative way of determining these matters. This suggestion was not heeded. Instead, the amendments incorporated new language directing that planning objectives in local and state plans should be even more quantitative than they had been in the past.[5] The amendments also introduced a specific new requirement that, except in "emergency circumstances," decisions on certificate-of-need applications shall be "consistent with the State health plan."[6] Although the amendments were clear in making competition an explicit consideration in the agencies' project-review activities, some interpolation is required to ascertain Congress's view of how plan development should be carried on in light of the new procompetition policy. At first glance, it might be concluded that the amendments, by insisting on quantitative plans, imply that central planning is preferable to competition and are thus internally inconsistent in simultaneously requiring that competition be highly valued. The issue to be discussed here is thus quite fundamental to understanding Congress's true meaning.

One line of argument that might be advanced to minimize the practical significance of the 1979 amendments' procompetition language would call attention to the fact that section 1502(b) frames the crucial question as being whether "competition appropriately allocates supply [of the service in question] *consistent with health systems plans and State health plans"* (emphasis added). The argument would be that such plans, which the amendments require to be specific and quantitative, are the ultimate reference point for assessing competition's efficacy and that Congress intended that competition should be used only if it was deemed the best way to achieve a particular numerical goal. This would be an extraordinary reading, of course, since competition as an allocative device is a process for discovering and giving effect to consumer preferences, not for hitting predetermined targets. The allocation of resources resulting from a smoothly functioning market, like the results of health planning-cum-regulation, is normally regarded as legitimized by the democratic character of the choosing process itself. Moreover, planners' methods for determining the configuration of services are themselves sufficiently questionable that the availability of an alternative way of identifying an appropriate allocation of services should probably be highly prized.

Although regulation and competition can be complementary in many respects, the dominant theme in the health planning amendments and their legislative history is that they are essentially alternative allocative devices whose relative utility varies with the circumstances. The logic of this way of looking at the issue and the illogic and peculiarity of the alternative view that competition is valuable only as a planner's tool, not as a way of discovering consumer wishes, are perhaps the best reasons why the results of relying on consumer choice should not be judged solely by their correlation with planners' preferences. Of course, whatever the conclusion reached on the law's meaning, planners will be strongly inclined to conclude that the market is not working well if they find, or anticipate finding, that the market outcome does not, or will not, coincide with the configuration of resources that they regard as ideal. Planners as a class, in other words, are unlikely to accept the market's verdict simply on the basis that the democratic choosing process validates the outcome. The reason for this tendency is, no doubt, their egalitarian leaning and their perception that the planning law embodies a congressional desire for equality of access to health services. Nevertheless, the clear tension between equity and efficiency goals should probably not be accommodated by setting up the planner-regulators as the ultimate judges of the acceptability of market outcomes. As a statutory matter, the regulators' opportunity to serve equity goals should probably be confined to exercises of their power to preserve internal subsidies required to meet essential needs.

These large issues are undeniably present here and will undoubtedly encourage some planners to evaluate the market's performance by appraising the outcome rather than the process. Nevertheless, Congress has made it rather clear that its preference for competition should be accommodated with health planning in a somewhat different fashion than by simply judging market outcomes in light of the planners' preconceptions. Thus, the House committee report addressed specifically the anticipated content of state and local health plans insofar as they deal with services that are deemed by the planners to be allocable by market forces:

> [T]he goals of the plan and the statement in those plans of changes in resources which are needed in the area ... might differ depending upon the agency's assessment of the extent to which, for a particular service, competition will limit the development of unneeded capacity and protect the public from its costs. For instance, plans could avoid establishing numerical goals or resource requirements by identifying where certain types of services are needed, or appear excessive, or by establishing a range for the number of new services needed.[7]

In similar fashion, the House report stated that an HSA's recommendations and findings in appropriateness reviews "could differ, as with health plans, depending upon the agency's assessment of the extent to which competition will allocate the supply of the service under review."[8] Under the approach implicit in the committee's concept of health planning, the planners would be expected to grant the market a degree of flexibility wherever it appears a promising mechanism. But in an appropriate case they could cite market outcomes departing from their expectations as evidence that the market is not working well or is more destructive of other values cognizable under section 1532(c) than had been anticipated. This approach seems to balance rather well the working market's presumptive claim to yield efficient outcomes that serve the public interest and the planners' statutory responsibility for the system's performance.

What Congress seemingly had in mind, then, was that health planners would affirmatively plan *for* competition, and for possible deregulation, by including, wherever feasible, in the plans themselves explicit findings covering the market's efficacy for controlling the supply of specific services.[9] The regulatory model adopted, while leaving the planners in charge—and indeed enhancing the authoritativeness of their plans—also gave them a new mandate to allow competitive forces to determine supply wherever, in their judgment as unbiased planners, competition would accurately reveal consumer preferences and would not unduly jeopardize other goals judged more important than the goals that competition itself can serve. Where the planners find the market likely to be serviceable in these terms, the regulators are instructed to refrain from command-and-control regulation of procompetitive new investment and market entry.

JUDICIAL REVIEW OF THE ROLE ASSIGNED BY PLANNERS TO COMPETITION

Although health planners have a new statutory duty to judge, on the merits and for each type of service, the value of the marketplace as a mechanism for revealing what the public wants, it is not altogether clear how this responsibility will be enforced. It is possible that DHHS, though long wedded to a conventional view of competition's value and desirability, will encourage the planning agencies to adopt a sanguine view. Perhaps Congress itself will be perceived as sufficiently single-minded on this issue that health planners will automatically respect its preferences. But, even if DHHS and Congress actively employ their powers of oversight on behalf of competition, they may not be able to affect behavior very much, because subjective judgments are involved and because abuses, now that HMOs are no longer subject to appreciable regulation, are not likely to be readily detectable. Thus, unless the courts are in a position to enforce stated congressional preferences, the effect of the new declaration of competition's desirability may depend mostly on its hortatory value.

There appears to be some question whether the courts will have an adequate opportunity to review health planners' conclusions on competition's value with respect to particular services. If such conclusions are embodied, either explicitly or implicitly, in a state health plan (SHP), a state agency's decision to deny a certificate of need on the automatic statutory ground of inconsistency with the SHP[10] might not be appealable on the basis that the plan's determination of competition's undesirability was not based on evidence or reasoned findings. Although the principles of administrative law usually allow attacks on agency rules that are inconsistent with the statute being implemented, the case here is peculiar in that the "rule"—if the state health plan can be analogized to a regulation—is not the product of the agency whose decision is being reviewed. Indeed, the state agency would not have access to or be able to provide to a reviewing court the full record on which the SHP was based. For these reasons, ordinary judicial review of certificate-of-need decisions would not permit the court to assess whether Congress's declared preference for competition had been given due weight in determining the outcome.

It is probable that some state agencies will allow certificate-of-need applicants a full evidentiary hearing on competition issues, addressing these issues de novo and thereby facilitating judicial review. This method of addressing specific competition questions would probably not lead to decisions violating the statutory requirement of consistency with the SHP since the plan would usually lack the necessary concreteness on such matters and the applicant would be entitled to a hearing in any event. Handling competition issues on such a case-by-case basis might, however, defeat the beneficial, discretion-limiting purpose of the consistency requirement. Moreover, such an approval would violate DHHS's instruction that "it is through the development of plans that planning agencies should determine whether a specific health service responds to competitive forces, not through individual determinations as applications are being reviewed."[11] It remains unclear how conclusions on competition's role that are reached in plan development are to be subjected to testing in light of applicants' evidence and to meaningful judicial review.

The remedy for a certificate-of-need applicant whose competitive entry is foreclosed by the SHP is to seek review of the SHP itself. This would have to be done administratively in the first instance, probably by applying to either the HSA or the statewide health coordinating council (SHCC), depending on where the SHP was in the three-year cycle of review and revision. Following the 1979 amendments, an applicant would probably be legally entitled to a hearing and a reasoned decision, supported by evidence, on his claim that competition would be valuable with respect to the particular service and in the particular market in question. Judicial review to determine whether this right had been respected might be deemed appropriate at either of two points. One possibility is that review would be allowed in federal court under federal law upon the HSA's contrary determination, on the theory that the HSA's health systems plan (HSP) was essentially final and open for revision by the SHCC only on matters affecting "statewide health needs."[12] Alternatively, the SHCC might be deemed the final decisionmaker, so that review would be granted, in state court under state law, only after that state instrumentality had acted.[13] In either event the decisionmaker should have to show that a record had been made that supported the outcome.

Although Congress has made no express provision for judicial review of the planning actions of either the HSA or the SHCC and has not made clear which is the final decisionmaker on localized issues, the better view would seem to be that the HSA, as a nongovernmental body, gives only recommendations; otherwise, a severe problem of unconstitutional delegation of legislative power to a private entity would exist.[14] A consequence of this reading would be to make the SHCC responsible for according due process to would-be competitors' claims that market forces should be allowed to operate with respect to particular services. Because, as Chapter 11 demonstrates, this is a matter amenable to proof by specific evidence, a hearing and findings of fact are appropriate. Moreover, because Congress has provided a clear legal standard for application to the facts surrounding a particular service, the SHCC's function in making the definitive choice between regulation and competition required by sections 1502(b)(2) and (3) is clearly adjudicative, not legislative, thus triggering due process requirements and the availability of judicial review. The conclusion that decisions on competition's value are reviewable obviously flies in the face of DHHS's suggestion that the health plan will settle all such issues, but due process considerations and traditional judicial concern that competition not be sacrificed without explanation make it likely that the right to a hearing and judicial review will be recognized.[15] Opponents of competition should be given the same standing to oppose provisions of the SHP that would encourage it.

The 1979 amendments' substantial changes in the character and responsibility of the SHCC, by giving it more formal status as an agency of state government and new duties to afford hearings and to decide disputed issues, would seem to confirm the view that the SHCC's decisions in promulgating the SHP are final and reviewable agency actions. The result is that aggrieved certificate-of-need applicants may in some instances have to pursue their rights, not before the state agency, but before the SHCC. Even though the peculiarities of this amalgam of regulation and planning make it hard to predict with certainty whether, where, and how the courts will intervene, judicial review of the SHCC's rulings on competition's value and efficacy should be available. Congress, as it strengthened the planners' hands by making the SHP conclusive on such matters as competition's role, also formalized the planning process so that it would not effectively foreclose private rights. It thus left the courts in a position to review, on appropriate application, the planners' disposition of claims to the effect that Congress's preference for allowing competition to operate wherever it is efficacious had been violated.

It remains to be seen, of course, whether state courts will be at all insistent on furthering Congress's desire that competition be given a fair hearing on its merits in formulating parts of the SHP. It is perhaps probable that most of them will defer to planners' conventional assessments, but, as the federal courts have done from time to time in reviewing administrative action,[16] they may sometimes be able to prevent the planners from selling out competition too quickly. Some substantive outcomes may therefore be affected. Nevertheless, it must be recognized that the courts cannot be counted on to revolutionize health planning. The ultimate check on anticompetitive regulation must be political. Whatever their precise legal meaning, the procompetition provisions in the 1979 amendments will only be important if they are backed by political as well as occasional legal sanctions.

IS PROTECTIONIST REGULATION STILL VALID?

The protectionist tendencies of all economic regulation have appeared strongly in the administration of certificate-of-need laws.

Some discussion is required to distinguish valid from invalid arguments for exclusionary regulation and to accommodate legitimate regulatory concerns with the new statutory mandate.

Conventional Justifications of Exclusionary Regulation

One provision in the 1979 amendments, whose implications for competition were not recognized in the report of the Senate committee where it originated, may be seen as strengthening the warrant for such anticompetitive tendencies. Under an amendment to one of the law's numerous decisionmaking criteria [section 1532(c)(9)], the planner-regulators, in passing on a new construction project, are to consider its impact "on the costs and charges to the public of providing health services by other persons." By legitimizing concern for a project's impact on services provided by "other persons," this provision invites the planner-regulators to protect incumbent providers from new competition. The criterion does not contemplate protectionism for its own sake or for the sake of incumbent providers but instead stresses possible effects on "costs and charges to the public." Nevertheless, the result is to enshrine two arguments for suppressing competition that have always carried great weight with health system regulators.

A leading source of support for protectionism in the health care industry has been the belief that excess capital facilities will be put to inappropriate uses for which the financing system, lacking the capacity to distinguish inappropriate utilization, will pay. The so-called Roemer effect, by which an available supply of hospital facilities is thought to generate demand for their use, thus supplies a special justification for adopting in this industry protectionist policies that are similar to those that have been adopted by regulators in other industries even without this particular excuse. By putting the Roemer effect and section 1532(c)(9) together, the appearance of a new competitor, such as a freestanding ambulatory care facility, can be contested on the simple ground that it will divert patients from hospitals. The theory is that the diverted patients may be replaced by others who would otherwise not be hospitalized, thus increasing "costs ... to the public of providing health services by other persons."

Among the planner-regulators' other articles of faith has been the belief that the cost of capital facilities, once incurred, will almost certainly be charged off to the public over time even if the facilities are underutilized. The perception is that institutional providers are protected against risk by third-party payment systems dedicated to reimbursing either providers' incurred costs or insureds' incurred charges. Not only does the "sunk-cost obsession" familiar in all economic regulation suggest to the regulators that allowing full recovery of capital costs is self-evidently fair,[17] but the dominant perception of how health care financing works suggests that recoupment of capital outlays from the public, even if not required by fairness, is inevitable. Again, one finds that health care regulators have available to them a rationale for protectionism that is significantly more alluring than the rationales employed in other industries where anticompetitive regulation has also taken hold. Thus, if they are so inclined, health system planners and regulators will find it quite easy to conclude that a new market entrant, by causing existing providers to allocate their fixed costs over a smaller number of patients, will increase "charges to the public of providing health services by other persons."

Belief in the Roemer effect rests on an unexamined assumption that the financing system will be unable to deal in the future with the demand distortions that it has freely underwritten in the past. Likewise, belief in the recoverability of all capital outlays reflects the premise that currently popular cost-reimbursement techniques will be employed to the same extent in the future. Even though these perceptions give the health care system's planner-regulators a powerful motive to prevent any competitively induced change that would reduce the use of existing capital facilities or render them obsolete, the 1979 amendments would seem to require a reexamination of such conventional assumptions. Not only did Congress perceive a hopeful potential for innovation in the financing system, but it is possible that the Roemer effect and the cost pass-through phenomenon have been overestimated in the past or have dwindled in importance in recent years. In any event, it is doubtful that the conventional wisdom of the planning community supplies a permanent justification for foreclosing competitively induced change. Indeed, section 1532(c)(9), while permitting these effects to be taken into account in the case of new construction projects, contemplates that their existence in particular cases must be established, not assumed, and that they must be balanced against other criteria, including those referring to competition. In keeping with this statutory structure, Chapter 11 is intended to help in making the necessary empirical assessments of particular situations.

The conventional arguments for using exclusionary regulation to suppress useful competition would seem to be defensible only if the various financing systems in place have no reasonable alternative but to be as strikingly perverse as these theories assume them to be. But, as is argued in Chapter 12, there may be many instances in which the planners and regulators should permit competitive market entry precisely for the purpose of stimulating competing third-party payers to defend both themselves and those who contribute their funds against higher costs. Automatic acceptance of existing financing arrangements as an excuse for suppressing desirable competition can prevent not only the appearance of efficient new providers but also changes in the financing system itself—changes that might ultimately restore enough backbone to the demand side of the market that command-and-control regulation could be largely dispensed with. Experience in transportation fields has demonstrated many times the harm to the public interest that can be done by regulators whose chief resourcefulness lies in finding reasons to discourage market entry by low-cost providers. One must hope that health system planners and regulators will prove resourceful enough in other ways to escape the trap of protectionism.

Congress has clearly demonstrated its preference for ridding health care regulation of its knee-jerk protectionist mentality. The 1979 amendments leave little doubt that exclusionary regulation, while often necessitated by perversities in the financing system, is now to be regarded as the exception rather than the rule. The new decisionmaking framework, carefully constructed so that the question of competition's efficacy must be addressed at the threshold, makes it clear that Congress, when it restated the planner-regulators' mission, had in mind the protectionists' excesses in other regulated industries. Even more important, Congress itself rejected powerful protectionist arguments when it relieved some HMOs of certificate-of-need requirements for new hospitals and narrowed the criteria for evaluating other HMO hospital investments so as to exclude the considerations reflected in section 1532(c)(9). Thus, HMOs are now free to enter the market without any regard to their impact on competitors or to the possibility that the Roemer effect and capital-cost recoupment will increase costs in the fee-for-service sector. In this way, Congress embraced the principle that providers who face meaningful competition, including competition based on price, can be trusted to make entry and investment decisions in the consumer interest and should not be suppressed because their competitors are less disciplined. The 1979 amendments must therefore be read, as a whole, to direct the planner-regulators' primary attention to actual and potential conditions on the demand side of the market and away from protectionist considerations.

Protecting Internal Subsidies

While the main props supporting regulatory protectionism are greatly weakened by the 1979 amendments, there is a remaining justification for protectionist policies in certification of need that retains some limited validity. This justification is the frequently perceived need to protect revenues that enable an existing provider to provide some service which the planner-regulators deem desirable but which cannot support itself. Such "internal subsidization" is common in hospitals, which price their various services without strict regard to costs. This practice exposes the hospital to the threat of competition from a new provider of the overpriced services and accounts for the common claim that a new entrant is "skimming the cream," taking the profitable business and leaving the existing hospital with the burden of providing needed but unprofitable services. Faced with such a claim, health system planner-regulators must make some difficult judgments concerning not only the short-run and long-run benefits of competition as an allocative mechanism but also some other possibly important values.

Although the planning law, as amended, provides no explicit instructions on how internal subsidies are to be regarded, there is no basis for treating them as illegitimate per se. Internal subsidies are common in all regulated industries. They have been compared to a system of taxation—in effect, an excise tax—whereby private firms charge monopoly prices to users of some services and apply the proceeds to support the provision of other services at a price below cost, or free.[18] This system of "taxation by regulation" can be criticized, however, both because the incidence of the "tax" may be inequitable and because the need for a public subsidy is not established through normal legislative channels. Moreover, the usual constitutional processes for levying a tax are bypassed, and the legislative steps of authorization and appropriation and the monitoring of expenditures are omitted. In the absence of the usual forms of governmental accountability, the responsibility of the planner-regulators in perpetuating the "tax" and the related subsidy would seem to be very great. When it is considered that all those currently benefiting from hidden subsidies are free to apply to the legislature for direct subsidies if their revenue source falls victim to competition, the appropriateness of a skeptical attitude toward protectionist policies seems clear.

It has been argued that hospitals, particularly nonprofit hospitals, employ internal subsidization to "compensat[e] for distortions and inequities in existing health insurance coverage."[19] As a general proposition, this is indisputable, but it raises many questions. If a gap exists in insurance coverage, one must inquire as to the gap's origin before judging that it is one that should be filled through an internal subsidy. For example, if consumers selected insurance plans that would not pay for experimental treatments, the hospital should not be permitted to subsidize those treatments by billing more for insured services; such a subsidy would amount to a rewriting of private insurance contracts and would violate the principle of consumer choice. Moreover, it would seem much sounder for the hospital to seek explicit subsidies for its experimental work. Similarly, educational costs should be isolated by making cost differences between teaching and nonteaching institutions more visible in a competitive market. Private insurance plans, reflecting consumer choice, can serve as efficient resource allocation mechanisms only if their exclusions from, and dollar limits on, coverage are respected and not cancelled out by protected provider monopolies milking the insurance system in order to indulge preferences of their own. Competitive entry eroding the spending discretion of monopolistic hospitals would contribute greatly to the emergence of consumer preferences as the dominant force controlling the performance of the hospital sector.

Probably the only internal subsidies that should ever be deemed to justify exclusionary regulation are those that benefit low-income patients. Despite the failure to enact a broad program of national health insurance, society has long recognized a commitment to meet the needs of patients lacking the means to purchase adequate health insurance. Private hospitals have filled a critical role in meeting this social commitment.[20] It is only relatively recently, however, that hospitals have come to expect that all their costs will be covered by their operating revenues. Previously philanthropy and public subventions filled the gap between costs and revenues, and many hospitals, both public and private, still depend on such sources. While expecting hospitals to turn to other subsidy sources would not be unreasonable—and there are signs that direct subsidies to threatened hospitals are increasing—established patterns may not permit planners and regulators to ignore the adverse effects that competition might have on vital services. In the absence of an adequate federal program covering disadvantaged persons, certain hospitals' capacity to carry on their charitable role probably needs to be protected in some measure. By the same token, enactment of national health insurance in some form, if and when it occurs, should be deemed to reduce, if not to eliminate altogether, the need to foster the hospital as a charitable monopoly. But, in the short run, the health care system's planner-regulators should probably not be criticized too roundly if they occasionally elect to exclude competition in order to preserve an existing hospital's ability to meet the vital needs of underserved and underinsured populations.

The regulatory problem here is substantial for several reasons. The existence and extent of subsidies are extremely hard to establish, particularly in the absence of uniform cost-accounting techniques. A hospital faced with competition from a certificate-of-need applicant could always threaten to close the service that the planner-regulators value most highly, even if many other services were also beneficiaries of subsidies of the type in jeopardy. The proper regulatory stance is to impose a heavy burden of proof on the hospital seeking protection from competition. Not only would its cost accounting have to be convincing and complete, but it should have to demonstrate that other, less defensible subsidies did not exist. Moreover, federal law is now interpreted to require that the states require regulatory approval for the closing of a service,[21] so that a hospital will not be entirely free to choose which service it would eliminate. In any event, it would be intolerable for the regulators to let a hospital hold an essential service provided to low-income patients as a hostage to get protection for its internal subsidization capability. Unless the hospital can show with reasonable clarity that it has no alternative candidates for closure, it should be denied the protected market position it seeks.

There are some indications that internal subsidies and the protectionism required to maintain them are not favored in the law. The 1979 amendments, by exempting HMOs from certificate-of-need requirements, revealed an unwillingness to trust the regulators to evaluate a procompetitive entrant against existing providers' claims. Moreover, Congress's grant to HMOs of the freedom to skim the paying patients without regard to possibly adverse consequences suggests that in other cases, too, this factor should not weigh heavily. Although the amendments expanded the statutory criteria to allow considerations of a construction project's effects "on the cost and charges to the public of providing health services by other persons," this provision, which was intended primarily to allow the regulators to assess Roemer effects and capital recoupment, does not amount to an acceptance of internal subsidies as a substitute for explicit subsidies. Moreover, no other prescribed criterion for decisionmaking clearly legitimizes protection of a competitor's capacity for subsidization. While it is true that DHHS has stretched certain statutory criteria to make "access" a crucial factor in certificate-of-need decisions,[22] the language seized on, however questionably, to make approval of the termination or introduction of a service turn on underserved persons' need for it provides no support for rejecting a procompetitive proposal because it jeopardizes a desirable redistribution of income.

The only reasonably explicit provision inviting regulators to protect internal subsidies from erosion through competition is the instruction in section 1502(b)(3) that competition be given priority only if "appropriate to advance the purposes of ... access." Weighing against interpreting this language too broadly, however, is Congress's expressed dissatisfaction with internal subsidies in the following language in Public Law 93–641's provisions looking toward development of a uniform cost accounting system [section

1533(d)(3)(B)]: "The system shall provide that revenues derived from patients in one category shall not be used to support the provision of services to patients in any other category." Although this principle is arguably inconsistent with the mandatory internal subsidies that DHHS enforces against hospitals that have received Hill-Burton assistance in the past,[23] those requirements may be rationalized as a way of assuring that past federal subsidies are applied as intended. In general, Congress would seem to have raised competition to a level where only a very compelling need for subsidy should be deemed to outweigh it as a value.

Given the propensity of most regulators to give in to protectionist temptations, a state certificate-of-need law should probably undertake to limit their discretion in this area. This could be done, for example, by stating that the regulators shall give no weight to a proposed service's competitive impact on an existing provider or on the ability of an existing provider to continue to offer services of another type. The innovative Utah law is not as clear as it might be in its attitude toward internal subsidization, but it appears [section 26–22–12(1)(f) in Appendix A] to require a finding that the "overriding public interest" is affected as well as an estimate of the hidden cost incurred. This approach implies an appropriate presumption against cross-subsidies and an insistence on visibility and justification. Even without a legislative instruction to approach internal subsidies in this way, agencies would be well advised to be explicit both in their findings of need and their justification for the amount of subsidy involved. In many instances, health planners might be helpful in finding new sources of support for services previously financed by hidden subsidies and thus in paving the way for competition that might otherwise have to be suppressed.

NOTES

1. Chapter 5 sets forth some specific proposed language from which the final language was derived.
2. See the discussion of internal subsidies later in this chapter.
3. 45 Fed. Reg. 69,771 (1980). Note how this reading glosses over the parallel references to "institutional health services." Since the reading is demonstrably untenable with respect to the latter (as

the text shows), it can hardly be valid for inpatient services. The construction of the statute challenged here received some mild support in a passing footnote by the Supreme Court in *National Gerimedical Hospital and Gerontology Center v. Blue Cross*, 49 U.S.L.W. 4672, 4675 n.13 (1981).

4. Chapter 5 describes the proposals made to committee staffs.

5. Public Health Service Act §1513(b)(2), *as amended*.

6. Public Health Service Act §1527(a)(5), *as amended*.

7. H.R. Rep. No. 96-190, 96th Cong., 1st Sess. 53 (1979).

8. *Id.*

9. DHHS seems to agree with this interpretation. *See* 45 Fed. Reg. 69,771 (1980).

10. As indicated earlier, Public Health Service Act §1527(a)(5), *as amended*, requires that certificate-of-need decisions be consistent with the SHP.

11. 45 Fed. Reg. 69,771 (1980).

12. Public Health Service Act §1524(c)(2)(A), *as amended*, charges the SHCC with preparing "a State health plan which shall be made up of the HSP's [health systems plans] of the health systems agencies within the State. Such plan may, as found necessary by the SHCC, contain revisions of such HSP's to achieve their appropriate coordination or to deal more effectively with statewide health needs . . . ."

13. The planning law does not specifically refer to the SHCC as a "state instrumentality," but it does contemplate that the governor will (1) appoint SHCC members; (2) select the SHCC chairman with the advice and consent of the state Senate; and (3) exercise a veto over any draft SHP that he "determines does not effectively meet the statewide health needs of the state as determined by" the state agency. Public Health Service Act §1524, *as amended*. Thus, the SHCC would seem to be for all practical purposes an agency of state government.

14. *Cf.* Simon v. Cameron, 337 F. Supp. 1380 (C.D. Cal. 1970).

15. If a private party were not entitled to a hearing and a reasoned decision, supported by evidence, on his claim that the health plan improperly foreclosed competition, the procedural rights granted by Public Health Service Act §1532, *as amended*, with respect to certificate-of-need reviews would be devalued considerably. Without at least some limited judicial review of health plans, the courts would be helpless to prevent arbitrariness in cases where the certificate-of-need decision is effectively dictated by the SHP.

16. *E.g.,* Continental Air Lines, Inc. v. CAB, 519 F.2d 944 (D.C. Cir. 1975); Northern Natural Gas Co. v. FPC, 399 F.2d 953 (D.C. Cir. 1968).

17. *See* R. Noll, *Reforming Regulation: An Evaluation of the Ash Council Proposals* 25–26 (1971).

18. Posner, "Taxation by Regulation," 2 *Bell J. Econ. & Mgt. Sci.* 22 (1971).

19. Harris, "Pricing Rules for Hospitals," 10 *Bell J. Econ.* 224, 225 (1979).

20. For an extensive discussion of the federal government's attempts to force hospitals receiving federal Hill-Burton funds to assume special burdens in this regard, see Newsom v. Vanderbilt University, No. 79–1026–27–28 (6th Cir. June 2, 1981).

21. 45 Fed. Reg. 69,746 (1980) (to be codified in 42 C.F.R. §123.404(a)). This regulation's construction of the pertinent statutory language is criticized in Chapter 7.

22. *See* 45 Fed. Reg. 69,752 (1980) (to be codified in 42 C.F.R. §§123.412(a)(5), (6) and 123.413).

23. *See* 42 C.F.R. §§124.501–512 and 124.601–607 (1980).

11 INDICIA OF A WORKING MARKET
"Factors Which Affect the Effect of Competition"

The 1979 amendments contemplate that planner-regulators will routinely make threshold determinations of the efficaciousness of market forces as part of both their plan-development and project-review activities.[1] Although a threshold finding of the market's utility with respect to a particular service appears to create a presumption in favor of allowing competition to operate, it does not obviate application of the decisionmaking criteria of section 1532(c) in reaching final decisions. Both in making the threshold determination and in applying the statutory criteria—in practice, these steps will undoubtedly be telescoped into a single judgment—, the planner-regulators should consider the specific characteristics of a service and its financing that affect the need for central allocative decisions. In so doing, they should take their cue from the new statutory criterion, appearing in section 1532(c)(11), which directs consideration of "the factors which affect the effect of competition on the supply of the health services being reviewed." This chapter sets forth ten such factors with a view to helping the planner-regulators carry out their new responsibilities.

The discussion here is concerned primarily with assessing, at a particular point in time, whether market forces are operating well enough to permit the relaxation of regulatory controls over entry and new investment. A recurring theme is the potential for changes in traditional payment mechanisms that may alter the need for regulatory intervention. However, the importance of weighing the possibilities for such reforms is not fully explored until Chapter 12. Whereas this chapter deals primarily with appraising market conditions as they exist at the time of inquiry, Chapter 12 argues that the planner-regulators should make allowances for future developments that have yet to occur. Throughout Part III, the reader will detect an urgency about using regulatory powers sparingly wherever the competitive private sector could, if properly stimulated, better perform the cost-containment and resource-allocation job.

The factors listed below are not discrete items so much as topic headings helpful in organizing a discussion of the complex dynamics of the health care marketplace. Thus, they should be used not as a checklist but as a guide to the exercise of judgment on the ultimate question: Would, under all the circumstances of a particular case, the encouragement of competition be in the public interest as Congress has defined it? The goal here is to give added concreteness to the analysis of specific markets beyond that appearing in the general discusion of competition's potential in Chapters 4 and 9.

FACTORS RELATED TO FINANCING

The first four factors relate to the way in which a service is paid for and the consequent impact on demand. The overriding importance of the inquiries suggested here is revealed by the new decisionmaking criterion in section 1532(c)(12), which directs particular attention to "improvements or innovations in the financing and delivery of health services which foster competition . . . ." Even though such financing system developments are easily encompassed in the statutory reference to "the factors which affect the effect of competition," Congress apparently felt it necessary to add the additional, more explicit criterion. It thus underscored its doubts about current payment practices, its hopefulness concerning future financing system reform, and the importance that it attaches to maintaining regulatory flexibility in the face of possible change on the demand side of the market.

An important implication of this discussion is the need for health planners to collect detailed information concerning the way in which different health services are bought and paid for. It will frequently be necessary to go into the specific terms of insurance policies and public program regulations and even behind the text of such policies and regulations to the administrative reality that ultimately determines the incentives that operate. Although considerable effort will be needed to estimate the extent and significance of the distortions of demand for particular services, the rewards of a fuller understanding of the payment system's defects and of its potential for change should justify the undertaking.

Factor 1: The Scope, Extent, and Form of Third-Party Payment

- To what extent is the service paid for by someone other than the patient?
- Do consumers have both an incentive and an opportunity to economize in purchasing the service?
- Even if third-party payment is extensive, does residual price competition for self-paying patients discipline providers and supply reliable and usable yardsticks for third parties' use?
- To what extent do third-party payments for the service take forms that leave consumers an incentive to ascertain the appropriateness of expenditures and to seek out a low-cost provider?
- To what extent are services of questionable value excluded from third parties' coverage so as to introduce market checks on questionable spending?
- Has coverage of the service under private health care plans been designed and administered under competitive conditions so that consumers' preferences may be deemed to have dictated coverage and the form of benefits and to have validated their cost effects?

A certificate-of-need law would seem inappropriately invoked to block the offering of a new service if the demand for that service is not significantly distorted by the payment mechanism. In selecting an HMO, for example, consumers usually have an opportunity, directly or indirectly, to evaluate the cost of what they are buying against the cost of an alternative, and, as discussed in Chapter 8, any regulator presuming to deny them the right to express their preferences under such circumstances bears a heavy burden of persuasion. Congress's sweeping exemption of HMOs from coverage of certificate-of-need laws in 1979 confirms the view that consumer choice under reasonably well-ordered incentives should ordinarily be deemed to make regulation inappropriate. The key factor obviating regulation of HMOs and their investments is the greater opportunity for the consumer to benefit himself, directly or indirectly, by an economizing choice. The principle thus recognized is an extremely important one, since it may be applied to any discrete service as to which consumers are reasonably aware of costs, have alternatives available to them, and have reason to economize in their purchasing decisions.

It will be noted that favorable treatment of an HMO is justified by regarding all its many services to have been purchased directly by the patient, even though he faces no cost at the point of consumption; it is the plan's integration of financing and delivery that makes it possible to regard the HMO itself as the seller of the service, thus removing the distorting third-party element that invites regulatory intervention. This point links the discussion of the payment systems for a particular service under this heading with the discussion of alternative delivery systems under factor 2. In either case, the issue is whether the consumer has both an incentive and an opportunity to economize in purchasing services—which he does not have where a third party unrelated to the provider is committed to pay the bill. The distinction between direct and indirect economizing—that is, between economizing in the purchase of discrete services and economizing in the selection of a provider group—accounts for the fundamental dichotomy that is drawn in the discussion of this and the following factor. These two factors together capture the full range of cost-containment strategies and should recall discussion in Chapter 9, which also stressed the conceptual distinction, often blurred in practice, between these two basic types of economizing.

The converse of the proposition that entry regulation on the basis of need is not called for where patients pay their own way is the proposition that regulation may be needed where the proposed service is one that, unlike services in an HMO, is commonly paid for by a passive and unquestioning third-party payer. However, if third-party payment does not cover the service in enough cases to induce substantial distortions, the planner-regulators should not deem demand factors to preclude reliance on competition. This may be a rationale for not imposing certificate-of-need requirements to control the location of doctors' offices, even though doctors, like hospitals, allegedly can "create their own demand." Other services also might be deemed sufficiently subject to discipline by patients paying their own bills that competition should be encouraged by admitting any competent provider to the market.

The judgment about when third-party payment is too widespread to trust the marketplace is difficult. For one thing, the costs and deficiencies of regulation should weigh against jumping too quickly to that conclusion. On the positive side, the existence of a substantial fringe of self-pay patients may provide valuable yardsticks for assessing the impact of third-party payment on utilization and price. Such yardsticks may help the regulators to judge the magnitude of third-party effects that may necessitate regulation. Moreover, the availability of a market yardstick may argue for relying on other kinds of controls instead of on entry restrictions to deal with any cost problem that exists. For example, prices and utilization patterns prevailing in that segment of the market where patients pay their own way might be deemed to provide reference points helpful to both public and private financing plans in determining what they will pay for, how much they will pay, and under what circumstances. On the other hand, it should be recognized that the widely used yardstick of "usual, customary, and reasonable" fees has not been a good guide for effective cost containment because under UCR systems no effort is made to distinguish between charges for covered and noncovered services; because the self-pay market is not viewed *alone* as a guide to the reasonableness of fees, charges to non-cost-conscious patients are allowed to inflate fee levels. Only where the self-pay market is large and typical enough to be regarded as a fair and reliable point of reference in assessing the reasonableness of pricing and utilization practices could it possibly serve usefully as a yardstick in administering public and private financing systems. A possibly insurmountable problem is the difficulty of obtaining reliable data on treatment patterns and charges to uninsured patients.

Third-party payment may take many forms, and each method of payment has different implications for costs and the problem of moral hazard. Perhaps the most destructive methods of payment involve retrospective cost reimbursement. Service-benefit and public financing plans that pay providers' costs incurred in treating their beneficiaries are a well-recognized cause of cost escalation, but commercial insurers' indemnity policies may be an even more destructive form of cost reimbursement. Because the latter plans reimburse patients' rather than providers' costs, they eliminate patient resistance to providers' overcharges without substituting either the cost of service as a criterion or the plan as an effective agent for bargaining with providers. Both cost-reimbursement approaches leave room, however, for contractual and administrative checks on automatic cost pass-throughs, so that planner-regulators, in attempting to assess the extent of distortions flowing from these payment methods, must look beneath the surface to estimate the payment systems' overall impact. It is quite possible that policy limits on payment obligations, technical wrinkles in service-benefit contractual arrangements with providers, statutory limits on public program liabilities, and administrative practices in plans of all types have greater cost-restraining impact than is usually supposed. Moreover, further evolution in the way services are in fact paid for, even under arrangements that ostensibly still call for cost reimbursement, might ultimately obviate the necessity for regulatory controls on entry and investment. As one example of a change that increases providers' risks and undercuts the conventional wisdom concerning the payment system's passivity, the Medicare law now includes authority for DHHS to focus on "reasonable" rather than actual costs[2] and may thus substantially reduce the federal government's obligation to keep hospitals whole for costs incurred in treating Medicare beneficiaries.

This is not the place to explore all the ways in which third-party payers can vary the terms and their administration of cost-reimbursement systems or can depart from cost reimbursement altogether. But planner-regulators charged with assessing the harms and benefits of allowing increased competition in the provision of particular services must be alert to the realities of payment mechanisms. Not only should they be aware of such obvious things as the use of cost sharing and fixed-dollar benefits, but they should identify elements in cost determination and limits on cost pass-throughs that put providers at risk. In this discussion of the scope and extent of third-party payment, the focus should be on the extent to which the form of such payments leaves consumers with an incentive to ascertain the appropriateness of the particular expenditure and to seek out a lower-cost provider. Things to look at include the use and magnitude of deductibles and coinsurance, which leave consumers responsible for paying many costs out of pocket and thus cost conscious enough to influence many provider practices and to deter many price and cost increases. A greater impact on the moral hazard would result if particular benefits were paid on a fixed-dollar basis, leaving consumers responsible for paying the marginal dollar and thus with an incentive to seek out less costly providers.

Besides altering the form of benefit payments, another way in which health plans can cope with moral hazard is to impose conditions and limitations on their liability to pay for particular services. In an insurance plan, such conditions and limitations operate as exclusions from coverage. Through careful design and administration, such exclusions could make the insureds self-insurers with respect to many services whose value is frequently questionable. If patients had to purchase such services, on medical advice, with the cost in view, concerns about their inappropriate utilization would be much reduced.

Thus, in looking at the scope of third-party payment for a particular service, significance should not be attached only to the percentage of persons having some kind of coverage for the service or to the percentage of services paid for by third parties. It is also important to determine whether mechanisms exist for limiting coverage in those cases where the service's cost-effectiveness and value are enough in doubt that insurance is inappropriate. Such mechanisms would include prior authorization requirements and arrangements for predetermination of benefits. Obviously, exclusions would not serve the desired purpose of inducing economizing behavior if they were at all complex and were invoked only retrospectively. It would seem that competition should stimulate efforts to design coverage limitations that could be fairly and effectively administered on a prospective basis so as to provide essential protection while also minimizing the impact of moral hazard on overall costs.

In considering whether the scope of third-party payment is narrow enough to trust market forces, it could probably not be concluded that the PSRO program, as presently administered, assures appropriately limited scope for Medicare and Medicaid benefits. Because PSRO reviews operate retrospectively for the most part and appear to limit the provision only of services whose prescription professionals would regard as bad medical practice, they probably do not prevent the programs from paying for many services whose costs exceed their benefits.[3] Moreover, PSROs' use of community practice as a yardstick is an unsatisfactory guide to efficiency or cost-effectiveness precisely because the standards of such practice have evolved in a market insufficiently disciplined by cost considerations. Furthermore, it is significant that the PSRO program is more often characterized as a quality-assurance than as a cost-containment program and that it is universally viewed as a form of regulation designed to catch irresponsible practitioners rather than as a device for putting reasonable limits on the obligations of a federal welfare system. A wide difference almost certainly exists between what is likely to be judged responsible practice and necessary care by professional standards and what the federal government should pay for to assure a satisfactory level of care for its beneficiaries. Thus, it must be concluded that the PSRO program does not provide enough limitation on the scope of federal third-party payment to support, by itself, a regulatory decision to allow competition to operate freely. Indeed, the program's implicit assumption that comprehensive benefit packages can be administered using professional standards and monopolistic peer review as the only controls on spending must be rejected as a manifestation of the precise problem that competition and decentralized decisionmaking—and regulation, for that matter—must be encouraged to overcome.

As to privately financed care, a particular service's coverage by third-party payment signifies a need for regulation only if prepayment plans are not designed and administered in a competitive setting allowing full recognition of the consumer's interest in cost containment. Thus, although scrutinizing plans' benefits, coverage, and administration may yield clues as to whether the worst regulation-inspiring fears concerning third-party payment are in danger of being realized, the more telling inquiry may be into the competitive conditions in which insurance and other plans are designed, sold, and implemented. On the one hand, there is no way of knowing when one is looking at the optimal level of cost-containment effort by third parties and when the lack of additional effort reflects high implementation costs and low consumer demand. On the other hand, planner-regulators should be able to estimate whether insurers and other plan organizers are in fact free to design and administer their benefits and coverage with a primary view to consumer preferences. In particular, they should consider whether competition among providers permits insurers to secure their cooperation in enforcing benefit limits or whether providers have conspired to resist limitations on their spending freedom. There is at the moment good reason to doubt that the market has been sufficiently free to respond to consumer interests in these respects.[4]

As long as the tax law subsidizes the purchase of excessive health insurance coverage and dilutes economizing incentives, it will be tempting to conclude that competitive conditions cannot reveal true consumer preferences and therefore that command-and-control regulation is essential. A respectable contrary view is that the impact of tax considerations should be ignored because, although they do produce a distortion in the demand for medical care and shift the market's equilibrium point, that consequence should be tolerated because it is the result of a considered social policy specifically intended to foster the consumption of medical care. If this latter view were adopted, the broad issue would be whether the marketplace was currently giving effect to the consumer's interest in containing his health care costs as well as to his interest in reducing his taxes. The factual inquiry would then be the same as that for assessing the need for regulation where the tax law was not a significant influence—namely, to determine whether the scope, extent, and form of third-party payment were being dictated by consumer choice or were instead a reflection of insurers' or providers' collective interests.

Factor 2: Progress of Alternative Delivery Systems

- To what extent are the financing and delivery of services integrated, either organizationally or contractually, so as to eliminate the demand distortions that accompany third-party payment?
- Are closed-panel HMOs or similar entities a substantial competitive factor?
- To what extent do third parties use provider participation agreements to integrate financing and delivery?
- Have private health care plans been organized and administered under competitive conditions so that consumers may be deemed to have selected, as optimal for their needs, the cost-containment mechanisms in place?

The market's efficacy would be most obvious in a market in which all care was provided through competing closed-panel HMOs or their equivalent. As noted above, HMOs' reliability as allocators of resources flows from the market check on their spending decisions that arises from their being offered to consumers in a competitive setting where purchases are made with costs in view. Even HMOs could not correct for the distorting effects of the current tax subsidy, however, so that this issue would still have to be confronted. Nevertheless, the broad exemption from certificate-of-need requirements extended to HMOs in the 1979 amendments suggests, at least tentatively, that Congress would be willing, despite the tax subsidy (which, after all, may be addressed separately), to trust a truly competitive market for health plans, where it existed, to allocate resources without regulatory assistance.

In recognizing the potential for financing system change as a factor requiring continuing review of the need for command-and-control regulation, the House committee report stated that HMO development was the type of financing system innovation most likely to permit regulators to relax their control (see Appendix B). Nevertheless, Congress's introduction of "improvements or innovations in the financing and delivery of health services which foster competition" as a new criterion in the same set of amendments that largely removed HMOs from the regulators' jurisdiction indicates a clear recognition that potentially important innovation can also occur in traditional modes of financing. Discussion of factor 1 indicated that health care plans based on traditional third-party models and bearing little resemblance to HMOs may indeed find ways to cope with the moral hazard problem well enough to obviate public oversight of capital investments and the introduction of new services.

Certain analytical benchmarks must be kept in mind in assessing the ability of the demand side of the market to discipline the supply side. To begin with, it is not enough to observe that all health care plans must be marketed competitively. Even though it might be assumed that competing plans cannot automatically pass on cost increases, interplan competition probably signifies very little if the plans are not able, or do not choose, to procure providers' services on a competitive basis. As noted in Chapters 4 and 9, the absence of active buying and selling—that is, competition—at the interface between health care plans and providers is an important aspect of the market failure that has seemed to necessitate regulation in this industry. Thus, a crucial question is whether health care plans are merely payers or have assumed, directly or indirectly, the role of purchasing agent for the consumer. Exemption of HMOs from certificate-of-need requirements is justified precisely because, unlike traditional insurers and most service-benefit plans, they have undertaken to act as cost-conscious purchasers of physician and hospital services in a competitive market. To the extent that other health care plans are *both* motivated by competition to control costs (as all plans presumably are in the absence of collusion, unless the tax subsidy is deemed to dilute cost-containment incentives excessively) *and* free to purchase needed inputs competitively, they and the providers doing business with them do not require regulatory oversight. In essence, any plan that deals effectively with providers as competitors, either hiring their services as employees or negotiating with them as independent contractors, meets the definition of an alternative delivery system for present purposes.

Indicia of effective health care plan competition in the procurement of provider services include, in particular, the use by competing insurers of provider participation agreements that specify both the price of services and administrative requirements necessary to implement utilization controls and coverage limitations. Because the use of such agreements implies either the exclusion of uncooperative or high-cost providers or payment for their services on less advantageous terms, they are potentially the most promising means of bringing competitive pressure to bear on providers. Planner-regulators assessing the need for regulation should consider the extent to which insurers and others are free to employ this vital cost-containment tool. Obviously, the market for providers' services cannot be classed as competitive if the only plans using participation agreements are under the control of organized providers or if the terms of contracts have been negotiated collectively.[5]

Other methods of dividing the provider community into competing elements may also be envisioned. For example, an insurer might quote lower, experience-based premiums for insureds who patronize only an identified hospital or multispecialty group practice or only those physicians and hospitals on an insurer-developed list. By this means, an alternative delivery system could be created, in effect, without the preferred providers' voluntary agreement. Nevertheless, the essential ingredients of effective competition would be present since both efficiency and the patronizing of efficient providers would be rewarded. New disincentives for investments unwarranted by consumer demand would appear, and regulation could correspondingly be withdrawn.

If insurers, provider groups, and others are relatively free to organize alternative delivery systems of all kinds and to use participation agreements and other measures that seemed cost-effective, it would not be essential that all care be paid for under such arrangements or through conventional HMOs before one could conclude that the market was capable of allocating resources well enough. Thus, rather than looking only at the extent of alternative delivery system development, planner-regulators should consider the competitive climate as a whole. If competitive conditions are truly healthy, with barriers to entry and innovation low, the market could be deemed to reflect consumer preferences well enough to validate the cost-containment mechanisms in place as optimal for consumers' needs. It is argued in Chapter 12 that, even though cost-containment mechanisms are not fully developed, the potential for innovation in payment and delivery methods may alone obviate command-and-control regulation.

Factor 3: The Cost Burden of Obsolete Capital Facilities

- Who bears the cost burden of unused facilities?
- Putting aside as irrelevant the question whether existing providers or their patrons bear the loss when new competition renders existing facilities obsolete, would the financing system effectively insulate *new* investors from the consequences of unwise investments, thus encouraging the creation of excess capacity?

One theory that has been widely used to justify protectionist entry controls in regulated industries is that, because the capital costs of existing facilities must be paid for by consumers in any event, allowing new competition that renders existing facilities obsolete may be unduly costly to the public. This theory has often been employed in health sector regulation to frustrate such competitive developments as the construction of ambulatory surgical facilities, which are deemed to drain patients away from existing hospitals without reducing their overhead. The special emphasis given by Congress to the need to control investments in "institutional health services" may signify a concern that the capital costs of facilities rendered obsolete by such competitive developments may be borne by the public anyway. On the other hand, Congress's 1979 grant of a broad exemption from certificate-of-need requirements to HMOs reflects at least a partial rejection of this theory. Even though HMOs' chief economizing skill is in substituting outpatient for inpatient care,[6] the impact of HMO competition on existing hospitals—and on those committed to pay their capital costs—was obviously not a matter that Congress viewed as a decisive consideration.

The 1979 amendments did, however, expressly authorize the planner-regulators to consider, as one factor in certificate-of-need decisions, the impact of new construction projects "on the costs and charges to the public of providing health services by other persons." This language in section 1532(c)(9) seemingly instructs the regulators to direct attention to the way in which the capital costs of providers adversely affected by new competition are handled by the financing system. If such capital costs are automatically passed through to consumers whether or not the facilities are used, they would appear to be a matter of legitimate regulatory concern. On the other hand, if the providers themselves must absorb losses due to obsolescence—as occurs regularly in unregulated markets—, the implication seems to be that the impact on existing firms should be ignored.

The best justification for drawing distinctions based on the actual incidence of losses attributable to capital obsolescence is not, however, as the quoted statutory language seems to imply, that such losses may fall on consumers rather than providers. (After all, all such costs are borne ultimately by the society as a whole.) Instead, a much more pertinent point is that, if providers themselves bear the risk of obsolescence, there is a strong market deterrent against the construction of facilities for which there is a doubtful need. The relevant subject of inquiry is therefore not the incidence of costs already incurred but the incentives affecting new or expanding firms. The points raised here may thus be viewed in conjunction with factor 4, which deals with the market deterrent to inappropriate investments—that is, with the incentives facing the firm proposing a capital project.

The argument here is of great importance. Whether or not an incumbent facility's sunk costs are subject to recoupment, creation of a competitive substitute for that facility will often be efficient. New investment will be desirable whenever the total costs of the new facility are less than the sum of operating costs and the opportunity costs (that is, any net revenue lost by forgoing alternative uses of the resource, including conversion or salvage) of the facility rendered obsolete. The problem is to know whether the market satisfactorily encourages investments likely to meet this test and discourages all others. This should be the regulators' sole concern.

Under a proper understanding of this issue, the inquiry has to do exclusively with the incentives influencing the new investment. Nevertheless, as long as the same financing system underwrites both existing and proposed facilities, no distinction is likely to be drawn in considering how fully the system reimburses providers for the capital costs of facilities that become obsolete. However, if the proposed facility is subject to incentives that are different from those of its competitors, distinctions should be drawn. It is quite possible that the new facility should be approved irrespective of how competitor sunk costs are treated. The HMO case, as reviewed in Chapter 8, is a classic demonstration of the operative principle. Although HMOs were relieved in the 1979 amendments of most regulation because they must be marketed as discrete packages to cost-conscious consumers, they have been left subject to a residuum of regulatory oversight precisely to protect against the risk that they might fall back on open-ended third-party financing systems to bail them out in the event of mistaken overexpansion. In contrast, facilities and services that are typically paid for by third-party payers have been left under strict regulatory control precisely because, presumptively at least, they lack accountability to consumers for costs incurred. Without question, the planner-regulators have the legitimate function of supplying a regulatory deterrent to overexpansion where the market does not yet threaten to devalue capital investments that ultimately prove to have been unwise.

The task of assessing whether the prevailing financing system adequately penalizes inappropriate investments can be quite complicated. On the one hand, if public utility rate setting were in effect in the health sector, the issue would be a purely technical one. But hospital rate setting, where it is in place, and cost reimbursement formulas are not usually so simple. The most common situation is that institutional providers have some, but incomplete, power to pass their incurred capital costs along. A final judgment on who would bear the cost of new facilities that ultimately prove or become unneeded may depend on a technical analysis of cost reimbursement formulas (for example, is overhead allocated on the basis of the actual or some assumed level of occupancy?) and of indemnification techniques (for example, do cost sharing and indemnification limits foster enough price competition to prevent costs of obsolete facilities from being freely passed along?). Not only are the regulators required to recognize new ways of paying for services when they emerge, but, as Chapter 12 makes clear, the regulators should recognize that existing reimbursement and indemnification practices are subject to change. Indeed, in assessing the market's deterrence to current investments, they should recognize that, even today, providers may no longer be able to depend to the same degree on future cost reimbursements and noncompetitive pricing for recoupment of sunk capital. Once prospective investors cease relying on outmoded financing systems to preserve their capital, market forces will adequately serve the deterrent function that the planner-regulators have sought to perform.

Factor 4: Price Competition as a Deterrent to New Capital Investment

- Are firms with unused facilities likely to engage in competitive price cutting, as they do in a normal market?
- Does a firm contemplating a new capital investment anticipate having to meet price competition and possibly having to sell below cost if it creates excess capacity?
- Does the anticipation of price cutting by firms with obsolete facilities serve to deter inappropriate investment?

In a normal market, obsolete facilities may be a powerful competitive factor. Except to the extent of any salvage value, the capital costs of such facilities are "sunk" or unrecoverable, and thus they will be largely ignored by the rational seller in future pricing decisions. The resulting threat of price cutting by firms whose facilities would be rendered worthless by new facilities will thus discourage the making of new capital investments and the creation of excess capacity. In a smoothly functioning market, a firm will enter or expand only where it has confidence in its greater efficiency or its product's greater attractiveness and thus can count on profitably riding out a period of depressed prices.

In the market for insured health services, however, things are apt to be different. As discussed under factor 3, most forms of cost reimbursement pay capital costs when they would no longer be recoverable in a normal competitive market and thus obviate competitive price cutting by the proprietors of obsolete facilities. Cost reimbursement may also effectively guarantee an expanding firm that its own prices need not fall below costs—as they might, at least temporarily, in a normal market with an excess of capital facilities. Moreover, because many forms of third-party payment effectively insulate the consumer from price concerns even at the margin, potential price cutting by the incumbent facility seeking to maintain its position is rendered ineffective as a competitive strategy and thus as a deterrent to a new entrant. It is for these reasons, essentially, that traditional forms of third-party payment have necessitated controls on capital investment.

Thus, unless the extent and forms of third-party payment vary substantially from traditional approaches, market forces will continue to be unsatisfactory allocators of resources. For this reason, careful analysis of financing techniques, particularly with respect to the reimbursement of capital costs, will be necessary to assess market functioning. Perhaps the ideal market is one in which competing health plans such as HMOs are engaged to a significant extent in purchasing the particular service on a competitive basis; indeed, this is reported to be occurring for hospital services in the Twin Cities area.[7] Nevertheless, other variations from the destructive reimbursement patterns of the past may also help to restore market forces to a useful role. Factors 1 through 4 are intended to help answer the crucial question: Does the third-party payment system in fact insulate providers from market risks associated with the creation of excess capacity, or do market forces adequately deter unneeded investment? Financing systems are in such a state of flux that this must be regarded as an open question to be answered empirically on a market-by-market, service-by-service basis.

CHARACTERISTICS OF THE SERVICE

Several features of the service in question may affect competition's value in allocating supply. The first three of the characteristics identified relate directly to the financing of the service and to the opportunities for private cost containment.

Factor 5: Nondiscretionary Versus Discretionary Services

- Is the service a "necessity" in the sense that its consumption would not be much affected by the availability of third-party financing?
- If so, is there nevertheless a risk that third-party payment will encourage the offering of more costly versions of the service?

- Have third parties addressed this problem by imposing fixed limits on what they will pay for the service? Should they be expected to do so?
- If the service is discretionary and not a necessity, why do third parties cover it at all (if they do)? Should they be expected to exclude the service from coverage?
- If the service is sometimes necessary and sometimes elective, do third parties attempt to limit their coverage to the former cases? Should they be expected to do so?

If demand for a particular service would not be much affected by changes in price—that is, if the service is a necessity and not discretionary—then the fact that it is covered by third-party financing should not much affect its consumption.[8] On the other hand, if new entrants are offering more costly versions of the same essential service, a different aspect of the moral hazard problem would still be present. The added increments of "quality"—if that is the right term to describe more costly equipment and heavier staffing—might not themselves be necessities, yet if the third-party financing system were ready and willing to reimburse the added costs, entry controls might seem appropriate. Nevertheless, the regulators lack jurisdiction over many qualitative improvements that existing providers of the service might introduce. Moreover, even where they have jurisdiction, they frequently find it hard to resist the claims of "quality."

Much the better means of cost containment in the use of non-discretionary services would seem to be for the third parties to impose a fixed limit on what they will pay for each essential service. If this limit reflected what the service could be obtained for from an efficient provider offering adequate quality, the consumer would have both the essential financial protection he requires and an incentive to evaluate any cost differentials that exist among providers. Thus, planner-regulators might well conclude that allowing free entry into the provision of such services would allow low-cost providers, such as abortion clinics or other ambulatory care services, at least to begin to compete effectively with high-cost providers. With such alternatives available, third parties might more quickly perceive the benefits of reimbursing providers or patients on some basis other than costs incurred. Conversely, restrictions on entry would have the effect of conferring a franchise on existing providers, putting pressure on third parties to cover their high costs. In addition to thus discouraging desirable change in the financing system, the planner-regulators' assumption of responsibility—a responsibility, moreover, which they probably cannot adequately discharge—would also contribute to the financing system's inertia by perpetuating the perception that health care costs are a public, not a private, responsibility.

Not all health services are nondiscretionary, of course. Indeed, some are so discretionary in all cases that their coverage by health insurance seems inappropriate in view of the magnitude of the moral hazard and the diminished need for financial protection—given that the service is never medically essential. Examples of such services include purely cosmetic surgery, the services of a health spa, and other services appropriately viewed as luxuries. Some such discretionary services might be extremely expensive and desirable enough in some circumstances that an insured group would elect (perhaps for tax reasons) to pay for covering them. An available technique for reducing the group's exposure to moral hazard would be to require a large (say, 50 percent) copayment; this strategy (which might be adopted for coronary bypass surgery,[9] for example) would assure that the service would be used only where the patient attached a high value to it. Because third parties have available the strategy of thus totally or partially excluding the service from coverage, regulation of the supply of such discretionary services by certification of need might seem unnecessary to protect against overutilization induced by third-party payment. Of course, such strategies may not be widely used because of tax considerations,[10] legal requirements,[11] or administrative problems in drawing lines.[12] In this event, regulation will appear appropriate, but it should still be deemed desirable—and possibly feasible—in the long run to allow the supply of such services to be allocated by the market.

The case for entry regulation is perhaps strongest where, judging in benefit/cost terms, the service is nonessential or discretionary in many cases but nondiscretionary in others. Coverage of the service by third-party payers would be appropriate only in the cases dictated by clear medical necessity, but for the health care plan to distinguish one case from another would often require complex administrative mechanisms, such as a second opinion ob-

tained from an insurer-designated physician, to verify necessity or
the presence of prescribed indications. Where such strategies are
not cost-effective, regulatory intervention to limit the supply of
the service and bring about its rationing by providers will seem
plausible.

In assessing the need for command-and-control regulation in
these instances, the planner-regulators must consider whether
third parties have taken, or might be expected to take, the initiatives needed to exclude highly discretionary services from
coverage. Although practical measures may seem available, special considerations may prevent third parties from adopting
them. Desirable innovation might be discouraged by fear of provider displeasure and retaliation, the natural disinclination of
oligopolists to compete in new and potentially disruptive ways,
the probability that rapid imitation will deprive the innovators
of a significant competitive advantage, and the likelihood that
some of the benefits of innovation will not be captured by the
innovator but will instead, as in the case of an innovation that
favorably affects the standard of medical practice in the community, accrue to others. Later discussion identifies the system's resistance to desirable change in such circumstances as a
market failure warranting the planner-regulators' invervention.
It is suggested, however, that the health planners consider intervening to break up the logjam, rather than simply seizing the
market's temporary recalcitrance as an excuse to assume a command-and-control role.

Factor 6: The Nature of Substitutes for the Service in Question

- Does the service substitute for a higher cost service, so that
  its increased availability may generate cost savings?
- Would the service's increased availability induce use by patients with lower cost alternatives?

Sometimes, the substitute service that is likely to be used
when a regulation-created constraint is encountered is more expensive than the competing service being regulated. The classic

instance is the use of hospitals to care for patients who cannot find a nursing home bed. When such a circumstance occurs, it invalidates a basic assumption underlying certificate-of-need requirements—namely, that reducing the availability of a service will result in the use of less costly alternatives and savings to the community. This problem is presented almost anytime the proposed new facility or service is one that substitutes for costly hospital care. Thus, restricting market entry for nursing homes, ambulatory surgery facilities, home health services, HMOs, hospices, abortion clinics, and many other competitive innovations can increase the demand for hospital beds. Similarly, each level of care is a substitute for a less costly one below it, making the problem a pervasive one except at the very top—the tertiary-care facility.

The identification of the low-cost provider is not always as easy as it may seem. For example, some cost savings may be achieved only by shifting costs to the patient and his family. Most important, unrecoverable capital costs should be ignored in making cost comparisons. Furthermore, the allocation of overhead and other joint costs must be done with an understanding of the issues involved. Ideally, some adjustment should be made for qualitative differences and convenience factors. Because specific cost estimates are extraordinarily difficult to make in the best of circumstances, it is likely that planner-regulators will rely on general studies of cost effectiveness. While everyone will certainly agree with the general principle that lower cost alternatives should be employed, arguments will continue over the current measurement of costs and the significance of qualitative factors.

If a community's supply of hospital beds had been closely tailored to fit its needs, then it might be reasonable to expect the system as a whole to find administrative ways to assure that patients are treated in the surroundings most appropriate to their specific condition; in such a tightly planned and controlled system, need factors alone might be considered, and the notion of offering competitive alternatives would seem out of place. But there are few places where hospital beds of each type are under such tight control. Moreover, providers lack incentives to allocate existing supplies to patients strictly in accordance with medical need. Also, the systems available for reviewing and controlling patient placement are not so developed or dependable as to justify confidence that total regulatory control will cause services to be rationed on a need basis and thus produce efficient performance. In the real world, therefore, regulatory discouragement of lower cost competitors may be quite destructive. Indeed, the scarcity of such lower cost alternatives will make it harder for the planner-regulators to control the growth of the hospitals themselves.

In most of the cases in which these problems are encountered, there will also exist the more commonly observed risk that the moral hazard will induce inappropriate utilization of the service in question by patients whose alternative is a lower cost (rather than a higher cost) service. In such cases, the regulators must compare the benefits and costs of regulation very carefully. In their assessments, they must not neglect to consider the ways in which the financing plans can themselves affect the system's performance. As later discussion develops more fully, third-party control on price and utilization may often be preferable to entry controls. The strong incentive for public and private plans to achieve correct placement of their beneficiaries and to reduce the impact of moral hazard can be a powerful ally of the regulators in improving the system's overall performance.

Factor 7: The Presence of Capital Investment

- Does the service involve an appreciable capital investment?
- Does the financing system continue to view capital investments as creating future obligations?
- Does rate-setting regulation, if any, view capital investments as presumptively recoverable?
- Are the resources in question, including any capital assets, mobile enough to dispel the felt necessity to protect the investment against obsolescence through competition?

Another factor that may decisively affect the need for regulatory command-and-control decisions on entry and expansion is the presence or absence of a significant capital investment. Obviously, third-party payment can induce inappropriate utilization and price escalation for all types of services without regard to their capital intensity, and Congress has acknowledged this by requiring that state certificate-of-need laws cover all new institutional health services, not just those involving capital expenditures. But capital investment creates claims on the future that regulation can appropriately seek to minimize, and it is this circumstance that makes a policy of uncontrolled entry especially dangerous in cases where large capital outlays are involved. A brief analysis of how large capital investments today obligate the public in the future may help to explain why services such as home health care, even though demand for it may be distorted by third-party payment, is much less in need of entry controls than the construction of a new hospital.[13] This discussion also suggests some reasons why Congress heavily emphasized the current need to use regulation rather than market forces to determine the supply of "inpatient . . . and other institutional health services."

To appreciate why capital investment requires special oversight, one must have reference to the dynamics of both regulation and the political process as well as to competition's long-term prospects. First, the existing financing system, including both private insurance and public programs, embodies a tacit and incomplete but still strong commitment to reimburse providers for capital costs. (Although a badly underutilized facility will usually not recover its full capital outlay in the form of depreciation, it will nevertheless be better off than its free-market counterpart, which has no assurance that even its out-of-pocket costs can be recovered.) Second, hospital rate-setting regulation, largely borrowed from the public utility field, seems to embody the same commitment to cover capital costs except under unusual circumstances.[14] Third, when a certificate-of-need agency permits a capital investment to be made, some implication arises that, as an outlay to provide a "needed" service, the investment is entitled to be recouped. Fourth, regulatory bodies of all kinds, reflecting a bias toward fairness at the expense of efficiency, have long indulged the "sunk-cost obsession," which causes them automatically to reject any competitive development that would reduce the present value of the investments of regulated firms.[15] Finally, the political process itself is probably more responsive to claims that investments would be devalued and bricks and mortar rendered obsolete than to claims of less tangible consequences flowing from strengthened competition. When all these factors are added up, the existence of excess capital investment looms as a considerable barrier—above and beyond the barrier posed by vested interests generally—to substantial change and, specifically, to the introduction of market forces.

It is ironic that, although regulation by certificate of need was introduced primarily to curb investments that create system obligations, regulation may itself strengthen the sense of obligation that is felt—and thus the urgency of strict control. The problem of seeming to guarantee recovery of capital costs is likely to be greatest in those states where rate-setting and certificate-of-need functions are integrated in the state bureaucracy, but may also exist where the programs are separately administered unless specific steps are taken to disabuse expectations. The well-regarded Maryland Health Care Cost Review Commission has been careful to deny any obligation toward facilities that obtain certificates of need.[16] In the Utah Pro-competitive Certificate of Need Act of 1979 [section 26–22–2(3) in Appendix A], the legislature stated its belief "that the need for health services should be subject to an independent test in the health services market" and directed that "nothing in this chapter shall be construed as requiring those purchasing health services to fully reimburse the costs of projects approved under this chapter."

Health services that do not involve significant capital investments, such as home health services, do not threaten to freeze the system because they are not themselves frozen in place. In an increasingly competitive market, they can expand or contract with relative ease. Moreover, they do not present the same risk of embarrassment that the planner-regulators face when a bricks-and-mortar facility is admitted to the market today and rendered obsolete by market forces tomorrow. Precisely because their admission to the market creates less of a political-economic barrier both to market-inspired innovations and to regulatory changes of direction, new health services that involve negligible capital outlays are less in need of strict command-and-control regulation than other facilities and services. This conclusion is confirmed by the provision, noted earlier, in the 1979 amendments that directs the regulators to consider the effect of new construction projects, which obviously involve capital expenditures, on the costs paid by the public for services provided by others.

Factor 8: The Benefits of Nonprice Competition

- Even if price is not an appreciable factor in purchasing decisions, is competition likely to yield improved quality or greater patient convenience and satisfaction?
- Might the benefits of nonprice competition be great enough to outweigh its cost-escalating tendencies, despite the clear congressional purpose to suppress the cost impact of such competition?
- Are providers sufficiently constrained in passing on incurred costs that nonprice competition could be expected to stimulate efficiency and discourage waste in the use of resources?
- On balance, can it be said that nonprice competition, because it stimulates attention to consumer needs and preferences and induces the husbanding of resources, is preferable to no competition at all (i.e., monopoly)?

Where price competition is ineffectual due to passive third-party payment, competition may still play a constructive role in stimulating providers to strive for improved quality, increased efficiency, and greater patient convenience and satisfaction. Because competition could be highly beneficial in promoting these values, regulators might be expected to establish the seriousness of countervailing hazards before engaging in exclusionary regulation.

Certificate-of-need requirements were introduced in large part because competition in health services tended to focus exclusively on nonprice factors and thus to have powerful cost-escalating tendencies. For this reason, competition to serve non-cost-conscious patients and physicans should not be encouraged unless circumstances suggest that, in the particular case, the threat of inappropriate cost increases is minimal due to the nature of the service or the way it is paid for, is minimized by regulatory or other checks built into the system, or is capable of being offset by competitively induced cost-containment strategies readily available to private third parties. But the benefits of nonprice competition are not to be totally ignored. Congress explicitly recognized the value of nonprice as well as price competition in the 1979 amendments, when it embraced as a national priority "the strengthening of competitive forces in the health services industry wherever competition and consumer choice can constructively serve . . . to advance the purposes of quality assurance, cost effectiveness, and access." Although the absence of any constraint at all on cost increases associated with nonprice competition will usually justify refusals to encourage competitive entry, the benefits of such competition are great enough that the regulators should be willing to tolerate some uncertainty concerning cost impacts and even some limited cost increases in order to obtain them. Planner-regulators should also perceive that efforts to strengthen consumer and provider cost consciousness through financing system reforms will benefit the public not only through cost reduction but in other ways as well.

Although the 1979 amendments do not preclude giving weight to nonprice benefits of competition, there are good reasons for not opening up every certificate-of-need proceeding to permit argument concerning such benefits. One way of confining the inquiry in a wide range of cases might be to give effect to a statutory presumption, such as that discussed in Chapter 10, against letting market forces operate with respect to "inpatient ... and other institutional health services." Under this approach, a proposed nursing home could not, without also showing significant changes in the methods of financing nursing home care, make the argument, suggested in Chapter 13, that competition is a particularly strong force for quality assurance. This is in itself a strong argument against making the presumption concerning inpatient facilities conclusive or rebuttable only by evidence concerning a service's financing. Nevertheless, the presumption may be valuable as a reminder that quality or other gains from nonprice competition are a suspicious circumstance, not an unalloyed blessing. Certainly the presumption should be strong enough that the burden of proof on the proponent of a service cannot be easily carried.

The possible benefits of nonprice competition include improvements in the quality of care, including not only the technical quality and intensity of services, but also amenities and accessibility. Claims of improved quality should be viewed skeptically, however, since regulation was designed specifically to curb this quality-oriented competition—precisely because, without cost constraints, it has gotten out of hand. Despite physicians' and others' frequent reference to quality and medical need as absolute values, the only defensible understanding of these concepts is in relative terms so that increments of quality must be justified in terms of their costs. It has been argued that market mechanisms are more likely than regulatory ones to be effective in addressing quality-cost tradeoffs, and this is perhaps the overriding reason why health system planner-regulators should attach a high value to getting market forces to work on resource-allocation problems. But, even in the absence of a developed capability in the private sector to address tradeoffs, competition can maintain high-quality standards. The regulators must be willing to assess, in appropriate cases, whether the qualitative gains likely to accrue from nonprice competition are mere frills or are truly valuable increments of quality deserving weight in a regulatory benefit/cost calculus.

Quality-promoting competition can also stimulate efficiency in the use of resources. Where any limitation exists on providers' ability to pass on particular costs—and such limitations are increasingly prevalent—nonprice competition with other providers can force providers to employ available resources to the consumer's advantage. Although the level of quality achieved—admittedly, the term *quality* is used loosely—may be excessive as a matter of allocative efficiency, under competition any excessive spending is more likely to benefit the patients being treated than to benefit the providers themselves or to be wasted through inefficiency. Nonprice competition promotes efficiency precisely because protected monopolists are not pressed to maintain high standards and may take some of their profits in the form of excessive staff, perquisites, and low productivity. Moreover, nonprofit firms with monopoly power, such as one finds throughout the health care industry, have even less reason, due to the absence of the profit motive, to be concerned about the quantity of resources they employ to produce a given output. In many situations, a strong argument can be made to the effect that nonprice competition, because it stimulates attention to consumer needs and preferences and induces the husbanding of resources so as to satisfy these needs and preferences better, is preferable to no competition at all.

ALTERNATIVE WAYS OF CONTROLLING THE SERVICE'S COSTS

Finally, even in the absence of major reforms in financing systems, competition's adverse impact on costs must not be too readily assumed. Thus, the existence of alternative methods of cost containment must be considered. Factor 9 calls attention to the possibility that public and other nonmarket controls may prevent competition from having undue cost-escalating effects. Factor 10 opens up a totally different line of inquiry by inviting attention to potential rather than actual cost controls that competition might stimulate in the private sector.

Factor 9: The Existence of Nonmarket Controls on Costs

- Does existing federal and state cost-containment regulation, such as state hospital rate setting, reduce providers' ability to pass through cost increases to an extent that makes some nonprice competition tolerable?
- Are government payments to providers of the service fixed without specific reference to costs, making nonprice competition less of a cost-escalating threat?
- Are existing checks on utilization abuses, including public and privately sponsored peer review mechanisms, sufficiently reliable to warrant relaxing supply restrictions and encouraging competition?

Given the benefits that may be derived from nonprice competition, planner-regulators might encourage it if the risk of cost escalation were deemed not to be great. One reason this risk might be acceptable is the existence of regulatory or other nonmarket cost controls. Cost is a function of both price and utilization, and, if these are both controlled to some extent, then nonprice competition should impose useful discipline on providers.

Considerable complexity is involved in assessing the efficacy of regulatory and other controls on cost and utilization. Hospital cost-containment regulation has been undertaken in various forms by a number of states and proposed at the federal level. Some state efforts are tied so closely to institution-specific costs that they would seem not to warrant lifting certificate-of-need determinations intended to establish the legitimacy of the costs that a hospital wishes to pass on. On the other hand, the well-regarded program in Maryland has largely ignored planning decisions in rate setting. This approach, plus rate setting that attaches only limited weight to a particular institution's actual costs, would permit the planners to encourage competition without fear that the public would be burdened with excessive costs. Thus, the Carter administration's original hospital cost-containment proposal,[17] had it passed, might have been deemed to provide a backstop justifying more widespread use of procompetitive strategies by planner-regulators for hospital-based services. On the other hand, later versions of the federal cap legislation would have encouraged automatic pass-through of the costs of all projects granted certificates of need.

Besides using direct regulation in some places, government seeks to control costs by various limitations on the price that it will pay for services rendered to beneficiaries of public programs, such as Medicare and Medicaid. While cost reimbursement is the dominant method of payment in these programs, there are some additional limits on what will be paid. Limitations to reasonable costs have been introduced for hospitals under Medicare,[18] and some state Medicaid programs pay nursing homes prospectively determined rates that are not adjusted to cover actual costs.[19] Such rate controls might be deemed, in specific cases, to diminish fears of cost-escalating impacts on public programs enough to warrant an increase in beneficial nonprice competition.

Regulators faced with a choice whether to allow a new entrant or a new service into the market as a competitive stimulus would also have to assess the risk that utilization could be inappropriately expanded. Thus, for example, if public controls over utilization effectively contained demand for the proposed service, it would be unnecessary to restrict supply in order to control inappropriate use. Some hospital rate-setting systems supply checks on utilization increases in their rate formulas and might thus be deemed to obviate concern on this score. There are as yet, however, no direct regulatory controls over utilization practices in the private sector, though the PSRO program serves, theoretically at least, to protect the Medicare and Medicaid programs against utilization abuses.[20] While incomplete in some respects, these various controls might be deemed to reduce the risk that serious overutilization would be induced by permitting competitive developments in a private sector that had not yet developed cost-containment mechanisms of its own.

Another set of nonmarket controls on price and utilization are embodied in voluntary cost-containment programs of industry groups. Professional organizations sponsor peer review systems that purport to police excessive fees, and hospitals and physicians have joined forces in the so-called Voluntary Effort in an attempt to slow the rate of hospital cost increases. In some places, PSROs, profession-sponsored "foundations for medical care," and local medical societies are already reviewing utilization practices for private insurers. These industry-sponsored cost controls are of debatable effectiveness and may serve more to legitimize higher costs and costly standards of practice than to curb inappropriate cost increases. In the last analysis, moreover, such private regulation is anticompetitive, and, to the extent that it addresses the sensitive matters of price and output, it probably violates the antitrust laws.[21] Nevertheless, although health system planners and regulators should resist the conventional view that such peer review measures are desirable reforms, it might not be amiss, in a specific case, for them to treat such industry-sponsored efforts as factors reducing the risks associated with procompetitive moves they might wish to make. The case where this view would be most appropriate would be one where the fee-for-service providers maintaining the controls—for example, through an individual practice association—faced meaningful competition from market-sensitive health care plans and thus had a real competitive incentive to contain costs.

Factor 10: The Service's Amenability to Competitively Inspired Cost Controls

This factor fundamentally shifts the focus from the market's current performance to its potential performance—that is, to the possibility that private cost controls which are not yet in place could effectively displace regulation and should therefore be encouraged. Because regulation that affirmatively seeks to realize the market's as yet unrealized potential is such a different kind of undertaking, it is the subject of a separate chapter. Chapter 12 includes a full exposition of this factor.

NOTES

1. Pub. L. No. 96–79, §103(b), *adding* Public Health Service Act §1502(b).
2. 42 U.S.C. §1396(b)(1976).
3. Havighurst & Blumstein, "Coping with Quality/Cost Trade-offs in Medical Care: The Role of PSROs," 70 *Nw. U.L. Rev.* 6 (1975).
4. Havighurst, "Professional Restraints on Innovation in Health Care Financing," 1978 *Duke L.J.* 303.
5. *Id.* at 375–77, 381–83. On the adverse competitive effect of profession-controlled IPA-type HMOs and foundations for medical care, see also Havighurst & Hackbarth, "Enforcing the Rules of Free Enterprise in an Imperfect Market: The Case of Individual Practice Associations," in *A New Approach to the Economics of Health Care* (M. Olson ed.) (in press).
6. *E.g.,* Luft, "How Do Health Maintenance Organizations Achieve Their 'Savings'?" 298 *New Eng. J. Med.* 1336 (1978).
7. *E.g., Hearings on S. 1968 before the Subcomm. on Health of the Senate Comm. on Finance*, 96th Cong., 2d Sess. 257, 278–81 (1980) (statement of Gary Appel, president of the Council of Community Hospitals, Minneapolis-St. Paul, Minn.).
8. For a conceptual discussion of how insurance affects the demand for different types of services, see Havighurst, "The Role of Competiton in Cost Containment," in Fedeal Trade Commission, Bureau of Competition, *Competition in the Health Care Sector: Past, Present, and Future* 359, 361–63 (W. Greenberg ed. 1978).
9. There has been considerable controversy over the cost-effectiveness of coronary bypass surgery. It has been rather clearly established that bypass surgery provides symptomatic relief (from angina pectoris), but its effect on heart function and on mortality and morbidity is less certain. *See, e.g.,* Kloster *et al.,* "Coronary Bypass for Stable Angina," 300 *New Eng. J. Med.* 149 (1979) (and sources cited therein).
10. The tax treatment of employer-paid health benefits provides a strong incentive for consumers to buy comprehensive coverage. Feldstein & Friedman, "Tax Subsidies, the Rational Demand for Insurance and the Health Care Crisis," 7 *J. Pub. Econ.* 155 (1977).
11. For example, state laws requiring minimum benefits may prevent extensive use of policy exclusions as a cost-containment device. Note, "Controlling Health Care Costs through Commercial Insurance Companies," 1978 *Duke L.J.* 728, 743–47.
12. *See generally* Havighurst & Hackbarth, "Private Cost Containment," 300 *New Eng. J. Med.* 1298 (1979).

13. A critical analysis of the case for subjecting home health care to certificate-of-need regulation is presented in Chapter 7.

14. Bauer, "Hospital Rate Setting—This Way to Salvation?," in *Hospital Cost Containment: Selected Notes for Future Policy* 324, 348 (M. Zubkoff, I. Raskin, & R. Hanft eds. 1978). There are, however, some notable exceptions to this general rule. *See, e.g.*, Demkovich, "Tough-Minded Cost Control Commission Keeps Lid on Maryland Hospital Rates," 11 *Nat'l J.* 1361 (1979).

15. R. Noll, *Reforming Regulation: An Evaluation of the Ash Council Proposals* 25–26 (1971).

16. *See* Demkovich, *supra* note 14.

17. S. 1391, H.R. 6575, 95th Cong., 1st Sess. (1977).

18. 42 U.S.C. §1396(b)(1976).

19. 3 *CCH Medicare and Medicaid Guide* ¶15,550 *et seq.*

20. The effectiveness of the PSRO program has been widely challenged. *See, e.g.*, Havighurst & Blumstein, *supra* note 3; Demkovich, "The Physician Peer Review Program—Does It Cost More than It Saves?" 12 *Nat'l J.* 733 (1980).

21. Havighurst, *supra* note 4, at 374–83; Havighurst & Hackbarth, *supra* note 5.

12 REGULATING TO STIMULATE FINANCING SYSTEM REFORM
The Market-Forcing Strategy

Prevailing methods of paying for medical care undeniably provide a strong warrant for imposing strict entry and investment controls. But, insofar as such controls have the desired effect of curbing the system's growth propensities, they also have the undesirable effect of reducing pressures on consumers, health care insurers, government programs, and others to discover and implement new methods of financing that curb, rather than fuel, cost escalation. A powerful tension thus exists between the need for regulation in pursuit of short-run cost savings and the desirability of long-run evolution in the direction of fundamental reform. This chapter offers a way of recognizing and accommodating that tension in health planning and certificate-of-need regulation.

CHOOSING A REGULATORY STRATEGY

Because there exist realistic, though still uncertain, prospects for competitively inspired private sector cost containment, health system planner-regulators' choice of a regulatory strategy requires careful consideration. Indeed, the regulatory stance adopted toward competition's role may be of crucial importance in determining the pace and extent of the financing system's evolution toward more cost-effective performance and thus the prospects for the eventual displacement of health-sector regulation by market forces. The strategic options available to the planner-regulators range from radical to conservative.

The Laissez-Faire Approach

The most radical position that health system planner-regulators might take is that, in view of the availability of private cost-containment techniques, price and utilization would be better controlled by competing financing plans and that entry controls can never adequately serve the public. On this premise, they would essentially withdraw from regulating new market entry and new investment on the basis of need. The goal of such deregulation would be to seek fundamental change exclusively through the unleashing of market forces. It is not at all clear that this radical strategy would be irrational or irresponsible. Little evidence, after all, supports the effectiveness of supply-side controls to keep costs and prices down or to squeeze inappropriate utilization out of the system.

Although a "let-'er-rip" policy could be defended as a responsible regulatory strategy, the mere theoretical possibility of private cost-containment efforts may be too speculative to warrant its adoption. Such a laissez-faire policy depends on strong, untested assumptions and is unlikely to work well without a major change in tax and other governmental policies and without effective antitrust enforcement. In any event, it is almost certainly inconsistent with the regulators' statutory mandate. The amended health planning legislation makes it quite clear that a policy of deferring to market forces must be justified on the basis of a reasonable expectation that such forces can and will serve the public adequately.[1] Moreover, case law involving other regulated industries indicates that, while regulators must give competition its due weight as a substitute for regulated monopoly, it cannot be embraced without stated reasons and without evidence indicating a probability that the public will be well served by competition in the specific case.[2] Legally, therefore, health system planner-regulators may be authorized to allow competition to operate only where an affirmative justification, supported by evidence, is given. Although Congress and the states might be well advised to repeal health-planning and certificate-of-need legislation as part of a broader strategy for letting market forces take over, as things now stand this is not an option that the regulators may themselves adopt.

The Easy Conservative Options

Far from leaning toward the radical laissez-faire approach, most health system planner-regulators will tend toward conservatism and resist accepting any responsibility at all for fostering competition. Although they may acknowledge a duty to recognize competition whenever and wherever it has become a potent and constructive force, most of them will regard that event as so unlikely to occur that it can be dismissed for practical regulatory purposes. Such assessments of competition's prospects would be partly an outgrowth of health planners' training and ideology and partly a result of political pressures and of the planners' need to obtain the cooperation of existing providers. Most planner-regulators will not perceive the highly conservative nature of their stance on these issues because the possibilities of fundamental demand-side change will have escaped their notice. Moreover, in doing battle with established interests on minor incremental issues, they will not realize the extent to which they have adopted their antagonists' assumptions concerning the rate and nature of contemplatable change and have allied themselves with those with whom they share power. It is noteworthy that planners and providers share many similar views on the efficaciousness of competition and the desirability of its encouragement.

A slightly more market-oriented approach that planners might adopt also lies toward the more conservative end of the scale. It would involve undertaking a careful and open-minded evaluation of the nine factors itemized in Chapter 11 and would contemplate employing a competitive strategy wherever market forces were found in fact to be working well. The trouble with this seemingly neutral position is that it accepts the market as it finds it and neglects even the most immediate and realistic possibilities for change in the way services are bought and paid for. More seriously, it implies that the financing system is, at any point in time, doing all that it can reasonably be expected to do about the cost problem and that further cost containment is the regulators' sole responsibility. Such implicit ratification of the current state of affairs would tend to freeze dysfunctional reimbursement practices in place, and this effect would be compounded if regulation were really effective in moderating costs. Thus, to the extent that regulation successfully protected existing financing plans from the consequences of their own inefficiency, it would ipso facto reduce both the incentive of traditional plans to change and the market opportunities of alternative systems. For these reasons, the regulatory attitude that looks only at the financing system as it is currently performing may be viewed as an important part of the problem that must be overcome. Given significant possibilities for competitive evolution in the financing system, regulation must be implemented in such a way that it serves as a catalyst of change, not as the private sector's best excuse for not changing.

Unfortunately, it is simply not possible for the planner-regulators to be neutral on the private sector's future cost-containment capability. While it would undoubtedly be easier for them to say that they will recognize that capability when and if it appears, current decisions that are based on the assumption that the prevailing market failure is irremediable, or on the assumption that it can cure itself without the planners' participation, could easily seal the fate of private sector change. On the other hand, a willingness to leave some things to market forces today would strengthen those forces and permit them to assume an increasingly substantial role in the future. Thus, because whatever prophecy is implicit in the regulators' basic approach could easily be self-fulfilling, the planner-regulators, unless they choose to be part of a market-oriented solution, could themselves turn out to be part of the market failure that is the ultimate problem. The ensuing analysis seeks to help the planner-regulators carry out their regulatory responsibilities in such a way as to promote rather than suppress competition's emergence. It would seem that they have been explicitly charged by Congress with a duty to approach matters in these terms.

The Moderate Path to Deregulation

Fortunately, a moderate approach, seeking fundamental change under regulatory supervision, is available to the health care system's planner-regulators. The proposed strategy, foreshadowed in earlier references to the financing system's potential for change, involves anticipating what the market can effectively do and withholding regulation that inhibits the market's adaptation. While this strategy of controlled deregulation is certainly the most difficult to employ for both political and technical reasons, its rewards are potentially great. Responsible regulatory decisions should therefore give full weight to the private sector's potential for controlling costs, and health planners should work hand in hand in nonregulatory ways with market-forcing regulation to assure that that potential is realized.

The 1979 amendments do not yield a clear signal on whether regulation can be relaxed in anticipation of the emergence of market forces. Whereas command-and-control regulation is mandated by section 1502(b)(2) whenever it is found that "competition does not *or will not* appropriately allocate supply," section 1502(b)(3)'s parallel directive to "give priority" to market-strengthening action seems to apply only where competition already "appropriately allocates supply." Obviously, however, it would be strange to read the latter section as expressing a preference for "actions which would strengthen the effect of competition" only where competition was already working well. Thus, it would seem to be easily within the statutory mandate for planner-regulators to take the position that, wherever they find market forces potentially capable of allocating services of a particular type, they "should in the performance of their functions under this title give priority . . . to actions which would strengthen the effect of competition on the supply of such services." This approach would also be consistent with other procompetition language in the 1979 amendments. Thus, there appears to be no statutory obstacle to the adoption of an affirmative market-forcing role, employing both regulatory and nonregulatory techniques to bring a competitive market into being.

In assessing the possibilities for competitively inspired demand-side reforms, planner-regulators should not attach undue weight to conventional assessments of the market's potential or to the predictions of those with a stake in keeping financing arrangements as nearly as possible in their present form. Most providers, most insurance carriers, most administrators of public programs, and even most established HMOs are not likely to be receptive to significant additional changes in financing and delivery arrangements. At best, these interests appear to favor gradual, incremental changes, presided over by regulators with whom they can negotiate the pace and direction of change and the details. By their very nature, competitively inspired developments, in addition to lacking the by-your-leave character of most regulation-sponsored change, are to some extent unpredictable and sudden, and they are thus intensely threatening to established industry interests. For these reasons, competition lacks a political constituency and able advocates within the industry and is systematically deemphasized as a possibility in the conventional wisdom. Although their political makeup and environment will make it difficult for them to undertake efforts on behalf of competition, the HSAs and the state agencies have an important role to play in keeping this promising idea alive and giving it a chance to show what it can do.

The argument here is that the private financing system's potential for change, developed in Chapters 4, 9, and 11, must be a central factor in every regulatory decision on whether to impose the regulators' own quantitative standards in controlling entry or, alternatively, to let market forces regulate entry, location, and survival. Perhaps the most significant fact about the health services marketplace today is that the private sector's capacity to introduce innovative cost-containment measures is steadily increasing. Wider availability of HMOs, greater cost consciousness on the part of employers and unions, active antitrust enforcement against provider-imposed restraints that have inhibited change in the past, and emerging legislative interest in increasing consumer opportunities to economize in the choice of a health care plan all point toward a dynamic potential that planner-regulators can help to foster—and should certainly not ignore—in their regulatory activities. As the financing system begins, at long last, to respond to consumer cost concerns, supply-side regulation must adjust to allow market forces to operate where they have previously failed to do so. Furthermore, as the planner-regulators recognize the potential for competitive responses even where they have not yet occurred, they have a responsibility not to stand in the way of such developments.

THE RELEVANCE FOR THE MARKET-FORCING
STRATEGY OF THE COMPARATIVE
INFLEXIBILITY OF FEDERAL PROGRAMS

Given recent alterations in the climate for privately initiated change, the private sector's adaptability to deal with artificially induced demand for services and with the higher prices that insurance encourages may be substantially greater than that of public programs such as Medicare and Medicaid. These programs are fixed in law and custom, are unwieldy in size, reflect bureaucratic inertia, and embody a political and social consensus that limits their ability to respond readily to changes in the economic environment. The issue thus arises whether health system planner-regulators must adopt attitudes toward competition that accommodate the specific needs of federal programs. If regulation were thus geared to the lowest common denominator—the system's least flexible parts—, the prospects for meaningful private sector change and reduced dependence on regulation would be greatly diminished. If, on the other hand, the regulators should pursue procompetitive policies in anticipation of significant demand-side change, the federal programs, being less adaptable in the short run, may incur some higher costs. Something of a dilemma is thus presented.

The mandate of the planner-regulators extends to the health care system as a whole, and it would not seem appropriate for them to confine themselves to acting in the interests solely of the Medicare and Medicaid programs if that meant inhibiting reforms beneficial to consumers in the private sector. Even though DHHS's current regulations implementing the procompetitive thrust of the 1979 amendments do not particularly encourage the taking of a long-run, systemwide view,[3] the department's stance may change and in any event should not be determinative. Its perceptions have been greatly influenced by its own fiscal concerns as steward of Medicare and Medicaid funds, by the cost-reimbursement dogma incorporated in these huge programs, and by a nonrecognition of distinctions between public and private mechanisms. Congress, on the other hand, in enacting the planning law and its amendments, has revealed wider concerns and has now squarely endorsed the concept of procompetitive change in the private sector. It would seem that this is the cue that health system planners and regulators should take. Admittedly, HSAs may find it difficult to ignore the preferences and regulatory philosophy of DHHS, to which they are accountable in many respects. But the federal statute, the state certificate-of-need law, and the state agency are all superior authorities, and one should expect that responsible procompetitive policies will not be frustrated. Indeed, DHHS has already indicated a desire for local planners to assess competition's potential for themselves.[4] Under the Reagan administration, DHHS may become an active promoter of the approach favored here.

It is also probable that strengthened competition in the private sector will prove to be in the long-run interest of the federal programs. Those programs have within them many mechanisms that would allow them to derive indirect benefits from positive developments in private sector cost containment. Thus, if "usual and customary" fees are kept down through strengthened competition, public programs and their beneficiaries would benefit. Furthermore, any increased institutional efficiency that is brought about by competition should show up in due course in Medicare cost reports. And changes in utilization patterns in treating private patients should ultimately be reflected both in medical practice generally and in PSRO norms that limit the exposure of federal programs. Proposals such as several to allow Medicare and Medicaid beneficiaries to enroll in HMOs at reduced expense to the federal government[5] demonstrate another way in which private sector developments can accrue to the advantage of federal programs. Chapter 14 indicates that more far-reaching proposals for moving toward market-oriented public programs are under serious consideration.

Private sector reforms, both by showing the way and by reshaping the industry along more cost-effective lines, could contribute nearly as much to fundamental change in public programs as anything that Congress or DHHS can easily do by legislation or regulation. Even if Medicare and Medicaid do encounter some higher costs under freer competition, that effect should simply induce Congress and the states to break finally with the cost reimbursement approach in those programs and to move toward more responsible payment methods. Moreover, if competition does take hold in the private sector, government would be less likely to yield to the temptation to control costs by becoming a dictatorial monopsonist, demanding adherence to its fee schedules and "reasonable cost" determinations and otherwise exerting its buying power over providers. With competition working, government could more readily move toward a voucher-type system in which consumers with subsidized purchasing power and incentives to economize would guide the system. Government could thus build on, rather than undercut, the private sector's strengths. Because changes of this kind are increasingly likely to occur, the planner-regulators have even less excuse than ever before for proceeding on the old assumptions concerning the deficiencies on the demand side of the market.

In the last analysis, encouragement of private sector change is probably the shortest route to reliable cost containment, which more and more appears to be a prerequisite for major changes in public programs and for enacting some form of universal health insurance. For this reason, health planners and regulators can in good conscience implement the market-forcing strategy with only passing regard for added costs that might accrue in the short run to private plans and public programs that remain wedded to antiquated methods of organization and payment.

THE STRATEGY OF ANTICIPATING AND ENCOURAGING CHANGE

Whereas most regulation contemplates only gradual, incremental, and consensual change, the market-forcing strategy involves allowing market pressures to build and to force innovation on unwilling health care plans and providers as a condition of competitive survival. Regulatory choices would be made on the basis of assessments of the feasibility of private measures to counter, directly or indirectly, the cost-escalating tendencies of third-party financing. Competitive entry would be encouraged whenever it was thought that effective countermeasures, including reorganization of the delivery system, were feasible at reasonable cost. Although adoption of this strategy is probably not mandatory, even under the 1979 amendments, it seems clear that planner-regulators would be acting well within their discretion and with Congress's approval if they should assign a high priority to competition's emergence.

An Analytical Framework for Weighing Competition's Benefits

Although a service's theoretical amenability to allocation by market forces could not alone justify abdication of regulatory responsibility to weigh need factors, it could support a decision to allow competition if other factors indicated that effective private cost controls, including the redesign of insurance benefits and the emergence of alternative delivery systems, could be expected to emerge within a reasonable time. Thus, in the absence of a vital internal subsidy whose protection could be justified within the principles discussed in Chapter 10, regulators could and should authorize entry and investment whenever indicated by the analysis prescribed below. It is assumed that the service in question is one that is covered to a significant degree by third-party payment. It should be reasonably clear how Chapter 11's discussion of "factors which affect the effect of competition" fits into the framework presented here.

Analysis should begin with the following two questions:

1. Are there in existence reasonably effective nonregulatory mechanisms, including cost sharing and other coverage limitations, for controlling the price and quantity of the service in question?
2. If not, are they a reasonable prospect?

If the answer to both of these questions is no, the issue is still not finally resolved against competition, because other factors then come into play:

3. Is nonprice competition in the provision of the service likely to yield substantial benefits to consumers, such as better quality, greater efficiency, or significantly increased convenience or satisfaction?
4. Is the public adequately protected by circumstances such as other regulatory controls against the risk that the market

will not immediately or adequately do its cost-containment job with respect to the service in question?

Given Congress's overriding concern about the costs associated with nonprice competition particularly in the provision of "inpatient ... and other institutional health services,"[6] an affirmative answer to either question 3 or 4 alone could probably not support a decision to encourage competition in the absence of an affirmative (even if somewhat speculative) answer to either of the initial questions. On the other hand, an affirmative finding on either question 3 or 4 could probably justify a lesser degree of certainty or immediacy in an affirmative answer to question 2.

Even in the face of negative answers to questions 1 and 2, affirmative answers to both questions 3 and 4 might alone warrant adoption of a policy of unrestricted entry. Although this is not entirely clear, it would seem within the range of the regulators' discretion for them to permit entry in a specific case on the affirmative basis that nonprice competition had potential value and that its cost-escalating tendencies were sufficiently curbed by such factors as existing limits on public program reimbursement, public rate setting, public or professional utilization controls, and incomplete private cost-containment measures. The case of nursing homes, discussed in Chapter 13, suggests how the benefits of nonprice competition might, if question 4 could be answered affirmatively, be deemed to justify a policy of unrestricted entry even though an inpatient service is involved and even though questions 1 and 2 probably must be answered in the negative. In general, it seems that, within a considerable range, the regulators will have their expertise and judgment on such complex matters respected if it is clear that all the relevant considerations have been weighed. Among the factors deserving special weight is Congress's expressed concern about the costs associated with capital expenditures and with new "inpatient ... and other institutional health services."

The primary focus in this analysis is naturally on the state of traditional financing mechanisms, whose dysfunctional payment methods have provided the rationale for entry and investment controls. To the extent that alternative delivery systems—defined broadly as plans that obtain providers' services on a competitive basis and not simply as HMOs—have become well established in the market, the actual progress of innovation among traditional private payers will be less important. This follows because, with such competitive plans present in the market, the prospects for competitively stimulated change are brighter. Thus, an affirmative answer to question 2 can be more confidently given. Because the availability to cost-conscious consumers of such alternatives can be deemed to supply the pressure needed to bring about desired changes and to give consumers the means of protecting themselves against higher costs, a policy of withdrawing regulation that shelters traditional mechanisms against the need to change can be regarded as a responsible one. Thus, the existence of alternative delivery systems, if they are truly competitive, may be a sufficient basis for lifting regulatory controls of practically the whole range of hospital and physician services. Until a market reaches that point, however, the recommended analysis should be undertaken on a service-by-service basis.

The foregoing analytical framework may also help to isolate the impact of government regulation and various types of professional self-regulation on decisions concerning competition's value. Because public and industry-sponsored controls over price and the volume of services are the antithesis of competition, under the law they probably cannot, in themselves, obviate entry controls. Government or industry-controlled private regulation might, however, serve in specific cases to reduce concern about exposing the public to high costs associated with otherwise beneficial nonprice competition or about the risk that the market will fail to develop—either promptly or at all—as great a cost-containment capability as the regulators may anticipate. On the other hand, because these same controls may give providers excuses for not competing, may actually facilitate collusion, and may protect inefficient health care plans against the full competitive consequences of their inefficiency, they may reduce the supportability of an affirmative answer to question 2 in a particular case. But, even though much existing regulation diminishes competition's prospects and makes it harder for regulators to rely on its emergence, Congress clearly meant for competition to be given a chance to show what it can do. Thus, because the prospects for competition are not wholly eliminated by existing forms of public and professional regulation, the regulators must assess those prospects in particular cases. It is believed that question 2 can frequently be answered in the affirmative, particularly by planners and regulators who take seriously their parallel responsibility for promoting changes in the way health services are bought and paid for so that price competition can indeed operate to the consumer's benefit.

Weighing Factor 10: The Service's Amenability to Competitively Inspired Cost Controls.

Analysis of the practical viability of private cost containment requires (1) an understanding of the techniques that might be employed, (2) an awareness of those characteristics of the service and its financing that affect the feasibility of private measures, and (3) a recognition of obstacles to the implementation of such measures. The first two of these essential items were discussed in Chapter 11 but are recalled here with a slightly different emphasis as a part of a discussion of the tenth item on that chapter's list of "factors that affect the effect of competition." Specifically, factor 10 is those market and nonmarket circumstances surrounding a service that make it more or less capable of having its costs controlled through administrative and other arrangements available to private third parties. This discussion puts special emphasis on the idea that planner-regulators should indulge in speculations concerning the future prospects for private cost control, whereas Chapter 11 was based on the assumption that regulators would await the market's demonstration of an actual cost-containment capability before abandoning their command-and-control function. In effect, it is contemplated here that the regulators should view their task as one of deciding which of the available public and private mechanisms, including the competitive market, has the greatest competence and capacity to address a specific problem of resource allocation. That would seem, after all, to be the most pertinent question.

An element here that was not present in Chapter 11's discussion of the market's current development is the specific impediments that may inhibit the emergence of private cost controls. Perhaps the only impediments that might have a conclusive impact in analyzing competition's prospects are regulatory restraints (other than those administered by the planners themselves) that foreclose or interfere with the development of private measures. For example, insurance regulation, such as that making certain health benefits mandatory, might take away insurers' flexibility in dealing with certain cost problems. Similarly, state legislation guaranteeing unlimited free choice of provider may be construed to prevent the formation of alternative delivery systems. Strained interpretation of licensure laws, such as recent rulings by dental examiners in Indiana precluding dental insurers' review of X-rays,[7] could interfere with legitimate cost-containment efforts. So could misapplications of state rules against the corporate practice of medicine or against interference with the doctor-patient relationship.[8] In general, planner-regulators should be alert to all kinds of constraints on effective private cost containment, and also to various ways of circumventing such constraints, since not all regulatory controls effectively stifle the prospects for change.

Private cost containment must address both price and utilization. Efforts to control prices would be foreclosed by hospital rate-setting regulation prescribing hospital unit charges, thereby obviating the efforts of competing health care plans to bargain with hospitals for lower prices. On the other hand, rate regulation that sets only maximum charges might permit negotiated rates if the various plans and hospitals could be persuaded to embark on competitive paths. This might be a doubtful prospect, however, given the state's overt price signaling to oligopolists on both sides of the market.

In the absence of public rate setting, competition would seem a reasonable possibility for dealing with the price element of the cost formula. Public and private third-party payers could seek to negotiate prices directly with individual providers of covered services, including both doctors and hospitals. If agreement was not reached, the private insurer could either refuse altogether to cover care rendered by a nonparticipating provider or could undertake to indemnify insureds who obtain care from such a provider only for a flat maximum amount for each service or on some other less advantageous basis. In a competitive market, such negotiations and such limitations on benefits might be as familiar as they are now exceptional, and the resulting consumer sensitivity to price differences at the margin would yield prices more accurately reflecting supply and demand factors. In such a market, new competitors could gain entrance to the market only if they met the going price, could persuade a cost-conscious health care plan to pay a higher price, or could supply a level of quality that attracted patients willing to pay a larger amount out of pocket. Certification of need would add no protection that the market would not supply at least as efficiently. Once such competitive mechanisms had taken hold for privately financed care, public programs would have better opportunities for shopping themselves and better yardsticks for establishing their own levels of reimbursement.

As to utilization, a range of private controls is available for competitive introduction if insurers and their customers want them. Although public regulation of utilization practices is not extensive enough to preclude private initiatives, a strong ethical norm appears to militate against independent financing plans' "interfering" in the "doctor-patient relationship." Widespread acceptance of this norm may be explained not only by legitimate concerns about effects on the quality of care but also by professionals' and insurers' respective feelings about the desirability of competition. If planners and regulators expected that this obstacle to competition, because it is embodied more in custom than in law, would break down under competitive pressures stimulated by consumer cost consciousness, they might take both regulatory and nonregulatory action to strengthen such pressures.

Though private controls over utilization abuses are not extensively employed at present, some private mechanisms, such as second-opinion plans, have been developed. Other arrangements, essentially ways of effectively implementing reasonable contractual limits on plan coverage, are also possible and have been aggressivley employed in other types of insurance, including dental coverage. Predetermination of benefits, in cases where it is feasible, would allow the patient and the provider to know in advance what services would and would not be paid for. Shifting the responsibility for paying for questionable services back to patients should serve to deter inappropriate spending without taking actual treatment decisions out of the doctor-patient relationship. Similarly, prior authorization by the insurer might be made a condition of coverage of elective hospitalization and surgery, again serving the useful purpose of prospectively limiting the availability of third-party financing in questionable cases. Such techniques for enforcing limits on coverage do not amount to the corporate practice of medicine or interfere with the relationship between the patient and the doctor, who remain free to design treatment as they see fit. No legal or ethical objection should lie where the plan simply limits the automatic availability of resources for some purposes.

As in private controls over providers' fees and charges, effective implementation of coverage limits would be easiest if the plan had entered into written participation agreements with providers that specified the plan's administrative requirements as well as mutually agreeable terms of compensation. Such agreements might not be essential, however, since a physician notified of the limits of his patient's financial resources might have a professional duty, enforceable at law, not to incur uninsured costs without advising the patient.[9] In any event, such agreements could probably be made attractive to physicians by sharing with them in the form of increased fees some of the savings from reduced utilization. At the same time, a lower insurance premium would compensate the patient for his willingness to patronize only participating providers and for his acceptance of the risk that some desirable hospitalization and treatments would not be covered or would be covered on less advantageous terms.

As the many possibilities for private cost containment are recognized, the opportunities for relaxing regulatory controls will seem more numerous. Planner-regulators must develop a facility in applying these concepts so that they may withdraw from portions of the field that market forces are able to occupy.

IMPLEMENTING THE MARKET-FORCING STRATEGY

The regulatory stance recommended here should be assumed not as a rigid or doctrinaire position but as part of a broad and constructive strategy designed to effectuate the new "national health priority" of strengthening useful competition and carrying out HSAs' newly assigned function of "improving ... competition in the health service area."[10] An appreciation of market dynamics and a certain amount of creativity will be required if the long-term benefits of competition are to be realized at minimum short-term cost. Nonregulatory efforts, some of which are suggested in Chapter 15, should be designed and undertaken to complement the regulatory policy adopted.

Where planner-regulators take the view that the price and utilization of a particular service can be better controlled in the private sector than through entry regulation, they might also find it appropriate to preside over the transition from public to private control in order both to stimulate the process of change and to assist affected parties in adjusting to it. For example, rather than simply opening up the market for such a service, they might announce their intention to do so at some future date—thus, the health systems plan might declare, "In two years, anyone can have a CT scanner." The planners could then actively assist employment groups, insurers, PSROs, and the rest of the community to prepare for that day, when effective price and utilization controls could be embodied in fee schedules and in coverage limitations in the insurance contract and implemented through provider participation agreements. It is an important insight that private sector change is likely to occur only if government and health planners have successfully disabused expectations that they alone will carry the cost-containment burden. To a large degree, the planner-regulators' job is one of establishing the credibility of their insistence that the private sector assume major responsiblity for controlling costs.

Fostering the Use of Participation Agreements.

In pursuing a strategy to bring about needed change, planner-regulators might give particular attention to overcoming a problem likely to be encountered in obtaining wider use of participation agreements by indemnity insurers and other health plan organizers—namely, providers' recalcitrance in accepting contractual limitations on their fees and on their freedom to prescribe covered services. If not the result of an actionable provider conspiracy in restraint of trade, such resistance to competition might best be met by the planners' announcing their willingness to allow new entry or investment by any provider of the service who has firm agreements embodying price and utilization understandings with third parties. Such a tactic would amount to exempting from need-oriented entry control those providers who had submitted to market control by bargaining with cost-sensitive representatives of the consumer's interest. The dynamic results of such a regulatory policy deserve some discussion.

If provider participation agreements were made the key to market entry, the third parties would suddenly be in a position to control entry by new providers. Moreover, they could confer other benefits by making the new provider alone eligible to provide the covered service or to provide it on the terms most favorable to the insured consumer. Because a new provider could thus be assured both a certificate of need and a high volume of business, he should be amenable to accepting lower fees and some accountability for utilization practices. Hospitals, physicians, and others, if barred by regulation from expanding or entering the market in the traditional way as nonaccountable providers, would for the first time be motivated to seek out third-party arrangements of the type visualized. The price of admission to the market would be, as it has not been heretofore, a willingness to submit to the discipline of a competitive regime in which price and cost factors are given due weight.

The automatic response of most health planners to this scenario would be that the new facilities contemplated would simply exacerbate the problem of excess capacity. But this argument fails to carry the scenario to its logical conclusion, since there would in fact be little risk that new facilities would actually be built. Instead, the effect of the recommended regulatory strategy would be to strengthen the bargaining power of third parties with existing providers by giving them a credible power to take their business elsewhere—to a new provider whom they might sponsor. As a result, third parties would enjoy an unprecedented opportunity to negotiate participation agreements with existing providers on favorable terms. Occasional invocations by third parties of their sanction of franchising a new facility, even if carried to the point of new construction, would have benefits for competition and cost containment that far outweighed any higher costs that the traditional financing system might have to bear. But it should be enough that the threat of competitive entry is credible. The need to carry out this threat should be rare indeed.

The tactic of deregulating entry and investment by providers integrated by contract with third-party payers is closely analogous to the exemption from certificate-of-need requirements granted to HMOs in the 1979 health planning amendments.[11] Substantial HMOs proposing to build a hospital were relieved of most regulatory oversight on the basis that they are accountable to consumers in the marketplace. Although this exemption apparently reflected a willingness to accept the costs that new HMO investments might impose on the traditional system, in fact there was little expectation that HMOs would build numerous new hospitals. Instead, it was anticipated that their opportunities to acquire or contract with existing facilities on reasonable terms would be enhanced. As discussed in Chapter 8, HMOs seeking to buy a hospital had frequently encountered unwilling sellers and high prices attributable in large measure to the existence of legal controls on the creation of new facilities. Threatened with possible new construction—that is, with potential competition—, underutilized facilities should be much more available for purchase or for hire.

During consideration of the HMO exemption in 1979, Congress entertained a proposal, included in the House-passed bill, to exempt all proposals backed by long-term contracts with a prepaid health plan, broadly defined. The so-called Gramm amendment, discussed in Chapter 8, thus embodied the essential principle proposed for adoption here. The failure of Congress to adopt this broad exemption in the final version of the law should not, however, be regarded as a rejection of the recommended regulatory strategy. Congress simply felt that the broad exemption was subject to potential abuse and that it could not through legislative drafting effectively prevent the exemption from becoming a loophole. But planner-regulators, looking at specific cases, should have no trouble determining whether particular contracts are bona fide and pose no serious risks to the public. Indeed, Congress has already shown how to make such assessments in laying down certain conditions that an HMO must meet before qualifying for the HMO exemption. The discussion of this subject in Chapter 8 should illuminate the issues presented here.

Deregulating entry and investment by providers associated by long-term contracts with third-party payers and other health care plans could do more than any other single thing to bring about the creation of alternative delivery systems, broadly defined as plans that purchase providers' services on a truly competitive basis. This tactic for implementing the market-forcing strategy would accomplish the deregulation of entry and investment at the precise point where the competitive threat would be meaningful and could be expected to force incumbent providers to compete even against their will. Potential competition could thus be restored to its crucial disciplinary role, and regulation could be removed as an impediment to effective competitive checks on provider performance. The crucial message is that planners who come to appreciate the dynamics of competition should be able, if they are willing, to force even the most recalcitrant providers and to engage in it. Planner-regulators who persist in believing that command-and-control regulation is essential for the foreseeable future have not thought the matter through.

Overcoming Obstacles to Insurer Innovation

Without health planners' active intercession in support of financing system change, the prospects for innovation by third-party payers may be diminished. Even though it seems that insurers could take effective measures that consumers would value, there may not be an adequate incentive for any single private insurer to take the needed first step. No innovation is without risk, and the kinds of innovation contemplated here may incur the wrath of organized medicine and some consumer resistance. Moreover, such innovations will certainly entail some costs in negotiating with individual providers, in selling the innovative plan to employment groups, and in developing and introducing new administrative procedures. In particular, conventional health insurers must restructure their operations in order to organize health services more effectively at the local level where cost containment must be effected. Finally, the benefits of the innovation may accrue to others besides the innovator and his customers. Thus, for example, innovation might have spillover effects on medical practice generally, changing doctors' approach to treating all their patients and not just those insured by the innovating insurer.[12] Alternatively, other insurers might find it relatively easy to imitate any innovations that proved effective, leaving the innovative firm to bear the costs of unsuccessful ventures without much hope of gaining a long-run competitive advantage from a successful one. All of these possibilities may make it unrealistic to expect that competition alone, unaided by the health planners, can easily bring about all potentially beneficial innovations.

Where insurers seem unable to capture a distinct competitive advantage from introducing certain cost-containment innovations, the planner-regulators, rather than seizing on the apparent market failure as an excuse for command-and-control regulation, might take facilitative actions. Directly addressing the market failure itself, they might attempt to trigger the process of change that the unassisted market was unable to get started. For example, their intervention might take the form of actively assisting the marketing efforts of any insurer that seeks to alter its payment methods—in effect subsidizing the insurer by reducing his selling costs and risks in innovating. Another alternative would be for the planner-regulators to cooperate with several insurers and perhaps the state insurance commissioner in simultaneously redesigning the insurers' coverage and approaches to claims review. Any collective action by competing insurers that might be involved, if temporary and properly confined to overcoming the identified market failure, should not offend antitrust principles.[13] In any event, if state regulators were involved, such action could probably be undertaken safely pursuant to the McCarran-Ferguson Act's exemption for the state-regulated "business of insurance." Given the arguable market deterrent to individual insurers' initiatives, these market-assisting approaches should be more constructive than direct regulation of supply. Where such efforts are made, it will be easier to adopt liberal attitudes toward new entry and investment.

Concentrating on Market Fundamentals

Even where a local market appears hopelessly noncompetitive and private cost containment is not immediately in prospect, permanent regulatory control of entry might still not be the appropriate remedy. Because competition may still be the best long-run hope and because nonprice competition can contribute significantly in the short run to quality and efficiency in local markets for health services, the planner-regulators might choose to encourage competition while also addressing fundamental market conditions that may in time stimulate the private sector to develop mechanisms for handling the cost problem. Competitiveness is determined by such supply-side factors as the number of sellers; the availability of information; the existence or absence of collusion; the interchangeability of services and the availability of substitutes for particular services; opportunities for granting hidden price or other concessions as competitive moves that are difficult for competitors to discover and imitate; and private actors' freedom to innovate without fear of sanctions imposed collectively by competitors or others.

Where competition has traditionally been weak, it may not be inevitably so, and planner-regulators at the local level might seek to trigger competition by taking nonregulatory steps to encourage aggressive negotiating by insurers (or employers or unions) and to break up collusive practices. They might also stimulate advertising and other forms of information dissemination, such as better disclosure of which providers would "accept assignment"—that is, accept various financing plans' fee schedules or other allowances as payment in full. There are many reasons to think that HSAs and their planning staffs might provide the greatest service to their communities by stimulating price and other forms of competition, by educating consumers and employers to private cost-containment possibilities, and by strengthening those forces that are most capable of offsetting the market power of providers and giving effect to consumer cost concerns.

Ultimately, planner-regulators might be inclined to lift all entry controls on the basis of the simple availability in the community of a significant number of alternative delivery systems—that is, competitive health care plans with developed cost-containment capability. Once such plans exist in sufficient number to give the consumer meaningful options, it should seem appropriate to let the market strategy work. The lifting of controls in such a competitive environment should further strengthen consumers' incentives to join an innovative plan, entrepreneurs' incentives to organize more such plans, and providers' incentives to participate in them. If Medicare beneficiaries have the means, under new legislation, of enrolling in an HMO (or in any other type of competitive health care plan) and benefiting themselves from any resulting saving, there would no longer be any convincing reason to protect the Medicare program or those beneficiaries who elect not to switch. The planner-regulators would simply have to judge what was a meaningful range of choice, whether competition, both among plans and among providers for the chance to serve the subscribers of such plans, was truly vigorous, and whether the plans would be capable of accepting increased enrollment if costs in the deregulated private sector should rise. If conditions are right, however, deregulation should cause no significantly increased costs, because would-be certificate-of-need applicants (and their lenders) would be deterred from making inappropriate investments by their recognition of the risks that newly effective market forces have created.

NOTES

1. Public Health Service Act §1502(b), *as amended.*
2. FCC v. RCA Communications, Inc., 346 U.S. 86 (1953); Hawaiian Tel. Co. v. FCC, 498 F.2d 771 (D.C. Cir. 1974).
3. *See* 45 Fed. Reg. 69,771 (1980).
4. *Id.*
5. *E.g.,* H.R. 4000 and S. 1530, 96th Cong., 1st Sess. (1979).
6. Public Health Service Act §1502(b)(2), *as amended.*
7. These opinions of the Indiana Board of Dental Examiners are briefly summarized and discussed in *Indiana Fed'n of Dentists,* Docket No. 9118 (FTC, March 25, 1980) (initial decision), at 100– 109.
8. For an overview of some of the potential legal barriers to private cost containment, see Note, "Controlling Health Care Costs through Commercial Insurance Companies," 1978 *Duke L.J.* 728.
9. *Cf.* Eisenberg & Rosoff, "Physician Responsibility for the Cost of Unnecessary Medical Services," 299 *New Eng. J. Med.* 76 (1978).
10. Public Health Service Act §1513(a)(5), *as amended.*
11. Pub. L. No. 96–79, §117(a), *adding* Public Health Service Act §1527(b).
12. *See* M. Pauly, *The Role of the Private Sector in National Health Insurance* 37–38 (1979).
13. This point is not clear, however. Under *National Soc'y of Professional Eng'rs v. United States,* 435 U.S. 679, 696 (1978), the test is whether concerted action "promotes" competition. Under this principle, efforts to overcome a market deficiency such as the free-rider problems identified here may be permissible so long as the effect is to make the market work better and not to prevent its

working. The FTC, though declaring ethical prohibitions against advertising and solicitation unlawful, has allowed professional groups to continue to prohibit and police "false and deceptive" advertising, presumably on the ground that consumer ignorance and gullibility is a market failure whose correction by concerted action will make market forces more reliable. American Medical Ass'n, No. 9064 (FTC, Oct. 12, 1979), at 58–60. *See also* American Medical Ass'n v. FTC, 638 F.2d 443, 452 (2d Cir. 1980) (enforcing, with minor modifications, the FTC order), *cert. granted,* 49 U.S.L.W. 3946 (1981).

13

THE CASE FOR COMPETITION WITH RESPECT TO SOME SPECIFIC SERVICES AND PROVIDERS

Health planners and regulators will confront competition issues in concrete factual settings in which the principles set forth in the foregoing chapters will not always be easy to apply. This chapter discusses the characteristics of some specific types of facilities, services, and providers with a view to further clarifying the analysis of competition-related issues. Although local market conditions, particularly the way specific services are paid for and the prospect for reform in such financing methods, will often be determinative, the benefits and harms of competition may be generally assessed with respect to particular services and the market settings in which they are typically provided. The discussion here is meant to be suggestive rather than definitive. Though not proceeding strictly in terms of the identified "factors which affect the effect of competition," it should assist the planner-regulators in employing the analytical framework already set forth.

AMBULATORY SURGICAL FACILITIES

Chapter 8 reviewed a number of plausible but ultimately unsatisfying arguments that can be advanced against allowing HMO entry into a market. Similar arguments can be leveled, with somewhat greater persuasiveness, against freestanding ambulatory surgical facilities (ASFs).[1] On the other hand, competition makes some persuasive claims of its own that must be weighed in establishing a policy toward ASF development. The ensuing outline of the arguments for and against ASFs largely avoids issues of the medical appropriateness and overall quality of care and focuses primarily on competition-related issues. The arguments reviewed here are similar to those raised by any certificate-of-need application by a provider who offers a lower cost outpatient service as a competitive alternative to inpatient care.

Regulatory Rationales

ASFs are subject to regulation because their services are very often paid for through financing mechanisms that encourage the development of overcapacity. It is of course an empirical issue whether consumers in particular local markets have an incentive and an opportunity to economize in the purchase of ASF services. In the typical market, however, the prevalence of cost reimbursement (of either the facility itself or the indemnified patient) will make it difficult to argue that ASF investments are adequately disciplined by market forces. Not only do most ASFs have a reasonable prospect of recovering their capital costs through cost reimbursement formulas or through charges to insured patients, but they also do not have to fear competitive price cutting by the hospitals with whom they compete. Because conventional financing arrangements usually permit hospitals to respond to ASF entry by raising their charges, by spreading their overhead over fewer cost-reimbursed services, or by increasing the volume of questionable services provided, the ASF need not expect to face prices based on short-run marginal costs, which is the usual competitive response of established sellers to the creation of excess capacity in their industry. Because such price cutting is unlikely to occur, a regulatory deterrent to excessive growth may be required to offset the lack of an adequate market deterrent.

Health planners have not specifically based their concern about ASFs on the weakness of the market deterrent to unneeded investment. Instead, the planners seem to fear that, under current financing systems, the hospitals' recoupment strategies are likely to work, causing consumers to support not only the hospitals at nearly their accustomed level of income but the ASF as well. One way of preventing this apparent cost-escalating effect would be to exclude the ASF as a competitor for the hospitals. This outcome has been widely regarded as an acceptable result for planner-regulators to reach. It has also been defended by calling the ASF a "cream-skimmer" and by expressing concerns about the safety of outpatient surgery lacking the immediate backup that a hospital provides. There are, however, good reasons for questioning the antagonistic stance that some planner-regulators have assumed toward ASF development.

The market failure allegedly warranting the ASF's exclusion is of course not primarily a failure of the ASF itself but of the financing system that allows institutional providers to maintain their revenues in the face of excess capacity and competition. An alternative to the common policy of admitting ASFs to the market only where needs are actually going unmet would focus on the incentive problems throughout the insured fee-for-service sector. For example, health system planners could adopt the view that allowing competition for the hospitals is a desirable way of increasing the pressure on public and private financing programs to make fundamental changes in their payment methods. Thus, even if market forces were deemed generally unreliable in the hospital sector, ASFs might be encouraged as part of an aggressive market-forcing strategy in the belief that financing plans could develop ways of protecting themselves against potentially higher costs. As suggested in Chapter 12, the planner-regulators might foster those ASFs that, unlike their hospital competitors, had submitted themselves to the market's discipline by accepting long-term contracts with competing, cost-conscious third-party payers, thereby providing market-validated evidence of need. To be most cost-effective, such contracts should probably be accompanied by third-party measures to induce consumers to elect the lower-cost service, thus introducing effective price competition where only nonprice competition had previously prevailed.

Although there are reasons to mistrust market forces as a deterrent to investments in ASF facilities, there are other reasons for wanting to see ASFs not discouraged by the planner-regulators. Many surgical services may be more cheaply provided on an ambulatory basis, making the ASF attractive as a substitute for higher-cost inpatient care. It is important to recognize, however, that appropriate cost comparisons would ignore (as "sunk") the cost of unrecoverable capital already invested in inpatient facilities. Thus, only if the ASF's total costs (including capital costs) are less than hospitals' avoidable costs of providing the same service, should the ASF be allowed to enter the market. But, if this condition is met, it should be allowed to enter without regard to its adverse effects on the hospitals and irrespective of whether hospital capital costs for obsolete facilities might be recouped in some way in charges to the public. Because it will seldom be possible to calculate comparative costs in specific markets, regulators will probably rely on the general consensus that ASFs are efficient.[2] Whether this consensus is so well founded as to be valid in every case is not known, but it is a plausible basis for regulatory policy.

Other values, such as the benefits of nonprice competition, may be even more important than static efficiency in supporting the case for freestanding ASFs. Thus, aggressive development of the possibilities of outpatient surgery is much more likely under competition than under monopoly. Also, many freestanding ASFs have lower costs due to lower overhead, more efficient management, and reduced use of tests and drugs.[3] Moreover, competition between ASFs has also been found to stimulate improved service and efficiency.[4]

The case for competitive ASF development has been investigated and stated at length in a study by ICF, Inc.[5] This study looked not only at comparative prices but also at comparative costs and found in favor of freestanding ASFs. It also reached reassuring conclusions on the quality of care, peripheral efficiencies, and patient and provider satisfaction. Though noting the possibility that unnecessary surgery could be stimulated by the presence of an additional provider, the ICF study strongly endorsed freestanding ASFs as a desirable competitive influence in local markets—one that promises long-range cost reductions in many circumstances. The specific criteria offered for ASF approval by HSAs and state agencies[6] were somewhat more conservative, however, than the study's findings seemed to warrant.

Among the other characteristics of an ASF's service that suggest regulatory tolerance are the probability that the ASF's facilities are mobile or readily convertible to other uses in the event competition should devalue them in their current location or use. Many of the services provided by ASFs are elective, thus raising the danger that availability will induce the provision of services that consumers would not be willing to purchase at their own expense. Nevertheless, surgical procedures are relatively discrete and identifiable and would thus seem to be subject to policing by the payers themselves through prior authorization requirements or otherwise. Moreover, benefits for such services can be and often are established on a basis that makes the consumer aware of cost differences at the margin. Competition may thus be able to operate usefully to prevent excessively costly versions of the service from being offered. The efficiency-enhancing prospects of such competition would seem entitled to substantial weight.

On balance, the case for allowing ASFs to compete with hospitals seems quite strong. The likelihood of cost savings and the substantial advantages of nonprice competition, when coupled with opportunities for third parties to control adverse cost effects, make regulatory decisions against ASFs highly questionable. Even where an ASF already exists in a community, additional ones should receive a full hearing. The correct stance in these circumstances would probably be to make contracts with established health plans the key to market entry.

Some Evidence of Regulatory Experience

Questionnaire responses obtained in 1977 in early phases of this study identified significant HSA resistance to ASF development and substantial control over the terms of entry. Of twenty-three HSAs which had encountered ASF applications at all, eleven had recommended their denial and one had compelled voluntary withdrawal. Six of the recommendations had not been accepted by the higher authority, however, and two had not yet been acted on. Some of the reasons given for rejecting the ASF applications were as follows:

1. "Unnecessary duplication."
2. "Incomplete applications; not enough service to the poor."
3. "Waiting for definition" (apparently found unreviewable for lack of criteria or guidelines).

4. "Sufficient facilities already extant."
5. "Not needed in rural area; nearby hospital outpatient surgery underutilized."
6. "Incomplete information."
7. "Three hospital-based ambulatory care facilities available."

Thus, in four instances, protection of existing facilities was an explicit basis for denial.

Recognition of ASFs' desirability, when coupled with regulatory instincts, can lead planner-regulators into a mediating role that they see as facilitative but that is in fact quite destructive of ASFs' competitive potential. The planner-regulators, hearing complaints from incumbent providers, are apt to seek a negotiated basis on which ambulatory surgery can be expanded without too much inconvenience to the hospitals. But such negotiations, even if successful, would allow the ASF to enter on more limited terms and probably at a higher cost. As with HMOs, the regulator's instinct for accommodation of competing interests is destructive of change, efficiency, and real competition. The added burdens that prospective ASFs would have to anticipate because of the planners' power to dictate the terms of entry would discourage initiatives, following the classic regulatory pattern.

Forced modification of ASF proposals seems common, judging from questionnaire responses showing eight instances, several of which were explained as follows:

1. "To assure as strong an application as possible." (Note that this response begs the question: what makes a "strong" application may make a weak or noncompetitive ASF.)
2. "Referred back to Blue Cross; general feeling that information was insufficient on this new animal; also, no criteria developed at that time."
3. "We recommended that they submit supporting data re quality review, back-up arrangement with hospitals; also financial data."
4. "Provision for indigent care."
5. "Related to description of planning, relative to other services, etc."
6. "Quality."

Assessment of these responses is difficult, but the regulatory mentality appears strong, with the consequence that increased costs and delay are incurred, incumbent providers are benefited, and incentives for innovation are curtailed.

Incumbents Versus New Entrants as the Provider of a New Service

One impulse common among planner-regulators is to have the hospitals themselves provide the day-surgery service. This approach conforms to the conception, sometimes advocated by planners, of the community hospital as the "hub" of a planned health care enterprise. It also minimizes the drain on the hospital's resources that would result from competitive cream skimming by ASFs and allows prices to include an element of cross-subsidy to support unremunerative hospital activities. A hospital's application for a certificate of need for such a new service also offers the opportunity to require the retirement or conversion of the beds that would be rendered unnecessary. These reasons will strike many health planners as sufficient to concentrate services in the monopolistic hospital, where they can be managed with less inconvenience and uncertainty.

Although health planners might appropriately seek to stimulate local hospitals' innovation in the area of ambulatory surgery, somewhat different considerations are presented where a certificate-of-need application is filed for a freestanding facility. A threatened hospital might at that point counter with a proposal of its own, and the question then becomes whether the hospital should be preferred. If the hospital's initiative was prompted by the competitive threat, it should be clear that deciding in its favor, allowing the monopolist to repel the competitive initiative, would destroy the incentive for others to mount similar initiatives in the future. It would seem the wiser policy, absent unusual factors, to reward the original proponent in these circumstances, even if the planner-regulators might have preferred to have the service provided by the hospital.

Competition in identifying and moving to meet an unmet need should surely be encouraged. A striking example of the value of such competition appears in a Nevada health planning decision.

Las Vegas physicians sought approval of a new specialty hospital to offer needed services that local hospitals had failed to provide but were now willing to offer. Denial of the certificate of need was recommended by the Facility Review Committee of the state planning agency with the following further recommendation: "That the physician applicants be praised for creating pressures which encouraged Las Vegas area hospitals to upgrade and to lay plans for futher upgrading health manpower, facilities and equipment for use in neurologic, thoracic, cardiovascular and orthopedic surgery procedures."[7] Even this pat on the back would not prevent this decision from exasperating the disappointed applicants. More importantly, it would also discourage other equally needed initiatives. The need to preserve incentives to initiate innovative proposals should be kept in mind in conducting comparative reviews under the new requirements for "batching" like applications.[8]

The ultimate question raised by ASFs' certificate-of-need applications is whether innovation will occur at all, or as soon, if independent, private initiatives are rejected and exclusive reliance is placed on existing institutions to initiate change, particularly cost-cutting measures that may be against their self-interest. Sometimes health planners may be able to appeal effectively to providers' better instincts or, with regulatory power, to establish an effective system of rewards and penalties. But regulation's record as a sponsor of change is not at all promising, and, even if the planners could persuade a local hospital to establish an outpatient surgical unit, it is doubtful that they could assure its efficiency or its maximum development as a substitute for inpatient care.

Much the better stance for health planners to take would be to encourage the development of freestanding ASFs as a destabilizing and ultimately procompetitive and market-forcing factor. They could certainly justify going so far in pursuit of competition as to discourage hospitals from offering new day-surgery services in order that ASF-hospital competition could spring up. Thus, the local health systems plan might make explicit provision for a freestanding ASF, thus inviting outside interests to start one as a competitor for the hospitals. It would also seem justifiable to deny a dominant hospital's application to provide outpatient surgery in the hope that a freestanding unit would materialize and contribute to the development of a competitive market.

The ASF case is a particularly interesting one for present purposes because it is a clear instance of how entrepreneurial initiatives can force the health care system and its regulators to face the pressures for desirable change that competition fosters. A planning agency's attitude toward ASFs can tell a great deal about whether it is committed to competition and rapid change or to monopoly, regulation, and only incremental departures from the status quo.

NURSING HOMES

The problems of long-term care are among the least tractable of all those facing the health sector. Given both the demographics of an aging population and the increasing willingness to view support of older citizens and the chronically ill as a public responsibility, government's role in long-term care is bound to grow. But, with the prospect of continuing financial stringency hanging over both income maintenance and health care programs for the elderly, the nation faces difficult policy choices in carrying out its commitments to the elderly and the chronically ill and assuring that their health care and related needs are decently and humanely met at a reasonable cost. Although long-term care issues are closely related to all other problems of the health sector, significant differences point to the necessity for a separate analysis.

The discussion here falls far short of being a treatise on the economics and regulation of nursing homes. The subject is quite complex, involving not only certificate-of-need requirements but also licensure, quality regulation, public reimbursement policies, private financing, problems of fraud and abuse, patients' rights and consumer protection, access regulation, and patient placement schemes. Moreover, the variety of extended care (skilled nursing facilities, intermediate care facilities, home health services) adds new complications that cannot be addressed here. The goal of this discussion is simply to begin a dialogue about how market forces might be harnessed to allocate this class of resources in appropriate ways. The 1979 health planning amendments require that these issues be addressed by health planners and certificate-of-need authorities, and the conventional bias toward regulatory prescriptions that nearly all recognized experts bring to this industry strongly suggests the need to stimulate some new thinking.

Competition and Quality

Low quality of care has long been regarded as a severe problem in the nursing home industry, and regulation often seems to have contributed more to raising costs than to improving the welfare of nursing home patients.[9] Indeed, the standard approaches used in assuring the quality of other types of medical care seem poorly adapted to maintaining the quality of care in nursing homes. Heavy reliance on regulatory specification of required "inputs"—facilities and manpower[10]—has proved insufficient to maintain quality, especially as measured along the subjective, "caring" dimension, so crucial in long-term care. "Process" measures, such as those employed in the conduct of medical audits and PSRO reviews, also seem not to get to the heart of the quality problem in nursing homes. Although everyone agrees that quality control would be best achieved by regulation geared to "outcomes" of care rather than "inputs" or "process," it is difficult to identify the desired outcome of much long-term nursing home care, where full recovery is rare and death is a common and natural occurrence. Unlike hospital care, which is generally short term and seeks to achieve a specific improvement in health status, nursing homes should be much more concerned with providing a decent quality of life for their patients. Although success in rehabilitating patients might be assessed, quality of care in nursing homes has many intangible dimensions that defy regulatory oversight.

Because regulation probably cannot be reliably based on measurements of outcomes or of the quality of life provided or of inmates' happiness, something can be said for leaving as much as possible to competition and consumer choice. Although it is obvious that nursing home patients are frequently in no condition or position to make intelligent decisions, one must be careful not to underestimate what might be achieved if HSAs and others worked to improve market conditions and the opportunities for informed choice. Although many nursing home patients would be incapable of meaningful choice despite an HSA's best efforts, not all customers need to be well informed in order for patient choice and competition to induce the provision of services of reasonable quality; it is the marginal rather than the average customer whose preferences most influence provider behavior.

There is some evidence that the growth of nursing homes in New York State in the 1950s demonstrated the possible value of more limited regulation and greater reliance on consumer choice.[11] Rapid growth of the proprietary sector occurred in New York while the voluntary sector was unable to meet the emerging demand attributable to the expanding state welfare program. Very uneven quality persisted while demand exceeded supply, but quality and efficiency began to improve as increased supply allowed competition to be effective in eliminating the poorer facilities. Though this experience was cited as a demonstration of quality failings, it also suggests that free entry and competition have virtues of their own, offsetting the effects of the much-maligned profit motive.

The suggestion that more emphasis might be placed on consumer choice obviously flies in the face of current policies aimed at restricting the supply of nursing home beds. Entry controls through certificate-of-need laws and the 1122 program have made it nearly impossible in many communities for patients to choose homes to suit their needs, since they are frequently lucky to get any bed at all; indeed, if this is not the case, the certificate-of-need agency can be accused of not doing its job of tightening supply to force rationing of beds. Restricting the growth of the nursing home industry by regulation thus unfortunately creates the seller's market that allows poor-quality care to flourish, largely immune to correction by other quality assurance mechanisms. (For example, license revocation is a useless sanction when patients have no alternative source of care.) Moreover, the limited resources available to health planning and regulatory agencies are strained by the necessity for reviewing in detail numerous nursing home applications, and it is quite possible that other activities, such as the market-reform efforts suggested in Chapter 15, would prove more productive of public benefits. A question of central interest here is whether weeding out unneeded, poor-quality nursing home beds could usefully be left, within wide ranges established by limited regulation, to the market under a liberal regulatory policy toward nursing home entry and expansion. A related question, not explored here, is whether input specification, even as a way for government to assure what it is buying for public beneficiaries, might be reduced in public programs, with more reliance placed on disclosure and consumer choice. Homes would then offer those services which consumers most want and would differentiate themselves so as to put a premium on shopping and choosing well.

Restricting the supply of nursing home beds has other adverse side effects, besides effects on the quality of care, that necessitate costly but largely ineffectual regulation. Where excess demand prevails, rather than consumers selecting homes to satisfy their needs, homes select patients. As would be anticipated, patients are chosen on the basis of their relative profitability. Under a system of fixed per diem rates, the least profitable patients from the homes' perspective are those that require the most care, and it is a common problem that many patients needing extensive nursing care remain hospitalized at high cost only because no nursing home will make room for them. As Feder and Scanlon put it, "When nursing home beds are insufficient to satisfy demand, the people most in need of the service have the greatest difficulty finding it."[12]

In a market with an adequate bed supply, homes would serve all patients whose care would not cause them a net loss; indeed, under conditions of excess capacity, some patients would be profitable to the provider only because the bed would otherwise be vacant, making only out-of-pocket costs relevant to the decision to provide the service. Thus, from the standpoint of the public interest, relaxation of certificate-of-need regulation for nursing homes would seem a desirable way—preferable to the regulatory measures frequently employed—of increasing willingness to treat the neediest patients. Moreover, removing these patients from acute care beds would lower costs, though whether costs would be lower overall with freer entry would depend on how well the problem of subsidy-induced demand could be dealt with by other means.

Hospitals and Nursing Homes Compared: The Prospects for Useful Competition

Not only does the nonprice competition precluded by certification of need for nursing homes seem potentially more beneficial to consumers than nonprice competition between hospitals is likely to be, but the other arguments that are advanced for limiting the supply of hospital beds as a cost-control measure do not apply with the same force to nursing home beds. Indeed, the tradition of noncompetitive operation of hospitals tends to color analysts' thinking about the entire institutional health care sector, causing them to miss relevant distinctions. For one thing, there are many more nursing homes than hospitals, which makes the homes both harder to regulate effectively and less likely to require regulation to control monopolistic performance. Moreover, the services offered by nursing homes are more likely to be comprehensible to the layman and to the patient experiencing the care.[13] By the same token, the patient or his family is more likely to take an active role in choosing a home than in choosing a hospital. In nursing homes, even more than hospitals, there is reason to think that "a bed is not a bed" and that regulation cannot assure the desired qualities sufficiently to make it safe to limit consumer choice.

The economics of nursing homes and the market for their services suggest that competitive conditions can be maintained more successfully than in the hospital industry. Economies of scale in nursing home operation seem to be less significant than for more sophisticated hospital care, and it is cheaper to start a nursing home than a hospital, so that entry costs (unlike entry regulation) pose no serious barrier to competition. Since nursing home operators are primarily private and proprietary, unlike the larger public and nonprofit hospital sector, operators should be more responsive to financial incentives and quicker to close an unneeded facility. And, being relative newcomers and rather fragmented in ownership and being held in generally low esteem, nursing home operators are much less capable of capturing any regulatory scheme or converting public controls into a protective shield against competition than are established physician and hospital interests.

Other relevant distinctions between nursing homes and hospitals relate to the financing of care. Significantly more nursing home care is purchased at some out-of-pocket cost to the patient. Not only do third parties provide only about 59 percent of total industry revenues[14] (as compared with over 94 percent of hospital revenues[15]), but even Medicaid patients must give up private means and cash benefits when electing nursing home care.[16] Moreover, the third-party payment that exists is less likely to be on a full cost reimbursement basis. Although rates set by states under Medicaid must be cost related, they are usually based on average, or reasonable, costs for a cross section of homes with reasonable levels of occupancy.[17] As a result, the costs of empty beds cannot be automatically passed on to the public but must instead be borne by the underutilized facility itself. In short, the features of the financing system for hospitals that most clearly invite the risk-free creation of overcapacity and most plainly justify regulation of their capital investments are lacking in the case of nursing homes.

Although marginal cost pricing is to be expected only in that part of an overstocked market that caters to price-sensitive buyers, nursing homes cannot be said to be immune to consumer cost concerns. Besides the substantial population of self-supporting patients, state Medicaid programs have proved to be aggressive and cost-conscious purchasers. Indeed, they have not always resisted the temptation to exert their monopsony power by holding reimbursement rates below fully distributed costs, thus forcing the homes to accept less than a full return on their capital. Although this practice has caused discrimination against Medicaid patients by the homes, it is usually the homes rather than the state that get criticized, and several states have sought to impose regulatory remedies against such discrimination.[18] The effect of such underpayment by the state and mandatory acceptance of Medicaid patients is that self-supporting patients must pay inflated prices, providing cross-subsidies to supplement the state's contribution. In general, the financing of nursing home care confronts their proprietors with real market risks that should discourage the wasteful duplication that certification of need is supposed to prevent.

For the reasons indicated in this comparison of the economics of hospitals and nursing homes, market forces may have a comparative advantage in disciplining this complex industry.

Solving the Problem of Induced Utilization

The obvious objection to freer entry and more competition in the nursing home industry is that, given an excess supply of beds and the availability to many patients of third-party payments—particularly under Medicaid—, patients will often seek nursing home care at public expense when it is not clear that such care is essential to their well-being.[19] Sometimes patients' desire for nursing home care results from the absence of public support for noninstitutional care, which they would otherwise prefer.[20] The objection that demand for nursing home care is a poor measure of need could of course be met by effective utilization review; indeed, with third-party payment structured as it is and with significant cost sharing unlikely to be regarded as feasible, direct control over utilization appears to be the key to carrying out a competitive strategy. Utilization review objective enough to cause the bed supply to adjust to it (rather than vice versa) would leave enough beds empty to put pressure on individual providers to upgrade quality as a means of keeping their own beds full. Strictly limiting the number of nursing home beds may well turn out to be a less efficient and less fair method of dealing with the problem of overutilization than is utilization review by disinterested doctors and other trained reviewers.[21]

A central issue in the development of a regulatory policy toward nursing homes is thus the prospect for adapting patient assessment technology to reviewing nursing home placements and care. Utilization control appears, at least on preliminary examination, to provide a possible key to a procompetitive policy that would yield significant cost-control as well as quality-of-care (in the broadest sense) benefits. A number of specific assessment techniques have been designed and are in use to facilitate correct patient placement in nursing and extended care facilities and in other social programs for the elderly.[22]

There would appear to be sufficient potential in utilization review to justify an HSA in exploring prospects for getting PSROs (or other reviewing bodies) to implement review on a sufficiently rigorous basis that entry restrictions on nursing home developments could be significantly relaxed. Unfortunately, PSROs are currently seen by physicians more as a regulatory mechanism designed to police their performance than as a device for putting reasonable limits on federal or state financing commitments.[23] Perhaps the largest challenge in making PSROs effective is to persuade physicians that PSROs were intended by Congress to control costs by limiting federal responsibility for nonessential spending and not to assure that the highest quality of care is enjoyed by all at the expense of an apparently bottomless public exchequer. Difficult as this would be as a general prospect, physicians may be less threatened by utilization review of long-term care than by PSRO oversight of hospital and outpatient care, in which the physician's professional judgment and self-interest are more directly implicated. Thus, a very real opportunity appears to exist for adapting public controls on utilization to offset the demand-increasing effects of public payment for nursing home care. Physicians in a PSRO should be much easier to persuade of a state's need to be protected against the costs of unnecessary nursing home stays than of the Medicare program's need to limit its responsibility to pay for medical services whose value may not exceed their costs.

Getting physicians to cooperate in imposing stringent utilization controls on nursing home beds would be easier if the judgments made did not appear to be exclusively medical. And, indeed, the appropriateness of patient placement in long-term care facilities is very often affected by social and economic factors—family and home circumstances in particular. Moreover, several of the available techniques for assessing patient placement attempt to weigh not just health status alone but the whole range of personal problems facing patients. Given this dimension of the needed assessment, a strong case can be made for allowing non-physicians to participate in utilization review for long-term care facilities. If physician cooperation can be obtained in implementing these approaches, responsible, publicly mandated utilization review may be feasible in the area of long-term care, even though the widespread skepticism about the effectiveness of the PSRO program as an efficiency assurance (as opposed to quality assurance) mechanism in hospital care remains justified.[24] An active HSA campaign to strengthen such review at the local level would seem essential, however, if a procompetitive strategy toward nursing home care is to be adopted.

In the course of this study, HSA directors were asked about the range of choice available to prospective nursing home patients in their areas. Forty-eight of the sixty respondents, not necessarily a representative sample, agreed that a range of choice for nursing home patients is desirable from a social standpoint and indicated that the resulting overutilization hazard should be controlled either by PSROs (twenty-seven respondents), by other utilization review (thirty-three), or by cost sharing (fourteen). Thirty-nine of sixty-one respondents indicated that non-Medicaid patients had a significant range of choice in their communities, whereas only fourteen thought that Medicaid patients had such a range of choice. These responses suggest that HSA directors may see some merit in the competitive policy suggested here.

Lest the foregoing assessment seem too sanguine, it must be observed that the rigor of the utilization review called for to make the competitive strategy work may well be more than can reasonably be expected from any set of reviewers.[25] Controls over utilization must be so rigorous that significant numbers of empty beds, appearing from time to time as the result of competitive new entry, will remain empty if patient needs are not sufficiently serious to warrant their use. The task must be seen not as rationing existing beds to their best use but as a wholly objective (and more difficult) task of determining whether the need for institutionalization rises to a level calling for a commitment of public funds. The fact that beds are available or that nursing homes are failing for lack of clientele must not enter into the decisions. It is probable, however, that the desire to take care of the marginally unfortunate will triumph, and certainly the courts would be hard to convince that some facilities should go unused and that a system to limit entitlements should be allowed to operate without cumbersome procedures.

Perhaps only if the reviewers are given a fixed budget within which to operate will effective utilization controls emerge. The development of such a fixed budget system is, of course, beyond the scope of HSAs, but such an approach to the public provision of long-term care benefits seems worth exploring. Not only would it impose a limit on the commitment of public funds to this costly area,[26] but it could be designed to allow competition a role in stimulating good performance in the nursing home industry itself.

A Strategy for Nursing Home Regulation

This examination of the issues in long-term care is meant to help health system planners and regulators recognize both the potential value and the limits of competition in the nursing home field. The costs of restricting competition would appear to be high, but the costs of a liberal policy toward entry might be high as well. Perhaps the best solution would be a policy permitting free entry by providers serving *private* patients primarily. Such homes present a reduced hazard of inappropriate utilization and drain on public funds. Moreover, private financing programs should find it easier than public programs to limit their coverage to cases of clear necessity, since the former's beneficiaries, unlike the latter's, usually have the option of financing the care privately if the third-party payer denies liability. Under an approach differentiating among homes along public-private lines, those relieved of regulatory oversight would have to be limited in their acceptance of public patients (say, to a third of the beds) so as to prevent the failing home from automatically converting to a Medicaid-only facility, increasing the pressure on public resources.

Absent reasonable assurance that stringent utilization review is possible, this approach, which the planner-regulators might find the legal means to adopt, would seem to leave competition a substantial role and to confine regulation to its appropriate sphere. Although some would argue that differentiating homes in this way would imply acceptance of two-class care and discrimination, that problem (if it is a problem) is unlikely to be satisfactorily resolved by regulation. Moreover, the presence of less heavily regulated homes that cater primarily to self-supporting patients would provide useful yardsticks by which to measure whether government was enforcing standards and maintaining adequate reimbursement levels in public programs. Given all the difficulties, the approach of confining regulation to the publicly financed providers may be the best one currently available to the planner-regulators.

PROPRIETARY INSTITUTIONS

The future role of proprietary institutions in the health services industry depends in part on how health system planners and regulators view them. The present uncertainty concerning the status of proprietaries already poses serious risks for them, and until the situation is clarified they cannot be expected to expand their role as much as market circumstances might warrant. Nevertheless, there remain some segments of the industry (such as nursing homes) and some local markets (such as California and some sunbelt states) where proprietary institutions are sufficiently well established that they can probably count on some kind of continuing role and can safely think in terms of increasing their investment.[27] And even though proprietaries have been discriminated against and phased or forced out of the market in many other places, there are a few signs that they may be making a comeback.[28]

Proprietaries have had good reason to fear the future, for at least a mild regulatory bias against them exists. Questionnaire responses in 1977, reported in Table 13–1, showed that a significant minority of HSA directors (or, in some cases, assistant directors) admitted to holding opinions adverse to proprietary hospitals and that these same directors detected somewhat stronger adverse opinions on the part of the members of their HSAs. Some HSA directors and board members even disagreed with the statement that proprietaries should be evaluated on their individual merits. As would be expected, some of the strongest antiproprietary views were expressed in those geographic areas where proprietaries are no longer a significant factor in the market.

The following discussion attempts to identify the reasons for antiproprietary attitudes and, by analyzing them, to encourage more balanced perceptions among health system planners and regulators. After discussing the two counts most often found in the indictment of proprietaries, the potential positive contributions of proprietary providers are explored, including their competitive input in an industry lacking in certain kinds of innovation and in incentives for achieving changes responsive to consumer preferences.

Table 13–1.   HSA Directors' Questionnaire Responses

| | You | | HSA Members | | | |
Proposition	Agree	Dis-agree	Most Agree	Most Dis-agree	Di-vided	Don't Know
Earning a profit is not an acceptable motive for operating a hospital.	18	37	18	11	18	7
The quality of care is apt to be unacceptably lower in proprietary hospitals.	6	48	9	16	15	13
No unacceptable qualitative differences are likely to exist between nonprofit and proprietary hospitals.	40	12	17	12	12	13
Apparent efficiencies in proprietary hospitals (e.g., lower assets per bed) are apt to reflect unacceptably lower quality of care or omission of desirable services.	19	34	15	15	8	13
Proprietary hospitals induce greater efficiency and lower costs in competing voluntary hospitals.	19	34	5	15	16	15
Proprietary hospitals are comparatively uncooperative with the planning process.	18	27	12	14	4	19

Proprietary hospitals "skim the cream" off the market, leaving voluntary hospitals to provide unprofitable but needed services.	38	11	26	4	10	12
Each certificate-of-need application by a hospital should be evaluated on its own merits without regard to its proprietary status.	48	3	31	6	5	8

Little space is devoted, however, to undermining such popular shibboleths as the view that no one should profit from the illnesses of others or the view, stated in the first entry in Table 13–1, that "earning a profit is not an acceptable motive for operating a hospital." It should suffice to say that these issues have little substance, "for physicians and other health personnel ... already 'profit' from the misfortunes of others, and there is no way of arranging things otherwise." [29] More to the point, such shibboleths have often been used to maintain physicians' monopoly over the industry's profits and to exclude entrepreneurs who threaten to reorganize the delivery system so that it better serves consumer interests. It must be recognized that, even where an enterprise is organized on a not-for-profit basis, it necessarily serves the employment and other proprietary interests of its personnel. Indeed, according to one widely accepted theory of nonprofit hospital behavior, the nonprofit hospital acts as a "physicians cooperative" whose primary purpose is to maximize the income of the medical staff.[30]

Even without the influence of profit-making physicians, the distinction between proprietary and nonproprietary facilities would not be at all clear-cut. Legally, a nonprofit corporation has no equity investors and cannot distribute its earnings in the form of dividends. This distinction may have little practical significance, however, because existing law does not effectively prevent a nonprofit corporation from paying out substantial amounts to its organizers in the form of salaries, lease payments, and management fees and from conferring perquisites and prestige. Managers of nonprofit firms are interested in growth, perhaps not so much for the sake of doing more good as for the pecuniary and psychic rewards that come with institutional size.. Undistributable earnings from operations contribute to such growth, whether reinvested as capital or used to subsidize added services that could not be supported by patient charges.

Although nonprofit firms may be just be as given to charging monopoly prices as for-profit firms, consumers may be able to rely on the different orientation imposed by the nondistribution rule for assurances that corners are not being cut for personal profit. Henry Hansmann, in important work reconceptualizing the foundations of the law of nonprofit corporations,[31] has argued that adoption of the nonprofit form should be viewed simply as a firm's way of reassuring consumers in this regard. So understood as a competitive strategy aimed at overcoming the problems that consumers face in evaluating complex services, adoption of the nonprofit form by a health care provider should carry with it no legal, tax, or regulatory advantages. As a general rule, nonprofit firms should rise or fall in competition with for-profits on the basis of their respective ability to attract patronage and capital. Hansmann makes a powerful case for rigorously enforcing the nondistribution constraint (in order to validate the firms's representation to consumers) but argues for otherwise fostering fair competition between nonprofit and for-profit providers.

Health system planners and regulators should not be too impressed by formal distinctions and should evaluate providers on their merits without regard to organizational or ownership forms.[32] When the profit-nonprofit distinction is pressed on them, planner-regulators should first be on the lookout for hypocrisy. Second, they should appreciate that choice of the nonprofit form is a competitive strategy aimed at allaying consumer fears and that consumers, not regulators, should judge whether the reassurance thus received is worth the possibly higher cost. Finally, they should recognize that the prejudice in the health sector against explicitly profit-seeking behavior may be based on a self-fulfilling prophesy that, by deterring ethical persons from certain lines of endeavor—for example, "commercial" forms of practice or professional advertising—, ensures the predominance in that line of endeavor of the less savory types.

Quality-of-Care Concerns

A for-profit enterprise might sometimes find it advantageous to sacrifice the quality of care it provides in order to increase profitability. Simplistic thinking can easily exaggerate this risk,[33] however, since there are many influences that limit the discretion that may in fact be exercised. Competition is only one of these influences, but it can be a substantial constraint, despite the consumer's relative ignorance about the technical quality of care. Certainly if the for-profit provider views itself as being in the market permanently and as needing to establish a reputation for good service, it cannot afford to skimp on quality, to risk malpractice suits, or to cause patients to doubt its commitment to their welfare. On the other hand, a provider with a shorter time horizon would have fewer constraints, and in certain circumstances may dupe consumers long enough to make a rapid and unconscionable profit at the expense of its patients' health—a "quick killing," so to speak.

It is also important to note that some health services—hospital care, for example—are typically purchased by consumers with the benefit of expert physician advice. Thus, a proprietary hospital seeking to turn a quick profit must not only dupe patients into accepting poor quality care but must also dupe their physicians. That would not be an easy task since the economic and professional incentives of physicians generally induce them to use institutions that, if anything, overserve, not underserve, their patients.

All things considered, opportunities for exploitation by proprietaries are most likely to exist where (1) there is inadequate competition, perhaps due to entry barriers, and consumers therefore lack alternative sources of care; (2) there is substantial uncertainty about providers' prospects for long-term viability or other conditions making market entry unattractive to more reputable or better established providers; and (3) largely ignorant consumers must purchase services with little or no professional advice.

An example of a market that proved inviting to the unscrupulous was that served by prepaid health plans (PHPs) under the California Medicaid program. That program, by funding a number of low-quality plans, created a scandal that has strengthened fears concerning proprietary HMOs and proprietary providers in general.[34] However, many of the unscrupulous PHPs contributing to the scandal were in fact nonprofit plans that funneled cash to for-profit enterprises offering physician services, management services, and the like.[35] Moreover, the "Medicaid-only" character of the PHPs, the medical profession's opposition to the plans (deterring involvement by ethical providers), and long-term uncertainty about the program (and about state and federal policy generally) contributed to the problems. In addition, the state appeared to be at fault in its haste to implement the PHP program, its lack of attention to assuring meaningful consumer choice, and its failure to monitor the quality of care. Finally, the scandals in California erupted before the competitive market had a chance to weed out the worst plans,[36] whose initial success may have been possible only because consumers had not yet gained sophistication and because demand temporarily exceeded supply.

It would appear that better understanding on the part of state officials about how competition works, and how it can fail, might have made the Medi-Cal PHP program a success. The experience is certainly one from which health system planners and regulators could learn a great deal. In particular, they should learn to distinguish between operators who seek to recover their investment immediately and those who are entering the market for the long pull. A corollary is that a regulatory objective should be to keep market conditions stable enough and governmental policy predictable enough to attract the latter type of investor. An important but unrecognized problem in the health care sector has been the vast uncertainty that confronts anyone undertaking nontraditional activities. Government has allowed itself to become a prospective enemy of all change that it does not sponsor, with the result that reputable innovators and investors are deterred from entering the market.

Having analyzed whether market conditions favor unscrupulous providers, planner-regulators should also give due consideration to nonmarket constraints on profiteering, including both governmental and professional controls. Though the efficacy of the quality control imposed by licensing, accreditation, and the like may sometimes be doubted, such controls would seem to place a floor on the proprietary provider's performance, and they can be improved if the necessity is felt and the will is found. Furthermore, local health planners and regulators are in a position to influence such regulatory activity, helping to assure that it is attuned to the needs of consumers and not called into play only when professional interests are threatened. The planner-regulators may also be in a position to insist that the standards applied in such quality-assurance efforts are realistic and not based solely on traditional providers' unverified belief in the efficacy of currently popular, and invariably costly, methods. Cost cutting, such as proprietary providers might be more inclined to attempt, is not objectionable per se. Health system planners and regulators should be alert to the difference between efficiency and legitimate cost containment, on the one hand, and "rip-offs," on the other, and should seek to make sure that restraints are imposed only on the latter. Unfortunately, regulators tend to have the greatest trouble in making such distinctions.

Internal Subsidies and the "Cream-Skimming" Issue

Unlike nonprofit institutions who frequently use higher than competitive prices for some services to subsidize other services that the public cannot or will not pay for, proprietary providers will normally eschew unprofitable activities, providing only those services whose costs can be recovered from their own charges. Because they do not subsidize money-losing services, proprietaries can often offer their profitable services at lower prices than competing nonprofit institutions. When price competition of this type occurs, proprietary providers are said to be skimming the cream off the market, leaving the unprofitable services without a source of funding.

Although proprietaries clearly have engaged in some cream skimming, nonprofits may also limit their provision of some uncompensated services—to indigents, for example—even while applying excess earnings from profitable services to uses that add more to the institution's prestige.[37] Moreover, proprietary institutions have on occasion been compelled, under regulation, to offer unremunerative services that they would not voluntarily provide; thus, the proprietary is made to assume the same burdens that the nonprofits may have voluntarily assumed. Indeed, the major chains of proprietary hospitals, often without overt compulsion but in recognition of their "image" problems, usually maintain emergency rooms and obstetric units even though they are not profitable. Finally, it is noteworthy that proprietary institutions, unlike their nonprofit competitors, pay taxes that help finance direct subsidies for the needy and for other worthy projects. In short, cream skimming is not limited to proprietary institutions, though they have frequently dramatized the issue; moreover, many proprietaries have accepted responsibilities that relieve them of the charge.

The cream-skimming phenomenon, discussed in different contexts in Chapters 1 and 10, has long been a feature of regulated industries. Indeed, the threat of cream skimming has been perhaps the leading rationale for suppressing competition in such industries, permitting regulators to exclude would-be entrants on the ground that their competitive low prices would erode the overall quality of service. When cream skimming is alleged, however, certain questions need always be answered: whether the services financed by internal subsidization are in fact economically appropriate and desirable objects of public subsidy; whether they could pay their own way if priced at cost—and, if not, why not; whether overcharges to users of the monopolized services are an appropriate and equitable revenue source for this purpose; and why subsidies, if truly needed to achieve a clear public purpose, cannot be provided by other means. By asking such questions, one can frequently raise grave doubts about the legitimacy of such "taxation by regulation." [38]

Internal subsidies in nonprofit hospitals and other health care institutions are sometimes, but not always, used to underwrite health care for the needy. When serving as the benefactor of the poor, the nonprofit hospital acts as a charitable monopolist—a sort of Robin Hood redistributing wealth from those who can pay for care to those who cannot. On the other hand, the beneficiaries of such hidden private subsidies have not always been poor. Services that paying patients would be unwilling to support but that doctors and hospitals deem desirable—perhaps for reasons of prestige—have also frequently been financed in this way. Furthermore, the burden of paying for the unprofitable services has not been evenly distributed. Some third-party payers have been strong enough to insist that they should pay nothing beyond the cost of care received by their beneficiaries. Similarly, patrons of hospitals lacking loss operations, such as proprietaries, have sometimes avoided contributing to the costs of such services. In short, the system has never had a clear rationale and has lacked clear legitimacy on equity or political grounds. The best thing that can be said about the monopolistic charity model of the hospital is that, despite the lack of accountability in taxing some for the benefit of others, internal subsidies have supported, among other things, some services that are widely identified as essential and that have no obvious alternative means of support.

Although planner-regulators might appropriately sanction and protect internal subsidies in particularly compelling cases involving care for the truly needy, the general illegitimacy of internal subsidization as a means of financing health care should be recognized. HMOs and ASFs, as well as proprietaries, cannot be systematically required to plow the gains from their efficiency back into internal subsidies benefiting one class of consumers at the expense of another without weakening the competitive effectiveness of the innovative provider used as the vehicle for such subsidies. Patrons of efficient providers must be allowed to benefit from their economizing choices if competition is to serve as a useful force for cost containment.

Of course, the thrust of the argument against internal subsidies is not that charitable instincts are bad or that an efficient system need suppress them. Rather, the point is that regulatory protectionism is a particularly inefficient way of providing for the needy and that it is best replaced by a more direct system of governmental and private subsidies. Indeed, it seems that protectionism really has very little at all to do with charity, at least on the part of the regulators and the protected providers. Regulators and protected providers, after all, are not footing the bill for the charity; the very purpose of protectionism is to facilitate shifting the costs of "charity" to buyers, whether they be financing plans or individual consumers.

The Costs of Suppressing Proprietaries

Planners and regulators should consider not only the validity of the objections that may be raised against proprietaries but also the benefits that may be lost if they are excluded from the marketplace. In formulating rules for proprietaries, decisionmakers can then balance the benefits to be derived from the profit-making form against the inherent possibilities of abuse.

One advantage proprietaries are often said to have is that they are more efficient than nonprofit firms; that is, they use fewer inputs to achieve a given output. Although the empirical evidence generally supports the view that for-profit hospitals are more efficient, it is at times ambiguous and subject to technical criticism.[39] (In particular, it should be noted that many proprietaries seem to have been of less than efficient size.) In addition, it is not implausible that under existing market circumstances nonprofits would be nearly as efficient. Health care financing systems that reimburse providers' incurred costs (or insurance beneficiaries' outlays for care) have systematically discouraged efficiency on the part of both for-profit and nonprofit providers. Moreover, even with third-party payment, many providers' budgets have been squeezed enough from time to time to enforce some efficiency, and it is possible that voluntary institutions have performed efficiently in those activities where the cost pass-through has not been automatic or complete. On the other hand, voluntary hospitals and nursing homes frequently have had other revenue sources—philanthropy and surplus earnings on particular services—with which to subsidize inefficiency or managerial slack. Also, managers of nonprofit firms may have sought to maximize institutional size and prestige as reflected in the size of the firm's budget and its staff as well as in the quantity and technical sophistication of the care rendered. Without investors to satisfy, they have been relatively free to neglect efficiency and to seek the material and other benefits that accrue to the administrators, trustees, and medical staff of a growing institution.

All things considered, technical input-output efficiency, while potentially yielding wherewithal for other kinds of institutional growth, would not appear to be as rewarding in the nonprofit firm as in a for-profit enterprise, where improved efficiency can frequently yield a direct profit to investors. Thus, as retrospective cost reimbursement declines and as prospective rate setting or contractual commitments to a schedule of charges enhance opportunities for profiting from efficiency, the strength of incentives for efficiency will likely be increasingly greater in for-profit enterprises than in the typical nonprofit institution. Of course, the strength of cost-cutting incentives will also depend in part on the competitive climate, because neither for-profit nor nonprofit providers are as apt to respond to the carrot of increased net earnings as to the stick of competition.

Whether proprietaries have a significantly greater instinct for cost saving, they appear clearly to respond more quickly than nonprofit organizations to changes in the demand for services.[40] The cost of neglecting market information is higher in profit-making institutions because a profit forgone is a loss. Nonprofit firms, on the other hand, do not respond as much to market signals as to their own perceptions of what is needed or desirable or what is in the interest of the institution. While nonprofit institutions are not slow to expand *in place,* they have not been as quick as proprietary providers to extend their reach by serving new market areas or entering new lines of endeavor. Moreover, new voluntary firms cannot be counted on as heavily to spring up to meet new needs, because the initiative needed for their appearance requires fortuitous circumstances in addition to the existence of a market opportunity.

Historically, when the voluntary health care sector has failed to generate needed initiatives and investment, the proprietary sector has responded, thereby serving an important function in meeting new needs at the margin. Thus, despite their substantial tax and other disadvantages, proprietary hospitals in the United States have long provided a fringe of relatively small facilities that have been more attuned to changes in the economic environment than the nonprofit core of the industry. Similarly, proprietaries have led the way in the rapid expansion of the nursing home industry that began in the 1950s, and such institutions still predominate in that industry.

Despite the current sense that additional expansion of the health care system is undesirable, it is important not to sacrifice the proprietaries' responsiveness to emerging health care needs.[41] Proprietaries have contributed substantially to improving the accessibility of care and have been somewhat less guilty than the nonprofit sector of concentrating on the qualitative growth that has produced the cost-escalating misallocation of resources that most concerns policymakers. Since further improvements in the accessibility of care are still necessary in the inner cities and rural areas, proprietaries' responsiveness to demand should be highly valued—particularly once a more rational set of subsidies is devised to give consumers in these areas sufficient means to purchase health care. By the same token, the needed reorganization of the health care financing and delivery system is less likely to occur if opportunities for making a profit are foreclosed or if for-profit innovators are excluded from the market either overtly or by a climate of antagonism. The disappointingly slow growth of HMOs has been ascribed to many factors, but discrimination against proprietary HMOs has certainly been an important part of the explanation.[42]

Not only will proprietary providers be more responsive to emerging health care needs as expressed in consumers' ability and willingness to pay, but they are also likely to be more responsive to a lack of demand and to the existence of overcapacity in local markets. Unlike nonprofit hospitals, proprietary hospitals can be expected to close down beds, or to go out of business altogether, once they have lost their market and have been replaced by more efficient or better located facilities. A for-profit firm has an incentive to stay in business only as long as its revenues cover its out-of-pocket costs plus at least a market rate of return on that portion of its capital that it could recover by ceasing business. (The remainder of its capital investment is "sunk," or lost already, and does not influence its decisions.) In contrast, managers of a nonprofit institution have little concern about salvageable capital; indeed, they are often prohibited by law from redirecting their capital to other uses. Thus, nonprofit managers will elect to eliminate their own jobs and positions only when cash flow is inadequate to meet the payroll and other out-of-pocket costs. Although health planners, frustrated in their efforts to close hospitals, have perhaps had more occasion to declare war on proprietaries (because of their small size) than on voluntaries, the latter's incentives incline them to even greater recalcitrance, ignoring clear market signals as well as the planners' preferences. The result of such perverse incentives is apt to be the perpetuation of obsolete nonprofit firms, unnaturally sustained by cost reimbursement and philanthropy, legally restricted in redirecting their capital, and reluctant to liquidate even when the market dictates that they should do so.

NOTES

1. Havighurst, "Regulation of Health Facilities and Services by 'Certificate of Need'," 59 *Va. L. Rev.* 1143, 1210–11 (1973).

2. Although there is a general consensus that ambulatory surgery is more efficient than inpatient surgery for some conditions, that consensus is based more on intuition than hard evidence. A recent survey of the literature on the cost and efficiency of all types of ambulatory care reported that there had been thirty-eight clinical studies of ambulatory surgery, including only five randomized controlled trials. Few of these studies properly measured the costs of ambulatory surgery, including the nonmonetary costs imposed on the patient and his family. Thus, the economic case for substituting ambulatory surgery for inpatient surgery must be regarded as unproven. *See* Berk & Chalmers, "Cost and Efficacy of the Substitution of Ambulatory for Inpatient Care," 304 *New Eng. J. Med.* 393 (1981).

3. ICF, Inc., *Selected Use of Competition by Health Systems Agencies* ch. 4, at 24 (1976).

4. *Id.* ch. 4, at 38.

5. *Id.* ch. 4.

6. *Id.* ch. 4, at 44.

7. Review of the Proposed Nevada Institute of Medicine and Surgery, Inc., Minutes of the Nevada State Comprehensive Health Planning Advisory Council, April 7, 1972.

8. 45 Fed. Reg. 69,743, 69,750 (1980).

9. *Cf.* Butler, "Assuring the Quality of Care and Life in Nursing Homes: The Dilemma of Enforcement," 57 *N.C.L. Rev.* 1371 (1979). This comprehensive review of regulatory approaches to quality assurance shows the complexity of the problem, documents regulation's past failures, reaches hopeful conclusions about the cost and efficacy of future regulation, and gives short shrift to consumer choice as a tool. The article is typical of the literature that sees regulatory failure only as evidence of the need to try harder.

10. *Cf.* 45 Fed. Reg. 47,368 (1980) (proposed Health Care Financing Administration regulations on nursing home participation in Medicare and Medicaid). *See also* Demkovich, "Government's Nursing

Home Rules—Better Care or More Bureaucracy?" 12 *Nat'l J.* 1846 (1980).

11. Paradoxically, some evidence in favor of limited regulation can be found in the writing of a proponent of nursing home regulation. *See* W. Thomas, *Nursing Homes and Public Policy: Drift and Decision in New York State* 155–58, 175, 261 (1969) (suggesting that when New York consumers were given a range of choice of nursing homes, some of the worst homes were in fact forced to close their doors).

12. Feder & Scanlon, "Regulating the Bed Supply in Nursing Homes," 58 *Milbank Mem. Fund Q.* 54, 58 (1980).

13. *Id.* at 56–57.

14. U.S. Department of Health, Education and Welfare, Public Health Service, *Health—United States, 1978,* at 402.

15. *Id.*

16. Feder & Scanlon, *supra* note 12, at 57.

17. Bishop, "Nursing Home Cost Studies and Reimbursement Issues," *Health Care Financing Rev.,* Spring 1980, at 47; 3 *CCH Medicare & Medicaid Guide* ¶15,550 *et seq.*

18. Feder & Scanlon, *supra* note 12, at 76.

19. *See generally* Scanlon, "Nursing Home Utilization Patterns: Implications for Policy," 4 *J. Health Pol., Pol'y & L.* 619 (1980).

20. Congressional Budget Office, *Long-Term Care for the Elderly and Disabled* 27–31 (1977).

21. *See* Willemain & Farber, "Nursing Homes and the Roemer-Feldstein Hypothesis," 14 *Med. Care* 880 (1976); Letters to the editor, 16 *Med. Care* 353–56 (1978). These references show that tightening supply does not contribute to more appropriate patient placement and that utilization controls are needed in any event. The "free market" approach is discussed in illuminating terms in a letter from Dr. Roemer, discoverer of the "Roemer effect," and in a reply from Willemain and Farber. *Id.* at 354–56.

22. *See, e.g., Multidimensional Functional Assessment: The OARS Methodology* (E. Pfeiffer ed. 1975).

23. *See generally* Havighurst & Blumstein, "Coping with Quality/Cost Tradeoffs in Medical Care: The Role of PSROs," 70 *Nw. U.L. Rev.* 6 (1975).

24. *See, e.g.,* Congressional Budget Office, *Impact of PSROs on Health Care Costs: Update of CBO's 1979 Evaluation* (1981).

25. For a pessimistic assessment of the prospects for utilization review, see Feder and Scanlon, *supra* note 12, at 75–76.

26. Underfunding is unlikely if ever more costly hospitalization is the alternative.

27. In the nation as a whole, proprietary hospitals account for only about 8 percent of all beds in nonfederal short-term general hospitals; nonprofit or voluntary institutions account for about 70 percent of the beds. American Hospital Association, *Hospital Statistics* 4–7 (1979) (figures for 1978).

28. *See, e.g.*, Demkovich, "Hospitals Adopting the Old Axiom—In Numbers There is Strength," 12 *Nat'l J.* 1316 (1980) (describing how for-profit hospitals have benefited from the growth of multihospital chains).

29. Havighurst, "Health Maintenance Organizations and the Market for Health Services," 35 *L. & Contemp. Prob.* 716, 757 (1970).

30. Pauly & Redisch, "The Not-for-Profit Hospital as a Physicians' Cooperative," 63 *Am. Econ. Rev.* 87 (1973).

31. *See* Hansmann, "Reforming Nonprofit Corporation Law," 129 *U. Pa. L. Rev.* 497 (1981); Hansmann, "The Role of Nonprofit Enterprise," 89 *Yale L.J.* 835 (1980).

32. For a more detailed challenge to the systematic legal bias in favor of the nonprofit form in the hospital industry, see Clark, "Does the Nonprofit Form Fit the Hospital Industry?" 93 *Harv. L. Rev.* 1417 (1980).

33. Clark compared nonprofit hospitals with for-profit hospitals in terms of rates of accreditation, facilities, incidence of malpractice, and the like. He concluded that when important variables such as size were controlled for, "such evidence as exists does not show nonprofit hospitals to differ from for-profits in quality." *Id.* at 1455 (and sources cited therein).

34. For a discussion of the growth and operation of HMOs in California under the Medicaid program, see Chavkin & Treseder, "California's Prepaid Health Plan Program: Can the Patient Be Saved?" 28 *Hastings L.J.* 685 (1977).

35. *Id.* at 724–25, 728.

36. Reports out of California at one time indicated to the author that consumers were reacting to poor service by changing plans. Unfortunately, the experience has never been analyzed rigorously except from a political point of view. *E.g.*, Chavkin & Treseder, *supra* note 34.

37. In an article generally critical of the "commercialization of health care," Relman acknowledged that nonprofit hospitals "in relatively well-to-do demographic areas"—that is, hospitals without the financial burden of caring for the poor—pose a competitive threat to teaching institutions that do care for the poor. Relman, "The New Medical-Industrial Complex," 303 *New Eng. J. Med.* 963, 968–69 (1980). The executive director of the Federation of American Hos-

pitals, the trade association of the for-profit hospitals, made a similar point in a letter responding to the Relman article. Letter to the editor from Michael D. Bromberg, 304 *New Eng. J. Med.* 233 (1981).

38. *See* Posner, "Taxation by Regulation," 2 *Bell J. Econ. & Mgt. Sci.* 22 (1971).

39. For an overview of this literature, see Clark, *supra* note 32, at 1455–62.

40. Kushman & Nuckton, "Further Evidence on the Relative Performance of Proprietary and Nonprofit Hospitals," 15 *Med. Care* 189 (1977); Steinwald & Neuhauser, "The Role of the Proprietary Hospital," 35 *L. & Contemp. Prob.* 817, 828–30 (1970).

41. Kushman & Nuckton, *supra* note 40, argue that proprietaries are likely to be discriminated against by health system planners and regulators and that they should not be. Their careful and well-documented discussion should be read to supplement the discussion here.

42. *Cf.* Institute of Medicine, *Health Maintenance Organizations: Toward a Fair Market Test* 21–23 (1974).

IV POLICY DIRECTIONS

IV FUTURE DIRECTIONS

14 FEDERAL POLICIES TO STRENGTHEN COMPETITION[1]

The failure of the 1970s to yield a coherent national health policy has produced in the 1980s a new willingness on the part of policy-makers to consider seriously the possibility that market forces can guide the evolution of the health services industry. But opening up the policy debate is only the first step. It may prove much harder to identify and finally bring about all the interrelated policy and behavioral changes that are needed to make the market alternative work satisfactorily. Whereas until recently it was legitimate simply to carp in academic terms about the unwisdom of the drift to regulation, it is now necessary for market advocates to offer a specific set of proposals that meets the tests of practicality and political feasibility.

This chapter discusses what needs to be done to establish competition as an effective allocator of health resources. The list of proposals here is less comprehensive and definitive than Alain Enthoven's innovative consumer-choice health plan (CCHP)[2] and the proposed National Health Care Reform Act[3] creatively developed by Congressman Richard Gephardt and former Congressman David Stockman, now director of President Reagan's Office of Management and Budget. Thus, the approach here, though including elements from several of the procompetition bills currently before Congress, lacks the programmatic character and identity that aid so much in getting attention in public debate. Nevertheless, it is argued that a piecemeal approach to policymaking, which addresses specific market defects and specific needs and problems on an ad hoc basis, will be more fruitful than an all-embracing legislative solution.

Even though the political climate now seems hospitable to a market-oriented national health policy, it remains to be seen whether the Reagan administration and Congress will in fact follow all the way through in implementing a procompetitive strategy. The antagonism to regulation that one senses is not the same thing as favoring aggressive efforts to rehabilitate the market as a force for changing the status quo. Indeed, a philosophical commitment to reducing government's role could easily undercut such necessary measures as antitrust enforcement and the provision of funds to replace desirable internal subsidies eroded by competition. Similarly, a philosophical propensity to return responsibilities to the states invites the continuation of regulatory patterns and state-supported professional control that have long diminished competition's force. Finally, government has great difficulty in pursuing any goal single-mindedly through the thickets of special interests. Unfortunately, a failure by the administration and Congress to carry the competitive strategy forward on all fronts could disappoint expectations for cost relief, causing the nation to return to the old path toward regulation. Although a competitive solution seems much easier to realize than a successful regulatory one, government's ability to act forthrightly and consistently on this or any other subject remains in doubt in the 1980s.

The unifying thread in the policy proposals in this chapter is the need to widen opportunities for consumer choice in such a way that providers will be forced to compete more actively than they do at present on the basis of both price and their willingness to submit to organized health plans' various cost-reducing measures. The key elements that must be addressed include, on the demand side of the market, the incentives of consumers and those who act as their agents in selecting or designing financing arrangements and in bargaining with insurers or providers. Also on the demand side, there are innumerable issues surrounding the manner in which beneficiaries of public financing programs can be motivated and permitted to economize without jeopardizing the objectives of those programs. On the supply side of the market, freedom to enter and to innovate must be assured so that the range of choice available to consumers is not unreasonably constricted. As discussed in Chapters 4 and 9, the causes of the current problems in the private sector include open-ended tax subsidies for employer-purchased health insurance, provider-imposed restraints on innovation and cost-containment initiatives, and employers' and unions' questionable representation of employee interests in purchasing decisions. The thesis of the policy discussion here is that these problems, as well as the additional complexities introduced by government financing and regulatory programs, are all amenable to effective governmental action. After a brief assessment of the likelihood that the private sector can be activated to address the problem of health care costs, the discussion focuses on the specific policy measures required.

ASSESSING THE PRIVATE SECTOR'S COST-CONTAINMENT CAPABILITY

Despite everything that has been said, it may still be possible to doubt the asserted premise that enhanced competition under appropriate incentives will bring about material changes in health care financing and delivery that will actually help in controlling costs. It should be a sufficient answer to such doubts to state that the real issue has nothing at all to do with the validity of such predictions. Instead, the only relevant question should be the feasibility of establishing a process that effectively reveals consumer preferences and induces providers and others to serve them. If such a process were in place, then it could be powerfully argued that the market's verdict should be accepted as an expression of people's wishes—even if the allocation of resources turned out to be no different than it is today.

Although it should not be necessary to provide assurances that the market, once unleashed, will in fact produce dramatic changes, there is a solid basis for confidence that it will. The crucial insight is that the way in which health services are currently paid for, though well established and familiar, is in no sense inevitable. Cost containment is a complex administrative and organizational problem that can be addressed in numerous ways, only a few of which have been given a fair market test. Evidence suggesting the potential for competitively stimulated improvements in the cost-effectiveness of private financing mechanisms can be gathered from many different places and is cumulatively convincing that demand-side changes hold the key to meaningful reform.

First, one can refer to theory and the powerful logic behind practical steps that might be taken but have not been attempted in medical care. Discussion in Chapter 9 conceptualized the ways in which health insurers, competing among themselves for the business of cost-conscious consumers, might go about the cost-containment task by redefining their benefits.[4] That discussion identified two essential strategies that, although they are conceptually distinct, might often be mixed in creative ways in practice. One approach is to use carefully designed exclusions from coverage, or limitations on payments (including cost sharing), to maintain cost awareness. The contrasting strategy, revealed in the HMO model in particular, is to limit the providers who are eligible to provide covered services. In a competitive world, one would expect, a priori, to find not only relatively pure models of both kinds—selective plans with large deductibles and copayments on the one hand and comprehensive group-practice HMOs on the other—but also a variety of hybrid plans. These hybrid plans would offer somewhat wider choice of provider than group-practice HMOs but would use participation agreements with preferred providers to control prices and to impose administrative controls on utilization—that is, to effectuate exclusions from coverage. Or they might find other ways to exclude high-cost providers from eligibility to treat plan subscribers on favorable terms. Obviously, administrative costs and consumer resistance will limit the realization of theoretical possibilities, but that is as it should be in a competitive market.

A second basis for confidence in the market's ability to change is evidence that insurers in closely analogous fields—including limited areas of health insurance (particularly dental insurance)—have taken effective action to curb the natural propensity of consumers and providers to spend the insurance fund on benefits not worth their costs. They have thus recognized the moral hazard phenomenon, characteristic of all insurance, as a problem that they must combat if they are to compete effectively. Among the techniques employed are insurance adjusters, multiple estimates, fixed cash benefits, and contracts with service providers (e.g., pharmacies and auto body shops). Although analogies to other types of insurance are far from perfect and the administrative costs of medical cost control would sometimes be prohibitive, the range of strategies neglected by medical care insurers still seems great enough to suggest that other inhibiting factors are at work. Specific examples of promising strategies, both theoretical and in use, are beginning to appear in the literature.[5]

An enlightening source of impressive anecdotal evidence that major change is possible is the antitrust enforcement effort, which is uncovering restraints by organized providers on specific moves attempted by individual insurers. In addition to revealing one reason why there has been so little innovation in the past, the antitrust enforcement agenda outlined in Chapter 4 suggests the potential for major change once providers and would-be innovators are convinced that providers' trade-restraining actions will be punished.

Historical research on how the financing system reached its present condition also provides convincing evidence that private institutional arrangements could have evolved differently and could be much more responsive to consumer cost concerns. The record reveals that the medical profession itself has long realized that third-party payment can be consistent with price competition in medical markets. Indeed, in the early days, the profession's leaders were candid about their purpose in moving to suppress competition generated by lay-controlled insurers seeking to secure medical services for their policyholders on advantageous terms.[6] These insurers certainly were not the passive payers we know today but rather were aggressive cost-conscious buyers of medical care. The history of prepaid medical care in Oregon, as gleaned by Goldberg and Greenberg from the record of an early antitrust case,[7] demonstrates powerfully the natural propensity of early third-party payers to control physician spending decisions; only strong concerted action by organized medicine made these early plans finally conform to the profession's preferences.[8]

Finally, promising signs of a revival of innovation in financing and delivery have begun to appear,[9] even though the tax law remains unchanged and even though antitrust enforcement is only beginning to deter professional resistance. HMO development has been steady and in some markets has created competitive conditions that reveal the market's promise.[10] Blue Cross and Blue

Shield plans have taken some steps in the direction of cost containment even though they have yet to be pushed very hard by either their competitors or their customers. Experimentation with second-opinion programs suggests that the innovative spirit is not wholly dead among commercial health insurers. HMO development by some insurers, innovative programs using a network of primary care physicians,[11] plans steering consumers to efficient preferred providers, and a few other scattered initiatives also reveal that some capacity for independent action exists.

Even though there is good reason to believe that dramatic change in the private financing system is possible, it must be recognized that employers, unions, and the private insurance industry are tightly wedded to dysfunctional payment methods.[12] Employers express no enthusiasm for grappling with health care costs,[13] and insurers reflect this attitude and strongly resist the assertion that they have a responsibility to challenge providers.[14] Moreover, insurers will find it hard to change as a practical matter; the HMO movement has shown that health services can be efficiently organized and integrated with financing only at the local community level, where traditional insurers are not accustomed, or currently well equipped, to function. Furthermore, breaking out of their current passivity in dealing with providers remains risky for insurers even though antitrust law now inhibits provider retaliation. Such innovation would require incurring substantial costs in devising administrative controls, in negotiating with providers on an individual basis, and in selling new types of coverage. If such efforts succeeded only in changing providers' general style of practice, the innovator's competitors would also benefit, and there would be no reward for the effort. Similarly, certain kinds of innovation, if successful, could be readily imitated so that investments in innovation could not be recouped. Also, where competitive moves are easily matched by competitors, oligopolistic interdependence deters such initiatives. Nevertheless, despite all these uncertainties surrounding the prospects for immediate change, the increasing cost consciousness of insurance purchasers, the large number of competing insurers, and the growth of alternative delivery systems all suggest that major change *is* possible if the right conditions exist.

Getting the conditions right to encourage private sector change is the concern of this and the final chapter and should be seen as the primary problem of health policy. On the demand side of the market, private purchasers' distorted economic incentives can be corrected by a change in the tax law, and public program beneficiaries can be offered new opportunities for cost-conscious choice. At the same time, the supply side's freedom to offer a full range of choice can be fostered by vigorous antitrust enforcement. Whether, if these things are done, anything else is necessary or desirable is the subject of much discussion below. Some proposals have sought to assure that all consumers have cost-saving options by maintaining, or by requiring employers to maintain, a structured system of choice. These proposals are questioned below except insofar as they would enhance the opportunities for cost-conscious consumer choice by the beneficiaries of public programs and by others falling outside the market for private group coverage.

Once all consumers have, directly or indirectly, an opportunity to choose health care coverage in an antitrust-conscious market with the relative costs in view, the market's response can almost certainly be depended on unless government interferes. Unfortunately, as Chapter 15 shows, government's continued presence as a regulator, major purchaser, and indecisive architect of the industry's environment may inhibit many of the private sector reforms that the market strategy seeks to trigger. Because true deregulation, particularly at the state level, will be hard to achieve, it may prove impossible to send anything but a mixed signal to the private sector. In the last analysis, government's inability to remove itself as the dominant decisionmaker in the health care marketplace could prove the Achilles heel of the market strategy.

CHANGING THE TAX TREATMENT OF EMPLOYER-PAID HEALTH INSURANCE PREMIUMS

The common element in all current procompetition proposals is a change in the tax subsidy for employer-paid health insurance. Why proposals to restore competition should put such emphasis on limiting this subsidy requires some explanation since the subsidy does not itself affect competition in any direct way. Current tax policy does, however, cause the market to seek a higher equilibrium level of health care spending than is probably appropriate. Because market advocates recognize that reliance on market forces is justified only if those forces are pulling us where we want to go, they would share others' doubts about strengthening competition in a market where purchasers substantially underestimate the cost of everything they buy. But market advocates also think that using regulation to frustrate the market's response to distorted price signals is a perverse policy if the cause of that distortion can be readily removed. Thus, market advocates are strongly attracted to the tax change both on resource-allocation grounds and as an alternative to regulation.

In addition to its merit in making the market a force for allocative efficiency, the right kind of tax change could directly strengthen the competitive process. If, by increasing the value of the dollars spent on marginal health insurance coverage, the tax change encouraged a large number of purchasers to reexamine their options, the sudden demand for innovation in cost containment would impart the impetus that is needed to overcome the inertia that currently depresses bargaining and competition in the industry. While antitrust enforcement can remove overt restraints on innovation, it may be that only a tax change strengthening bulk purchasers' pressure for cost containment can break down the tacit conspiracies, ignorance, irrational attitudes, and other obstacles to competition that also exist. It is thus possible to view a tax change as a valuable, even necessary, way to break the existing logjam and speed up the competitive process.

The Tax Subsidy: Piling One Distortion of Demand on Top of Another

It is difficult to measure the magnitude of the distortions created by the exclusion of employer-paid health insurance premiums from employees' wages subject to income and Social Security taxes,[15] but it seems quite substantial. Although the subsidy is generally greater for upper-bracket taxpayers and minimal for low-income persons with little tax liability, the fact that the Federal Insurance Contributions Act (FICA) tax benefit does not accrue to higher-bracket employees makes the effective discount for services purchased through insurance (with untaxed dollars) fairly uniform (and substantial) across a wide spectrum of taxpayers. In 1977, Martin Feldstein and Bernard Friedman estimated that the tax law provided an average discount (before administrative expenses) of roughly 35 percent for all health services purchased through an insurance plan.[16] Because of inflation-caused "bracket creep" and FICA tax increases, the average subsidy reached 43 percent in 1980, according to Congressional Budget Office (CBO) estimates.[17] The size of this discount means that people have a powerful and increasing incentive to pay as many bills as possible through employer-purchased insurance, rejecting coinsurance and deductibles and seeking coverage for services that could readily be paid for out of pocket. In other words, insurance is valued not simply as a means of obtaining essential financial protection but as a vehicle for obtaining federal help in paying routine bills.

The overinsurance that results from the tax subsidy has consequences whose magnitude far exceeds the dollar amount of the revenue loss, which, being estimated by CBO at about $28 billion for 1982 (exclusive of state tax consequences),[18] is itself hardly a negligible figure. By inducing the purchase of additional insurance, the tax subsidy extends third-party payment's distorting effect on the demand for medical care to a much wider range of health care transactions than would otherwise be affected. Feldstein and Friedman describe this piling of one demand distortion on top of another as providing "a subsidy of a subsidy."[19] The effect on overall health care spending of unnecessarily removing cost considerations from provider and patient decisionmaking is probably incalculable, but it is certainly very large.

Overinsurance induced by the tax law takes other forms besides discouraging cost sharing and encouraging overly comprehensive coverage. Excessive liberality on the part of insurers in the payment of claims, less than optimal use of dollar limitations on indemnity payments, and an undue preference for paid-in-full service benefits are other consequences of the tax law's penalization of out-of-pocket payments. By the same token, cost-containment efforts by third parties are not valued as highly as they should be, since any saving in premium that is achieved and paid out as increased wages becomes taxable income. Thus, because a dollar saved is not a dollar earned, insurers have been unduly passive in dealing with providers and attempting to curb manifestations of moral hazard. Although much of the passivity of third-party payers has resulted from restraints of trade imposed or threatened by providers, the tax law has greatly reduced the incentives of insurers and consumers to resist provider dictation.

The tax subsidy has also induced many employers to bear the entire cost of health insurance and not to require employee contributions, at least for individual coverage. Employees have thus been rendered unconscious of plan costs and lulled into an entitlement mentality. Cost-saving initiatives are much more difficult under such circumstances.

This recitation of the ways in which the unlimited tax subsidy for private health insurance has distorted the industry's performance suggests why a change in the tax law would be in the public interest. The contention is simply that, with consumer incentives to economize appropriately strengthened and the market freed of professionally imposed restraints on innovation in the financing system, private initiatives could reasonably be expected to move us toward efficient levels of spending on health care. Obviously, overall allocative efficiency would also require redesign of public programs, but that redesign should be easier if pressures from newly cost-conscious bulk purchasers of health coverage and self-supporting consumers have already stimulated competition in insurance and provider markets. Thus, high-priority attention to triggering this impetus for change is desirable. The resulting innovations in private financing mechanisms would pave the way both for comparable administrative changes in public programs and for greater reliance in those programs on cost-conscious consumer choice. Moreover, greater efficiency and competitiveness in the larger market might facilitate expansion of public programs by freeing resources to meet, and reducing the cost of meeting, currently unmet needs.

The policy agenda set forth in this chapter is intended to satisfy the minimal conditions that must exist before the competitive market can be deemed to serve consumers well. Whether a tax law change is one of those essential preconditions to primary reliance on competition and consumer choice is an important question because any significant tax change faces political obstacles. Whereas many observers would argue for regulation on resource allocation grounds if the tax subsidy could not be curtailed,[20] it is also possible to argue that continuation of the existing tax subsidies for the purchase of health insurance would not automatically justify government regulation, which may still be criticized as more self-aggrandizing than socially imperative. Tax subsidies are common in the overall economy and do not, in themselves, invalidate reliance on the marketplace to allocate resources. Moreover, if government lacks the will to change tax rules to improve private incentives, it is fair to ask that it accept the consequences of that choice and not meddle further in the private market. Even with the tax laws as they are, the private market can be made to function usefully, although the equilibrium it seeks will obviously be affected by the tax subsidy. In short, heavy-handed regulation is not even a second-best strategy when compared with the market's ability to correct the defects in private insurance that are not tax-induced.[21]

Although a change in the tax law is an extremely important policy measure, it should not be regarded as a sine qua non for reliance on competition to allocate health resources. Congress should recognize, however, that rejection of a substantial tax change would imply a judgment that society should spend substantially more on health services for employed persons than those citizens spending only their own money would elect to spend. Moreover, continued reliance on competition without a tax change would probably be irresponsible without regulation of employer health plan offerings and encouragement of individual choice. Later discussion of arguments for mandating multiple offerings of health plans to employees and uniform employer contributions deals with whether these measures are needed in addition to a substantial change in the tax law. They would seem essential if the tax change is not adopted.

Proposals for Change

The obvious remedy for the law's inducement of excessive health insurance coverage is to put some kind of limit on the exclusion of employer contributions from taxable income. With such a limited subsidy, the purchase of basic protection would still be encouraged, but beyond some fixed point the marginal dollars spent by an employer on health insurance would have the same after-tax value to employees as dollars paid in wages. Among the various proposals to reduce the tax law's demand-stimulating impact, the most common approach is to place a flat dollar limitation on the amount of employer-paid premiums that may be excluded from income. For example, Senator Durenberger's bill would include in a family's taxable income for income tax purposes any employer contribution over $125 per month, or $1,500 per year (in current dollars).[22]

Putting an absolute limit, or cap, on the tax exclusion, though beneficial, would stop short of changing incentives throughout the entire range in which economizing might be appropriate. Indeed, whereas the limit of the Durenberger bill was chosen for the express purpose of subsidizing the purchase of comprehensive coverage through either an HMO or traditional insurance with modest cost sharing, it is arguable that employees should not be discouraged by tax considerations from purchasing even cheaper types of coverage. It is quite possible, for example, that many consumers would rationally prefer plans featuring large deductibles and copayments or strategic departures from comprehensiveness in benefit design. For this reason, although some would object to inducing undue risk selection, it might be desirable to strengthen economizing incentives even further than under the Durenberger bill. Some proposals, such as one originally introduced by Secretary (then Senator) Schweiker in the Ninety-sixth Congress,[23] would do this by excluding from taxable income any rebate of premiums received by employees who select a plan that costs less than their employer's most expensive one. The following paragraphs briefly set forth a somewhat different approach.

The approach suggested here, primarily to highlight the issues that need to be addressed, is, first, to allow an exclusion from taxable income and wages for both employer- and employee-paid premiums limited to some amount, say $1,800 per family per year (the "maximum total exclusion"); unlike the $1,500 exclusion in the Durenberger bill, this proposed exclusion would not apply just to employer-paid premiums, and the limit would apply for FICA as well as income-tax purposes. The more distinctive new feature of the proposal, however, is an additional exclusion from taxation for up to, say, $800 of the unused maximum total exclusion—that is, the excess of $1,800 per year over the taxpayer's annual health plan premium. Like the proposals for tax-free rebates, the effect of this tax exclusion for cash income would be to extend employees' incentive to economize over a wider range, by making the taxpayer see the last $800 spent on premiums below the $1,800 level as whole dollars. This proposal has the advantage over others that it would break the link between the predominant tax subsidy and the employment relationship,[24] thus treating equitably the self-employed and others who are currently denied the full tax subsidy. It would also greatly increase the number of employees who are fully cost conscious at the margin over the number that would be affected by the Durenberger proposal.

Although the cash exclusion feature may seem peculiar, it is in fact a quite logical extension of the perception that employees should receive tax free any saving achieved by selecting a low-cost rather than a high-cost option. Taking the tax-free rebate approach, however, as in the Schweiker proposal, would simply induce employers to offer new high options with premiums equal to the maximum exclusion (in order to shelter as much income as possible). To avoid this effect, it becomes logical to reward an employee for spending less than the maximum amount whether or not his employer offers the high-option plan in fact. Also, extending the tax reduction to employees who lack access to a high-cost plan is more equitable. Finally, the automatic cash exclusion approach greatly simplifies the administration of the tax law, the paying of taxes, and the employer's situation.

Changing the tax law to limit the exclusion of employer contributions and to provide for tax-free rebates (or the equivalent) presents several difficult technical and policy problems that deserve brief comment:

- *Calculation of the employee's taxable share of the employer's contribution.* It is arguably inequitable to tax each employee on his proportionate share of his employer's health plan contribution since the plan's value to individuals varies with their age, health status, and family situation. Also, if employee shares of the employer contribution are calculated in this way, younger employees could obtain a tax-free windfall by shifting to a limited-coverage plan, while older workers would have to supplement the employer contribution to obtain the same coverage that they had before. In order to reduce the new cost and tax burdens borne by older workers and the windfalls to younger ones, the tax law might set a lower cap or reduce the tax-free rebates for younger employees and for those with fewer family responsibilities. The employer could then be allowed to allocate his total costs to the prescribed actuarial categories before apportioning them to individuals.

- *Identifying costs in self-insured plans.* As a practical matter, employers who self-insure or otherwise bear the risk of cost overruns could not readily compute a monthly or annual cost per employee in time to determine the employees' taxable income. Although employers could avoid these problems by cutting benefits to assure that contributions would not exceed the cap or by changing to a prospectively priced plan, such discouragement of self-insurance would be unfortunate. Presumably, cash-method accounting would be an acceptable way of arriving at an annual cost figure.

- *Regional cost differences.* A uniform exclusion cap would have greater and arguably inequitable effects in areas where costs are high; in low-cost areas, the cap might have little or no effect. This is more a political than a policy problem, however, since high costs are precisely the problem to be addressed. Although the cap could be varied by region, it would be difficult to be completely equitable because costs can vary greatly within regions and even within states. Moreover, varying tax burdens by region would create undesirable complexities, and there would be strong resistance to regional variations that might carry over as a precedent to other tax issues.

- *Indexing the cap.* Even a high exclusion limit could achieve the desired effects in time as inflation brought more and more people up against it. Nevertheless, there would be pressure to index any cap. The choice of a method of indexing (by the gross national product deflator, the consumer price index, or a health cost index) should depend on whether the original cap is low enough to affect purchasing behavior to the desired degree.

In discussing exclusion-limiting proposals, it is important not to lose sight of another, somewhat simpler way to improve cost consciousness with respect to the marginal dollar of insurance premium. In many ways, the soundest approach of all (adopted, it should be noted, in the Enthoven proposal) would be to replace the present open-ended exclusion with a limited credit against the insured's taxes. All or some stated fraction of premiums paid up to the limit of the credit would then be subtracted directly from the insured's tax bill, and all additional premiums would be paid with after-tax dollars. One of the advantages of this approach would be to end the disproportionately favorable tax subsidy for employed individuals in higher brackets. Moreover, a system of limited tax credits would make it possible to allow progressively larger credits for lower income taxpayers and could easily provide refundable credits for those persons who had income taxes insufficient to absorb the credit. The availability of a new tax credit would prompt the purchase of basic insurance protection by those persons who are not now covered adequately, yet the fixed limit on the credit would mean that people would be spending their own after-tax money for additional coverage beyond a certain point. If a complete shift to the use of credits is impractical, credits might still be used to assist those who pay their own premiums, thus supplementing rather than replacing the currently inequitable subsidy limited to employer-paid premiums. The Gephardt-Stockman bill adopts this promising approach.

The political prospects of any of the foregoing proposals are problematical. The cash exclusion approach has the arguable advantage over the Durenberger bill that it can be made to accomplish a net tax reduction rather than a tax increase. (Moreover, the raising of the maximum exclusion—to $1,800 from $1,500 in the example given—reduces the number of employees who would perceive the change as a new tax on hard-earned benefits.) On the other hand, the loss of revenue implied could be a potent argument against both this and the tax credit approach. Although the revenue effects could be controlled somewhat by adjusting the numbers, the revenue loss could be substantial, particularly since both approaches would almost necessarily have to extend favorable treatment to nonemployees previously discriminated against. One could also expect organized employer and union interests to complain of inequity if their burdens were increased (by lowering the maximum total exclusion) to offset the revenue loss. In addition to confronting specific problems of this kind, any proposal to change the tax laws as a health policy measure is likely to run into the larger political cross currents that already beset tax and fiscal policy in the 1980s.

The Reagan administration and Congress should not allow political difficulties and technical complexities to deter the adoption of a tax measure that heightens the hitherto suppressed econo-mizing incentives of a critical mass of consumers. In addition to promoting allocative efficiency by facilitating unbiased expression of consumer preferences, such a tax change would stimulate a needed reevaluation of employee health benefit programs. That rethinking would in turn prompt competitive responses in the pri-vate insurance market and among providers. A useful rule of thumb for evaluating tax change proposals would be whether at least half of the employed population would be placed in the posi-tion of having to reconsider the value of their marginal purchases. Another goal should be to assure that basic medical and hospital coverages, and not just dental and other similar insurance, are reexamined.

It would be unfortunate if, in pursuing these immediate goals, policymakers should lose sight of the attractive possibilities for using the tax law to assure virtually universal basic coverage of the entire self-supporting population. By providing taxpayers a limited tax credit or exclusion for premiums paid to plans provid-ing at least satisfactory catastrophic coverage, one essential goal of national health insurance could be readily achieved very soon. Ultimately refundable credits, perhaps payable in advance to solve cash flow problems, could serve as vouchers allowing low-income persons to participate in private health plans at public expense. One must hope that the expedient tax change to be un-dertaken now to straighten out the incentives of the employed population will be designed so as not to foreclose such future steps to assure universal cost-effective coverage. Professor En-thoven's plan and the Gephardt-Stockman bill provide helpful models for extending coverage when it is possible to do so.

THE ROLE OF GOVERNMENT IN STRUCTURING CONSUMER CHOICE

Most of the proposals to alter the tax treatment of employer-paid health insurance premiums obviously contemplate continuation of the tradition, largely traceable to the tax law itself, that most health insurance is purchased through employment groups as a fringe benefit.[25] On the other hand, both Professor Enthoven's path-breaking consumer-choice health plan and the Gephardt-

Stockman bill look ahead to a day when employers would have no role in the design or selection of their employees' health plans, which would no longer be purchased through employment groups but would instead be chosen by individuals from a government-sponsored array of private plans. Other pending proposals would preserve some employer decisionmaking (and thus also collective bargaining) with respect to health benefits but would narrow the employer's discretion or limit the employer's ability to make the final choice. Thus, some proposals contemplate heavy regulation of health plan content, whereas others would structure the choice situation so that, while employers and unions would have a responsibility for providing a menu of choices ("multiple choice"), the final choice from that menu would be made by the individual employee. In view of these policy options, a useful discussion can be organized around the theme of the relative roles of government and employment groups in designing health care plans.

The analytical key here is how consumer ignorance can best be overcome in a competitive system based on consumer choice. Under one possible approach, government would serve in a regulatory capacity to prevent consumers from being victimized by deceptive and inadequate health care plans or from making unwise choices. Alternatively, it might be concluded that employers (and unions, where they are present) can be counted on to bring expertise to bear and to assure that workers get maximum value for their compensation dollar. The conclusion reached here is that employers should be left free to play a major role in choosing or in structuring choices without substantial regulatory restraint and that government should assume a consumer protection role only with respect to the market for individual, as opposed to group, coverage.

The Likelihood of Undue Uniformity in Regulated Health Plans: Minimum Benefit Requirements

One approach to the problem of consumer ignorance would be to have government preside over the market for health plans. A procedure for qualifying plans would seek to assure that plans met minimum requirements, were financially sound, made full disclosure of their special characteristics, and so forth. Professor Enthoven's CCHP embodies this approach, drawing heavily on the model of structured consumer choice represented by the Federal Employees Health Benefits Plan (FEHBP). Within such a government-sponsored system of structured choice, the approach could be highly regulatory or permissive, depending on perceptions of consumer competence and whether other values besides competition were being promoted. In general, the Gephardt-Stockman bill, which also contemplates government sponsorship and control of the choosing process, appears to promise less regulation than the Enthoven proposal.

The question to be considered here is whether government can be expected to offer consumers both a meaningful range of choice and sufficient information to assure wise choices. Unfortunately, the necessarily large number of choices would probably itself be deemed confusing to consumers unless the plans varied only along two or three easily understood dimensions. Enthoven's CCHP would keep choices simple by prescribing minimum benefits and by allowing competition only over price, cost-sharing obligations, and supplemental benefits. Closed-panel plans would also differ with respect to convenience, style, and service as well as the identity of the providers whose services would be paid for, but competition along other dimensions, such as coverage of discretionary services, would not be allowed. It is not known whether an insurance plan with strict prior authorization requirements (which would, in effect, deny coverage for some physician-prescribed treatments) would be excluded for failing to provide minimum benefits, but the desire for a uniform basic benefit package to simplify consumer choice may imply regulatory restrictions on plans' experimentation with both explicit and implicit coverage limits.[26]

Another reason (besides simplification) why the range of consumer choice would probably be limited in a government-structured system is that government, in its role of consumer protector, would want no plan offered that would be an inappropriate choice for any offeree. Because one's ability to self-insure certain risks is largely a function of income and savings, some plans would be appropriate only for middle- or upper-income persons. Thus, catastrophic-only "major-risk" insurance would be clearly inappropriate for persons with low incomes, who (alone) clearly require comprehensive coverage. Such plans might well be excluded from being offered on the ground that they were traps for the improvident. The Enthoven proposal, while requiring comprehensive benefits, would allow cost sharing by consumers of a maximum of $1,500 a year. It is doubtful, however, whether Congress or the presiding regulators would allow such plans to be offered to, say, Medicaid beneficiaries. Thus, unless limitations were placed on the offering of some plans to lower income individuals (something that has never been proposed), the regulators might be inclined to put even stricter limits on cost sharing. Similarly, although the Gephardt-Stockman proposal explicitly eschews regulation of minimum benefit packages, it is doubtful that Congress would enact a plan that left low-income and perhaps other persons in a position to make serious mistakes.

A third reason for limiting the range of consumer choice—and the one that predominates in Enthoven's thinking—is concern about "adverse selection," whereby consumers, anticipating their probable needs, choose or switch plans to take advantage of differences in coverage. Obviously, if all plans had the same benefit package, consumers would have no reason to choose on the basis of their expectations and would base their choices on other factors. As noted below, concerns about segmentation of the insurance market through adverse selection spring not only from the need to prevent competition among plans from focusing on risk selection rather than efficiency but also from the natural governmental impulse to use the insurance system to achieve the social objective of forcing the healthy to subsidize the less healthy. Although substantial variations in cost sharing among plans also invite adverse selection, Enthoven would permit such variations, apparently as a concession to the need for some variety in a competitive system that must serve consumers with different needs. Nevertheless, his endorsement of a minimum benefit package and his restrictions on cost sharing are traceable in large measure to a concern about adverse selection.

The experience of the FEHBP supports the expectation that government-structured choice systems cannot simultaneously promote both variety and well-informed choice. Although federal employees are offered many choices, it is not clear that the *range* of choice is meaningful. Thus, for example, although "high-option" and "low-option" plans are offered, good catastrophic-only

plans—with, say, an annual deductible of $1,000—are not general-
ly available to federal employees.[27] Moreover, in order to get satisfactory catastrophic protection, it has usually been necessary to
purchase a high-option plan covering many easily budgetable expenses. One possibility is, of course, that major-risk coverage is
simply not demanded, federal employees being among the most
risk-averse of citizens. But it is also possible that such plans have
been discouraged because the Office of Personnel Management,
which controls the choices, has been wedded to comprehensiveness as a way of simplifying choices and minimizing adverse selection and has regarded such plans as inappropriate, at least for the
lower income persons among the offerees.

The danger of undue uniformity among competing health plans
is offset to some degree by the variations that can appear in the
practice patterns of the providers in different delivery systems.
For example, although an HMO contracts to provide all needed
services, its doctors' style or its internal incentives might discourage hospitalization so that the subscriber is not "covered" for as
much hospital care as he might obtain in a traditional insurance
plan. The CCHP model depends heavily on such implicit benefit
limitations for its effectiveness and relies on consumer assessments of provider groups to make the market work. Nevertheless,
because choosing a prepaid provider may be seen as riskier than
selecting a fee-for-service doctor (because of the former's incentive to skimp on treatment), regulation might be invoked to suppress corner cutting, thus forcing all plans into a conservative
mold and reintroducing uniformity. Even if implicit variations
among plans might yield a sufficient range of choice in a government-structured system, it is still hard to see why the consumer
should be allowed to select plans featuring implicit, provider-dic-
tated exclusions from coverage yet denied the chance to choose a
plan with explicit exclusions, fully disclosed.

Regulatory prescription of a minimum benefit package in a
government-structured system of choice would significantly restrict innovation by third-party payers, whose ability to curb excessive spending may depend on their ability to limit their
coverage of discretionary services. Enthoven's belief that competing physician groups (HMOs, etc.) can introduce enough variety
to obviate concern about regulation-imposed uniformity depends
for its validity on the success achieved in dividing the physician

community into such groups. Although this is happening in some places, the progress is slow, and it would therefore seem desirable that traditional insurers be left free to innovate in ways that do not require fragmenting the provider community but increase competition in other ways. Although a minimum benefit requirement would not preclude all insurer innovation—some cost sharing would apparently be tolerated—, it could limit the use of major-risk insurance, strategic coverage exclusions, and utilization controls (such as prior authorization and predetermination of benefits) that could be construed as benefit limitations. Despite Enthoven's different judgment based on concern about segmentation, competition's prospects would seem dimmer if regulation blocked or limited the adoption of these insurer strategies. As discussed below, segmentation in insurance markets is not objectionable per se. Even in a market with several organized health plans, allowing insurers to seek out preferred risks and to employ other market-segmenting strategies would add to the market's overall competitiveness.

A final argument against regulation-induced uniformity focuses on the problems of assuring meaningful competition in concentrated markets. Many markets will feature only a handful of organized health plans, and the vigor of competition among them may be diminished if a legal requirement of uniform benefits so narrows the forms that competition can take that interdependent parallel pricing is fostered. Price rigidity develops in concentrated markets when opportunities for varying the product are eliminated and competitors have to worry that price reductions will be so quickly imitated that they will bring no new business. One cannot be sure that, with product uniformity reinforcing other rigidities, this would not be a problem in local health plan markets.

Complications Introduced by Government's Pursuit of Other Goals: Open Enrollment and Community Rating

A different set of reasons for objecting to government sponsorship of the choice mechanism relates to government's propensity to pursue other goals besides competitively induced efficiency. For example, efforts to curtail adverse selection could be carried to extremes unrelated to the needs of a competitive insurance market and justified only by a redistributive impulse, a desire that some groups be subsidized by others. Strong sentiment naturally exists for using insurance mechanisms to impose what are in effect hidden taxes on low utilizers for the benefit of high utilizers. Whereas, in a free market, insurance allows similarly situated consumers to pool their roughly comparable risks, regulation would frown upon narrow groupings of risks, viewing such segmentation as a way of letting preferred risks escape their fair share of the cost of caring for the sick.

As in economic regulation of other kinds, preserving cross-subsidies would probably be an important goal of any government program to structure choice. Even the conservative Gephardt-Stockman bill embraces the public utility model in this regard, requiring "open enrollment" and "community rating" (within actuarial categories). By imposing a utilitylike duty to accept enrollees without regard to health status and not to "discriminate" in price, the Enthoven and Gephardt-Stockman proposals seek by regulation both to overcome the individual risk selection problems that group coverage currently minimizes for much of the population and to facilitate internal subsidization as a way of advancing social objectives.

There is no denying the attractiveness of using regulation to supply hidden funding for uninsurables and the poor, particularly in view of government's chronic unwillingness to provide adequate subsidies from tax revenues. Indeed, this way of subsidizing care for those who cannot pay their own way might seem valuable as a way of replacing those revenue sources currently being relied on that will be eroded by increased competition. This answer to revenue shortfalls has problems of its own, however. Most serious is the strong incentive given plans to avoid higher risk patients. Regulation probably could not prevent plans from targeting their marketing—advertising, for example, a "stay-well" philosophy that implicitly stigmatizes the sick—or from locating their facilities with this goal in mind. (Someone has facetiously suggested a fifth-floor walk-up clinic.) Such evasive actions would defeat regulation's dual purposes of assuring access to care and equitably distributing cost burdens. Moreover, the redistributive effects of cross-subsidies may not always be as progressive as they seem. Indeed, the high utilizers may sometimes turn out to be people who, far from being sicker, have better access to care, higher expectations, and higher income. For example, when Duke University combined its health plan for hourly-paid workers with its plan for faculty and staff a few years ago, the cost of the plan to individual faculty members fell dramatically; under the new "community" rate, hourly-paid workers subsidized the faculty. Despite the strong temptation to convert private insurance into social insurance, a great deal can be said for maintaining group coverage with experience rating, for seeking additional ways within employment groups of rewarding lower utilization and patronage of efficient providers, and for using alternative mechanisms to achieve redistributive goals.

Additional objections to using open enrollment and community rating requirements to foster internal subsidization have to do with these requirements' destructive effects on price competition and the vigor of competition generally. By scrapping group purchasing in favor of universal individual choice, the Enthoven and Gephardt-Stockman proposals would remove the bulk purchaser not only as a decisionmaking agent of the consumer but also as a force for obtaining price concessions and stimulating innovation. Moreover, the elimination of experience rating for groups, in addition to making a plan's price reflect its enrollees' risk profile more than its efficiency, makes it much harder for a plan to engage in price competition. Because each plan's price is posted and must be uniformly adhered to, it cannot be varied in selective competitive moves. Furthermore, oligopoly theory predicts that price cuts are less likely to occur if they would be easily noticed and met by competitors. Since health plan markets are likely to be highly concentrated, foreclosure of plan pricing flexibility could significantly reduce the chances for price competition, particularly if the product is also made artificially homogeneous by regulatory prescription. Finally, regulatory restraints on traditional insurers' use of market-segmenting strategies would limit their entry potential and value as a destabilizing competitive factor in otherwise concentrated and highly insulated local markets.

When it is considered that desired cross-subsidization can be achieved and that the needs of the poor and uninsurable can be met through direct public subsidies, through actuarially adjusted tax credits (as in Enthoven's CCHP), and in other ways that do not undercut competition and efficiency, the attractiveness of using regulation to impose hidden taxes seems much reduced. If properly designed, pooling and assigned-risk programs could distribute the residual poorest risks more equitably than open enrollment, leaving prices to reflect efficiency more than success in avoiding high utilizers.

Conclusions on Government's Role in Structuring Choice

The Enthoven and Gephardt-Stockman proposals have materially advanced understanding of both health policy choices and the role of competition. Nevertheless, analysis suggests that, contrary to those proposals, government is not the best vehicle for structuring consumer choice and minimizing consumer ignorance. Because most consumers have access to better assistance in procuring the financial protection most appropriate to their personal circumstances, government should allow these alternative mechanisms—primarily group purchasing through employment groups—to operate. Subsequent discussion presents the affirmative arguments for preserving for employers an important decisionmaking and choice-structuring role.

A government-sponsored system of consumer choice along the lines envisioned in the Enthoven and Gephardt-Stockman proposals seems the best available alternative for persons who cannot purchase more advantageously through some employment group or otherwise. Among those who would have the option of enrolling in private health plans through the government-sponsored system would be workers without employment-based coverage, the self-employed, the unemployed whose employment-based benefits have been exhausted,[28] Medicaid beneficiaries, veterans, and dependents of military personnel. (Medicare beneficiaries might be kept in a separately structured system with somewhat different rules.) Possibly the most feasible arrangement would be to make the consumer-choice system (referred to below as the "CCS") available to anyone for whom it offered a better opportunity. Thus, public program beneficiaries could stay in the basic program or opt to have government enroll them in a private plan selected through the CCS. Small employers unable to qualify for advantageous group rates might elect to cash out their health plans, letting their workers enter the CCS, or they could seek to pool employees with other employers. The CCS might best be organized through local clearinghouses similar to Project Health in Oregon, which has had some limited success in offering choice to both public beneficiaries and self-supporting enrollees.[29]

The degree of regulation in the CCS should be kept to a minimum for the same reasons noted above. With a strong private market showing which plans have in fact earned consumer support, the regulatory task should not be as difficult as it would be if government were forced to judge plan acceptability on a priori grounds. Thus, for example, consumer protection might take the form of a requirement that no plan could be offered that did not have a minimum number and percentage of premium payers enrolled otherwise than through the CCS. Perhaps the only additional restrictions needed would be those preventing low-income persons from selecting plans whose coverage gaps and cost-sharing provisions made them suitable only for the well-to-do. Care must be taken to prevent the CCS from becoming a catch-all for uninsurables and a vehicle for achieving redistributive goals. Thus, the scheme should be administered so that prices and risks would not particularly discourage consumers and plans, respectively, from participating. Thus, open enrollment (without screening for health status) and community rating (without actuarial adjustments) should probably not be required. Instead of trying to force bad risks on plans participating in the CCS, pooling and assigned-risk mechanisms involving all insurers and plans should be employed to deal with the residual population. The mechanics and financing of such mechanisms should not present insurmountable problems, though some complexity must be acknowledged.

Obviously, fully specifying a CCS is well beyond the scope of this discussion. It appears, however, that government does have a responsibility to intervene in the market for health care plans to assure both informed purchasing and, ultimately, universal coverage for all citizens. It has a collateral responsibility, however, to limit its involvement to those areas where it can serve usefully and not to displace private mechanisms that are fully capable of serving consumers well. The following discussion demonstrates that employment-linked health coverage should not be substantially interfered with.

THE ROLE OF EMPLOYERS IN DESIGNING HEALTH BENEFITS

Employers represent the only generally available alternative to government as an aid to the consumer in protecting himself against health care costs. Not all consumers are in a position to enlist an employer's aid, of course, but enough protection is bought through employment groups that, if a vigorous competitive market could be maintained to serve group demands, an infrastructure of efficient health care plans would exist to serve the needs of the remainder of the population, including the beneficiaries of public programs. Obviously, where a labor union exists to represent employee interests in dealing with the employer, the union, too, serves to assist the individual consumer in overcoming his ignorance in purchasing a complex product.

The key insight here is that employers and unions can achieve economies of scale in searching the market and bargaining with plans while possibly avoiding the diseconomies of larger scale and political organization that appear to limit government's ability to serve in the same capacity. They are also in a position where they can either make the final purchasing decision on the employee's behalf or perform the service of structuring the employee's choices so that inappropriate options are excluded and the remaining options are carefully explained. The latter role, while still unfamiliar, is closely analogous to the role visualized for government in the Enthoven and Gephardt-Stockman proposals but seems more promising. Whereas government must maintain a lengthy and therefore inherently confusing menu of plans for individuals to choose from, employers can limit the number of choices, selecting with care from a larger universe but leaving the individual to make the final choice. Paradoxically, this unique ability to offer fewer choices selected in a competitive environment allows the employer to offer the consumer, safely, a wider *range* of choices than government would see fit to make available. Quite simply, the consumer who is offered only a few preselected and well-defined options in an environment where he can share

experiences with coworkers would be less handicapped by ignorance than the person participating in a government-structured
system of consumer choice.[30] No better proof of this assertion is
required than experience under the FEHBP. Despite the Office of
Personnel Management's extensive disclosure requirements, almost any federal employee—even including some who are health
care experts—will admit to being mystified by the choices available. A private-employer-sponsored system of structured choice
promises material improvements.

There may be some drawbacks, however, to relying on employers and unions to act for consumers. Before addressing technical
issues, it is necessary to consider some problems concerning the
incentives at work in vicarious (employer) and collective (union)
purchasing of health benefits. In fact, there are reasons why one
might doubt that employer and union interests are sufficiently
congruent with worker interests that they should be relied on to
act as their purchasing agents. Moreover, if employers become increasingly engaged in self-insurance or in the direct provision of
care for their employees, their interests may differ enough from
their employees' that their plans will not be able to deal effectively with the cost problem. This is not to say that employers
should not experiment with new techniques of financing and delivery as a way of stimulating competition among providers and
encouraging change. It will be argued, however, that employers
and unions would usually do better not to act as providers or as
final decisionmakers and should confine themselves to structuring
systems of individual choice.

Employers and Unions as Agents for the Rank and File

The reasons why employers and unions are ultimately in a poor
position to choose on employees' behalf are similar to the reasons
why government is a poor regulator of health care costs. As Chapter 2 shows, it is difficult for anyone in a political relationship
with the consumer to say no on the basis of cost considerations to
more and arguably better health services. Similar inhibitions on
economizing also apparently afflict employers and unions in
purchasing health benefits. Their paternalistic or quasi-political

relationship with the rank and file, combined with the powerful symbolism surrounding medical care, have made comprehensive health benefits and hassle-free administration the norm in most industrial settings.[31] Individual employees, choosing for themselves, might well have preferred more selective and less costly coverage.

It is quite understandable that employers and unions, facing sensitive decisions, would fear the repercussions of "type I" errors (visible hardships due to economizing) more than "type II" errors (excessive but well-spread and hidden costs). Almost inevitably, the health plan's costs and the tradeoff with take-home pay are so effectively hidden from the workers that economizing usually appears only to enrich the employer or the insurer—at the expense of those whose coverage is revealed to be inadequate. To complicate matters further, powerful ideologies frequently operate, and even where an employer or union becomes concerned about costs, past rhetoric and carefully nurtured expectations get in the way of change. Finally, all collective decisionmaking carries with it the risk that some minority preferences will be neglected and that other minorities with a powerful incentive to assert their interests will be served at the majority's expense.

In light of all these vagrant influences distorting the purchase of health insurance in the employment setting, one can reasonably suggest that the market failure we are witnessing is not really a problem of health policy at all. Instead, the difficulties seem to lie deeply embedded in employee-management relations and in a tax system that, by subsidizing coverage purchased through employment groups, has made spending on health care a hostage to collective bargaining and the strange dynamics of the employment relationship. So understood, the problems presented by vicarious and collective purchasing of health benefits would appear to be solvable by somehow substituting individual choice, thus better internalizing the costs and benefits of specific decisions. But, because extending economizing opportunities to individuals is a strategy that employers and unions could have adopted voluntarily, it is important to consider why they have not done so in the past and what it might take to encourage them to do so in the future. The question for consideration next is whether regulatory prescription of the employer's role is needed to overcome the perversities observed in their behavior.

Mandating Multiple Choice and Equal Contributions

Under several pending procompetition bills, employers above a certain size would be required by law, if they offer their employees any kind of health plan, to offer a minimum of three, allowing the individual employee to make the final choice. Employers would also have to make the same dollar contribution on an employee's behalf whichever plan he selects and to refund to the employee any excess of that contribution over a chosen plan's actual premium; the employee would pay any additional premium required. The declared object of these proposals is to substitute individual for collective choice and to assure that the employee has both an opportunity and an incentive to economize. Although the rationale for these regulatory measures is usually stated in this simple way, it seems obvious that the unstated rationale is a lack of faith in the ability of employers and unions to act in the employees' interest. As previously noted, concerns on this score are not ill founded.

Despite its plausibility, the case for thus regulating employer and union behavior is not finally convincing. It rests largely on perceptions of employers' and unions' past performance and does not adequately allow for the possibility that changes in the environment and in the operative incentives will be sufficient to induce the desired behavioral changes. As long as provider-imposed restraints of trade prevented the market as a whole from offering meaningful alternatives, multiple choice made little sense, and employers can hardly be criticized for not having adopted it and for falling instead into the present pattern. Now, however, with antitrust enforcement and increasing cost pressures, new options are appearing in many markets, and some employers are showing signs of responding to these new opportunities. Finally, a tax change raising the cost of marginal health coverage for a majority of American workers would surely stimulate many more employee benefits managers to reconsider their options.

Judging employer behavior at the present time is difficult, not only because people differ over whether a glass is half full or half empty, but also because, in this case, we have no way of measuring the contents of the glass or of knowing how fast it is filling. Some reports indicate that most employers and unions are still locked in the old pattern, expressing attitudes that suggest they are unlikely to change soon.[32] Moreover, as Enthoven has reported, some employers and unions have seemed recalcitrant in not offering HMO options when they were available or have undercut employees' economizing incentives by making unequal contributions to different plans.[33] Nevertheless, we have no empirical basis for concluding that such attitudes and perverse behavior would continue indefinitely under changing conditions and changed incentives or that education would not address the problem at least as well as regulation.

Where competition's critics see predominant disinterest, it is possible also to see hopeful signs of change, since some employers and unions are already making major changes in their purchasing habits. A few have voluntarily established multiple-choice systems to let employees profit directly from economizing in the purchase of a health plan, while others have adopted a "cafeteria" approach to fringe benefits generally, eschewing paternalism and allowing employees to shop rather widely with their tax-free dollars. Interestingly, employers and unions do not expressly view these choice-oriented systems as a means of escaping quasi-political responsibility for the shortcomings of lower cost options—that is, type I errors. Yet that would appear to be the best practical reason for shifting from vicarious or collective purchasing to a choice-structuring role. In any event, while most employers remain reluctant to consider taking away benefits previously granted, others are coming to understand that letting employees have wider options and an opportunity to profit directly from an economizing choice increases rather than decreases their aggregate welfare. In the not too distant future, employers who withhold desirable opportunities for economizing may be at some disadvantage in the labor market. A substantial tax change should certainly hasten that day.

With the tax subsidy changed so that employers and employees were spending their own money on marginal health benefits, it could be strongly argued that government should ignore any remaining problems rather than intervene further by mandating multiple choice. This argument would hold even if it were true that—as has been argued by a spokesman for the United Auto Workers, for example[34]—incentives make no difference and that, even with a different tax rule, employers and unions would choose the same kinds of cost-escalating insurance they now have. If auto workers did choose to spend their own after-tax money on the most expensive kind of insurance, that should surely be regarded as their business. Even if they did so because their union gave them no opportunity to economize—by failing to provide multiple choice or to rebate any saving from choosing lower cost options—, that would be a problem solely between them and their union's leadership and should not concern the government. The important goal for health policy should be to make sure that the supply side of the market is not precluded from making a full range of choices available and that demand does not reflect government-induced biases. Since these conditions can be reasonably well satisfied by antitrust enforcement and a substantial tax change, regulation of fringe benefit programs seems unnecessary as a further assurance that the market's verdict is a true expression of people's preference.

A more practical objection to mandatory multiple choice is that it would probably not be sufficient, without more extensive regulation, to effect a material change in market outcomes. An employer who introduces multiple choice only in response to compulsion is unlikely to perform his screening and choice-structuring role in a manner helpful to his employees. Indeed, a common practice might be to turn compliance over to an insurance broker who would have no incentive to observe the spirit of the law. Experience under the mandatory dual-choice provision of the 1973 HMO Act already establishes that such regulation does not automatically lead employers and unions to serve employee interests better. Thus, HMO advocates report that requiring employers to offer federally qualified HMOs has been of little value in attracting HMO enrollment in employment groups where the employer does not take an affirmative interest in promoting the HMO alternative. Although mandatory multiple choice would probably help to open some employers' minds as well as their doors, its contribution would probably be slight.

If Congress should perceive that compliance with the letter of the multiple-choice requirement does not in itself bring about informed consumer choice among meaningful alternatives, it would be tempted to go further and specify the particular options that must be made available. Indeed, several of the procompetition bills, like the dual-choice provisions of the HMO Act, already do this. Whether such regulatory specifications, including those in the HMO Act, are a sound idea depends once again on one's assessment of employers' and unions' ability to recognize, in due course, the desirability of offering meaningful, competition-promoting choices. The conclusion here is that, even if mandatory multiple choice is deemed desirable, the additional regulatory burdens needed to guarantee a range of alternatives would be excessive. For similar reasons, the HMO Act's dual-choice provision should be repealed; while having only limited value for fledgling HMOs—it is greatly valued by established HMOs, of course, as a way of locking up employment groups against new HMOs—, the dual-choice requirement has forced innovation into unduly narrow channels. Even if it were thought necessary to prod possibly recalcitrant employers and union leaders to offer desirable new options, certainly such regulatory intervention should stop short of specifying all choices and of defining the mandatory offering too restrictively.[35]

Achieving multiple choice through regulation also runs risks that important employer options will be foreclosed and unanticipated problems created. For example, in the interest of forcing competition there would be an inclination not to count as more than one offering the multiple plans that might be offered by a single carrier; as long as one visualizes only recalcitrant employers who resist assuming the screening function, this rule makes sense, but employers who shop carefully in a competitive market should not be foreclosed from concluding that a single carrier's multiple lines represent the best value and the best way to implement individual choice. Similarly, the equal-contributions requirement, while well intended, could easily be drafted in a way that forecloses particular solutions to adverse-selection problems. Other problems necessitating cumbersome and possibly overly restrictive regulations would be presented by employers who provide services directly or self-insure and by union-sponsored health plans. Regulatory problems more difficult than any encountered in implementing the HMO Act's dual-choice provision would arise if it was felt necessary to define what is a bona fide choice, to prevent employers or unions from biasing choices in their own interest, and to assure fair pricing.

On balance, the case for mandatory multiple choice does not seem strong enough to warrant the additional regulatory burdens needed for it to make an appreciable difference. Whereas the most that could be hoped is that such regulation might speed up competitive developments somewhat, this possible gain seems more than offset by the reciprocal risk that employers facing the prospect of regulation would refrain from acting on their own initiative, thus retarding the very process sought to be accelerated. Thus, while Congress was pondering the proposed legislation and while the bureaucracy was developing its regulations, employers who would otherwise be changing their approach to fringe benefits would be waiting to be told what to do. Again experience under the HMO dual-choice requirement confirms that this is not an imaginary danger. As Paul Starr reports, "confusion over the implications of the law caused employers throughout the country, including 73 per cent of the *Fortune* 500, to hold up making any arrangements with HMO's, since it was unclear which health plans would qualify under the statutes." [36]

Dropping the idea of mandatory multiple choice would go a long way toward disabusing employers of the idea that government either is going to solve the cost problem itself or is going to tell employers how to go about doing it for themselves. Only when consumers, employers, and unions are convinced that health care costs are their problem alone will they proceed to do anything about them. There is a great deal they can do, and government's role should be simply to motivate them—by changing the tax law—to get on with the job. If multiple choice is really a good idea, employers and unions will adopt it, filling the key screening and choice-structuring role that is increasingly and appropriately visualized for them. If government feels a need to give multiple choice an additional boost, allowing employers a one-time tax credit for each employee offered multiple choice with equal contributions before, say, 1985 would be the preferable way of doing it.

Solving the Problem of Adverse Selection

The feasibility of multiple choice has been questioned on the ground that adverse selection would occur whenever several plans with substantially different benefits were offered. It is suggested that, because of this problem, most employers would not voluntarily offer more than one plan or, if compelled to do so, would not voluntarily offer a meaningful range of choices, offering instead plans with substantially identical benefit packages and similar cost-sharing obligations. Because adverse selection could be the weak link of the multiple-choice approach, it is crucial that a solution to it be available.

The adverse selection problem exists on several levels. The basic problem, which exists in the field of insurance generally and is effectively neutralized by the device of group insurance, takes two forms. First, there is the likelihood that consumers will "game" a system of choice, switching plans as they perceive potential needs. In addition, there is a general tendency for low risks to isolate themselves in limited-coverage plans and for high utilizers to congregate in the more comprehensive plans. These various tendencies do not seem likely to ruin the prospects for a system based on multiple choice, however, because administrative measures can be taken to limit them to manageable proportions. Thus, premiums can be actuarially adjusted to narrow selection opportunities, and administrative rules and financial penalties can be imposed to limit switching. (Paul Ginsburg has proposed a financial penalty for shifting from a low-cost to a high-cost plan.[37]) Once these administrative adjustments are made, any remaining selection is probably tolerable. Indeed, decisions to opt out of a high-cost plan frequently reflect a willingness to forgo consumption and thus represent economizing behavior that should be rewarded. Moreover, it is not necessarily inappropriate for people with similar risks to be grouped together for insurance purposes. Although the issues involve value judgments as well as empirical questions, it is not obvious either that risk selection has no place in a competitive market or that it would dominate efficiency considerations as a basis for competition among plans in a multiple-choice system.

There remain, however, some special problems peculiar to the employment setting that complicate employers' voluntary decisions to adopt multiple choice or to offer real variety. As poor risks became increasingly isolated in a high-option plan, an employer would be under pressure to increase his per capita contribution to cover that plan's higher premium; indeed, if he did not do so, he could fairly be accused of reducing those employees' benefits. At the same time, the employer would perceive the savings realized by the low utilizers migrating to a lower cost plan as a windfall to them, representing funds currently contributed by the employer to defray the cost of higher risk employees. The employer's special problem stems from his traditional orientation toward giving each employee equal benefits whatever his risks, not equal value. Thus, a shift to a system of multiple choice with equal cash contributions would threaten established compensation patterns. An employer would be naturally reluctant to offer a low-option alternative that would cause low utilizers to leave the high-cost plan, raising its per capita cost to the disadvantage of the high-utilizing employees and implicitly increasing the low utilizers' wages.

Fortunately, these special problems faced by employers, while real deterrents to the offering of meaningful choices, are essentially transitional and could be solved by a creative approach, such as one that Ginsburg has proposed. Ginsburg suggests that the rebates to employees choosing a low-cost option be actuarially adjusted so as to make the low-cost and high-cost options equally attractive to each employee.[38] Thus, an older employee would receive a greater rebate than a younger one in recognition of the greater self-insurance risk that he assumes. The effect of such actuarially adjusted rebates would be to eliminate the windfall that younger employees receive if savings are cashed out in the form of equal per capita rebates.

It would appear that a substantial change in the tax law would provide an appropriate occasion for employers to reexamine their compensation arrangements. One result of such a reexamination might be a system of rebates along the lines Ginsburg proposes. Another might be a cashing out of a substantial portion of the employer contribution along the same actuarial lines that Ginsburg suggests. Thus, the employer might increase take-home pay by amounts that vary on the basis of age, sex, and other actuarial factors, thus maintaining all employees in essentially the same relative position in terms of overall compensation. While one can imagine that increasing the wage differential between young and old might complicate collective bargaining and give rise to other problems, the benefit of shifting to a system of individual choice might be great enough in many circumstances to be worth the trouble. Undoubtedly some employers would be able to move more quickly than others, but all would seem to have an incentive and some opportunity to alter current patterns. Some employers will undoubtedly prefer, as a matter of employment policy, to continue to offer a single plan with implicit cross-subsidies; with the tax law changed, such choices should not be questioned since, if employers are willing to bear the costs of such policies, they must know something we do not know about their own or their workers' preferences or about the costs of doing otherwise.

This is not the place to explore these possibilities further. Because methods appear to be available for overcoming adverse selection problems in an employment group, voluntary adoption of multiple choice is not precluded. Although some of the problems identified are unique to the employment setting, they seem sufficiently manageable that it is not necessary to incur the costs and rigidities that would accompany a shift to a universal government-structured system of consumer choice. Moreover, even if it was decided to make multiple choice mandatory, employers could probably be left to cope with the adverse selection problem for themselves. Particular care should be taken to avoid requirements concerning equal contributions, the taxation of rebates, open enrollment, or community rating that would preclude employer solutions to the selection problem. Once again, the regulatory complexities confronted in complying with this injunction argue strongly for not regulating at all.

PUBLIC PROGRAM REFORMS

Although changed incentives for private purchasing of health care coverage would trigger the process of innovation, the larger volume of services rendered at government expense would be affected only indirectly, if at all. Indeed, the net effect of increasing stringency in private programs would be harmful to public programs if providers sought to maintain their incomes by exploiting the public programs more than ever. Not only to protect the public pocketbook against new exploitation but also to assist in stimulating supply-side innovation, the federal government and the states should begin adapting their programs to fit the larger procompetitive policy. Whether the initial procompetitive changes in the Medicare and Medicaid programs should be made in the same legislative package as the tax law amendments would depend on political strategy, but it could be counterproductive to try to solve all of the health sector's current problems in one legislative stroke. It might be preferable to seek prompt enactment of the tax change legislation as a sign of the new policy emphasis and to proceed to deal with the more complicated Medicare and Medicaid programs independently, though as expeditiously as possible.

It is not intended to spell out here a program of specific changes in Medicare or Medicaid or to specify the consumer-choice system to which the federal government might ultimately move in order to offer choice and appropriate subsidies to populations that lack access to private group coverage. Obviously, fundamental changes will require a great deal of thought. Professor Enthoven has recently proposed a far-reaching plan under which current Medicare beneficiaries would be offered a chance to opt out of the basic program, which would be phased out as that population dwindles. New beneficiaries would have to choose a private plan in a government-structured system of choice under which open-enrollment and community-rating requirements would assure universal coverage. This method of phasing in a new system would seem to have much merit. Moreover, if feasible, the use of regulation to assure universal coverage for the elderly would not be subject to as many objections as a similar system covering the entire population; although there would be some hidden cross-subsidization, most of the money would come in the form of explicit subsidies.

There are a few reasons why Congress might be reluctant to enact legislation along the lines of the Enthoven proposal. Cashing out the Medicare program entirely into a voucher-type system (as the Enthoven proposal would do for new beneficiaries) would impair the program's basic and politically important entitlement character; arguably (though not obviously), it would be easier for Congress to reduce the cash value of the vouchers than it has been for it to reduce benefits, thus causing beneficiaries to worry that the program's value to them will erode under budgetary pressures. On the other hand, if the basic Medicare entitlement program were kept in place as an available option (which the Enthoven proposal would do for current beneficiaries), the federal government would face an adverse selection problem similar to that faced by an employer implementing multiple choice. Thus, the government would want to be sure that it could assign actuarially correct values to the vouchers so that only efficient plans could give more benefits for the voucher than the basic program; otherwise, the government's total cost could rise substantially solely because of adverse selection.

With respect to the Medicaid program, some problems are raised by the current interest of the federal government in shifting more of the cost burden to the states. A corollary policy is the granting to the states of relief from some federal requirements that have limited their flexibility in controlling costs. A hopeful possibility is that new flexibility would encourage the states to employ such innovative procompetitive techniques as paying providers on the basis of negotiated prices rather than costs and limiting beneficiaries' freedom of choice so as to exclude high-cost providers. Ultimately, some states, overcoming concerns about the higher costs that might arise from adverse selection, might let beneficiaries enroll at state expense in competitive health care plans. Despite these possibilities, the greater likelihood is that most states will simply reduce benefits and eligibility. Moreover, as Chapter 15 highlights, states might simply tighten regulatory controls over the system as a whole, threatening the success of the larger market strategy. For these reasons, Medicaid reforms should not be left entirely to the states.

It is important that efforts to restructure public programs be undertaken with sensitivity to the important social values at stake and not with an eye solely to economizing on public expenditures and promoting competition without regard to its side effects. Later discussion of the need to maintain the social "safety net" indicates some additional ways in which needed restructuring of public subsidies, if responsibly undertaken, will probably result in government's incurring some new direct costs. It is argued that responsible political leaders should recognize that some of the savings that self-supporting consumers derive in a competitive system are properly appropriated to cover the costs of improved public programs. Even if government is unimpressed by high-minded reasons for making new funds available for public programs, perhaps the need to reassure providers concerning the impact of procompetitive policies will force attention to these issues.

It is possible that the perceived complexities involved in developing a universal voucher-type system of structured choice for public programs will make piecemeal measures to establish the feasibility of the concept seem to be all that is currently feasible. Demonstrations, some of which are already under way, should not be undertaken as an excuse for delay, but, if further experimentation is deemed necessary, it should be clear that the goal is to determine how, and not whether, to run a market-oriented public financing plan. In order to make sure that the right message is given to the private sector, there should certainly be an immediate departure from the anticompetitive principles of assured cost reimbursement and unlimited free choice of provider for public beneficiaries. Thus, "prudent purchaser" strategies should be adopted, and various other incentive mechanisms, perhaps including the preferred-provider approach, should be tried. An important goal should be to convince the private sector that the days of cost reimbursement are numbered and that competitive purchasing and bargaining can be expected to increase. There exists no surer way of curbing the health care system's historic propensity to grow without adequate regard to supply and demand conditions. Moreover, the threat that public programs will increasingly exercise their concentrated buying (monopsony) power should make providers much more receptive to the idea of installing a voucher-type system of structured choice.

ITEMS ON THE UNFINISHED FEDERAL AGENDA

With the tax subsidy for private health insurance appropriately limited, the principles of competition and choice introduced in public programs, and the supply side of the market free, under antitrust protection, to respond to the new demand for economizing, the federal government would have only a few more things to do to put the health services industry on a permanent competitive footing. While everything discussed under this heading is extremely important, none of the recommended actions is a prerequisite to substantial success in stimulating competition and private innovation. In this sense, the identified agenda items are loose ends that, though they must be tied up soon, are not as urgent as the tax change and the initiation of public program reforms. Some of the measures recommended below address residual incentive problems that result from minor, though ultimately important, market failures. Others are needed to offset some predictable adverse side effects of intensified price competition whose rectification, though somewhat deferrable, should be considered an essential and integral part of a responsible procompetitive policy.

It is important to disentangle the initiatives discussed above from the agenda items identified here. Because there is no longer any idea of imposing pervasive new controls on the industry, it should be possible to present the tax change and the new emphasis on choice in public programs as a clear signal to the private sector that the cost problem is now entirely in its lap and that nothing remaining in the federal policy pipeline will interfere with private cost-containment initiatives that might be taken. If such a signal were given, needed private innovations would not be held in abeyance pending completion of federal action on the complex issues remaining for attention. In view of the overriding need to relieve uncertainty in the private sector, the Reagan administration should expressly disavow the idea of a comprehensive legislative proposal and should instead announce that it will address particular problems one by one, always with a view to improving rather than interfering with the basic operation of the marketplace. Only if this can be done convincingly will private actors have a basis for confidence that their investments in innovation will pay off and will not shortly be devalued or rendered obsolete by some new federally sponsored surprise.

Mandating Protection Against the Costs of Catastrophic Disease

A particular problem addressed by several of the procompetition proposals, including the Enthoven and Gephardt-Stockman plans, is the adequacy of citizens' protection against the sometimes staggering costs of catastrophic illness. Some other bills have also sought to address this problem by providing governmental coverage of such costs or mandating private coverage.[39] These bills have been simply modified versions of national health insurance,

designed to appeal to middle-class voters fearful of medical catas-
trophes, and, as such, would not be compatible with the development of competition. Furthermore, these bills have revealed little
understanding of the nature and incidence of high-cost illness and
an inadequate appreciation of the cost problem, which they
would exacerbate.[40] The focus here is not on assuring financial
protection for all but on a narrower set of concerns that arise in
the context of implementing a procompetition strategy.

Regulatory attention to the adequacy of catastrophic coverage
is warranted because persons whose coverage proves inadequate
are frequently treated without charge at the expense of the
health care system as a whole and ultimately of the general public. In light of this fact, a strong case for regulatory intervention
can be made under standard economic analysis by characterizing
the situation as a "free-rider" problem. The argument has been
stated as follows:

> Through a variety of charitable acts and public agencies, as a society
> we do often act to help those who have not helped themselves. Know-
> ing this, many individuals might not buy insurance, however readily
> available and fairly priced, because they know that some protection
> already exists in the willingness of others to come to their aid in an
> emergency. For persons having other uses for the cash, forgoing insur-
> ance might be quite rational, and mandating contributions by all may
> be the only way of preventing such "free riders" from taking advan-
> tage of society's good nature in this way. Moreover, regularizing fi-
> nancial support for such services better distributes these social costs,
> relieving particular providers, notably community hospitals, of their
> disproportionate financial burdens and of the even greater burden of
> turning away needy patients when the available resources are
> insufficient.[41]

Thus, a regulatory requirement of adequate catastrophic coverage
would be justified and should be imposed, either in a regulated
system of choice modeled after Enthoven's CCHP or as a condition of tax benefits in a system featuring a wider role for private
decisionmaking.

Nevertheless, while the need for public intervention to assure
catastrophic protection is clear, the nature of the appropriate regulatory requirement is not. Moreover, there appears to be a great
risk that, in compelling catastrophic coverage, government will
act to insulate the affected consumer from all costs, thus freeing

providers from cost constraints and inviting serious cost escalation. Thus, the approach prevalent in most of the proposals to date appears to preclude many of the ways whereby insurers might cover catastrophic risks in a cost-effective manner. These proposals would simply require that consumers be insulated from all costs after some initial outlay, in effect introducing a high deductible which, once satisfied, would allow the patient to have unlimited free care. Because the incremental costs of most significant hospitalizations would be covered, cost constraints would remain diminished in the acute care setting, and victims of chronic disease would lack any incentive to seek cost-effective care or to avoid unhealthy behavior.[42] Thus, the approach of mandating an ironclad guarantee of free care once some threshold is crossed carries with it a powerful threat of cost escalation and would invite continued regulation of system capacity or treatment methods and appropriateness to contain the costs and ration the availability of catastrophic care. Congress has so far been oblivious to the immense problems that these proposals potentially present despite their political appeal.

It is far from easy to design a regulatory requirement that satisfactorily balances the clear need for financial protection against the need to contain the impact of moral hazard. The crucial insight from which analysis must proceed, however, is that, even in the treatment of catastrophic disease, tradeoffs matter.[43] It is always possible in such cases to use a slightly higher priced input, to provide a little more service, and to spend a little more money in the hope of improving the outcome. Moreover, without some constraint, providers will inevitably feel ethically or legally compelled to incur expenses that are not justified in benefit/cost terms. It has been observed that ethically troublesome but nevertheless legitimate questions about the value of such expenditures arise on at least three levels:

First, doubts can be raised about the effectiveness of, and necessity for, many of the particular medical services which would be subsidized: Not all possible medical services contribute meaningfully or in the same measure to patients' survival.

Second, the value of the benefits derived in individual cases is highly variable: Not all catastrophic disease is actually life-threatening; not all lives threatened are in fact saved; and not all prolongations of life achieved are quantitatively or qualitatively alike, since some patients are maintained in states of health which they would not value highly.

Third, once a program has made us feel collectively responsible, we may over-exalt particular lifesaving efforts, almost independently of their benefit to patients, as a way of affirming our society's deeply felt reverence for the sanctity of life.[44]

The quoted source develops at length the social dilemmas presented by such tradeoffs, arguing that the cost consequences of making "tragic choices" [45] in public forums would be high and that, for reasons similar to those reviewed in Chapter 2, regulation and other mechanisms of explicit public choice will fail to solve the problem. It also explores some possible ways of framing a requirement for minimum coverage of catastrophic costs without placing government in the impossible position of having to use regulation to limit implicitly the entitlements it has explicitly mandated. Although this is not the place to retrace those arguments, it cannot be emphasized too strongly that government must find a way to deal with the free-rider problem that does not foreclose private measures to counter the moral hazard problems that would be unleashed. The cited source provides some suggestions, all relevant to the implementation of mandated catastrophic coverage in the context of a system based primarily on consumer choice and private decisionmaking.

Perhaps government could be comfortable in mandating less than open-ended coverage of the costs of catastrophic illness if it recognized

that exhaustion of a patient's benefits or his inability to meet a cost-sharing obligation would not automatically be fatal, both because not all catastrophic illnesses threaten imminent death and because providers would frequently continue to take care of many such patients without charge, much as they do now. Indeed, preservation of the financial ability of providers to furnish some uncompensated services would seem desirable as a means of softening the impact of benefit limits imposed . . . in a catastrophic insurance plan. Moreover, providers, in rationing their limited discretionary funds, might engage in precisely the kind of benefit-cost balancing that is so difficult to achieve in more formal mechanisms, choosing perhaps to serve those patients who could be saved most cheaply or those who could be restored to the most useful existence or to the most satisfactory quality of life. This reliance on providers, where benefits are exhausted, could

be an important buffer against pressures on government to expend
unlimited sums to save a single (identified) human life ....[46]

The point here is of great practical and political as well as conceptual and ethical significance. Once government perceives that
the system's charitable impulses provide a buffer against hardships occasioned by stringency, it should be able to tolerate methods of covering catastrophic risks that leave some cost constraints
in place. It should be clear that the recognition accorded here to
the system's ability and willingness to render free care is not inconsistent with encouraging competition that erodes the system's
monopoly returns heretofore relied on so heavily to finance basic
services. The idea is not that charity should be fostered and protected or that providers' charitable instincts should be exploited
to fill gaps in coverage that government is unwilling to fill. Instead, the point is that government should not forget that it is
addressing only a free-rider problem and lapse instead into a paternalistic mode of thinking that would cause it to prohibit any
catastrophic disease insurance that does not go as far as possible
in removing financial and health risks.

At least the first step in assuring adequate catastrophic coverage could reasonably be taken in the legislation proposing a tax
change—by making such coverage a condition of favorable tax
treatment. This feature would probably attract some provider
support, especially from hospitals, because of its beneficial effect
on their bad debts. Efficiency gains might result from shifting
coverage away from first dollars.

Subsidizing Private Innovation in Cost Containment

Even with changed incentives and antitrust sanctions against
providers' attempts to restrain it, innovation in the financing and
organization of health services might be suboptimal for technical
reasons. The problems lie in the riskiness of innovation and the
difficulty of capturing the gains of successful undertakings. The
resulting reluctance of potential innovators to break out of familiar patterns suggests a need for government financial support of

competitive initiatives that promise to raise consumer cost consciousness, change provider behavior, or trigger provider competition.

Experience under the HMO Act suggests both the promise and the pitfalls of government subsidization of innovation in the organization of health services. In particular, the HMO Act may help to explain why commercial health insurers, where they have been willing to innovate at all, have seemed to emphasize HMO development over other kinds of innovation. Although in many cases the risks of provider retaliation and competitor imitation have been avoided by working closely with organized medicine in establishing IPA-type HMOs, other HMO initiatives have had a more competitive thrust that may have owed something to government's intervention in the market. Through the HMO Act, government has legitimized the HMO model, carried some of the burden of public education, and subsidized development costs. Moreover, by giving the first federally qualified HMO in an area an inside track under the HMO Act's dual-choice provisions and by de facto limiting subsidies to only one HMO per community, government has maintained substantial barriers—comparable to patent protection—to further HMO growth, thereby reducing the risks associated with the first initiative.

If obstacles to innovation by insurers are in fact as great as suggested above, perhaps other governmental strategies similar to the HMO Act would be helpful. Indeed, the HMO Act itself might be adapted for the purpose by expanding the types of innovation that it would encourage. Alternatively, demonstration grants, perhaps under authority already possessed by the Health Care Financing Administration, could be used to support promising experiments. Another possibility, mentioned in Chapters 12 and 15, is that competition-sensitive health planners might assist unspecified innovative ventures in local markets. Obviously, support for innovative strategies should be temporary and designed only to get the process of innovation started. Care should be taken not to preclude, or cast doubt on the legitimacy of, change that occurs without government sponsorship. Unfortunately, the HMO legislation, by seeming to bless only one type of innovation, had the effect of discouraging innovations that it failed to encourage.

Replacing Lost Subsidies for Education and Research

Competition that increasingly focuses on price considerations will seriously jeopardize those institutional providers that have heretofore relied on excess revenues from patient care to support the training of medical personnel and the generation and dissemination of new knowledge. Although protecting the welfare of these institutions is not a sufficient reason for restraining competition, the threat posed to their valuable educational and research activities must be recognized as a major policy problem. The major university medical centers are an important national resource that must not be allowed to fall victim to a policy that places undue faith in competition and the free market to allocate resources. It must be recognized that a competitive market is frequently unable to generate optimum levels of investment in education and research.

The reasons why competitive markets may underproduce research and education are similar to those that would justify government intervention to compensate for underinvestment in cost-containment innovation. Medical research, the results of which are widely publicized in accordance with scientific traditions, yields "public goods," which economic theory tells us will be underproduced without subsidy because inventors cannot capture the welfare gains that their discoveries generate. Although one can imagine several ways in which researchers could retain a proprietary interest in their discoveries and market them profitably, the costs of limiting their availability to other researchers and to the general public would be great indeed. The need for public subsidies and philanthropic support for medical research is already well established, of course, but it is important to recognize that much additional research and development, particularly the less formal variety that occurs through the interactions of skilled clinician-scientists in major medical centers, has been supported through internal subsidies. Government, private foundations, and private donors must all recognize the legitimacy of some of the hardship pleas they are already beginning to hear.

Education, too, has been subsidized from patient care revenues that are threatened by the strengthening of competitive forces. Arguably, professional training is a private, not a public, good and could be left to seek its own level in a competitive world. On the other hand, it can be argued that the public benefits from subsidizing excellence in medical and other health professional training, that the high cost of an unsubsidized medical education would bar entry by nonaffluent individuals, and that inappropriate values would be fostered by undue commercialization of the educational endeavor. The problems facing medical education are exacerbated by the probability that the medical schools have overexpanded, largely in response to past government subsidies, and should probably not be sustained at their present level of output. Competition provides a convenient, nonpolitical mechanism for eliminating the industry's excess capacity, but this process could prove as painful for medical schools as it has been in other industries. Government might be wise to use grants and other subsidies to prevent demoralization of the finest programs during the inevitable shakeout.

Solutions to these impending problems will not be easy, but it would not be inappropriate for government to recognize an obligation to compensate in some way the most deserving institutional victims of its procompetitive policy. The efficiency gains from that policy should certainly be great enough that the public would still enjoy a net profit after compensating the losers. Of course, subsidies to education and research need not be thought of exclusively in this way since the public also stands to benefit directly from preserving centers of research and educational excellence.

Filling Widening Gaps in the "Safety Net"

Competition will also erode the health care system's ability to generate the resources needed to provide care for the underinsured. This loss of hidden cross-subsidies will in turn impose on government an obligation to repair the holes that develop in society's "safety net"—that being the Reagan administration's term for the basic protection against financial hardship that it has promised to maintain for all citizens. Preservation of the safety net in a competitive world will require more than simply maintaining existing programs. New money will have to be provided. In an era when new social initiatives do not attract much support, it is particularly important to observe that the competition strategy could easily generate serious hardships for many Americans who, though ineligible for care under any public program, have had their basic medical needs more or less attended to by institutional providers practicing socially sanctioned cross-subsidization. As those providers become less and less able to pass on their unreimbursed costs and bad debts to increasingly cost-conscious payers and patients, government must accept some responsibility for shoring up the system's ability to continue serving those who cannot pay.

A great strength of the Enthoven and Gephardt-Stockman proposals is that they both make complete provision for subsidizing, as necessary, the enrollment of all citizens in private financing plans. Thus, if either plan could be enacted in toto, the problems identified here would not arise. On the other hand, this chapter, reflecting in part a concern about political feasibility but primarily concerns about how to ensure the dynamism of a competitive market, has suggested a piecemeal legislative approach and has argued for the preservation of an intermediary role for employers and for encouraging cost-conscious employer and consumer choice in a largely unregulated environment. This prescription would necessarily lead, through increased segmentation in insurance markets and hard bargaining with providers, to a substantial expansion of the opportunities for self-supporting consumers to escape the necessity for contributing funds to meet the needs of the underinsured. Thus, an important negative implication of the policy approach recommended here is the increased danger that self-supporting consumers, in addition to profiting from increased efficiency in the system, will also gain at the expense of the medically needy. Moreover, because this danger is implicit, not explicit, and will materialize unless specific measures are taken, government must be specifically urged not to ignore these side effects of its procompetition strategy. While society is entitled to seek the efficiency gains that will flow from competition, it would be small-minded for it not to return some of its efficiency dividend to those whose life-support systems competition would jeopardize. Indeed, an important justification for exalting efficiency and competition should be their effect of lowering the social costs of meeting equity goals and of increasing the wealth that enables those goals to be met.

Because it will be difficult to recapture the private gains arising from the elimination of desirable cross-subsidies, it is important to address the need for new explicit subsidies as early as
possible, preferably in the legislation limiting the current tax subsidies for private health insurance. Although the proposed exclusion cap would yield some additional revenue, it would not be
enough to offset the loss of cross-subsidies. Consideration should
therefore be given to levying a tax on enrollment in any tax-fa-
vored health benefits plan and earmarking the revenue thus
raised for strengthening and expanding public programs.[47] Since
some of the private gains from the economizing behavior fostered
by competition will reflect an escape from hidden taxes that the
system has heretofore successfully imposed, it is entirely reasonable to regard some of those savings as legitimately recouped by
new explicit taxes to meet social needs. As in the case of cross-
subsidies for education and research, there should be early and
explicit recognition of an obligation to compensate those who suffer losses as an indirect result of the new procompetitive policy.
The public would still enjoy a net gain due to the efficiency improvements that competition generates.

Despite these equity arguments, one cannot be sanguine about
political leaders' willingness or ability to make the case for re-
newing and regularizing society's commitment to the poor. If
there is a flaw in the competition strategy as proposed in this
chapter and as it is most likely to be pursued by the Reagan administration, it lies in these uncertainties. If government cannot
address the social issue forthrightly and assure a decent minimum
standard for all, then the competitive strategy could become,
whether inadvertently or not, a vehicle for exacerbating social in-
justice. Although reliance on competition to allocate health resources does not necessarily imply a neglect of health care for the
needy, society must be careful, in the present circumstances, not
to default on its obligations.

Implicit in even a well-designed competition strategy is an
acceptance of a class-differentiated medical care system. There is
no reason for competition advocates to apologize for this aspect
of their program, however. After all, the present system falls far
short of achieving true equity. Moreover, nothing but an extreme
political preference would lead one to favor a true single-class system, and in any event it is highly doubtful that class differences

could be much reduced even in a system that paid lip service to equality as a symbolic goal. But, even though reliance on willingness to pay is an entirely legitimate way to assure that people get what they want and what society can and should afford, the problem of serving those who cannot pay must be met as an independent social issue.

This is not the place to explore the technical issues of how to strengthen and extend the safety net. Some of those issues have already been confronted in debating proposals to cap the federal Medicaid contribution and to convert other categorical programs into block grants. One risk in shifting responsibility to the hard-pressed states is that they will be led into cynical competition to underserve the poor, reducing services in order to avoid attracting new users and perhaps to shift the burden elsewhere. It is to be hoped that a basic federal commitment to support a decent minimum standard of care will ultimately emerge out of efforts to structure a government-sponsored consumer-choice system for federal beneficiaries and others along the lines indicated in earlier discussion. These issues of social justice promise to be among the most wrenching that the 1980s have in store.

CONCLUSION: SENDING THE PROPER SIGNAL

The success of the market-oriented policy outlined in this chapter depends heavily on convincing independent actors in the private sector that they, and not government, are responsible for controlling private health care costs and that their cost-containment efforts and efficiency will be rewarded even in the provision of care under public programs. Employers and the employees whose interests they represent must be led to recognize the savings that are derivable from careful purchasing. Insurers and other health plan organizers must be persuaded that not only private purchasers but public program beneficiaries as well will soon be beating a path to the door of those who achieve cost-effectiveness in benefit design and in plan organization and administration. Providers must become convinced that newly cost-conscious consumers will soon be seeking and finding effective ways of rewarding efficient providers and penalizing inefficient or unduly expensive ones. The strategies proposed in this chapter would go quite far toward communicating proper signals to the various parties whose conduct must change in material ways if costs are to be given appropriate weight in consumption decisions in the health care industry.

No attempt has been made here to offer political advice on how to get Congress to undertake the policy initiatives suggested. Nevertheless, it has been argued that government should eschew launching a single legislative reform proposal. One reason for proceeding on a piecemeal basis is simply the need to get on with privately initiated reforms as soon as possible. More important, however, is the need to shift the burden of cost containment and decisionmaking back to the private sector and off government's shoulders, where it has rested too long. A prompt tax change to strengthen purchasers' economizing incentives and some significant moves to establish cost-conscious choice in public programs would together signify a clear and almost certainly irrevocable decision to transfer responsibility and would make palpable the rewards (or penalties) to private actors who get (or fail to get) the message. Any more substantial legislative package would run the risk that, by keeping government as the center of attention, it muddies the signal and delays the effective date of the new policy.

Sending a clear and correct signal to the private sector also requires establishing a convincing formula for deregulation of the industry's economic organization, performance, and development. Unless it is carefully designed and administered, regulation perpetuates the insidious perception that government and not the private sector is somehow ultimately in charge of health care costs and of dictating private efforts to reduce such costs. In order to dispel this perception, the policy proposed here has another crucial element, namely the adoption of a market-forcing deregulation strategy analogous in some respects to the regulatory strategy outlined in Chapter 12. The goal is once again to convince the various independent actors in the private sector of the necessity for changing the dysfunctional ways in which health services are currently bought and paid for. Unfortunately, deregulating the health care industry will be difficult because of the necessity for orchestrating so many substantial changes in public policy at different levels of government. Chapter 15 seeks a realistic path to the goal of deregulation.

NOTES

1. This chapter benefited from thoughtful comments by Alain En-thoven, who does not share some of its conclusions. It contains some material adapted from a paper prepared for a conference at the Hoover Institution, Palo Alto, California, March 28–29, 1980, and published by the Hoover Institution as Havighurst, "Increas-ing the Role of Competition in the Market for Health Services," in *National Health Policy: What Role for Government?* (I. Ehrlich ed.) (in press) (adapted with permission). Some of the substantive conclusions reached here differ significantly from those in the ear-lier work.

2. A. Enthoven, *Health Plan* (1980); Enthoven, "Consumer-Choice Health Plan" (pts. 1 & 2), 298 *New Eng. J. Med.* 650, 709 (1978).

3. H.R. 850, 97th Cong., 1st Sess. (1981).

4. *See also* Havighurst & Hackbarth, "Private Cost Containment," 300 *New Eng. J. Med.* 1305 (1979); Havighurst, "Private Cost Con-tainment—Medical Practice under Competition," 1979 *Socioeco-nomic Issues of Health* 41 (G. Misek ed.).

5. *See* Havighurst, "Professional Restraints on Innovation in Health Care Financing," 1978 *Duke L.J.* 303, 321–26; Havighurst, "Health Insurers and Health-Care Costs: Can the Problem Be Part of the Solution?" 5 *Health Communications and Informatics* 319, 320–31 (1979); S. Caulfield & P. Haynes, *Health Care Costs: Private Ini-tiatives for Containment* (Gov't Research Corp. 1981).

6. *See, e.g.,* Christie *et al.,* "Minority Report Number One," in Com-mittee on the Costs of Medical Care, *Medical Care for the Ameri-can People* 151 (1932). *See also* Note, "The American Medical Association: Power, Purpose, and Politics in Organized Medicine," 63 *Yale L.J.* 937, 967–97 (1954).

7. United States v. Oregon State Medical Soc'y, 343 U.S. 326 (1952).

8. Goldberg & Greenberg, "The Effect of Physician-Controlled Health Insurance: *U.S. v. Oregon State Medical Society,*" 2 *J. Health Pol., Pol'y & Law* 48 (1977).

9. *See* Caulfield & Haynes, *supra* note 5.

10. *See* Christianson & McClure, "Competition in the Delivery of Medical Care," 301 *New Eng. J. Med.* 812 (1979).

11. *See* Moore, "Cost Containment through Risk-Sharing by Primary-Care Physicians," 300 *New Eng. J. Med.* 1359 (1979). In addition to the plan created by the Safeco Insurance Company, the Group Health Plan of Northeast Ohio and the HMO of Pennsylvania use this model.

12. *See generally* Havighurst, "Professional Restraints," *supra* note 5, at 336–43, and references therein.

13. *See* Sapolsky, Altman, Green, & Moore, "Corporate Attitudes toward Health Care Costs" (1980) (to be published in *Milbank Mem. Fund Q.*, 1981). *See also* R. Munts, *Bargaining for Health* (1967). Employer and union motivations are discussed later in this chapter.

14. *See* C. Morrow, *Health Care Guidance: Commercial Health Insurance and National Health Policy* (1976).

15. 26 U.S.C. §§106, 3121(a)(2)(1976).

16. Feldstein & Friedman, "Tax Subsidies, the Rational Demand for Insurance, and the Health Care Crisis," 7 *J. Pub. Econ.* 156 (1977).

17. Ginsburg, "Altering the Tax Treatment of Employment-Based Health Plans," 59 *Milbank Mem. Fund Q.* 224, 226 (1981). The percentages represent the sum of the average marginal income tax rate and the combined rate of FICA taxes. They do not, however, reflect the reduction in income tax rates enacted in 1981.

18. Congressional Budget Office, *Reducing the Federal Budget: Strategies and Examples, Fiscal Years 1982–1986,* at 130 (1981). Again, this estimate does not reflect 1981 tax reductions.

19. Feldstein & Friedman, *supra* note 16, at 174.

20. *E.g.* Altman & Weiner, "Regulation as a Second Best," in *Competition in the Health Care Sector* 399 (W. Greenberg ed. 1978).

21. Havighurst & Hackbarth, *supra* note 4, at 1305.

22. S. 433, 97th Cong., 1st Sess. (1981).

23. S. 139, 97th Cong., 1st Sess. (1981) (reintroduced by Senator Hatch).

24. *See generally* Enthoven, "Consumer-Centered v. Job-Centered Health Insurance," 57 *Harvard Bus. Rev.* 141 (1979). Unlike Enthoven, the proposal here does not seek to discharge employers from a decisionmaking role. Even if the tax law's artificial inducement for employment-based purchasing were removed, employers' intermediary role would probably not be much lessened. Not only would the economies of group purchasing remain substantial, but, as noted below, the employer's comparative advantage in obtaining advantageous arrangements, screening options, providing information, and structuring choices would probably prevent substantial departures from traditional patterns.

25. *See* note 24 *supra*.

26. *Cf.* Medical Soc'y v. Toia, CCH Medicare & Medicaid Guide ¶28,364 (E.D.N.Y. 1977) (federal law requires state Medicaid programs to cover all "customary" services, *rev'd on other grounds,* 560 F.2d 535 (2d Cir. 1977).

27. In this market, unlike the larger one, the unavailability of such "major-risk" insurance cannot be attributed to the tax laws, since the federal contribution is largely fixed and employees pay for extra coverage out of pocket.

28. A good argument can also be made for requiring employers, as a condition of favorable tax treatment, to provide some continued coverage for workers who leave employment and would otherwise be temporarily uninsured.

29. A. Enthoven, *Health Plan* 88–89 (1980).

30. *Cf.* Pauly & Satterthwaite, "The Effect of Provider Supply on Price," in U.S. Department of Health, Education and Welfare, Health Resources Administration, *The Target Income Hypothesis and Related Issues in Health Manpower Policy* 26 (1980) (discussed in Chapter 4).

31. *See* Sapolsky, *et al., supra* note 13.

32. *Id.*

33. A. Enthoven, *Health Plan* 73–77 (1980).

34. *See* "Republican Cure Would Aggravate the Malady, Labor Leader Testifies," *Nat'l Health Ins. Rep.,* Feb. 22, 1980, at 2.

35. For a proposal that one of three mandatory choices be a "cost-sensitive health plan" and a definition thereof, see *Proposals to Restructure the Financing of Private Health Insurance: Hearing on H.R. 5740 before the Subcomm. on Health of the House Comm. on Ways and Means,* 96th Cong., 2d Sess. 139 (1980) (statement of Clark C. Havighurst).

36. Starr, "The Undelivered Health System," 42 *Pub. Interest* 66, 77 (1976).

37. Ginsburg, *supra* note 17, at 240.

38. *Id.* at 240–41.

39. *E.g.,* S. 350, 96th Cong., 1st Sess. (1979) (Senator Long); S. 748, 96th Cong., 1st Sess. (1979) (Senator Dole).

40. *See* Zook, Moore & Zeckhauser, " 'Catastrophic' Health Insurance: A Misguided Prescription?" 62 *Pub. Interest* 66 (1981).

41. Havighurst, Blumstein & Bovbjerg, "Strategies in Underwriting the Costs of Catastrophic Disease," 40 *L. & Contemp. Prob.* 122, 130–31 (1976).

42. Zook *et al., supra* note 40, at 72–80.

43. *Id.*

44. Havighurst *et al., supra* note 41, at 139.

45. *Cf.* G. Calabresi & P. Bobbitt, *Tragic Choices* (1978).

46. Havighurst *et al., supra* note 41, at 180–81.

47. Because of the way in which the benefits of competition distribute themselves, such a tax should probably be a flat amount on each insured rather than a percentage of premiums. Although a tax of the latter type might seem to accentuate price differences and thus to encourage desirable economizing, it would fall more heavily on those insureds most harmed by increased segmentation.

15 DEREGULATING THE HEALTH CARE INDUSTRY

As long as regulation remains a central fact in the health services industry, the ultimate success of a market-oriented health policy cannot be assured. This is true not only because regulation directly precludes much desirable innovation and competition but also because it protects private actors against the necessity for changing their traditional ways. In general, because regulation appears to treat established practices as immutable, it ratifies conventional views concerning how health services are bought and paid for. With regulation as a pervasive reality, employers and unions may assume that it represents the best available protection of their interests and perceive neither a necessity nor any real opportunity to take new action to protect themselves. Insurers, reluctant to change their traditional attitudes and methods, may value regulation for seemingly legitimizing both their inaction and the costs they pass on in premiums. Providers, though naturally railing against regulation, value both its anticompetitive features and its cost-legitimizing effects. In general, the existence of extensive regulatory controls confirms government's apparent assumption of cost-containment responsibility. Even if that responsibility is not discharged in fact, the mere presence of pervasive regulation creates a psychology that is likely to cause private actors, who hold the best keys to cost containment, to stay their hands.

435

Thus, without actual deregulation or a credible governmental commitment to move aggressively toward it, the effects of eliminating the tax law's inducement to overinsure and of introducing choice in public programs may be disappointing. Indeed, without substantial deregulation, the private sector will probably make only the most obvious incremental moves in response to changed purchasers' incentives. Probably one could expect little more than increased cost sharing, a continuation of gradual HMO development, and cutbacks in such benefits as dental and vision care. More fundamental changes, affecting such matters as the symbolism surrounding employee health benefits and the relationship between plans and providers, would probably occur very slowly. As long as government continues to define the cost problem and to do so in necessarily conventional terms, the private sector will see more risk than profit in embarking on costly reeducation and fundamental reform. Regulation, therefore, in addition to posing specific barriers to competitive development, also threatens to confuse government's signals to the private sector and to disrupt, perhaps fatally, the projected transfer of cost-containment responsibility.

Unfortunately, regulation is quite pervasive in the health services industry and for a variety of reasons cannot be readily dismantled. This chapter considers the various ways in which deregulation might be achieved, focusing particularly on certification of need, which is the most directly anticompetitive form of regulation. But, before confronting the barriers to deregulation, it will be useful to review briefly the various federal and state regulatory programs that require substantial rethinking in light of competition's new role.

REGULATORY RESTRICTIONS THREATENING COMPETITIVE DEVELOPMENT

Because adoption of a competition-oriented strategy would substantially shift the foundations of national health policy, all of the structural elements thereof should be reexamined to see if they can support the industry in its new competitive condition. In particular, there are regulatory programs at both the federal and state levels, but primarily in the states, that, though arguably well designed when prevailing policies were different, now allow inadequate flexibility. Because governmental policies must be consistent if the strategy of encouraging private-sector change is to work to maximum advantage, one would hope that the federal government would take the lead in eliminating obsolete regulation. The discussion here simply highlights some contradictions and conflicts that require attention if a federal policy of promoting competition is to work well.

Hospital Rate Regulation

Hospital rate setting, which has been employed with some apparent success in a number of states,[1] may easily, but does not inevitably, prevent useful price competition. As such regulation usually operates, hospital rates reflect their individual costs, and substantial price differentials may exist. Thus, if purchasers' cost consciousness increases, high-cost institutions will be subject to losing business even though their high rates are legitimized by regulation. Moreover, such regulation has usually involved setting only maximum charges, leaving opportunities for aggressive health plans to bargain for preferential rates. While rate setting might facilitate collusion by hospitals seeking to avoid such competition, rate-setting programs are not themselves designed to curb price cutting. Unlike the regulators of transportation rates in the past, hospital rate setters do not usually have the power to set minimum or uniform rates. For these reasons, one might expect that protectionist regulation undertaken to minimize price competition would take the form, not of rate setting, but of entry restrictions under certificate-of-need laws. On the other hand, commercial insurers are beginning to complain about so-called cost shifting, whereby their insureds are allegedly forced to pay more than fully distributed costs while others pay less.[2] Out of such rumblings are likely to come proposals to enforce minimum rates, thereby relieving insurers of the need to compete in obtaining hospital services on reasonable terms.

As federal policy threatens to shift more of the Medicaid cost burden to the states, many people are predicting that the states will turn increasingly to hospital rate setting as a way of protecting themselves. It would seem that their better strategy, at least from the procompetitive standpoint, would be to adopt the prudent purchaser approach of dealing selectively with institutions and to explore the prospects for a voucher-type system of structured consumer choice. Nevertheless, many states will be attracted by the opportunity that a rate-setting system offers for building into paying patients' charges the free-care and bad-debt burdens incurred by hospitals in filling the gaps in Medicaid eligibility and benefits. Such regulation, if coupled with protectionist entry controls, would represent a classic case of cross-subsidization to achieve public purposes—"taxation by regulation" in Posner's phrase.[3] The convergence behind such regulation of the interests of the states, commercial insurers, hospitals, and subsidized populations suggests the likelihood of a powerful movement to legitimize cost shifting and to assure that the burden is shared equitably among the patrons of a given facility. The threat to competition from further entrenching the charitable monopoly model of the hospital could not be clearer.

Regulation of Health Insurance and Health Plans

State regulation of health insurance and federal and state regulation of HMOs and other alternative delivery arrangements and organizational forms feature many elements that are difficult to reconcile with the maintenance of a competitive environment. If continued at all, these regulatory schemes would benefit from being administered with an explicit regard for competitive values. State insurance regulation, for example, should encourage (or be prevented by federal law from discouraging) competitive innovation in the design of benefit packages, in reimbursement practices, in the implementation of utilization controls, in relationships with providers, and generally in giving insured consumers a chance to benefit from appropriate economizing in the choice of a plan, a provider, or a treatment. Legal restraints on organizational innovation, particularly on the use of corporate forms and salaried personnel to provide professional services, should be lifted. The McCarran-Ferguson Act's exemption of the business of insurance from the federal antitrust laws increases the responsibility of state regulators to foster competition. Although the exemption has not proved an absolute barrier to important antitrust suits in the health care industry,[4] its repeal or clarification might send a useful signal to insurers. (Certainly granting a more extensive exemption, such as insurers claim to need to allow them to confront providers, would be a grave mistake.[5])

Insurers frequently allege that so-called "freedom of choice" laws in the states prevent them from excluding costly providers from eligibility to provide covered services. It is true that such laws force insurers to cover services of such nonphysician providers as clinical psychologists, podiatrists, and chiropractors, but insurers seem guilty of intentionally overstating the laws' impact as an excuse for their failure to compete. (Indeed, their agreement on a sweeping but questionable legal interpretation may be a form of collusion to suppress competitive innovation.) Although judicial interpretations might differ among states, those laws do not appear to preclude preferred provider plans or the exclusion of individual practitioners who refuse to sign participation agreements or to cooperate with utilization controls.[6] In any event, such laws should probably be clarified to allow plans to act as consumer agents in screening providers and forcing them into unwonted competition. States should certainly resist the predictable pressure from physicians to intervene in defense of the presumed right of patients to "free choice of physician." Few things could be as destructive of competition's prospects.[7]

State and federal regulation of HMOs should not stifle their competitive viability or their innovative potential, particularly their organizational flexibility, and should not impose undue fiscal burdens. State and federal laws must also be reviewed for neutrality as between providers of different types, making sure that any preferences are justified on the basis of policy. One target for reform would be the premium-tax exemptions that some states extend to Blue Cross and Blue Shield plans. Invidious distinctions between for-profit and not-for-profit providers should also be eliminated.[8]

Public Program Cost Controls

Federal and state controls designed to contain the costs of Medicare and Medicaid should be distinguished for present purposes from regulation, which governs care provided and paid for in the private sector. Although providers are inclined to characterize such cost controls as regulation in order to discredit them, it is obvious that government must protect itself against provider exploitation of entitlement programs. On the other hand, government may sometimes use its great bargaining power under these programs to exploit providers, obtaining their services at less than a competitive price. In such cases, providers have a complaint analogous to those of producers in other industries who have been victimized by maximum price regulation. Nevertheless, the reform of Medicare and Medicaid to foster choice and competition is not deregulation in the strict sense. It is, however, very much a part of the procompetition strategy. Given the potential for monopsonistic exploitation that exists in any system where government pays providers directly, this aspect of the market strategy is the one most likely to benefit providers as a class.

Although proposals to repeal the PSRO legislation have been made in the name of deregulation, they would not advance that purpose. Strictly speaking, PSROs are not engaged in regulation at all but are part of the administrative apparatus of the Medicare and Medicaid programs—being charged, in effect, with defining those programs' coverage.[9] Thus, unless PSROs' function of limiting government's payment responsibilities is otherwise performed, their elimination would amount to, not deregulation, but an expansion of Medicare and Medicaid benefits. Moreover, such a liberalization would benefit providers more than the patients receiving the care whose appropriateness PSROs might question. Obviously, one can doubt the wisdom of giving organized medicine so much power to specify government's obligation to pay for professional services. Obviously, too, the argument against PSROs can have nothing to do with government's abuse of its monopsony power; if anything, government has erred on the side of accepting the professional monopoly and of assuming too readily PSROs' ability to overcome their inherent conflict of interests.[10] Until government moves to a voucher-based competitive system, some mechanism must perform the function that PSROs are currently assigned.

Professional Self-Regulation and Standards

The health care system's self-regulatory and peer review activities, which often receive explicit or tacit support in legislation or administrative practice, must be reviewed in the light of anticompetitive hazards. For example, federally mandated utilization review and quality-assurance efforts under the PSRO program should not permit local doctors to use their powers anticompetitively.[11] Also the responsibility assumed by organized medicine for determining for insurers the reasonableness of fees or utilization practices should be curbed in order that competing plans can initiate their own cost-containment measures, thus triggering provider competition.[12] Much of the needed review of practices in this area may be undertaken under the antitrust laws,[13] but state and federal legislation may insulate some practices from such scrutiny. In other cases, antitrust rules may not reach subtle or tacit restraints that operate without overt collusion or coercion. Policymakers and antitrust courts should not accept all professional self-regulation at face value.

In general, regulatory and self-regulatory institutions should be reviewed to reduce insistence on a single, professionally defined standard of quality and utilization in medical care. Innovation can occur only where some flexibility exists. Whereas regulation and professional dominance have historically kept change in narrow channels, it must now be assumed that market mechanisms can supply enough accountability that many regulatory and professional controls can be relaxed. In this connection, too, some formal attention should be given to the law of medical malpractice and its tendency to enforce a single standard of care that, being drawn from community practice under inappropriate incentives, may be too costly and demanding.[14] A general realization that there is usually not "one right way" to diagnose and treat patients would be a helpful step in paving the way for conscientious cost-containment efforts. Obviously, abuse, negligence, and incompetence must be punished, but the role of the organized medical profession as ultimate arbiter of medical practice must be diminished. Competing organizations of physicians must feel free to adopt cost-effective practices in good faith without fear of professional, regulatory, or judicial sanction.

Manpower Regulation

Health manpower policies must also be reassessed in light of competition's requirements. Seemingly, government could pay less attention to controlling the number of personnel trained than it has in the past, trusting the market to yield price signals that will ultimately bring demand and supply into appropriate equilibrium. The increasing physician supply carries with it a considerable potential for change as physicians are forced to compete for business in a cost-conscious environmnet. Whereas reductions in subsidies to medical education are appropriate, artificial restrictions on aggregate supply and specialty training should be avoided. The antitrust laws should be applied to curb private restraints in this area.

Quality-oriented licensure and regulation of health personnel would seem less important as a protection for consumers once more organized systems are in place and institutions are more reliably pressed by market forces to find the right balance between cost and quality. Furthermore, regulation of health personnel must not unduly restrict attempts to improve efficiency by substituting one type of personnel for another or by developing unique types of personnel to fit particular needs.

Professional certification and accreditation programs should be valued as sources of potentially valuable information to guide consumers and other in assessing qualifications, but certification schemes should be freed of professional domination that precludes overlap—that is, competition—among occupational groups and the appearance of bona fide new specialties and occupations. Also, government should be wary of ceding responsibility to private certification programs and converting voluntary certification into something very much like exclusionary licensure.

Certification of Need and Health Planning

Obviously, the regulatory schemes with the greatest implications for the emergence of competition are health planning and certificate-of-need programs. The remainder of this chapter is primarily concerned with possible alternative futures of health planning-cum-regulation. But its examination of the special problems of achieving true deregulation of the health care industry also illuminates the possibilities for eliminating the anticompetitive elements in the various regulatory schemes discussed above.

PROSPECTS FOR ELIMINATING REGULATION AS A BARRIER TO COMPETITIVE DEVELOPMENT

It might seem that the nation is currently well positioned to shift cost-containment responsibility convincingly to the private sector by combining an incentive-altering tax change and expanded consumer choice with affirmative deregulation. Certainly the Reagan administration would be generally believed if it should foreswear regulation and declare that government's cost-containment responsibility extends no further than its own programs. Congress, having declined to pass hospital cost-containment legislation in 1979, now seems as unlikely to enact new regulation as the Reagan administration is to propose it. Indeed, the administration and Congress moved in 1981 to eliminate budgetary support for existing regulation and to scale down past regulatory initiatives. The federal government's retreat from regulating this industry seems real enough that, if its substantive policies were all that mattered, the signal to the private sector would be both definitive and clear. Unfortunately, federal health policy is not the only issue.

Historically, the states have contributed in many important ways to the foreclosure of competition in the health care industry. Unless the states' anticompetitive impact can be reduced either by preemptive action at the federal level or by new state legislation in support of procompetitive federal policy, the market strategy will not pay all the dividends that might otherwise be reasonably anticipated. There are reasons for pessimism concerning the prospects for obtaining appropriate deregulation by means of either federal or state action.

Federalism Concerns

It would be easy enough, as a matter of constitutional law, for Congress preemptively to invalidate state laws that impair the development of a competitive health care industry. Thus, most of the state regulatory programs whose review and revision were recommended above could be swept aside or restricted in their impact if Congress were so inclined. Indeed, the Gephardt-Stockman bill would explicitly preempt state laws governing a wide range of matters, including the regulation of provider prices, health plan characteristics and premiums, and the availability of services and facilities. Substantial questions exist, however, concerning Congress's willingness to enact such preemptive legislation.

An important tenet of the Reagan administration's conservative political philosophy is the restoration of state sovereignty. With respect to many matters, the administration launched early moves to return important responsibility to the states. In health care, it sought to have categorical programs combined into block grants so that states could perform the task of allocating resources in accordance with local needs and preferences. Rejecting the idea of "federalizing" Medicaid, the administration also sought to fix the federal Medicaid contribution, thus increasing the states' fiscal burdens, and to reduce limitations in the Medicaid law on the states' administrative and cost-containment flexibility. The Ninety-seventh Congress, elected in 1980, appeared to share many of the administration's philosophical views on the relationship of the states to the federal government and went along with many of the administration's proposals to shift costs and responsibilities away from Washington. In these circumstances and in light of the political trend they reflect, there would seem to be only a small likelihood that the federal government will see fit to deprive the states of their traditional powers to regulate the health care industry. Not only is there a reluctance to interfere with the states' traditional authority, but the shifting of new costs to the states might make any infringement on their regulatory powers seem doubly burdensome and unfair.

Controversy surrounding the FTC has highlighted some of the new political interest in protecting state regulatory schemes against federal invalidation. The commission has in recent years taken a substantial interest in state regulation affecting the health professions, threatening to adopt rules that override state action that is, in the FTC's view, incompatible with the procompetitive policies of the Federal Trade Commission Act. In one trade regulation rule, the commission sought to invalidate state restrictions on the advertising of eyeglasses. The federal court reviewing that rule remanded it for further consideration, indicating some doubt about the scope of the FTC's powers to invalidate state laws.[15] That action by the commission and several other investigations, including one involving state restrictions on denturists, prompted some members of Congress, concerned about the federal bureaucracy's sitting in judgment on state laws, to launch efforts to curb commission powers.

The obvious rejoinder to the conservative challenge to FTC authority to preempt state laws is that the commission's target is overregulation by the states, which has been shown to be highly destructive of economic liberties and competition, harmful to consumer interests, and immune to judicial scrutiny.[16] This argument may ultimately prevail. James C. Miller, III, President Reagan's choice as FTC chairman, has generally approved the commission's efforts to weaken the market power of professional groups and is a well-known critic of anticompetitive legislation. Moreover, recent legislation subjecting FTC rules to congressional veto[17] weakens the claim that the FTC, as a bureaucratic agency, exercises excessive power over state legislatures. If Congress itself has the final say on such rules,[18] their preemptive impact may be more acceptable.

Despite the current sensitivity of federalism issues, it should still be tolerable for the federal government to dictate selectively to the states wherever necessary to prevent the subversion of a specific and well-formulated federal policy. As long as the state regulatory rules targeted for preemption are narrow ones and are not at the core of traditional state concerns, the preemptive measure would carry few enough political implications to be acceptable as an aid to the implementation of another policy generally favored by conservatives—the promotion of competition. Among the particular state-imposed restraints whose invalidation would materially assist in this effort without doing undue violence to principles of federalism are the following:

- Prohibitions on the provision of professional services by corporations
- Inhibitions on independent insurers' ability to practice selectivity in deciding which providers are eligible to provide covered services

- Restrictions on competitive price cutting that might begin to appear in state rate-setting programs
- Unduly restrictive reserve and other requirements imposed on alternative delivery systems
- Discriminatory premium taxes

These and perhaps a few other state-sponsored restraints on price competition and organizational innovation should be specifically overridden by federal legislation implementing the procompetition strategy.

There exists some precedent for preemption of the states in aid of procompetitive health legislation. Though enacted at a time when federalism concerns were not taken so seriously, the HMO Act of 1973 specifically overrode state laws restricting HMO development.[19] Perhaps more significantly, the 1979 health planning amendments, in addition to rescinding the previous federal requirement that the states regulate HMOs under their certificate-of-need laws, took the further step (described in Chapter 8) of barring such regulation. It is true that this move was not preemptive in the literal sense of invalidating state laws but instead took the form of imposing a new condition on the receipt by states of federal funds. Nevertheless, the federal HMO exemption from state regulation constituted a clear recognition of the necessity for curbing states' anticompetitive tendencies as part of a larger policy of relying on market forces. This legislation, which was sponsored by conservative Representatives Phil Gramm and David Stockman, suggests that selective invalidation of state laws in aid of a procompetitive federal policy is not infeasible. Mr. Stockman's sponsorship of the Gephardt-Stockman bill's sweeping preemptive provisions also indicates that he, at least, has higher priorities than states' rights.

The initial deregulatory impulse of some conservative policymakers (including Mr. Stockman and Mr. Gramm) following the elections of 1980 was to eliminate funding for HSAs, which were widely viewed as an unwelcome federal presence in local decision-making, and to repeal or greatly curtail the scope of Public Law 93–641, as amended. While such moves might be defensible on some basis, they would certainly not in themselves achieve deregulation or foster competition, since the state regulatory programs established under prior federal compulsion would remain in place. Under such federal policies, regulation's threat to desirable competitive developments could be dispelled only if the states repealed their certificate-of-need laws or the regulators changed their behavior in important and unlikely ways.

It would be ironic indeed if the federal government, after having forced the states to adopt certificate-of-need laws under Public Law 93–641, should now, under a states' rights rationale, simply repeal the compulsions of the federal statute, leaving those state laws in place. Although the states would be free to repeal or modify their laws, the federal government's responsibility for the pervasiveness of regulation cannot be so lightly avoided. Indeed, if its policy is premised to any degree on a desire to promote competition, the federal government's responsibility would seem to extend at least to the point of assuring that, before they are turned loose, state programs are brought into compliance with the procompetition provisions of the 1979 amendments. Because of the time lag necessarily built into those amendments and the deadline extensions subsequently enacted, it could happen that the states would be given their freedom to regulate without ever having had to comply with the 1979 requirement that they introduce competition as a factor in their regulatory decisionmaking. For these reasons, any impulse to recognize states' rights on this issue at this juncture would seem misplaced and unnecessarily destructive of both federal policy and coherence in public policy generally. The uncertainty created for the private sector by triggering a new round of political battles in the states would be certain to perpetuate the psychology of inaction, delaying meaningful reforms and frustrating an otherwise sensible federal strategy.

The Likelihood of State Action in Support of Competition

One possibility is, of course, that the states will come to agree with the federal procompetitive policy and will repeal or restructure their regulatory programs in aid of it. This possibility seems more theoretical than real, however, because the states have been chronically more neglectful of competition's prospects in most industries than the current Congress is inclined to be. This point was concisely made to a congressional committee by Professor Uwe Reinhardt in responding to the question whether, granting that the various professions' market behavior must be regulated to protect competition, a federal layer of regulation such as the FTC provides is needed:

> A shift to exclusive reliance on state regulation should not, *in theory*, imply an associated shift towards less competitive health care markets. A careful reading of history, however, will suggest that the organized professions have generally found it easy to push successfully for state regulation that fosters their preferred (less competitive) market structure.[20]

Discussing organized medicine's interest in measures to curb the FTC's powers in order to permit regulation to be undertaken at the state level, Professor Reinhardt stated, "I am persuaded that its push for state regulation rests on the hope that, without vigilance on the part of the FTC, [the administration's] pro-competitive initiative can be more effectively thwarted."[21]

Thus, it is hard to be optimistic about the prospects of achieving policy coherence by relying on the states to see the wisdom of the federal government's market strategy. Few states could be expected to embrace a clear and affirmatively procompetitive policy, and, even where a state took seemingly definitive action, political forces would seek the earliest opportunity to undo it or to subvert it by seemingly innocuous changes at crucial points. Although each instance of arguable state infringement on competition must be considered separately to make sure that valid state policies are not being sacrificed,[22] the argument for preserving FTC oversight and for selectively preempting the states in aid of specific federal policies seems quite strong. In any event, it is clear that what pass for pious expressions of federalism concerns are very often special pleading by or on behalf of groups, particularly professional groups, that have too long enjoyed the benefits of anticonsumer overregulation. Thus, there would seem to be important limits to the proposition that the success of the federal procompetition strategy should be left hostage to local politics, in which provider interests so often have the strategic advantage. Even if provider interests were not always successful in blocking or subverting the deregulation movement, the inevitable delays and uncertainty in getting the states to go along would discourage the private sector changes that, more than the deregulatory legislation itself, are the key to competition's success.

Whether states should be left entirely free to determine the necessity for certificate-of-need regulation and the tone, substance, and thrust of their respective programs is the issue of paramount concern here. Such laws are usually opposed by physicians but are often favored by the established institutional providers, who are primarily attracted by their protectionist features. Because providers' views may be divided and because other organized groups vary in both their attachment to such laws and their political influence, political outcomes are hard to predict. Moreover, even outright repeal of a certificate-of-need law would not necessarily signify a strong state commitment to competition. Thus, repeal might occur simply because the regulators had become unpopular either by successfully frustrating providers' costly projects or by not giving them much protection against competition. By the same token, of course, the regulatory programs left in place might be those that are least effective in containing costs and most protective of established interests.

As the states face heavier burdens under their Medicaid programs, they may come to share the attraction felt by institutional providers and some others for the suppression of price competition through tight restrictions on market entry. Thus, a state may discover that by employing such regulation to preserve internal subsidies against erosion by competition, it can skimp on its own Medicaid outlays, counting on providers to fill the gaps and to tax the costs of so doing to the paying population. Seldom have state governments had such a strong reason for engaging in "taxation by regulation" and for curbing the competition that would frustrate regulated firms' collection of monopoly revenues to be applied to industry good works. Thus, there is a strong possibility that state regulation will become more rather than less restrictive if federal policy leaves the states free to implement their own solutions to the problem of Medicaid costs and to respond to provider pressures.

If the states are in fact left free to determine their own regulatory policies, the proposals for employing competition-sensitive regulation offered in this book would be directly relevant to the debates on appropriate state policy. Indeed, the book's value would be once again what was anticipated in its earliest stages—

when regulation seemed a fait accompli and the goal was simply to make regulators somewhat more receptive to desirable competitive developments. Although total deregulation can now be realistically advocated under a market-forcing, signal-giving rationale, the alternative strategy of pursuing phased deregulation under regulatory oversight also remains a strategy available for adoption by the states. It is unfortunate that success in getting the federal government to adopt this general regulatory approach in the 1979 amendments may not have finally carried the day, perhaps leaving the same battle to be fought all over again at the state level.

THE FUTURE OF CERTIFICATE-OF-NEED REGULATION

In view of the poor chances for reaching the goal of true deregulation through federal invalidation or state repeal of certificate-of-need laws, this book concludes that Public Law 93–641, as amended (and as it could be further amended), is probably the best vehicle for achieving a coherent and reliable national health policy favorable to competition and thus for sending the appropriate signal to the private sector. It is important, however, that, if regulation is to be continued at all, it proceed under a new and substantially different rationale. Only if residual entry regulation is made an integral part of the new federal initiative on behalf of competition will it not continue to operate as a primary obstacle, both tangible and psychological, to the market changes that competition is supposed to trigger.

The Importance of Continuing Regulation Under the Right Rationale

The argument advanced here for preserving the regulatory apparatus is substantially different from the arguments advanced by the health planners and regulators in support of their own retention. Whereas the conventional argument is that regulation and planning are needed to protect against a short-run cost explosion that would follow deregulation and to assure a smooth transition to a market-oriented system, the argument primarily relied upon here is of the second-best variety. Because state certificate-of-need regulation probably cannot be eliminated altogether, the best remaining option is to maintain regulation as a federally controlled initiative, thus allowing implementation of Congress's already declared preference for competition and responsible deregulation. Clear-cut adoption of this deregulatory strategy should convey the right messages to the private sector.

The argument that continued regulation is needed to prevent a cost explosion is an interesting one. Its premise that regulation effectively controls costs is probably false, yet health planners purport to sense a pent-up demand for building and expanding facilities. Even a skeptic about regulation might be reluctant, despite the evidence that regulation is ineffective in controlling costs, to put that hypothesis to the test of suddenly lifting the controls. In all probability, however, the lifting of controls as part of a credible procompetitive policy would not trigger an unwarranted building boom. Even if a hospital's trustees thought that deregulation was a green light for expansion, it is doubtful that the capital market to which the institution would have to turn for funds would be willing to ignore the risks present in the new, potentially competitive environment. Hospital bonds have enjoyed favorable ratings in the past precisely because regulation has protected those investments and because the financing system has provided special implied assurances that debt-service payments will be made. Even though a few institutions and lenders would undoubtedly underestimate either demand elasticities or the prospects for real demand-side changes and price competition, deregulation coupled with meaningful incentive changes and expanded opportunities for choice should trigger caution, not a building binge. The key factor, once again, is psychological, and success depends greatly upon the clarity of the signal given to the private sector about government's purpose and its seriousness. Once it is perceived that price competition is certain to intensify, the system should check its own growth propensities, allowing expansion only where consumers having new opportunities for choice are still willing to support it.

Unfortunately, advocates of competition have sometimes abetted the regulators by conceding that the market will not immediately be able to carry the full load of allocating health resources.

In stating that the necessary financing-system reforms may take ten years or more to occur, they have invited the regulators to claim that their services are needed during the transition period. Moreover, market advocates, fearful that their theories will be deemed discredited by short-run cost increases, have been reluctant to call for immediate and total deregulation. But their ten-year forecast, which may also result from fear of a backlash if they should promise more than they can deliver, could diminish the urgency of the signal being given. By thus weakening the very forces that they seek to strengthen, they may increase the chances that their policies will be deemed a failure.

If regulation is maintained under the rationale that, although it may be dispensable ten years hence, it is needed to protect against cost increases today, the private sector will maintain the same wait-and-see, do-nothing attitude that retarded change throughout the 1970s. Regulation must therefore make a clear new departure under a procompetitive rationale if it is not to discourage rethinking and new initiatives. The 1979 amendments provide a statutory framework for procompetitive, market-forcing regulation that could—with only minor adjustments to achieve true clarity of purpose—assure that the federal government's continued support for certificate-of-need regulation will not be viewed as a sign of doubt about competition's prospects or as evidence that things are not going to be so different after all. To the greatest extent possible, the administration should present its regulatory reforms as part of its procompetition package and as the best way of bringing about true deregulation. Attention to presenting regulation in this way will convey that it is being kept on as a part of the new strategy and not as a vestige of the old. Such packaging should prevent the apparent inconsistency from weakening both the administration's arguments for its position and its signal to the private sector.

Some Procompetitive Changes in the Federal Regulatory Mandate

In general, the regulations under Public Law 93–641, as amended, and the statute itself should be reviewed and, where necessary, amended with an eye to establishing a new procompetitive rationale for regulation. The goal should be to eliminate all vestiges of the previous presumption that the market has failed beyond redemption and to replace it with a new presumption in favor of letting newly reliable private sector decisions guide the investment of capital and the flow of resources. A few specific amendments of the regulations under Public Law 93–641, designed to clarify, reinforce, or strengthen the procompetitive thrust of the 1979 amendments, are suggested here:

- The regulations should be rewritten to clarify that, as Chapter 10 argues, "inpatient ... and other institutional health services" are viewed by law as among those facilities and services that are potentially subject to appropriate allocation by market forces. The suggestion in the current regulations[23] that the statute embodies an opposite and irrebuttable presumption should be overturned.
- The 1979 amendments should be reinterpreted as *not* requiring states to regulate service terminations and bed reductions.[24] Chapter 7 discusses why that construction was gratuitous.
- The Carter administration's regulations requiring regulators to attach great weight in need determinations to a service's availability to underserved persons[25] should be rewritten to narrow the circumstances in which public utility principles can be invoked. The discussion of protectionism in Chapter 10 provides some guidance.
- The policy unfavorable to protectionist regulation should be underscored in other respects so that states will be preempted from relying broadly on cross-subsidization and "taxation by regulation" rather than on explicit subsidies to carry out public responsibilities.
- The regulations should acknowledge the appropriateness of market-forcing regulation, as described in Chapter 12. This change is particularly important as a help in overcoming the regulators' natural tendency to continue business as usual until such time as someone persuades them that market forces are working perfectly.
- The regulations should specify who has the burden of proof on competition's efficaciousness in particular circumstances and should ensure that decisions on such questions are made

on the basis of hearings and explicit findings of fact and are subject to judicial review.

- The criteria for decisionmaking should be explicated more fully so that all "factors that affect the effect of competition" will be recognized and given due weight.

The most important change that could be made in Public Law 93–641, as amended, would allow states to dismantle their certificate-of-need programs altogether; unrepealed programs would still be required to conform to federal standards. With this change, the federal legislation would serve only to control over-regulation by the states and not to confirm the continued necessity for entry controls. Such a move, while restoring state control over the decision to regulate or not, would go as far as is apparently possible toward preventing state regulation from nullifying the federal policy favoring competition. Even though a few states might repeal their laws to appease providers frustrated by regulatory constraints and not primarily to foster competition, the federal government should tolerate such action. The long-run market-forcing effects of such deregulation, which would be made more probable by the projected incentive reforms and expanded opportunities for choice, must be presumed to outweigh any short-run gains that providers might derive.

Final Thoughts on the Prospects for Competition-Sensitive Regulation

The 1979 health planning amendments restored appropriate balance to federal health policy by putting Congress on record for the first time in favor of relying on competition to allocate resources wherever it can serve congressionally declared goals. The door to ultimate deregulation was thus opened, and this book has attempted to show the path that the health system's planners and regulators are now invited to follow. Congress revealed in 1979 that its continued support for certificate-of-need regulation does not imply that it automatically accepts the use of command-and-control methods throughout the length and breadth of the regulators' jurisdiction. Instead, Congress now expects regulation to incorporate a preference for using and strengthening market mechanisms wherever that is a responsible policy. Indeed, developments since 1979 suggest that the rationale for continued federal support for certificate-of-need regulation has shifted even further, so that it should now be viewed as primarily a protection against overregulation by the states. Being reluctant to invalidate state regulation altogether, the federal government should adopt a stance of tolerating it within prescribed limits designed to prevent competition from being frustrated.

In concluding this book's discussion of state regulators' federal mandate, some attention must be given to how it can be enforced, since an act of Congress may not be enough to change the behavior of health system regulators. Even though the 1979 amendments are quite clear in embracing competition as an alternative tool for identifying and giving effect to the public interest, they necessarily leave a great deal to the regulators' judgment. Because of the subjectivity involved in judging whether competition and consumer choice can serve public objectives well, the new legal mandate cannot be enforced in such a way as to deprive the regulators of all discretion. Experience in other industries has frequently revealed the resourcefulness of agencies in clinging to old ways in the face of new statutory directives.[26] Because health planners and regulators, as a class, are probably even more resistant than other regulators to the idea that competition and consumer choice can be constructive influences in their industry, it may seem futile to harbor the hope that a meaningful deregulation movement can be launched under the 1979 amendments.

Despite the difficulty of changing deep-seated values and perceptions by a statutory amendment, it is still possible to sketch a plausible scenario culminating in something like total deregulation of the health services industry. One hopeful fact is that health planning and regulation are highly decentralized, being carried out by numerous HSAs and other bodies and by state agencies in every state. Although planners and regulators are unlikely to be converted en masse to the cause of wholeheartedly promoting competition, a significant minority of these planning and regulatory bodies will undoubtedly, by design or default, give effect to the new mandate.[27] By tolerating and even encouraging vigorous competition and fostering financing reforms, these agencies might lay the groundwork for changes that would spread to other areas. Through the deregulation of particular services in particular markets and through nonregulatory initiatives, market-oriented health planning and innovative regulation could yield valuable regulatory experience and foster innovations in private cost containment that are transferable to other markets. Thus, the deregulation movement might benefit from persuasive natural experiments, much as airline deregulation was helped along by the obviously superior performance of unregulated intrastate carriers in California and Texas.[28]

The other development lending hopefulness to the deregulation scenario is a political climate increasingly receptive to market-oriented strategies and increasingly unsupportive of traditional forms of regulation and planning. This deregulatory climate could easily prove decisive in the health care sector just as it has in other regulated industries. Like the Civil Aeronautics Board, which under Alfred Kahn's chairmanship took the lead in deregulating the airlines, health system planner-regulators must now sense that the wind is blowing strongly in the direction of the market strategy. Many of them can be expected to chart their course so that the wind is at their backs. At the same time, the federal government's difficulty in establishing a clear regulatory rationale and in influencing state legislatures may make it hard to convince state regulators that their political future depends upon their accepting the deregulatory mission. Thus, federal policy alone is probably not enough. Federal leadership will also be required. It will still be necessary to win state legislatures and state regulators to the view that introducing competition is a promising strategy for achieving substantive reforms and cost containment.

THE FUTURE OF HEALTH PLANNING

The fate of certificate-of-need regulation seems severable from the future of the health planning agencies. Because HSAs are creatures of federal law, they enjoy little of the protection given to state certificate-of-need programs by federalism concerns at the federal level. Although the local character of HSAs might seem to make them attractive in an era when decentralization of power and devolution of responsibility are favored, their reliance on federal money and the extent of federal control weaken their claims in this regard. Instead, it is widely asserted that needed planning efforts can be organized and supported without federal involvement.

Targeted for early extinction by the Reagan administration's budget cutters, HSAs received a reprieve of sorts in the Omnibus Budget Reconciliation Act of 1981.[29] Funding for HSAs in fiscal year 1982 was set at $65 million dollars,[30] about ten times the amount that the administration had sought for phasing out HSAs during that year. Although the new level of support was much lower than in earlier years, it promised to keep enough HSAs in existence that Congress, in deciding whether to extend the health planning program or to let it expire by its terms in 1982, would not be faced with a fait accompli. In addition to reducing HSAs' funding, Congress took some steps to streamline the program. States were given the right to dispense with HSAs altogether[31] and were invited to consolidate them into a smaller number of agencies.[32] States were authorized to raise the dollar thresholds for certificate-of-need review so that fewer capital investments would require planners' and regulators' attention.[33] The secretary of DHHS was given the power to waive certain HSA duties, such as appropriateness review, review of proposed uses of federal funds (PUFF), and the collection and dissemination of hospital charge data.[34] In another step designed to allow HSAs to function with reduced federal funding, HSAs were authorized to receive funds from health insurers to supplement the federal contribution.[35]

Although the future of HSAs remains in grave doubt, it is still open for discussion. Moreover, even if HSAs as we have known them are doomed, health planning may reappear in other forms, either as particular HSAs go through a metamorphosis or as other planning bodies appear in their place. The discussion here focuses first on the rationale for continuing any kind of health planning in a market newly disciplined by competition, suggesting that there are certain market-assisting initiatives that planning agencies might undertake. It then considers the types of agencies that might be employed for such purposes.

Finding a Raison d'Etre for Health Planning under a Procompetitive Health Policy

Like regulators' arguments for continuing certification of need, health planners' arguments for continuing to maintain a publicly or privately supported health planning effort have largely depended on the claim that market forces are not yet capable of stimulating efficiency and appropriately allocating health resources. One version of this argument is that planner-assisted regulation is required until such time as market forces can be relied upon. This book cautions against too-ready acceptance of this view, because it provides a warrant too easily used for continuing traditional anticompetitive regulation with only lip service to competition. Like continued federal sponsorship of state certificate-of-need programs, federally supported health planning requires a new rationale if it is to survive without undercutting the competition strategy. The traditional, central-planning concept must be discarded.

A more acceptable rationale for health planning under a market-oriented health policy is that competition will take effect sooner and work better if private actors are given external assistance in adapting to the new conditions. Faced with new political imperatives, the American Health Planning Association (AHPA), which represents the nation's HSAs, began in the spring of 1981 to stress the role that HSAs might play in encouraging competition. AHPA president James R. Kimmey told a congressional committee:

> In the absence of the community health planning structure, the process of reorganization of the [health care] delivery system and of activating consumers' interests in and understanding of, the advantages of competition would be measurably slowed. A truly competitive market may not need external planning, but moving to a competitive market from the current disorganized approach to health care delivery is a planning challenge of the first magnitude.[36]

Congress had, of course, already indicated its awareness that planners might help to improve the operation of market forces when, in the 1979 amendments, it introduced "preserving and improving . . . competition" as a new mandatory function for HSAs. There would indeed appear to be room for some kind of locally based effort to hasten and smooth the transition to competition.

Many of the functions that health planners might perform on behalf of competition would represent major departures from HSAs' current activities. In view of the funding cutbacks for HSAs, it may be hard to imagine their assuming important new functions. Nevertheless, HSAs have been granted some relief from their previous burdens and some new flexibility. Because DHHS is unlikely to penalize HSAs that embark on a procompetitive course, some of them may reorder their priorities so as to undertake procompetitive actions as a new primary responsibility. On the other hand, many of the procompetitive activities suggested below might be more readily carried out by organizations that have a different heritage and makeup and are thus less likely to be troubled by ideological doubts or conflicting loyalties. Before addressing the nature and sponsorship of the organizational mechanisms required, it will be useful to review the agenda of constructive actions that might be taken.

The procompetitive function that today's health planners would most naturally embrace would involve advising providers and others of community trends and probable future needs. Potential lenders in particular would find such advice useful. Indeed, because planners are concerned about excessive capital spending, they could be expected to warn would-be investors about potential risks associated with competition's emergence and impending reforms in the financing system. For such warnings to work, however, the planners would have to demonstrate their own commitment to deregulation, to strengthening market forces, and to increasing cost consciousness on the demand side of the market. If credible, that commitment should serve as a stronger deterrent to inappropriate growth and cost escalation than regulation has ever been.

Local planners could also advance the cause of competition by educating the public on the problem of health care costs and possible solutions to it. Simply by showing how local experience compares with experience elsewhere, planners could heighten awareness of the problem and receptivity to new ideas. The planners could also prepare the way for desirable changes by directing educational efforts to specific community groups. Consumers could be introduced to new concepts, such as HMOs, and shown how health plans differ and how certain kinds of economizing may make more sense than others. A planning organization might also educate employers and unions on specific economizing opportunities and on the desirability of collaborative action to expand options in the local market. Thus, planners might help employers and unions to understand such matters as why it is important that employees be offered multiple choice, why an HMO ought to be supported despite its seemingly high initial charges, why additional HMOs ought to be encouraged, why an IPA-type HMO sponsored by the local medical society is not necessarily a desirable development,[37] and why a joint effort by employers to offer multiple choice might be more beneficial to all than a unilateral effort would be to any one of them. A local agency might educate employers by sponsoring forums on private cost-containment measures and site visits to communities where particular progress had been made. A nationwide network of agencies engaged in such employer education would facilitate the spread of ideas. If such agencies were publicly supported, the information would perhaps flow more freely than if businesses had to rely on private consulting organizations.

A planning organization that developed the right expertise might also serve individual employers by reviewing their health benefits and advising on such matters as how to deal with adverse-selection problems in a multiple-choice system. In performing such functions, the planners would be competing with insurance brokers and employee benefits consultants but would bring a community-wide, reform-oriented perspective to bear. A credible planning organization might also assist an employer in educating his employees on the desirability and techniques of economizing, showing them how less is sometimes better. Another cooperative effort that planners might facilitate would be the formation of a coalition of purchasers that could perform for the community many of the functions suggested here.

A local planning body could be directly instrumental in organizing new institutional frameworks and in stimulating provider cooperation that generates efficiency without unduly sacrificing competition. Assistance to developing HMOs and other innovative health plans, including help in marketing them, would be useful in overcoming artificial entry barriers. Encouragement of shared-service arrangements and other cooperation among hospitals would be useful if carried out with antitrust principles in mind. A planning body might also help to create or even operate a clearinghouse through which health benefit plans could be offered on a multiple-choice basis to the employees of small businesses and others who need the assistance of a sophisticated intermediary.[38]

Other services to competition that planners might perform in local markets would involve the collection and dissemination of information. Several HSAs have developed physician directories containing such basic information as physician fees, office hours, specialties, and board certification.[39] Additional facts of interest to consumers include whether the physician accepts Medicare and Medicaid patients or accepts Medicare allowances as payment in full. Information on these and other subjects is extremely valuable to consumers, who are for the most part denied the benefits of physician advertising.

Planning bodies might also assist employment groups in collecting and evaluating utilization and cost data, comparing it with the experience of other groups and with the performance of efficient high-quality providers. A planning body might also encourage and coordinate the collection by employers of provider-specific utilization data and indicia of quality. Insurers have generally not collected such data because of opposition from provider organizations. Presumably providers fear the potential for competition once differences in the performance and cost experience of individual physicians and hospitals become recognized. Provider-specific data would indeed be extremely valuable in organizing cost-containment efforts, particularly those that depend on steering patients to efficient providers. Planners might also participate with insurers in pooling data for such purposes. Although the interpretation of such data should, for antitrust reasons, be left to the individual insurers, its collection and pooling are highly desirable activities and would be less likely to raise antitrust questions if carried out by an independent body.

In addition to helping employers, unions, and individual consumers become aggressive, informed, and cost-conscious buyers of financial protection and health services, local planning bodies could also promote competition by advocating before state legislatures and regulatory agencies the elimination of existing legal barriers to a more competitive marketplace. A planning body that was sensitized to the needs of a competitive market and to the subtle ways in which governmental policy can subvert it could serve as a true consumer advocate, offsetting to some degree the power of organized providers. Although there are some legal limitations on lobbying by nonprofit planning bodies,[40] much could be done within exceptions for the sharing of nonpartisan analysis and for the provision of requested technical advice. Moreover, an agency might act by alerting others to the problems perceived, relying on them to participate actively in the political process. To a large extent, the outcome of many battles in which competition has been sacrificed by the states has been determined by the failure of consumers and those who pay for health care to recognize the potential costs to themselves of the measures being debated.

A final area where a local planning group might improve competition's prospects would be in identifying and combatting private restraints of trade. Although such a body might feel uncomfortable in instituting antitrust litigation or inviting public enforcement against local providers, such action would be appropriate where a provider group was recalcitrant or engaged in conduct deserving a public rebuke. Often the objectionable practices might be terminated simply by pointing out the existence of a probable violation to the providers involved.

Most of the activities contemplated here are obviously not the kind of activities that are usually thought of under the heading of health planning. Neither are they the kind of activities that have predominated in the work of HSAs. Nevertheless, it is not inevitable that health planners will engage in central planning premised on the concept of a monolithic system or in activities associated with command-and-control regulation. Indeed, some HSAs have prepared physician directories and reports on HMOs and have helped employers through direct advice and in forging purchaser coalitions. Moreover, health planning has always involved a great deal of guiding, cajoling, and consensus building—though such efforts have usually been focused only on the supply side of the market. In theory at least, health planning is neutral between regulation and competition and chooses its methods on the basis of what is most appropriate under the circumstances. Thus, as the policy and operational premises of the industry change, health planning's focus should shift as well—away from command-and-control efforts and coordination of the supply side and toward improving the demand side's signals to providers. If planning is conceived of as doing whatever circumstances and the public interest require, then procompetitive actions of the kind outlined above would seem to be appropriate undertakings for agencies organized to do health planning.

Organizing for Health Planning in a Competitive Market

Because market reform is neither a traditional nor a natural function of health planning agencies, whether an agency will undertake the activities suggested above depends mostly on its motivation. Obviously, market reform would be resisted by an agency controlled by the natural enemies of competition. This discussion considers the types of organizations that might be counted on to perform constructive services to implement a procompetitive policy.

The chief advantage of relying on HSAs to perform market-reform tasks is their accountability to the federal government, which could, at least theoretically, redirect their efforts. HSAs also have a local presence and knowledge of local conditions and are in a position to work closely with large purchasers of care in the community. Furthermore, because HSAs are built into the certificate-of-need process, they might somewhat improve the quality of regulation by checking the otherwise wide discretion of the state agencies.[41] If they could be made to serve as agents of the federal policy of promoting competition, their presence as expert analysts of regulatory issues might reduce the impact of provider pressures and protectionist impulses at the state level.

Although one should not underestimate the difficulty of converting HSAs to the cause of competition, it is conceivable that they could become more an asset than a liability. Some HSAs have already taken actions on behalf of competition and seem sincerely interested in its possibilities. Moreover, the new political realities and close DHHS oversight could surely inspire many more HSAs to embrace competition as a value. As noted earlier, competition's success does not depend on universal acceptance of the concept by planners and regulators, since, if innovation can proceed in some local markets, its successes will eventually become apparent and will spread. Even though HSAs may not be ideal vehicles for implementing federal regulatory policy and performing market-reform tasks, Congress might still see fit to continue them as market reformers and as procompetitive influences in a regulatory system in which competition is always in danger of being sacrificed.

On the other hand, the arguments against retaining HSAs are quite strong. Threats by the Reagan administration to discontinue their federal funding induced many of their most capable staff to find other employment, and it is unlikely that many agencies any longer possess an organizational vigor worth preserving. Moreover, HSAs are far from being natural allies of the federal government in the deregulatory effort. They are staffed by persons largely unfamiliar and uncomfortable with the idea of competition, and their governing boards were recruited for quite different purposes. The heavy involvement of providers alone suggests a wholly inappropriate orientation, as does the origin of HSAs in a burst of now-exhausted 1970s enthusiasm for politicized central planning. Although HSAs could conceivably be restructured legislatively to remove the anticompetitive influences and to express a new kind of consumerism, the effort would require such a fundamental reconstitution of the agencies that it might not be worth the cost. Whether HSAs are provider-dominated or consumer-dominated or reflect a balance of interests, most of them have thoroughly internalized the idea that issues existing between consumers and providers or among providers are to be resolved through negotiations and consensus building. This orientation is so totally at odds with the idea of introducing robust competition into the market that any restructuring effort using such raw material might have little success.

As federal funding for HSAs is reduced, the federal government's power to control their activities will also diminish. Indeed, in encouraging HSAs to seek funding from private sources, the federal government may be driving HSAs into the arms of those most likely to resist competition's emergence. While HSAs are still barred from seeking financial support from providers,[42] they are increasingly invited to obtain funds from employers and health insurers. Although HSAs could perform valuable procompetitive services for individual employers on a fee-for-service basis, the greater likelihood is that an agency would be funded by an employer group to undertake traditional planning. Many employers shrink from the prospect of redesigning their health benefits and prefer not to rely for cost containment on their own and their employees' purchasing in a more competitive market. Their preference for collective cost-containment measures is traceable to a reluctance to reopen their health plans as an issue in collective bargaining and to the quasi-political problems, noted in Chapter 14, that deter employers from seeming to economize in purchasing health benefits. Some employers with this preference have actively supported such community-wide endeavors as health planning and PSROs in an effort to achieve cost containment indirectly, thus avoiding direct responsibility by getting someone else to do the job.[43]

The new federal provision allowing HSAs to receive contributions from health insurers is even more ominous in its implications for competition. Certainly insurers have no interest in educating employers and employees to buy health insurance more effectively in a competitive market. Moreover, they have a large stake in preserving HSAs as the entities responsible for organizing the market's supply side. As long as HSAs fill that role, insurers can continue to evade their responsibility for transmitting demand-side signals to providers through competitive bargaining. Like some employers, insurers' highest priority appears to be to place the burden of disciplining the supply side on someone else. In this way, insurers can avoid competing among themselves in the highly risky and uncertain area of cost containment. Insurers' current interest in getting PSROs to assume new utilization-review functions reflects this same preference for turning cost-containment responsibility over to others—in this case to entities directly accountable to the organized medical profession.[44] Insurers' support for any collective cost-containment measure should arouse a strong suspicion that that measure is antithetical to competition and a barrier to its emergence.

HSAs' future will be determined when Congress reviews Public Law 93–641 in 1982, in which year the entire federal health planning and certificate-of-need program will be up for reauthorization. Although it is possible to conceive of HSAs as agents of the procompetition strategy, their retention would be more likely to indicate to the world a lack of congressional commitment to that strategy. Because it would be hard to preserve them without sending the wrong signal concerning federal policy, HSAs are probably of greater symbolic than practical importance. Moreover, because of their strong identification with a central-planning, command-and-control philosophy, their explicit sacrifice as outdated and unneeded influences might serve the cause of competition better than their retention in a new role could ever do. In short, the effort needed to reorient the HSAs and to mobilize them in the fight for competition would probably not be worthwhile even if there were good reasons for thinking that it would succeed.

If HSAs should disappear, they might be replaced by, or might themselves evolve into, local voluntary planning agencies. This would represent simply a return to the model of the original health planning agencies, which acted primarily as conveners of local hospitals and as facilitators of efforts to work out collective solutions to the hospitals' mutual problems. Acceptance of this model, which has considerable appeal to providers, would greatly threaten competition, however, since it has many of the earmarks of a provider cartel. Even if other interests are allowed to participate, the operative premise of such planning is that negotiation is always preferable to competition in the marketplace. Local providers are seen as parts of a "system" that must be coordinated, not through bargaining and integration in response to market forces, but through centralized decisionmaking by the industry elite. Enforcement of the antitrust laws would prevent this conception of planning from being carried very far, but, as long as its premises continue to dominate thinking, competition will not prosper. Obviously care should be taken to avoid legitimizing this model of planning through legislation.

Perhaps the most promising vehicle for undertaking the health planning agenda outlined above is the purchaser-sponsored coalition. Such coalitions are being organized voluntarily in many communities.[45] The most promising ones are those that involve only the purchasers of care. Even though many major employers fail to recognize their direct stake in promoting competition, employers are still the most likely source of an impetus for procompetitive change. Moreover, they can pursue their goals more effectively and single-mindedly if they control their own organization. In contrast, a coalition including providers would almost certainly be oriented toward trying to persuade them to pursue cost containment and not toward forcing them to do so by applying competitive pressure. Insurers, too, would seem inappropriate participants in a coalition, since competition requires that they work independently, not collectively, to deal with the cost problem. Although it is conceivable that HSAs could ultimately reorganize themselves to operate in the manner of purchaser coalitions, the substantial participation of providers in HSAs suggests that the coalitions emerging from such a metamorphosis would not be the most helpful kind.

Government support for the coalition movement might be endorsed on the basis that the participation of a critical mass of purchasers may be difficult to obtain in particular communities. "Free-rider" problems might be confronted as some employers hang back in the hope of benefiting from the efforts of others. Also, an employer simply might not fully understand its stake in a collective effort to improve competitive conditions in the community. For example, a local plant manager of a large national firm might lack the authority or the interest needed to participate. Although independent funding might be desirable as a way of overcoming these arguable problems, government might not be the appropriate source of such subsidies. For one thing, government is somewhat committed through the HSA movement to the inclusion of providers in any such efforts. More importantly, employer groups have already been formed in many locations without government help. The John A. Hartford Foundation gave early support to such endeavors, and the Robert Wood Johnson Foundation and the National Chamber Foundation have supported the creation of a Health Coalition Exchange by the U.S. Chamber of Commerce. Not only is the private sector already proving capable of organizing a credible effort, but, as costs pinch harder, as new lessons are learned, and as evidence of success spreads, the coalition movement should receive all the impetus that is necessary.

It remains to be seen whether coalitions will place their primary emphasis on reshaping health care financing and strengthening competition or will instead engage in more traditional planning. Because many employers apparently prefer to control health care costs by collective action rather than by redesigning their benefits, not every purchaser coalition will represent a procompetitive force. Although many coalitions will undoubtedly begin with a preference for collective action, they are likely to discover that this approach is only marginally effective. For one thing, although they can offer recommendations on certificates of need, the effectiveness of such regulation remains in doubt, partly because, as Chapter 3 shows, the cost balloon can bulge at other places even if major capital investments are successfully controlled. Even hospital rate setting will prove a disappointing tool if, as is most common, it simply ratifies the passing on of incurred costs and cannot control utilization.

Upon discovering regulation's inadequacies, a frustrated coalition of purchasers would be tempted to take things into their own hands by demanding that providers control their prices and utilization. But such demands would be ineffectual without a sanction, and a coalition would be barred by antitrust law from exercising its members' collective buying power to coerce adherence to their preferences.[46] Lacking authority to sponsor concerted refusals to deal against uncooperative providers,[47] coalitions will have to rely primarily on persuasion. Under such circumstances, they are likely to find that negotiations with providers over prices and utilization practices yield very little improvement in industry performance.

It might seem that organized purchasers possess another sanction that they might threaten to use against providers without objection from antitrust enforcers—namely, their ability to adopt the aggressive market-reform strategy suggested above. Indeed, if providers viewed a coalition's threat to adopt such a procompetitive strategy as credible, the coalition should be able to persuade them to reduce their prices and utilization to levels close to those that would prevail under competition. Once again, however, the antitrust laws would frustrate the collective solution, since a local medical society would risk legal attack in attempting to control doctors' prices and utilization practices.[48] It would thus not be in a position to deliver improved performance even if it should want to do so.

Because it appears that the antitrust laws stand in the way of seemingly desirable cost-containment measures on both sides of the market, some comment is needed to show that antitrust courts and prosecutors would be justified in frustrating collective action and in holding out for the competitive solution. Even if the antitrust laws were relaxed to permit profession-sponsored cost containment, it is still improbable that organized buyers could achieve competitive price and output levels by merely threatening to institute competition. Although it would not be impossible to achieve the equivalent of a competitive market's performance by allowing organized buyers and sellers to confront each other across a bargaining table without antitrust constraints, that desirable result is not assured, and there would be no way of knowing whether it had been obtained in a particular case. Because so many fortuitous factors could influence the results of such bargaining, antitrust enforcers should not be satisfied. Although antitrust prosecutors have some discretion to look the other way when enforcement of the law's strict insistence on competition[49] would be destructive of consumer welfare, this is not such a case. Because a true competitive solution is feasible and will materialize only if collective actions are frustrated, the antitrust authorities would be remiss if they did not insist on actual competition.[50] In the law's contemplation, cost containment is not a legitimate excuse for anticompetitive actions on either the buyers' or the sellers' side of the market. Moreover, because the law is ultimately concerned with effects on competition and not with specific effects on prices and output, it should not be necessary to prove that prices or utilization differ from competitive prices or utilization before a violation can be found.[51]

As purchaser coalitions learn that the antitrust laws block both organized providers and themselves from addressing the cost problem through anticompetitive collective action, they should ultimately find that their best strategy is an aggressively procompetitive one. Thus, coalitions should concentrate on demystifying employee health plans, fostering consumer choice in a multiple-choice setting, and forcing insurers and providers into unaccustomed forms of bargaining and price competition. As their efforts become increasingly sophisticated and bear fruit, a truly competitive solution will finally be possible. The nation (and courts facing antitrust questions) should settle for nothing less.

FOCUSING ON THE DEMAND SIDE OF THE MARKET—FOR A CHANGE

Most of the keys to deregulating the health services industry lie on the demand side of the market. Whereas regulatory strategies of the past have concentrated on controlling the supply side, that approach should now be viewed as a misguided and discredited attempt to treat the symptoms of a problem that is inherent in a financing system that effectively insulates consumers and providers from the cost consequences of their consumption decisions.

With new understanding of where the root causes of the problem lie, the highest priority should now be assigned to correcting incentives, to opening up ways for consumers directly or indirectly to express their cost concerns, and to facilitating the creation of mechanisms for transmitting those concerns to competing providers.

Conventional health planning and certificate-of-need regulation, with their emphasis on structuring a centrally directed system on the supply side of the market, have no future in a competitive industry. In a competitive environment, health planners' energies, if exercised at all, should be primarily directed at encouraging innovation in the financing system and fostering wiser purchasing of financial protection by employers and individuals, all with a view to improving the signals given by the market to providers. Likewise, certificate-of-need regulation, if retained at all, should be relaxed wherever and whenever the demand side of the market becomes reasonably capable of disciplining the supply side. Planners and regulators should cease seeing their job as one of protecting those on the demand side of the market who are capable of helping themselves through wiser purchasing and those on the supply side who seek to avoid competition. If planners and regulators cannot assist in promoting competition's emergence and continue to stand in its way, their services should be dispensed with.

Ultimately, deregulation of the health care marketplace requires that the planners and regulators (and everybody else) cease to think in terms of a unitary system inevitably unresponsive to consumer demand and embrace the market model instead. What is needed is a new conception of health care as appropriately the product, not of a monolithic system, but of a pluralistic industry comprising, either now or potentially, a variety of competing systems organized and operated on various principles but all ultimately accountable in the competitive marketplace for their overall performance. Once this conception is established, neither government nor the medical profession will be needed any longer as a regulator. Although we will, in the nature of things, have discovered a whole new set of policy problems, we will at least have laid a foundation on which, instead of continually tinkering with the old structure, we can reliably build for the future.

Although it may seem anomalous, amid all the talk about supply-side economics in the 1980s, to advocate the emergence of a demand-side strategy in the health care sector, there is no contradiction at all. In the larger economy, the problem that has called forth a supply-side strategy has been underinvestment and lagging productivity and employment due to policies aimed at fostering consumption rather than saving. If it were appropriate to judge the health care industry by its ability to attract investment, to grow and provide jobs, and to generate wealth, it would be seen to perform well. But these are standards by which we appropriately judge the national economy, not a particular sector of it. Until subsidies and institutional arrangements distorting the demand for health services are reexamined and restructured, there is a strong basis for thinking that consumers of health services are paying more than is necessary for many services and are not getting commensurate value for much of their expenditure. The nation's welfare requires that attention be given to the apparently severe misallocation of resources and maldistribution of wealth that we usually refer to as the problem of health care costs. It would seem that the nation now has an unprecedented opportunity to address this important problem in a fundamentally sound and responsible way. Whether its political institutions and leadership are capable of capitalizing on this opportunity remains, of course, to be seen.

NOTES

1. *See* Biles, Schramm, & Atkinson, "Hospital Cost Inflation under State Rate-Setting Programs," 303 *New Eng. J. Med.* 664 (1980); Sloan & Steinwald, "Effects of Regulation on Hospital Costs and Use," 23 *J.L. & Econ.* 81 (1980).
2. *E.g.,* "Katz: Hospital Cost Shifting #1 Health Industry Problem," *Nat'l Underwriter,* Aug. 22, 1981, at 4.
3. Posner, "Taxation by Regulation," 2 *Bell J. Econ. & Management Sci.* 22 (1971).
4. *Compare* Pireno v. New York State Chiropractic Ass'n, 1981-1 Trade Cases (CCH) ¶64,047 (2d Cir. 1981) *with* Bartholomew v. Virginia Chiropractors Ass'n, 612 F.2d 812 (4th Cir. 1979), *cert. denied,* 446 U.S. 938 (1980). *See also* Virginia Academy of Clinical Psychologists v. Blue Shield, 676 F.2d 476 (4th Cir. 1980); Arizona

v. Maricopa County Medical Soc'y, 643 F.2d 553 (9th Cir. 1980), *cert. granted,* 49 U.S.L.W. 3663 (1981).

5. *See* Havighurst, "Professional Restraints on Innovation in Health Care Financing," 1978 *Duke L.J.* 303, 339–42.

6. *See* Insurance Commissioners v. Mutual Medical Ins., Inc. 241 N.E. 2d 56 (Ind. 1968); Herring v. American Bankers Ins. Co., 216 So. 2d 137 (La. App. 1968). *See also* Havighurst, "The Role of Competition in Cost Containment," in *Competition in the Health Care Sector* 285, 297–98 (W. Greenberg ed. 1978).

7. *See* Olson, "Introduction," in *A New Approach to the Economics of Health Care* (M. Olson ed.) (in press).

8. *See* Frech, "Health Insurance: Private, Mutual, or Government," in *The Economics of Nonproprietary Organizations* 61 (K. Clarkson & D. Martin eds. 1980); Clark, "Does the Nonprofit Form Fit the Hospital Industry?" 93 *Harv. L. Rev.* 1417 (1980); Hansmann, "The Role of Nonprofit Enterprise," 89 *Yale L.J.* 835 (1980).

9. *See* Havighurst & Blumstein, "Coping With Quality/Cost Trade-Offs in Medical Care: The Role of PSROs," 70 *Nw. U.L. Rev.* 6, 54–60 (1975).

10. *Id.* at 20–30, 38–68; Havighurst & Bovbjerg, "Professional Standards Review Organizations and Health Maintenance Organizations: Are They Compatible?" 1975 *Utah L. Rev.* 381, 401–21.

11. *See id.*

12. *Cf.* Havighurst & Kissam, "The Antitrust Implications of Relative Value Studies in Medicine," 4 *J. Health Pol., Pol'y & L.* 48 (1979).

13. *See id.*; M. Pollard & R. Liebenluft, *Antitrust and the Health Professions* (F.T.C. Office of Policy Planning 1981). *See also* Pireno v. New York State Chiropractic Ass'n, 1981–1 Trade Cases (CCH) ¶64,047 (2d Cir. 1981); Arizona v. Maricopa County Med. Soc'y, 643 F.2d 553 (9th Cir. 1980), *cert. granted,* 49 U.S.L.W. 3663 (1981).

14. *See* Bovbjerg, "The Medical Malpractice Standard of Care: HMOs and Customary Practice," 1975 *Duke L.J.* 1375 (1976); Havighurst, " 'Medical Adversity Insurance'—Has Its Time Come?" 1975 *Duke L.J.* 1233, 1234–41 (1976). The latter article describes a compensation system that a cost-conscious health plan, such as an HMO, might adopt by contract as a substitute for the malpractice remedy, thus reducing pressure to practice "defensive medicine." *See also* American Bar Ass'n, Comm'n on Medical Professional Liability, *Designated Compensable Event System* (1980).

15. American Optometric Ass'n v. FTC, 626 F.2d 896 (D.C. Cir. 1980).

16. *See* B. Seigan, *Economic Liberties and the Constitution* (1980).

17. Federal Trade Commission Improvements Act of 1980, Pub. L. No. 96–252, §21, 94 Stat. 374 (1980).
18. Questions have been raised about the constitutionality of the legislative veto. *See* Nathanson, "Separation of Powers and Administrative Law: Delegation, the Legislative Veto, and the 'Independent' Agencies," 75 *Nw. U.L. Rev.* 1064 (1981); Scalia, "The Legislative Veto: A False Remedy for System Overload," *Regulation*, Nov./Dec. 1979, at 19. The legislative veto would seem peculiarly appropriate, however, where the regulation in question purported to override state action.
19. 42 U.S.C. §300e-10 (1976).
20. Letter from Uwe E. Reinhardt to Sen. Robert W. Kasten, Jr., Chairman, Consumer Subcomm. of the Senate Comm. on Commerce, Science, and Transportation (July 20, 1981) (emphasis added).
21. *Id.*
22. Legal principles for accommodating state legislative policy with federal antitrust policies have been developed in case law. *See* 1 P. Areeda & D. Turner, *Antitrust Law* ¶¶207–218 (1978).
23. 45 Fed. Reg. 69,771 (1980).
24. 45 Fed. Reg. 69,752 (1980) (to be codified in 42 C.F.R. §123.412(5)(ii)).
25. 45 Fed. Reg. 69,752 (1980) (to be codified in 42 C.F.R. §§123.412(a)(5)-(6) and 123.413).
26. An often cited example of an agency resisting a change in its statutory mandate was the ICC's reluctance to permit vigorous competition between railroads and other modes of transportation, even after Congress amended the ICC's statutory authority in an apparent effort to encourage intermodal competition. *See, e.g.*, ICC v. New York, N.H. & H.R.R. Co., 372 U.S. 744 (1963) (overturning an ICC decision limiting intermodal price competition); American Commercial Lines v. Louisville & N. R.R., 392 U.S. 571 (1968) (upholding an ICC decision limiting intermodal price competition). For a description of the leading cases and legislative history, see W. Jones, *Regulated Industries* 656–716 (2d ed. 1976). It is noteworthy, however, that the ICC's mandate to promote intermodal competition was less clear than the health planners' and regulators' new mandate to promote competition in the health care sector.
27. Utah's Pro-competitive Certificate of Need Act (see Appendix A) indicates that state's receptiveness to competition.
28. *See, e.g.*, Note, "Is Regulation Necessary? California Air Transportation and National Regulatory Policy," 74 *Yale L.J.* 1416 (1965);

W. Jordan, *Airline Regulation in America: Effects & Imperfections* (1970).

29.   Pub. L. No. 97–35, 95 Stat. 357 (referred to hereafter as Pub. L. No. 97–35). *See* H. Rep. No. 97–208, 97th Cong., 1st Sess. 822–23 (1981).

30.   Pub. L. No. 97–35, §933, *adding* Public Health Service Act §1537.

31.   Pub. L. No. 97–35, §935, *amending* Public Health Service Act §1536.

32.   H. Rep. No. 97–208, 97th Cong., 1st Sess. 822 (1981).

33.   Pub. L. No. 97–35, §936, *amending* Public Health Service Act §1531(5)-(7).

34.   Pub. L. No. 97–35, §934(b).

35.   Pub. L. No. 97–35, §935(d), *amending* Public Health Service Act §1512(b)(5).

36.   Testimony presented before the Task Force on Human Resources and Block Grants of the House Budget Comm., 97th Cong., 1st Sess. (March 13, 1981).

37.   *See* Havighurst & Hackbarth, "Enforcing the Rules of Free Enterprise in an Imperfect Market: The Case of Individual Practice Associations," in *A New Approach to the Economics of Health Care* (M. Olson ed.) (in press).

38.   Possible models include Project Health in Multnomah County, Oregon, and the Massachusetts Businessmen's Association.

39.   *See* Health Systems Agency v. Virginia State Bd. of Med., 424 F. Supp. 267 (E.D. Va. 1976); ICF, Inc., *Selected Use of Competition by Health Systems Agencies*, ch. 5, app. D (1976).

40.   *E.g.*, Public Health Service Act §1513(a)(5) *as amended*; I.R.C. §§501(c)(3), 4911 (1976); 2 U.S.C. §§261–270 (1976).

41.   The concept of "checking" agency discretion is drawn from the work of Kenneth Culp Davis. *See* K. Davis, *Discretionary Justice* (1969).

42.   Public Health Service Act §1512(b)(5) *as amended*.

43.   The Washington Business Group on Health (WBGH) typifies this attitude on the part of large employers. Organized by the Business Roundtable, the WBGH also reflects the views of commercial health insurers, who, though admitted to membership as employers, wear another hat in making WBGH policy. The WBGH has actively supported the continuation of health planning and PSROs and expressed skepticism about competition. *See* Iglehart, "Drawing the Lines for the Debate on Competition," 305 *New Eng. J. Med.* 291, 295 (1981).

44. *See* Havighurst & Blumstein, *supra* note 9. On the antitrust implications of turning economic decisions over to organized providers, see text accompanying notes 11–13 *supra*.

45. *See* J. Kingsdale & P. Haynes, *A Report on Coalitions to Contain Health Care Costs* (Government Research Corp. 1979); "Controlling Health Care Costs: The Coalition Approach," *Medicine & Health (Perspectives)*, June 22, 1981.

46. Private regulation enforced by coercive sanctions is unlawful. *E.g.*, Fashion Originators' Guild v. FTC, 312 U.S. 457, 465 (1941) ("the combination is in reality an extra-governmental agency, which prescribes rules for the regulation and restraint of interstate commerce").

47. A concerted refusal by employers to deal with a hospital that refused to accept a coalition's planning decision would be a more obvious violation than the unilateral refusal to deal involved in *National Gerimedical Hosp. & Gerontology Center v.. Blue Cross*, 49 U.S.L.W. 4672 (1981), discussed in Chapter 6.

48. *See* cases cited in note 13 *supra*.

49. The law is correct in always insisting on competition, because competition is nearly always the best long-run solution. To allow exceptions would put courts in the position of having to make impossible judgments. For a discussion of the law and prosecutors' discretion, see Havighurst & Hackbarth, *supra* note 37.

50. *See id.* for a full discussion of the legality of profession-sponsored efforts allegedly designed for cost containment.

51. This question is raised in a case awaiting decision by the Supreme Court. Arizona v. Maricopa County Med. Soc'y, 643 F.2d 553 (9th Cir. 1980), *cert. granted*, 49 U.S.L.W. 3663 (1981).

APPENDIX A

Excerpts from the Utah Pro-competitive Certificate of Need Act
[This statute, orignally enacted in 1979 (1979 Utah Laws ch. 95), was repealed and reenacted with editorial and a few substantive changes by 1981 Utah Laws ch. 126 §§1, 21. Section references are to Utah Laws Annotated, 1981 Interim Supplement.]

[Legislative findings]

§26-22-2. (1) The legislature finds that duplication and excess investment in and supply of health facilities, equipment, and services contribute to the rising cost of health services and the financial ability of the public to obtain necessary care. The legislature also finds that the prevailing systems of public and other third party payment for health care sometimes provide inappropriate economic incentives for new investment and service development and inadequately deter duplication and overinvestment. The legislature concludes that development of a facility for the provision of health services is affected with a public interest and such development should be granted only on an affirmative demonstration of the desirability of such facility and the services rendered therein, its necessity, and its economic appropriateness.

(2) The legislature finds that regulation of the growth and development of health services will not obviate the need for maintaining competitive conditions in local markets for health services and financing. The legislature also finds that the degree to which competition and consumer choice can serve the public purposes of quality assurance, cost containment and responsiveness to consumers' preferences varies from service to service and place to place. The agencies administering this chapter shall consider and make findings as to the effectiveness of such forces in protecting the public interest.

(3) The legislature recognizes that the definition of need for a health service or facility depends on judgments about acceptable medical practices, the importance of patient comfort and convenience, expense of services, the priority of services within the community, and the efficacy of competition. The legislature believes that the growth and development of health services is most likely to be effective if it is based on the rigorous application of health planning principles that consider these factors in defining need. The legislature also believes that the need for health services should be subject to an independent test in the health services market and directs that nothing in this chapter shall be construed as requiring those purchasing health services to fully reimburse the costs of projects approved under this chapter.

(4) The purposes of this chapter are: to promote effective health planning; to provide a method to resolve questions about the necessity for new health care facilities, equipment, and services including the construction and modification of health care facilities where economic forces are inadequate for this purpose; to increase competition and improved market conditions to the extent possible; and to assure that necessary and adequate health care facilities, equipment, and services are available and accessible.

[Definitions]

§26-22-3.   As used in this chapter:

. . . .

(10) "Market conditions" or "markets" means that:

(a) Conditions exist in which consumers and their agents in making decisions with respect to the purchase of health services have information on the quality and price of the services and the availability of alternatives;

(b) Consumers and their agents are purchasing services with sensitivity to the quality, price and availability of alternatives thereto; and

(c) Providers are considering in their decisions concerning the type or level of services to be offered, consumer preferences regarding quality, price, and availability of alternative services.

. . . .

[Decisionmaking criteria]

§26-22-12.   (1) Every health systems agency and the department shall prescribe by rule, and utilize as appropriate, criteria for conducting the reviews covered by this chapter. Such criteria shall include consideration of:

. . . .

(c) The need of the population served or to be served for such project; in considering need, the prospective benefit to the public demonstrated by the applicant of an innovation in the delivery of health care services which promotes significant cost savings or avoidance or is an advance of substantial magnitude in the delivery of health care services meriting a test in the marketplace notwithstanding possible impact on existing health care services shall be given a preponderant effect;

. . . .

(f) The relationship of the proposed project to the existing health care system of the area in which the project is proposed to be provided, including the effect of the proposed facility or service on the maintenane of competitive conditions in the local market; in assessing the relationship of proposed services to the existing health care system, any consideration given to the ability of an existing provider to continue to offer services of this or a similar type shall be contained in the findings required by section 26-22-7, including a statement of overriding public interest justifying such consideration and the estimated cost to the public of such consideration;

. . . .

(l) With respect to services of the type involved in the proposed project, the existence and capacity of market conditions in advancing the purposes of quality assurance, cost containment, and responsiveness to consumers' preferences;

(m) With respect to services of the type involved in the proposed project, the existence and capacity of public or private reimbursement and utilization review programs, and other public and private cost control measures to give effect to consumer preferences and establish appropriate incentives for capital allocation;

. . . .

APPENDIX B

Excerpts from the Report of the House Committee on Interstate and Foreign Commerce on the National Health Planning and Resources Development Amendments of 1979
   (H. Rep. No. 96–190, 96th Cong., 1st Sess., May, 15, 1979)

[p. 4]
   The bill recognizes those circumstances in which competition may serve to allocate the supply of health services and encourages planning agencies to work to strengthen market forces.

[pp. 51–56]
THE ROLE OF COMPETITION IN THE ALLOCATION OF HEALTH SERVICES AND THE APPLICATION OF THE ANTITRUST LAWS TO HEALTH PLANNING AGENCIES

The Congress enacted the National Health Planning and Resources Development Act (Public Law 93–641) to deal with a range of health care problems two of which continue to plague our health care system—access and cost. In that Act Congress stated that (1) "the achievement of equal access to quality health care at a reasonable cost is a priority of the Federal government," and (2) "increases in the cost of health care, particularly for hospital stays, have been uncontrollable and inflationary and there are presently inadequate incentives for use of appropriate alternative levels of health care, and for the substitution of ambulatory and intermediate care for inpatient hospital care."

In addressing these two problems Congress established planning agencies. These agencies are (1) to develop and implement health systems plans, which describe goals for a healthful environment and health system (including all necessary health services) which are responsive to the unique needs of the areas, and State health plans; (2) to determine the appropriate supply of institutional health services by recommending and approving only those new services and facilities that are needed (certificate of need); (3) to review existing institutional health services and determine their appropriateness (appropriateness review); and (4) to review the proposed uses in the area of Federal funds to develop new health services.

In establishing this health planning system the Congress did not address the role of competition in the planning or allocation of health services or the application of the antitrust laws to these planning agency activities. This lack of Congressional direction, particularly respecting the application of the antitrust laws, has created some confusion and concern about the legality of planning agencies undertaking the functions required of them in Public Law 93–641.

The committee's bill would make several clarifying amendments and the committee seeks, through this report, to explain the appropriate relationship between title XV of the Public Health Service Act and the antitrust laws and the appropriate interaction between health planning and competition.

Role of competition

In section 103 of the bill the committee sets forth findings that the market forces of supply and demand for many health services have been distorted and that, as a result, the interplay of purchaser and provider decisions regarding those services has not resulted in an appropriate allocation of supply of those health services. The section identifies (1) extensive coverage of health services by health insurance plans and (2) the methods of paying for health services by those health insurance plans, as specific sources of market distortion for inpatient health services and other institutional health services. The result has been duplication and excess supply of those services (and facilities) as well as excessive use of those services. Primarily because of these third party reimbursement arrangements, individuals often make decisions respecting their use of institutional health service with almost no regard to the price of the services, and providers make decisions respecting the supply of institutional health services substantially unaffected by the usual financial incentives and risks which exist in other personal service industries. The committee notes that there are other factors which contribute to this distortion of market forces for institutional health services. The urgent nature of the need for some institutional health services, the rapid development of new technologies for the delivery of institutional health care services, and the predominant role of physicians in making purchasing decisions on behalf of the patient, thereby reducing the patient's opportunity to consider less costly alternatives, are all important factors.

This section of the committee's bill would make clear that for inpatient health services and other institutional health services for which market forces of supply and demand do not or will not appropriately allocate supply because of the effect of health insurance coverage and the methods of paying for institutional health care services under that insurance (and the other factors mentioned above), health systems agencies and State health planning and development agencies should take the actions authorized by title XV to allocate the supply of those services. The section also makes clear that for health services for which the market forces of supply and demand have not been distorted and will appropriately allocate the supply of those services, health systems agencies and State health planning and development agencies should in the performance of their functions under title XV give priority to actions which would strengthen the effect of market forces on the supply of those health services.

The committee believes that consideration in health planning of the role of competition can be integrated into current activities by the health planning agencies. The distortion of market forces has occurred primarily in the market for inpatient health services and for most other institutional health services. All institutional health services are currently required by title XV to be included in State certificate of need laws; and the committee's bill does not alter those coverage requirements. Where State certificate of need laws extend coverage beyond that required by title XV to non-institutional health services, the committee expects that the health planning agencies in those States would evaluate the factors which distort the market forces of supply and demand for those covered services. If an agency found that individuals, in making decisions respecting their use of those health services, are sensitive to the price of the service, and that any provider which developed services or facilities of that type would be at financial risk for low levels of utilization and the costs associated with excess unused capacity, then the planning agency should make certificate of need decisions which would strengthen the effects of market forces on the supply of those services. The committee would expect, however, that those health planning agencies would make a positive finding that market forces will appropriately allocate supply.

This new section would establish a fifth purpose of health systems agencies and an additional criteria for use by health system agencies and State health planning and development agencies in conducting their reviews. This new purpose describes the new responsibility which the committee's bill places on planning agencies to consider the role of competition in carrying out its functions. For those institutional health services for which an effective market does not function, planning agencies would use the certificate of need process to restrain increases in the cost of health services (section 1513(a)(3)) and prevent unnecessary duplication of health resources (section 1513(a)(4)). For other health services among which there is competition based on price and for which an effective market operates, planning agencies would strengthen the effect of those market forces of supply and demand by awarding sufficient certificates of need so that those market forces could operate to allocate the appropriate supply in response to consumer preferences.

The committee's decision to not include home health services or clinical laboratory services in the title XV requirements for coverage by State certificate of need programs, and its decision to prohibit coverage by State certificate of need programs of health maintenance organizations (HMOs), was based partially, in the cases of home health and clinical labs, and entirely, in the case of HMOs, on the committee's belief that the supply of those services would not be excessive if they were not regulated and that market forces of supply and demand may appropriately allocate them.

It is the committee's view that the scope of the planning agency functions of planning and appropriateness review would not be substantially altered by these new requirements. The health systems plan and the State health plan would include all health services, but the goals of the plan and the statement in those plans of changes in resources which are needed in the area (per section 115) might differ depending upon the agency's assessment of the extent to which, for a particular service, competition will limit the development of unneeded capacity and protect the public from its costs. For instance, plans could avoid establishing numerical goals or resource requirements by identifying where certain types of services are needed, or appear excessive, or by establishing a range for the number of new services needed.

The agency's review for appropriateness would include all institutional health and home health services, as required by this bill, and other services the agency chooses to include. The recommendations and findings could differ, as with health plans, depending upon the agency's assessment of the extent to which competition will allocate the supply of the service under review.

As the committee has pointed out, the market forces affecting institutional health services are sufficiently diminished that planning agencies should play a role in allocating the supply of those services. If however, an innovative financing, reimbursement or service delivery arrangement affecting institutional health services, were designed so that the method of payment by patients (1) created incentives for patients to respond to prices charged and (2) placed the providers at financial risk for unnecessary or excessive services; the committee would expect that planning agencies would, in awarding certificates of need, consider whether the effect of that new arrangement will be to properly allocate the supply of those services. The committee expects that these types of new arrangements would likely involve a population enrolled with a provider on a prepaid basis for the delivery of a comprehensive range of services, including institutional health services.

The committee notes that its bill is consistent with the thrust of the January 1979 report of the President's National Commission for the Review of Antitrust Laws and Procedures. That report calls for increased competition to allocate supply wherever it will do so effectively. The committee generally agrees with the goals of the President's Commission and believes it has complied with them; but the committee is also convinced that there are distortions in the market forces of supply and demand for institutional health services which do not occur in other personal service industries. For this reason the committee believes that the health planning process, and particularly the certificate of need process is a necessary and effective regulatory mechanism to control the supply of institutional health services.

Antitrust laws

The basic objective of the antitrust laws, broadly stated, is to eliminate practices that interfere with free competition. The laws are designed to promote a vigorous and competitive economy in which each business has a full opportunity to compete on the basis of price, quality, and service. As noted previously, questions have been raised as to the relationship between title XV and the antitrust laws.

The committee believes that the antitrust laws should be aggressively enforced to ensure a vigorous and competitive economy where there is reason to believe that business will in fact compete on the basis of price, quality, and service. However, as indicated by the reported bill and this report, the committee believes there is currently little, if any, competition based on price among institutional health services. For those services unfettered competition could further aggravate existing health system problems—duplicative and unnecessary services and facilities and rapidly rising costs.

While the application of the antitrust laws to promote competition is and should be the general rule, the committee believes that a practical and realistic analysis of the health care industry argues for exceptions to the rule. In 1974 in enacting Public Law

93–641. Congress found that "[i]n recognition of the magnitude of the problems (of access and cost) . . . and the urgency placed on their solution" a system of health planning with certain well defined regulatory authority had to be established. As described in the second paragraph of this section of this report. Congress *required* health planning agencies to carry out specific functions and established a financial penalty for States which failed to comply with the requirements. Those statutory requirements and penalty indicate that Congress did not expect the antitrust laws to be applied to agency actions, which might otherwise be in violation of the antitrust laws, if those agency actions were necessary to carry out the prescribed functions. On the other hand, however, agency acts which are not necessary to carry out such functions or which are outside the scope of title XV are not authorized and therefore not immune from the application of the antitrust laws.

In carrying out these functions, agencies will receive the views of providers and consumers at public hearings, develop health plans, make appropriateness review findings, and make recommendations and issue certificates of need for new institutional health services, capital expenditures, and major medical equipment. It is the committee's view that when health systems agencies, Statewide Health Coordinating Councils, and State health planning and development agencies carry out these functions by acting within the scope of the authority of title XV, there should be no doubt that Congress intended for no other Federal or State law, including antitrust laws, to prohibit those agencies from so acting.

Section 103 of the reported bill helps clarify this position of the committee on this matter. Under section 103, Congress calls upon HSAs and SHPDAs, when dealing with inpatient health services and other institutional health services, to substitute their judgement regarding the proper supply of those services for market forces of supply and demand which would otherwise allocate that supply. When recommending and issuing certificates of need for institutional health services, HSAs and SHPDAs would be strictly limiting supply to those services which the agencies determine are needed. In developing health systems plans and State health plans to cover institutional health services (including those which specifically identify excess or needed resources at specific institutions) and in recommending and making appropriateness review findings regarding institutional health services (including findings which identify specific institutions), HSAs and SHPDAs (and SHCCs) would be indirectly affecting the market forces of supply and demand for those services by advising consumers and providers as to their determination of the proper supply. In developing plans covering health services, other than institutional health services, for which there are reasons to believe there is competition based on price, HSAs, SHCCs and SHPDAs would establish goals which would strengthen the effect of the competitive forces. In those States where other than institutional health services are covered by certificate of need, HSAs and SHPDAs would award certificates of need in accordance with section 103 by considering the role which market forces of supply and demand play in allocating supply for the services under review. Even though such States have gone beyond the requirements of title XV by covering more than institutional health services (and HMOs before these amendments deleted them), it is the committee's understanding that the antitrust laws are not applicable because those planning agencies are acting under the requirements of State law.

The committee notes that the only Federal court decision to date on the relationship of the antitrust laws to health planning agencies is a March 1979 decision by the United States District Court for the Eastern District of Michigan in the case of *Huron Valley Hospital, Inc. v. City of Pontiac, et al.* That case involved the disapproval of the certificate of need application of the plantiff (Huron Valley Hospital) and a subsequent award of a certificate of need to defendant, Pontiac General Hospital. The court found that the activities of the defendant HSA and State planning agency of recommending and awarding a certificate of need were within the scope of the authority of Michigan law and title XV and therefore were not violative of Federal antitrust laws.

To further resolve this issue the committee would amend section 1512(b)(4) (see section 110 of the bill) to provide immunity for the health systems agency from liability for the payment of money damages under any Federal or State law when the member of the board or the employee of the HSA who acted on behalf of the agency acted within the scope of his duty, exercised due care, and acted without malice. The committee included this provision to insure that when HSAs act within the specific authority of title XV the agency would not be subject to money damages, including treble damages under the antitrust laws.

[p. 76]

The committee specifically considered and rejected a proposal to include home health services in the minimum requirements for a satisfactory certificate of need program. The committee feels that where competition can be encouraged in the health care industry, regulation of supply through certificate of need in unnecessary. Certificate of need regulation should be extended to only those services where the market forces of supply and demand will not appropriately allocate the supply of that service. The committee feels that home health services is a developing field and that competition between those who provide home health services should be encouraged. The committee will continue to examine whether market forces are at work to appropriately allocate supply and may return to this issue to evaluate more critically the structure of the home health services system.

[p. 106]

Section 103. The role of competition in the allocation of health services

Section 103 (a) amends section 1502 by finding that extensive coverage by health insurance, particularly of inpatient health services, and the prevailing methods of paying for health services through health insurance have: resulted in decisions respecting the use of health services being made without regard to price; diminished the effect of market forces on decisions respecting the supply of health services: and consequently encouraged duplication and excess supply. For health services such as institutional health services, for which market forces do not or will not appropriately allocate supply, HSAs and SHPDAs should take actions to allocate the supply of health services. For health services for which market forces appropriately allocate or will appropriately allocate supply, HSAs and SHPDAs should give priority to actions which would strengthen the effect of market forces.

Section 103(b) amends section 1513(a) by adding to an HSAs purposes the strengthening of the effect of market forces in cases where they can appropriately allocate the supply of health services.

Section 103(c) amends section 1532(c) requiring that HSAs, SHPDAs and SHCCs consider the effect of market forces on supply and demand in their project review activities.

INDEX

ABOUT THE AUTHOR

Clark C. Havighurst is professor of Law at the Duke University School of Law. A native of Evanston, Illinois, he is a graduate of Princeton University and Northwestern University School of Law. After several years of New York law practice, he entered law teaching at Duke in 1964. Serving as Editor of the journal *Law and Contemporary Problems* from 1965 to 1970, he developed an interest in economics and public policy, an interest that has come to center on the health services industry. Since 1969, Professor Havighurst has directed Duke's federally funded research program on Legal Issues in Health Care. In 1972–73, he served as scholar in residence at the Institute of Medicine of the National Academy of Sciences. In 1978–79, he spent another year in Washington as a part-time consultant to the Federal Trade Commission's Bureau of Competition. He is a member of the Institute of Medicine and is an adjunct scholar in law and health policy of the American Enterprise Institute for Public Policy Research. In addition to teaching in the fields of public regulation of business and antitrust law, Professor Havighurst offers seminars in health care law and policy. His publications include articles on most phases of regulation in the health services sector, the "no-fault" alternative to the tort of medical malpractice, the role of competition in the financing and delivery of health care, and antitrust issues arising in the health care field. He is known as an advocate of policies that would depend less on government and more on competition and consumer choice to guide the health care industry's development.